KU-736-922

A Handbook for Teaching and Learning in Higher Education

Enhancing academic practice

Fourth edition

**Edited by
Heather Fry
Steve Ketteridge
Stephanie Marshall**

LIS LIBRARY

WITHDRAWN

Date
15/9/14   nm-Clac

Order no
2 500243

University of Chester

Routledge
Taylor & Francis Group

LONDON AND NEW YORK

Fourth edition published 2015
by Routledge
2 Park Square, Milton Park, Abingdon, Oxon OX14 4RN

and by Routledge
711 Third Avenue, New York, NY 10017

Routledge is an imprint of the Taylor & Francis Group, an informa business

© 2015 Heather Fry, Steve Ketteridge and Stephanie Marshall

The right of the editors to be identified as the authors of the editorial material, and of the authors for their individual chapters, has been asserted in accordance with sections 77 and 78 of the Copyright, Designs and Patents Act 1988.

All rights reserved. No part of this book may be reprinted or reproduced or utilised in any form or by any electronic, mechanical, or other means, now known or hereafter invented, including photocopying and recording, or in any information storage or retrieval system, without permission in writing from the publishers.

Trademark notice: Product or corporate names may be trademarks or registered trademarks, and are used only for identification and explanation without intent to infringe.

First edition published by Routledge 1999
Second edition published by Routledge 2003
Third edition published by Routledge 2009

British Library Cataloguing in Publication Data
A catalogue record for this book is available from the British Library.

Library of Congress Cataloging in Publication Data
A handbook for teaching and learning in higher education : enhancing academic practice / edited by Heather Fry, Steven Ketteridge, Stephanie Marshall. – Fourth edition.
   pages cm
Includes bibliographical references and index.
1. College teaching–Handbooks, manuals, etc. 2. College teachers. 3. Lecture method in teaching. I. Fry, Heather. II. Ketteridge, Steve. III. Marshall, Stephanie. IV. Title: Handbook for Teaching & learning in higher education.
LB2331.H3145 2014
378.1'25–dc23   2014006845

ISBN: 978-0-415-70995-8 (hbk)
ISBN: 978-0-415-70996-5 (pbk)
ISBN: 978-1-315-76308-8 (ebk)

Typeset in Palatino
by Sunrise Setting Ltd, Paignton, UK

Printed and bound by CPI Group (UK) Ltd, Croydon, CR0 4YY

Contents

Accession no.
36202438

378.
125
FRY

A Handbook for Teaching and Learning in Higher Education

This entirely new edition of a very successful book focuses on developing professional academic skills for supporting and supervising student learning and effective teaching. It is built on the premise that the roles of those who teach in higher education are complex and multi-faceted. *A Handbook for Teaching and Learning in Higher Education* is sensitive to the competing demands of teaching, research, scholarship and academic management.

The new edition reflects and responds to the rapidly changing context of higher education and to current understanding of how to best support student learning. Drawing together a large number of expert authors, it continues to feature extensive use of case studies that show how successful teachers have implemented these ideas. It includes key topics such as student engagement and motivation, internationalisation, employability, inclusive strategies for teaching, effective use of technology and issues relating to postgraduate students and student retention.

- Part 1 explores a number of aspects of the context of UK higher education that affect the education of students, looking at the drivers of institutional behaviours and how to achieve success as a university teacher.
- Part 2 examines learning, teaching and supervising in higher education and includes chapters on working with diversity, encouraging independent learning and learning gain.
- Part 3 considers approaches to teaching and learning in different disciplines, covering a full range including arts and humanities, social sciences and experimental sciences through to medicine and dentistry.

Written to support the excellence in teaching and learning design required to bring about student learning of the highest quality, this will be essential reading for all new lecturers, particularly anyone taking an accredited course in teaching and learning in higher education, as well as those experienced lecturers who wish to improve their teaching practice. Those working in adult learning and educational development will also find the book to be a particularly useful resource. In addition it will appeal to staff who support learning and teaching in various other roles.

Heather Fry is Director (Education, Participation and Students) at the Higher Education Funding Council for England (HEFCE), UK.

Steve Ketteridge is the former Director of the Learning Institute, Queen Mary, University of London, UK.

Stephanie Marshall is Chief Executive of the Higher Education Academy (HEA), UK.

Illustrations

FIGURES

TABLES

Case Studies

Contributors

THE EDITORS

Heather Fry is currently Director (Education, Participation and Students) at the Higher Education Funding Council for England. She joined HEFCE in 2008, initially as Head of Learning and Teaching. She has responsibility for HEFCE's work in learning and teaching, widening participation, student success and collective student interest. Before joining HEFCE she worked as an academic at various universities. She started her career in Nigeria and subsequently she worked at the Centre for Higher Education Studies at the Institute of Education, University of London, Queen Mary, University of London and Imperial College London where she established its first Certificate in Learning and Teaching. She has published and researched extensively in higher education policy and teaching and learning in higher education and professional education, with her most recent book being *Surgical Education – Theorising an Emerging Domain* with Roger Kneebone (Springer 2011).

Steve Ketteridge retired as Director of the Learning Institute at Queen Mary, University of London in 2012. He spent his full-time career working in the higher education sector, first as Lecturer in Microbiology, later moving into human resources, working on policy and development, before establishing the Learning Institute. He was actively involved in strategy development and led projects on the enhancement of teaching and learning. At Queen Mary he initiated the Postgraduate Certificate in Academic Practice and a range of other development programmes for staff and researchers, including the High Potential Leaders Programme for high flying academic and professional staff. Currently his professional interests span a number of sectors but are centred around the world of further and adult education: he is a governor at Morley College London and Chair of the Board of Trustees of the Open College Network London which, amongst other things, awards Access to HE Diplomas regulated by the QAA.

Stephanie Marshall is Chief Executive of the Higher Education Academy (HEA), a Principal Fellow of the HEA and Professor of Higher Education at the University of Manchester. Previous to joining the HEA Stephanie was Director of Programmes at the Leadership Foundation, where she developed an extensive portfolio of executive leadership programmes and activities. Commencing her career at the University of York, she joined the Department of Educational Studies where she researched and lectured in 'new forms of teaching and learning', 'policy into practice' and the 'leadership and management of change'. It was from this position that she was recruited to develop and deliver the university's first training programme for academic staff – the York Certificate of Academic Practice (YCAP), which was one of the first programmes to be accredited by the Institute for Learning and Teaching. Stephanie progressed to become a college provost – a position she held for ten years.

THE AUTHORS

Ruth Ayres is Dean of Learning Enhancement and Innovation at the University of Derby. Qualified as a biologist, she has extensive experience of designing and teaching undergraduate and postgraduate programmes. She has held various senior posts in academic practice.

Veronica Bamber is Professor and Director of the Centre for Academic Practice at Queen Margaret University, Edinburgh. Prior to working in educational development, she was a lecturer in Spanish for 18 years, teaching in four different universities around the United Kingdom. Her current research is in universities as organisations, the development of academic staff and the evaluation of academic work.

Sue Bloxham is Professor of Academic Practice at the University of Cumbria. She has taught in higher education for many years, developing a particular interest in assessment. She is a National Teaching Fellow and has researched and published widely on higher education assessment.

Sam Brenton has been helping people and organisations teach and learn online since the 1990s. He was for many years responsible for technology-enhanced learning at Queen Mary, University of London, and is currently Chief Academic Officer for Academic Partnerships International.

Roni Brown is a design historian and Executive Dean of the Faculty of Art, Media and Communication Design at the University for the Creative Arts. She was a member of the Group for Learning in Art and Design (GLAD) between 2007 and 2013. In this role, she convened a number of national conferences, developed publications and research and acted in an advocacy role supporting practitioners of arts, design and media in HE across the UK. She is a Fellow of the Higher Education Academy and Royal Society of Arts.

Chris Butcher is a National Teaching Fellow and leads the Staff and Departmental Development Unit's Learning and Teaching Team at the University of Leeds. He is responsible for credit-bearing courses and the University's Teaching Fellowship scheme. He has taught in the United Kingdom and abroad, and provided educational development in 30 higher education institutions worldwide.

Lucie Byrne-Davis is a Chartered Psychologist and Lecturer in Assessment and Psychometrics at Manchester Medical School. Her current research interests are in how students learn in clinical learning environments, the role of m-technologies in clinical learning and cognitions associated with assessments.

John Davies is Professor of Civil Engineering at Coventry University. He has 30 years experience as an academic, following 8 years practicing as a civil engineer. He is editor of *Engineering Education*, a journal of the Higher Education Academy, and since 2012 has been a National Teaching Fellow.

Graham Gibbs retired as Professor and Director of the Oxford Learning Institute, University of Oxford in 2008. He is currently a (very part-time) Professor at the University of Winchester. He is author of *Dimensions of Quality*, a report that summarised research evidence that has been used by universities, and by government, to make policy decisions on how to improve quality in higher education.

Sarah Hamilton was previously a lecturer at BPP Business School, specialising in Human Resource Management. She is now the Assessment Enhancement Manager in the Learning and Teaching team at BPP University (a private for-profit university in England). Her particular research interest is in the development of education for emerging professions.

Rebecca Huxley-Binns is Professor of Legal Education and Co-Director of the Centre for Legal Education at Nottingham Law School. She is a National Teaching Fellow, Chair of the Association of Law Teachers and was Law Teacher of the Year 2010.

Paola Iannone is a Senior Lecturer in the School of Education and Lifelong Learning at the University of East Anglia. Her research has primarily focused on teaching and learning mathematics at university level, with particular attention to proof and proof production, and assessment of mathematics at university.

Anna Jones is Reader in Education at the Centre for Research in Lifelong Learning at Glasgow Caledonian University. Before that she worked at King's College London and the University of Melbourne. Her research interests include graduate attributes, disciplinary cultures in higher education, academic identity and the role of higher education in society.

Maria Joyce is a Senior Lecturer with responsibility for student admissions onto the nursing programme at the University of Lincoln. Her recent achievement of an EdD in Educational Leadership and Management focused on personal and professional experiences influencing the career trajectory of women professors of nursing.

Camille B. Kandiko Howson is a Research Fellow in Higher Education at King's College London. She works on projects to enhance higher education, teaching and learning, and the student and staff experience. She leads the King's Experience Internship scheme for undergraduate students and previously worked in the United States on the National Survey of Student Engagement (NSSE).

Michael Kelly is Professor of French and Head of Modern Languages at the University of Southampton. He is Director of LLAS, the Centre for Languages, Linguistics and Areas Studies at Southampton and Director of the government-funded Routes into Languages programme.

Margaret Kiley is a Visiting Fellow at the Australian National University and has a conjoint position at Newcastle University Australia. Her research and teaching interests are in the area of research education including the examination of doctoral theses, the experience of international students undertaking research degrees and candidates' and supervisors' perceptions of research.

Martyn Kingsbury is the Head of the Educational Development Unit at Imperial College London. He comes from a biomedical research background and his research interests include the research–teaching nexus, problem-based learning and concept mapping of new learning, particularly around threshold concepts.

Paul Kleiman trained and worked as a theatre designer and director. He was a founding tutor of the Liverpool Institute for Performing Arts and, for 11 years, was Deputy Director of PALATINE, the Higher Education Academy's Subject Centre for Dance, Drama and Music. He is currently the Higher Education Academy's UK Lead for those disciplines.

Colin Lumsden is a Senior Lecturer and Honorary Paediatric Consultant based at Lancashire Teaching Hospital and the Academic Lead for e-learning in Manchester Medical School where he has pioneered the use of iPads in undergraduate medicine. He has a Masters in Medical Education from Cardiff University.

Sue Mathieson works on Academic Quality and leads on Enhancement at Northumbria University. She holds a PhD in Educational Research from Lancaster University, focusing on the nature of academic cultures of learning and teaching.

Jonathan Parker is a Senior Lecturer in Politics at Keele University. He writes about higher education policy, particularly around research methods. He won the University Award for Teaching in 2005 and became a National Teaching Fellow in 2009.

Nathan Pike is Discipline Lead for Biological Sciences at the Higher Education Academy. He was formerly Degree Co-ordinator of the Masters-level Biology degree programme in Integrative Bioscience at the University of Oxford. He is now a Senior Research Associate within the University's Department of Zoology.

Adrian Simpson is a Reader in Mathematics Education in the School of Education at Durham University. He is also Principal of Josephine Butler College. His research has primarily focused on students' thinking across transition from school to university mathematics, the transition to independent graduate study, and mathematical logic and rationality.

Fiona Stephen is currently Honorary Research Associate at the London School of Economics. For the past 16 years she worked at Queen Mary, University of London and Aberystwyth University, and before that The Open University. Her book *A Farewell to Arms: From long war to peace* was nominated for the Gravenor Prize (United States) in 2003. Previously she worked on integrated education during the years of the troubles in Northern Ireland.

Tim Stewart started his career as a business practitioner within the Unilever Group. Tim moved into academia in 1997 and is Dean of Learning and Teaching and Dean of the Business School within BPP University (a private for-profit university in England).

Stan Taylor retired in 2013 from the Directorship of the Centre for Academic and Research Development at Durham University. He previously taught and researched in the social sciences at the University of Warwick. His publications include *A Handbook for Doctoral Supervisors* (2005) co-authored with Nigel Beasley. He is a Senior Fellow of the Higher Education Academy.

Richard Tong is the Dean of the Cardiff School of Sport at Cardiff Metropolitan University. He is Professor of Sport and Exercise Science and a National Teaching Fellow. Richard has a particular interest in curriculum design and assessment.

Julie Williams is Director of Nurse Education at the University of Lincoln, following posts at the University of Liverpool and the University of Chester as Head of Department. Her current interests include education research and the issue of academic identity in professional and vocational disciplines.

Richard Winsley is Director of Education in Sport and Health Sciences at the University of Exeter. Alongside his interest in learning style, he also teaches exercise science and clinical exercise physiology. He was made a National Teaching Fellow in 2012 and is a Senior Fellow of the Higher Education Academy.

Case study authors

Colette Balmer, University of Liverpool
Caroline Barnes, University of Westminster
Christopher Benjamin, Bournemouth University
Ken Booth, Aberystwyth University
Jo Ann Boylan-Kemp, Nottingham Trent University
Alan Cann, University of Leicester
Tim Cappelli, University of Manchester
Aldwyn Cooper, Regent's University London

Andrew Cooper, University of Salford
Hazel Corradi, University of Bath
Michael Cox, London School of Economics and Political Science
Chris Craggs, University of Lincoln
Luke Dawson, University of Liverpool
Peter Day, University of Wolverhampton
Uwe Derksen, University of the Creative Arts
Mike Dickinson, Lancashire Teaching Hospitals NHS Foundation Trust
Naureen Durrani, University of Sussex
Joseph Gray, University of Glasgow
Jacky Hanson, Lancashire Teaching Hospitals NHS Foundation Trust
Peter Holgate, Northumbria University
Nigel Horner, University of Lincoln
Mark Huxham, Napier University
Katherine Jarman, King's College London
Celia Jenkins, University of Westminster
Phil Jimmieson, University of Liverpool
Steve Jones, Leeds Trinity University
Witney Kilgore, Academic Partnerships
Maria Krivenski, Goldsmiths, University of London
Geoff Layer, University of Wolverhampton
Varunika Lecamwasam, Ealing NHS Trust
David Llewellyn, Harper Adams University
Roger Lloyd-Jones, Sheffield Hallam University
Martha Mador, Kingston University
Philip Martin, Sheffield Hallam University
Ben Mason, University of Liverpool
Beverley Milton-Edwards, Queen's University Belfast
Jane Mooney, University of Manchester
David Nicholls, Manchester Metropolitan University
Berry O'Donovan, Oxford Brookes University
Caroline Pearman, University of Leeds
Clare Peddie, University of St Andrews
Mark Pimblett, Lancashire Hospital NHS Foundation Trust
Stephanie Pitts, University of Sheffield
Georgia Prescott, University of Cumbria
Gerald Prescott, University of St Andrews
Elena Rodriguez-Falcon, University of Sheffield
Kay Sambel, Northumbria University
Michael Sandal, Harvard University
Kerstin Stoedefalke, Colby-Sawyer College, NH, USA
Niki N. Tariq, University of Central Lancashire
Stephen Tawse, Northumbria University

Ann Thanaraj, University of Cumbria
Mark Thorley, Coventry University
Geoffrey Timmins, University of Central Lancashire
Owen Tomlinson, University of Bath
Clive Turner, City College Norwich
Gwen van der Velden, University of Bath
Evelyn Welch, King's College London
Paul White, University of Sheffield
Sarah Wood, Lancashire Teaching Hospitals NHS Foundation Trust
Abigail Woods, King's College London
Claire Worthington, University of Central Lancashire

Case study teams

Languages and Area Studies, University of Portsmouth
Languages and Social Sciences and International Placement Team, Aston University
METAL Mathematics for Economics: Enhancing Teaching and Learning project
Modern Languages, University of Southampton
National Teaching Fellowship Scheme project team, Keele University
Quality Assurance Agency for Higher Education, UK

Acknowledgements

The editors wish to acknowledge all those who have helped us in the production of the fourth edition of this handbook. In particular, we are especially grateful, as before, to our team of expert contributing authors who together provide a wealth of expertise and experience from across the higher education sector and different perspectives on the challenges and issues that the higher education sector is facing. We are pleased to have brought in new members to our team and benefitted from their fresh ideas. We are also indebted to all those practitioners from the United Kingdom and beyond who have provided the case studies included in the chapters. We are aware that the case studies enrich the handbook, add interest and relevance for our readers and have contributed to the success of the previous editions over the years.

Thanks are also due to two others who have helped complete the task of assembling this fourth edition of the handbook. First, Nicole Nathan helped us with the initial organisation of this project. Second, special thanks go to Lucy Marsh at the Higher Education Academy who worked as our editorial assistant in the final stages to bring the manuscript together for publication. Her professionalism and high-level skills have been invaluable to us. We would also like to thank Fiona Gray at the Higher Education Funding Council for England.

We also thank all others who have helped in the project not specifically named above. In particular, we have to acknowledge the patience and support given by our families and friends for bearing with us whilst we produced the handbook and have been otherwise neglectful of them.

Heather Fry
Steve Ketteridge
Stephanie Marshall
January 2014

Foreword

For any book to go into a second edition is a considerable achievement but to be invited to bring out a fourth edition suggests that the previous volumes have been a great success, that people have found the volume very helpful, that the topics 'teaching and learning' are high on the agenda of the higher education community and that the publisher has sold lots of copies. But there is more. The editors have done it again by bringing together a new collection of essays that will be invaluable to the new lecturer, as well as to those who have worked in the sector for many years, because their guides are leaders in the world of teaching and learning in higher education: Director of Education, Participation and Students at the Higher Education Funding Council for England (Heather Fry); Chief Executive of the Higher Education Academy (Stephanie Marshall); and the former Director of the Learning Institute in a research intensive university (Steve Ketteridge).

For anyone new to teaching, this will be the definitive guide. It is quite rightly described as a handbook that conveys the idea that it is a book for dipping into rather than reading from cover to cover. In this respect, it is an excellent sourcebook that pulls together material addressing many of the questions that higher education colleagues frequently raise at the start of their careers: how do you work with diverse groups? How do you engage students in the learning process? How do you supervise postgraduate research students? Here, the beginner will have the opportunity to explore ways that teaching, learning and assessment fit together because the essays include practical exercises and point towards areas of further support.

All together, these essays give the teacher the opportunity to reflect on some of the key questions and basic issues before turning to a series of discipline-based examples from the experimental sciences, the social sciences, arts, humanities and law, as well as the creative arts and vocational subjects such as Medicine and Dentistry. These essays contain case study material alongside questions about practice that will stimulate the beginning teacher while acting as a timely reminder, for those with greater experience, about ways to develop and enhance their practice.

Overall, Heather Fry, Steve Ketteridge and Stephanie Marshall have done it again. They have produced a splendid volume that highlights the importance of teaching and learning in higher education.

Sir Robert Burgess
Chair of the Higher Education Academy
Vice-Chancellor
University of Leicester
United Kingdom
January 2014

Part 1
The current world of teaching and learning in higher education

1 A user's guide

Heather Fry, Steve Ketteridge
and Stephanie Marshall

SETTING THE CONTEXT OF ACADEMIC PRACTICE

This book starts from the premise that the roles of those who teach in higher education (HE) are complex and multifaceted. Teaching is just one of the roles that readers of this book will be undertaking. It recognises and acknowledges that academics have contractual obligations to pursue excellence in several directions, including teaching, research, scholarship and knowledge exchange, supervision, academic management and leadership. Many must also maintain their professional status within a vocational career, such as teaching or nursing. Academic practice is a term to encompass all these facets.

The focus of this book is on teaching, supporting student learning, assessment and the supervision of students. It is intended as a guide for anyone who teaches in HE and demonstrates how to best facilitate learning and contribute to the student learning experience. We stress the role of the academic as teacher (rather than any of their other roles) in both the title and text of this handbook, but effective teaching (and supervision, assessment and so on) has to be based on a clear understanding of how students learn for teaching to be successful.

The editors and authors all recognise the changing environment in HE in the United Kingdom. The greatest change since the last edition of the handbook has been in how teaching is funded, and the consequent increase in fees paid by many students. There is now more diversity across the four nations of the United Kingdom in how HE is funded, but the nations retain shared aims of purpose and outcome. Universities and colleges are now more fully involved in partnerships to deliver HE on overseas campuses and to recruit staff and students globally. Students are now viewed far more as 'partners' in their education to be engaged in all aspects of teaching and learning. Teaching to a diverse student body has been more widely embraced across the sector and strategies for inclusive teaching adopted. Initiatives to improve the flexibility of delivery and access to students have increased markedly. Online learning is now a normal component of many UK degree programmes. Academic staff may be routinely teaching students face-to-face as well as distance learners. Some will also be travelling to teach on their university campuses overseas. The teaching strategies of universities have also changed since the last edition of the handbook. There is now more emphasis on preparing students for employment with far greater engagement with employers or the local economy in more rural institutions. We have aimed to incorporate and reflect all of these types of changing agendas within the various chapters in this latest edition of the handbook.

PURPOSE OF THIS HANDBOOK

As with our previous editions, this book is intended primarily for relatively inexperienced teachers in HE in all types of institutions. Established lecturers interested in exploring recent developments in teaching, learning and assessment will also find it a valuable resource for updating their own practice. It is also intended that it will be of interest to the wide range of other professional staff working in HE, including those working in communication and information technology, library and technical staff, graduate **teaching assistants** and research staff. It has much to offer staff working outside HE who may have a role in teaching university students in the work place, such as clinicians, engineers and research scientists. Those joining universities after working abroad or perhaps returning from a career in industry or the professions will find the Handbook a helpful introduction to current practice in university teaching.

We know that previous editions of the handbook have been extensively used overseas in universities that have evolved from the British tradition. This edition has been written with these readers in mind to ensure it is fully accessible to audiences further afield. Previous editions of the handbook have also been translated into other languages for our non-English speaking readers.

The book is not based solely on the UK system and is informed by best practice from other countries and different types of institutions and providers of teaching, learning and assessment. It is underpinned and informed by appropriate references to research. The chapters are written by authors from a wide range of disciplinary traditions and reflect those styles in approach. The focus is primarily on teaching at the undergraduate level in England, that is levels 4, 5 and 6, but much will also apply to Masters (level 7) teaching, and there is a chapter solely dedicated to research supervision (level 8). A particular feature of this book is that it reviews the more generic issues in teaching and learning (such as effective lecturing or giving feedback to students) that will be common to most practitioners (in Part 2), and explores practices in a range of major disciplines or disciplinary clusters (in Part 3). Over the years, the editors have changed the particular disciplinary areas to some extent to showcase practices in newer and emerging disciplinary areas. Chapter 14, written by Professor Graham Gibbs, is slightly different to the others in Part 2. He takes a broad overview of how to maximise student learning gain and considers some of the key methods of enhancing student learning. Readers will find his chapter useful in extending their knowledge and understanding of the complexities of the HE system in the United Kingdom, as well as contrasting it with features in other systems, most notably that of the United States.

This fourth edition of the handbook has been completely rewritten for a new audience. The chapters with titles similar to those in previous editions have all been written afresh to incorporate the latest ideas and research findings. The handbook reflects current systems and processes operating in the UK HE sector and includes new case studies based on latest practice. The editors have written new chapters in Part 1 that provide an introduction to the context of teaching practice and developing a career that involves HE teaching. They draw extensively on their most recent knowledge and experience at national and institutional level.

It is now usual for new staff to complete an accredited teaching programme of some type when taking up a post for the first time in HE where teaching will be a significant part of the role. This handbook has been particularly designed with those in mind and should be a useful and thought-provoking resource. It specifically supports those in the United Kingdom where the teaching programme is linked to gaining professional recognition through an Associate Fellowship or Fellowship of the Higher Education Academy (HEA).

The editors have drawn together authors from across a range of different institutions in the UK HE sector. The authors work in different types of roles in their institutions and collectively they offer a wealth of knowledge and experiences based on their expert practice. They have taken care in writing to avoid overusing jargon, but to introduce key terminology and to make all generic text accessible to all disciplines. The editors have sought to ensure that the Handbook provides a scholarly and rigorous approach, while maintaining a user-friendly format.

For the purposes of this handbook, the terms 'academic', 'lecturer', 'teacher' and 'tutor' are be used interchangeably and should be taken to include anyone engaged in the support of student learning in HE.

NAVIGATING THE HANDBOOK

An important feature of the handbook is that each chapter is written so that it can be read independently of the others and in any order. Readers can select and prioritise, according to their interest, although Chapter 5 (Student learning) should be essential reading at an early stage.

Part 1: The current world of teaching and learning in higher education

Following this user's guide, this section has three principal chapters aimed at those new to university teaching in the United Kingdom. Chapter 2 sets out the UK context within which HE teaching occurs. It will help to demystify some of the national bodies and acronyms in everyday use in institutions. Importantly, it draws attention to different ways in which students now engage with their institutions. Chapter 3 reviews the international dimensions of UK HE from the perspectives of staffing, students and overseas operations. Lastly, Chapter 4 considers success as a university teacher and considers career routes, personal development, rewards for excellence and recognition as an excellent teacher.

Part 2: Learning, teaching and supervising in higher education

Chapter 5 provides essential information about student learning. It is based upon theories of student learning in HE and how to use them in practice. It is followed by nine chapters that set out the major facets of teaching and/or learning from a more general perspective, rather than a particular disciplinary bias. They represent the essential toolkit for teaching, supervising, working with groups, course design, assessment and feedback for the less experienced teacher.

Part 3: Teaching and learning in the disciplines

This section includes 13 chapters that consider and explore teaching and learning in the major disciplinary groupings and current aspects of successful practice. They are written by academic staff who have taken a particular interest in the pedagogy of their own disciplines and include detailed case studies to showcase aspects of innovative practice from across the sector and from outside the United Kingdom. These chapters generally assume some background knowledge and understanding, such as from reading the chapters in Part 2.

DISTINCTIVE FEATURES OF THE HANDBOOK

Case studies

The case studies contained in each chapter are a particular strength of the handbook. In most cases, these include the names of the contributing case study authors. These exemplify issues, practices and research findings mentioned in the body of the respective chapters. The case studies are drawn from a wealth of different institutions, involving the everyday practice of their authors and their colleagues to demonstrate how particular approaches can be used successfully.

Interrogating practice boxes

Each chapter features one or more instances where readers are invited to review aspects of their own institution, school, course, students or practice. This is done by posing short questions or prompts to the readers under the heading 'Interrogating practice'. This feature has a number of purposes: first, to encourage the reader to audit their own practice with a view to enhancement; second, to challenge the reader to examine critically their conceptions of teaching and workplace practice; and third, to get the reader to engage actively with a new idea and perhaps reflect on practice. In addition, they aim to ensure that readers are familiar with their institutional and/or school policies and practices. Readers are free to choose whether or not they engage with these personal interrogations.

Glossary

There is a glossary after Part 3 listing technical terms and educational acronyms in common usage that have been used in chapters. In each chapter, the authors have put such terms in **bold** to indicate that a brief definition of the meaning of words or terms may be found alphabetically listed in the glossary. Authors have been careful to use such technical words or terms sparingly so as not to overload the reader coming from a different background, but many are terms that will be encountered and need to be used in teaching in HE. The glossary may be used in conjunction with reading the chapter or (as many of our previous readers have found) used as a separate resource. The glossary entries include new terms in the fourth edition plus others from previous editions, which have been refreshed and renewed.

FURTHER READING AND/OR REFERENCES

Each chapter has a final section that includes suggestions for further reading. In some cases, this will be a few carefully selected review articles and books. In other cases, the reader will be referred to key journal publications and primary sources. There are also many links to online resources.

2 UK institutional teaching contexts

Policies and practice

Heather Fry, Steve Ketteridge
and Stephanie Marshall

INTRODUCTION

This chapter seeks to describe the wider context within which higher education (HE) teaching in the UK occurs. Some understanding of this wider context is vital because academics are not free agents to teach students whatever and however they wish. Teaching takes place within the context of agreed curricula and within UK agreed norms and expectations. Institutions have their own characteristics (e.g. size, subject mix, location) and mission that affect the education they offer. Disciplines too have characteristics and differences about their teaching and learning practices. Such matters are reflected in what is taught, how it is taught, and which students are selected for admission to particular courses, etc. Students also have an effect on what happens because their behaviour affects outcomes and they influence programme development through feedback to staff and teaching committees.

Teaching is used here to refer to curriculum design, face-to-face teaching, use of digital technology, assessment and all forms of interaction with students that relate to their academic experience. It is also taken as a given that the purpose of all these activities is to enhance student learning by creating, constructing and facilitating learning environments that students engage with and that will produce informed, analytical, creative and employable graduates. On occasion, 'teaching' may be used more broadly to include the supervision of research postgraduates.

Although there are national variations within the UK (England, Northern Ireland, Scotland and Wales), HE follows a similar pattern in many important respects. While this chapter draws attention to a few key differences, its content is generally applicable across the UK. There are also some differences in the way HE operates in institutions that are generally described as 'publicly funded' and those often dubbed 'alternative providers'; however, there is much diversity within both sets of institutions and considerable overlap and similarity between some in each set.

This chapter has four case studies, each written by institutional leaders of teaching policy and practice, but coming from institutions of very different size, mission and length of operation. They serve to demonstrate the range of educational diversity, the importance of institutional policy but also the commonality of certain characteristics and approaches that bear testament to there being a distinctive HE approach ('brand') in the UK within which the practice of individual academics is assured and organised.

The work an academic carries out can be described as **'academic practice'**. This term encompasses teaching, supervision, research, scholarship, administration and various forms of consultancy, knowledge exchange or community engagement (see also Chapter 4). This chapter focuses on policy and practices that relate primarily to teaching.

Although these matters act as a constraint on how individual academics teach, teaching also affords considerable freedom to the individual within these norms. The newly starting academic is likely, for example, to 'inherit' a curriculum and certain set-and-agreed ways of doing things but over time, through participation in school/departmental and institutional teaching activities, their understanding of teaching and learning grows and can have much more influence over a wider range of teaching and learning matters. This scope for change encompasses not just their own classroom but also curriculum development and creating new programmes, as well as shaping teaching polices at an institutional or national level. An important part of developing expertise in teaching in HE is about much more than becoming comfortable with a range of teaching methods, assessment approaches or understanding how students learn (see Chapters 7, 8 and 5, respectively) – it involves understanding what effective educational innovation and change to bring about student learning looks like, and being adept at incorporating effective institutional and national norms into one's own practice, as well as being constructively critical of such norms to enable their enhancement.

The University of Sheffield is very clear about the importance of this 'creative balance' that mixes central involvement with individuality to maximise benefit for students and the university. The Sheffield case study also demonstrates the increasing role of **students as partners** in their learning experience and of **student engagement** (see also Chapters 9 and 14).

Case study 2.1: From the local to the global: institutional drivers for learning and teaching at the University of Sheffield

My predecessor as Pro Vice-Chancellor at the University of Sheffield once described the learning and teaching environment in the institution as something of a cottage industry. Everyone did their own thing, often in imaginative and creative ways, but with little co-ordination with others or thought for what the overall objectives should be for students. This mirrored the research environment for many staff able to secure funding for projects that today seem small scale and individualistic.

That was ten years ago. In both research and teaching at Sheffield, and at many other research-intensive universities, the landscape has changed. In teaching, this results from a stronger central emphasis on outcomes and strategy and the marketing of clear messages about the university's student 'offer'. But there has also been the sharing of good practice and creative discussion across the university at a grass roots level, and teaching strategies have been created generally through collaborative discussion rather than through top–down command.

Specific catalysts have been important. The first was arguably the introduction of the university's first virtual learning environment and the decision to let students be the drivers for its introduction across departments through their demands for parity with the experience of their friends who happened to be taught by more innovative lecturers.

A second catalyst lay in the two Centres for Excellence in Teaching and Learning (CETLs) awarded to the university. These created spaces for staff and students together to explore the possibilities of enterprise learning and of inquiry-based learning across the whole university. Student involvement was particularly important because this led to a strong view of the benefits of what is now labelled 'student engagement' – exemplified in Sheffield's award-winning Student Ambassadors for Learning and Teaching (SALTs) who work on teaching enhancement projects with staff support.

A third catalyst occurred in 2005 in the centenary celebrations of the university's royal charter. This led to renewed interest in Sheffield's civic origins, but also to a recognition of how far the university had come since 1905 in establishing itself as a global leader. The City of Sheffield has thus been increasingly seen as a resource to be drawn upon to give students opportunities for not just the clinical experiences of our medical and dental schools but also work with local disabled residents (in Engineering), students in English analysing oral histories from local people and students from across the university working with local small and medium-sized enterprises on enterprise activities.

At the same time, advice from the university's global employers (Rolls Royce, Santander Bank, DLA Piper and others) has encouraged university-wide consideration of students' 'cultural agility' and the desire to give graduates the skills to compete in the global labour market. Alongside the civic engagement agendas, this has reinforced the role for cross-university projects to galvanise local teaching practice to meet institutional goals, themselves derived from consultations with all interested parties including a strong student voice.

Today's **Learning and Teaching Strategy** at the University of Sheffield is entitled 'Global Education in a Civic University'. We want our students to understand the global context for their studies and to seek future experiences anywhere in the world, but we want to ground their learning through contact with clients, customers and communities within our own city.

The words 'local' and 'global' can also be applied to the learning and teaching environment across the university. Local initiative is still strongly encouraged, as it was ten years ago, but now within shared university-wide (or global) perspectives on what we want to achieve.

(Paul White, Pro Vice-Chancellor for Learning and Teaching)

Interrogating practice

- When you first started teaching in HE, how aware were you of the broader context (including institutional) within which teaching operates?
- How have/are you acquiring knowledge and understanding of this context?
- As your understanding of this wider context within which teaching occurs grows (grew), have you been surprised positively or negatively by its impact on how you conduct your own teaching?

THE STUDENT POPULATION

UK higher education has grown rapidly over the last twenty years in particular. The following data refer to 2011–12 and are published by the Higher Education Statistics Agency (HESA) on their web pages (Higher Education Statistics Agency, 2013):

- In 2011–12 there were 2,496,645 total enrolments at UK higher education institutions (HEI). This total is smaller than that of all those studying higher education at UK institutions (for example, this data was not collected from alternative providers).
- 568,505 of this 2011–12 total were postgraduate students.
- Taking undergraduate and postgraduate students together, 775,240 students were studying part-time.

- Of young, full-time, first-degree entrants in 2011–12, 88.9 per cent were from state schools.
- 83 per cent of all students were UK domiciled, 5 per cent EU domiciled and 12 per cent from countries outside the EU.
- Of the 2,061,410 UK domiciled students, 1,636,395 declared themselves to be of White ethnicity, 121,855 Black, 176,450 Asian, with 46,525 not known and 80,185 Other (including mixed).
- Of those obtaining qualifications in 2011–12, 115,610 were female and 73,045 male.
- There were 378,250 staff working in HEIs; 181,385 of these being academic staff. (Chapter 4 elaborates further on matters relating to higher education staff and staffing.)

This statistical snapshot is the most recent available at the time of writing and does not include a time series to show changes over time in these data.

THE DIVERSITY OF INSTITUTIONAL AND QUALIFICATION TYPES IN HIGHER EDUCATION IN THE UK

Within the UK there are three main types of providers of higher education, usually described as:

- Publicly funded higher education institutions (mainly universities)
- Publicly funded further education colleges teaching higher education
- Alternative providers that have generally been founded and developed without public investment, some of which are for-profit companies.

Within each of these categories there is considerable variation and examples can be found within each group that are very similar to examples from a different group. Some of the factors that promote homogeneity are the possession or otherwise of **degree-awarding powers**, size, mission and student profile. The second case study in this chapter is written by the Vice-Chancellor and Chief Executive of an alternative provider with a strong international focus (see also Chapter 3).

> ## Case study 2.2: Regent's University London: an 'alternative' provider approach to learning and teaching

Regent's University London (RUL) is the largest campus-based private, non-state funded, not-for-profit university in the UK with a current student base of about 4,000 full-time equivalent degree-seeking students and an expectation of doubling in size by 2020. It has a broad portfolio of both British and American validated programmes offered at all levels. By 2020, it is expected that it will have gained UK Research Degree Awarding Powers and US accreditation.

RUL was reorganised substantially in 2007 to provide a single structure, gain university title and strengthen its distinctive approach to learning, teaching and research. The learning experience at the university is focused primarily around on-campus face-to-face interaction or off-campus projects and visits, with an average of 20 contact hours per week of study. Contact hours do not include online activity, which acts as a supplement to contact.

RUL has a broad and diverse student base with students drawn from more than 140 countries around the globe. The learning is enhanced by ensuring that all students are integrated fully into the collegiate life of the campus. Learning is structured to ensure that students learn from each other as well as learning from academic staff and visitors.

RUL believes that there should be a strong interaction between learners and academic staff. It maintains a staff-student ratio of better than 15:1 on average. Students should have a high level of access to academic staff. Seventy-five per cent of contact hours are delivered by permanent full-time or high-fractional staff, although the contribution made by visiting lecturers is valued because many bring current practical experience and knowledge to enrich programmes. Alumni are engaged globally in mentoring graduating students.

Academic staff are required to maintain scholarly activity to ensure continual improvement and relevance of the learning experience. Staff are encouraged to become engaged in innovative research, both for publication and to continually refresh the programmes on which they teach. Funds are available to pump prime research, and successful research staff see the profile of their activity rebalanced to afford them time for research.

Face-to-face instruction is supported by cutting edge application of digital technologies, including broad access to online knowledge products, appropriate applications and the university's implementation of the Blackboard Managed Learning Environment (MLE) used on all programmes of study.

RUL teaches ten economically important languages through its Institute for Language and Culture and promotes international experience strongly across the campus, with more than 30 per cent of students required to learn a new language and to study for two semesters in a country where that language is used.

RUL is teaching focused but research engaged. A research environment is being generated across the institution. To assist in this, a new unit is being established to co-ordinate further 'Research, Learning, Teaching, Assessment and

Academic Development' with a new professorial level appointment to direct these activities.

The approach taken by RUL is repaid by the high level of graduate employment around the world at higher than average graduate salaries.

(Aldwyn Cooper, Vice-Chancellor and CEO)

Most institutions are charities, including those from each of the three types; some are postgraduate only and some are specialist with a focus on a single subject or a small range of related subjects (specialist institutions).

Publicly funded universities (or more strictly publicly funded higher education institutions because not all are universities) will typically conduct both research and teaching and may receive government money for these functions from a national funding council or similar (the Higher Education Funding Councils for England and Wales; the **Scottish Funding Council**, which funds both further and higher education; and the Department for Employment and Learning in Northern Ireland). Among this group of institutions there are some that are more research intensive than others and for staff working there who have a broad academic contract they will be balancing these two main arms of activity. The staff of all higher education providers in the UK (as in Case study 2.2) should be engaging in scholarly activity that keeps them up to date about their field of activity, be this theoretical or applied. Those teaching in more applied disciplines are also likely to need (or be encouraged) to engage in practicing their chosen profession or vocation (doctor, school teacher, artist, pianist, etc.). For all, but especially the new higher education teacher, progressing these various career strands in parallel imposes a considerable strain and tension (see Chapter 4).

Institutions with full degree-awarding powers issue their own degrees. All higher education qualifications are described as belonging to a particular level, as set out in the national frameworks for higher education qualifications, and having a particular number of credits (such as 360 for an honours degree) at the prescribed levels. Research degrees (such as the PhD) and more practice-orientated professional research degrees with a higher taught element (such as those in education called EdDs) are described in England as being at level 8. Masters degrees operate at level 7, a full Bachelors honour degree is at level 6 and a **Foundation degree** at level 5. The first year of higher education study (for a full-time programme) is calibrated at level 4.

Institutions with degree-awarding powers set standards against national norms and use the **subject benchmark statements** within disciplines as their reference point to ensure minimum national standards are maintained. The **Quality Assurance Agency** (QAA) compiles and operates the national frameworks, academic credit arrangements and benchmarks for the higher education sector and these, along with other chapters, make up the **UK Quality Code for Higher Education**. Institutions with degree-awarding powers can validate degrees that are taught by others, as well as franchise out their own degrees. There are also long-standing non-degree awards, such as the Higher National Certificate and Diploma (levels 4 and 5, respectively) that are run by EdExcel (owned by Pearson).

THE ORGANISATION AND GOVERNANCE OF TEACHING WITHIN HIGHER EDUCATION PROVIDERS

What follows in this section may appear as information of little interest or concern to many new teachers in higher education, but it is important. The structure of educational governance has a large impact on how teaching is conducted in each institution and hence on each member of teaching staff. For teaching staff who attended a UK higher education institution as a student, some of this may be familiar, but although students are increasingly becoming knowledgeable about these structures and arrangements, many staff, especially those who may have completed their own undergraduate degree a decade or more ago, will have less familiarity with it and will have perhaps seen these arrangements through a different lens than their current staff perspective. Newer higher education teachers from overseas may find much of this section unfamiliar territory.

UK higher education providers are generally regarded as being autonomous, that is there are many areas of their operation that are not governed or regulated by 'higher authorities'. Many national policies and norms operate through more or less willing consent on the part of institutions. A high degree of autonomy creates opportunity for diversity, and local variation is one of the strengths of the UK approach to higher education. However there are some restraints on autonomy, for example in ensuring accountability for public money. Arguably, such constraints have grown over the last fifty years (Shattock, 2012). Higher education providers employ their own staff and have full autonomy from government over admissions decisions, assessment, the content of programmes, etc.

Various professional bodies (such as the General Medical Council) **accredit** programmes of study, often granting those completing such programmes a 'licence to practice'. They will usually operate a system of periodic review to grant and re-grant accreditation and their expectations influence department decisions about teaching. Institutions in the UK are generally required to accept the QAA process of review to give assurance about quality and standards in educational provision at a national level (the exceptions may be some non-publicly funded providers).

To simplify drastically, institutional organisation of teaching will be influenced by and approved in broadly the following ways:

1   An institution or organisation will be governed at the highest level by a board or council. The head of the institution or organisation will attend and participate in meetings of this body. Alternative providers owned by another entity (such as a parent company) will have another level of governance sitting above this structure.

2 There will often be a senate or similar that considers academic matters and will usually be composed only of staff members, along with some student representation.

3 There will be at least one person who has leadership and management responsibility for education and students who reports to the head of the organisation. In the publically funded university sector, the most usual title at this level is Pro Vice-Chancellor.

4 Admissions, programme regulations, and so on, can be operated at school/department level (depending upon the terminology used), but are often operated through faculty or institutional level 'administrative' departments.

5 Schools/departments are usually organised into faculties (also, confusingly sometimes called schools), with there being a head of each level. There may or may not be a faculty or department lead below the head with responsibility for teaching/education/students.

6 Schools/departments and/or faculties may have teaching committees, as will the institution as a whole generally. It is in these committees that many institutional teaching policies and practices are developed, agreed and set down, including a strategy document about the learning and teaching aims of the institution or faculty. Such a committee may also create and update a document setting out the responsibilities of the institution to students and the expectations the institution places on students (a 'student charter'). These or different committees will also operate policies in relation to quality assurance of teaching, including approving new programmes and reviewing or revalidating existing programmes periodically (typically every five years). There will almost always be student representation on these types of committees.

7 For institutions without degree-awarding powers, validation of degrees will happen outside the home organisation.

8 At course or programme level, each programme will generally have a lead academic who has overall responsibility for it. There should be formal arrangements for course or school/department level meetings of those engaged in teaching, often once a term/semester.

9 Taught courses should also have a staff–student committee to enable the exchange of feedback and information about the course and to seek enhancement of the course. There will also usually be an examiners panel or meeting that considers assessment outcomes and will include an **external examiner**.

10 In terms of research degrees (i.e. those in which the main pedagogic method is supervision rather than teaching), there will usually be a parallel set of committees. (Taught postgraduate courses, e.g. Masters degrees, will rarely be considered to be part of the research degree structure.)

11 In smaller providers of higher education, there is likely to be a flatter hierarchy of committees and leaders involved in setting the parameters within which teaching occurs. In providers that also offer other levels of education, there will generally be separate structures that cover all of these aspects in relation to higher education.

NATIONAL ORGANISATIONS THAT HAVE AN IMPACT ON THE ORGANISATION AND PRACTICE OF TEACHING

National governments within the UK determine the broad approach to higher education through the various policies, regulations and funding approaches they adopt; however, they operate much of this overall, broad policy landscape through other bodies, rather than directly. This part of the chapter mentions a number of these bodies and provides web links for those who want to find out more about them.

Since devolution of higher education matters from Westminster, there are an increasing number of differences across different countries in the UK. Typically, the government ministers with responsibility for higher education will set out their vision in a White Paper. This means that as government changes, broad overall directions of policy may change. England has seen such a change with the coming to power of a coalition government in 2010, the decision to raise tuition fees and a subsequent White Paper (Department for Business, Innovation and Skills, 2011), which the government is seeking to implement, perhaps ultimately through changed legislation around higher education.

There are also a number of organisations that are less restricted by any government direction that influences how education works. These are generally organisations that large parts of the higher education sector subscribe to. An example of such an organisation is the Universities and Colleges Admissions Service (UCAS).

The following box mentions some of the key organisations that are particularly important.

There are various national organisations that have an impact on the policies and organisation of higher education teaching in the UK. Some of these key organisations are listed and their web details are given at the end of this chapter:

Funding Councils England, Scotland and Wales each have their own funding council for higher education, with Scotland's council operating across higher and further education. A government department operates a similar function in Northern Ireland. The councils distribute government funding for teaching and research in higher education according to the broad approach set out by their government and also operate various regulatory and enhancement functions, including holding the statutory powers in relation to quality assessment, which they operate through the QAA.

Higher Education Academy (HEA) champions excellent learning and teaching in higher education and supports the higher education community to enhance the quality and impact of learning and teaching. It is a national and independent organisation, funded by the four UK HE funding bodies and by subscriptions and grants.

National Union of Students (NUS) is a voluntary membership organisation aiming to make a difference to the lives of students and its member students' unions. It is a confederation of 600 students' unions, amounting to more than 95 per cent of all higher and further education unions in the UK. The NUS promotes, defends and seeks to extend the rights of students and to develop and champion strong students' unions.

Figure 2.1 Some key organisations with an influence on higher education in the UK (continued)

Office for Fair Access (Offa) is an independent public body that helps safeguard and promote fair access to higher education. It does this by approving and monitoring 'access agreements'. All English universities and colleges that want to charge higher fees must have an 'access agreement'.

Office of the Independent Adjudicator (OIA) is an independent body set up to review student complaints. Free to students, the OIA deals with individual complaints against higher education institutions in England and Wales.

Quality Assurance Agency for Higher Education (QAA) safeguards quality and standards in UK universities and colleges so that students have the best possible learning experience. It offers advice, guidance and support to help UK universities, colleges and other institutions. It conducts reviews of institutions and publishes reports detailing the findings. It also publishes a range of reference points and guidance to support standards and promote quality enhancement.

Universities and Colleges Admission Service (UCAS) is the organisation responsible for managing applications to higher education courses in the UK, providing application services across a range of subject areas and modes of study. It is funded by subscriptions from members and focuses on admissions services for students.

Vitae focuses on the career and professional development of researchers. It works in partnership with higher education institutions, research organisations, funders and national organisations to the benefit of researchers and their careers, including supporting higher education providers to train and develop researchers appropriately. It is supported by Research Councils UK (RCUK), and UK HE funding councils.

Figure 2.1 Some key organisations with an influence on higher education in the UK

DISTINCTIVE FEATURES OF UK TEACHING ORGANISATION AND PRACTICE

This section elaborates further on some of the national norms and expectations referred to in the earlier sections.

There are three main ways in which the standards of UK higher education awards are assured. These are through degree-awarding powers, an external examining system and parts of the QAA quality code.

Degree-Awarding Powers

A large number of higher education providers, especially the largest, have their own degree-awarding powers (DAPs). This means they can create and validate degrees that are accepted as meeting national expectations. Some institutions have these powers in perpetuity because of historical circumstances. Nowadays, any new applicant for DAPs receives them for six years after which they have to be renewed. The QAA makes recommendations to government about granting new DAPs and carries out the review for renewals. This process acts as a safety mechanism to ensure UK degrees operate a similar approach to standards. There are different types of DAPs – for foundation degrees, all taught degrees and research degrees. An institution may have DAPs for one or more type of degree.

Case study 3 comes from a higher education manager at a provider of publically funded higher education that does not have DAPs, offering degrees validated by providers who do have them, as well as other higher level qualifications. These arrangements do not stifle local innovation but may promote it and enable an institution to be responsive and agile, as in the case study.

Case study 2.3: Innovation in teaching, learning and assessment at City College Norwich

Significant delivery of higher education takes place within further education colleges. Such provision is generally characterised as vocational and having a student population which is markedly different to the typical 18–21-year-old undergraduate population of universities. The courses on offer have evolved rapidly over time and, with the introduction of foundation degrees some ten years ago, have required colleges and their validating partner higher education institutions to engage much more closely than ever before with employers in the design of curriculum, the introduction of new mechanisms and devices of assessment, to adopt a new or at least significantly modified pedagogy and to devise and deliver a range of student support mechanisms.

The imperative to develop curricula and learning and teaching strategies – which are not only academically rigorous but also develop specific knowledge and skills for an employment context or development need that itself is dynamic and, as experience shows, can be short-lived – has been the motivator for the development of approaches to teaching and assessment that are flexible and adaptable to these rapidly changing contexts.

At City College Norwich we have introduced, for example, a 60 credit major project in four of the five 'top-up' (from foundation degree) honours year programmes developed in the last two years. The approach was informed by the experience of the BA Professional Studies more generic top-up degree developed earlier with the University of East Anglia. The project is assessed in stages and incorporates group work, individual presentations, a literature review and project scoping exercise, a written report and a final presentation/viva. Student peer assessment is used in the early stages and employers are invited to comment on the written reports and to observe the final presentations. Whilst none of these initiatives is unique, the combination of activities, coupled with supporting workshops spread over the whole period of the 10-month project, makes this a valuable and worthwhile experience for students and tutors alike.

Other innovative approaches to teaching and learning have been prompted by the changing requirements of a professional body. The team running our social work qualification, a Bachelor's degree in Applied Social Work, have introduced a number of notable initiatives, including inquiry-based learning that features small groups of students investigating one of seven different and variously funded community projects over the course of their three-year degree. Each group produces a report at the end that has to identify and evaluate contemporary transformative influences/developments in social work. This also reflects the college's commitment to enterprise. Social work students make use of our 'Start Up Lounge' to conceive and create social enterprise organisations, which gives them practical insight into the variety of forms that social intervention and support can take, as well as into teamworking, the development of communication and a range of 'soft skills'. 'Service User Learning Groups' bring a service user perspective and add relevance to student learning. Small groups of students (five or six) meet a service user twice per term throughout their programme.

Other examples of distinctive learning and assessment techniques include professional discussions, reflective practice logs, small business start-ups and poster presentations.

(Clive Turner, Higher Education Manager, City College Norwich)

External examining (see Chapter 8)

Any type of assessment that counts towards the final degree outcome should be assessed by more than one person and moderated by someone external to the home institution – the external examiner. External examiners are typically academics with strong discipline and education experience. They use their knowledge of standards in other higher education providers to cross-check how marking was conducted and sample mark some assignments/examinations. They then use their judgement to help keep standards across the country similar by advising assessment panels about their marking or, on occasion, seeking alteration to the marks of a cohort of students. External examining for research degrees operates to similar principles, but with one or two externals often also conducting an oral examination of the candidate (see Chapter 13).

The QAA has a considerable influence on how academic practice takes place, through assurance work and through establishing norms.

The UK Quality Code for Higher Education (see references)

The QAA takes the lead to work with panels of academic experts and then, through wider consultation to seek UK-wide consensus and agreement, to subject benchmark statements, frameworks relating to qualifications, the credit points that relate to different qualifications (all referred to earlier), a code about how matters such as teaching, assessment, admissions and supervision practice should be conducted and guidance about the provision of information about higher education. The subject benchmark statements set out statements about the level and types of outcome expected at a threshold level for obtaining a degree in different disciplines. The frameworks describe the level of achievement expected at each year of HE study. It is expected that higher education providers adhere to the code and for this to be demonstrated when the QAA visits an institution for quality assurance purposes. At the time of writing this chapter, the code was in the midst of being updated, having evolved from a predecessor known as the Academic Infrastructure. By August 2014, all updating should be complete and the code comprised of three parts (relating to standards, quality and information about higher education). Various chapters set out the expectations that practices in each of these areas should conform to. This is a form of co-regulation or consent to regulation.

Quality assurance at a national level

This builds on the various arrangements that institutions have in place, such as the periodic review of courses mentioned previously. The QAA operates within each devolved administration to conduct periodic assurance and enhancement visits to institutions to consider how each is meeting national norms and expectations with regard to the learning opportunities on offer and the standards of awards (and other aspects in different countries of the UK). It does this in a manner that has been agreed through consultation with the higher education sector and under powers held in each country by the funding bodies with respect to publically funded providers, and in various ways (or not) with alternative providers. The teams who visit are largely composed of peers of the teaching staff. Subsequent to visits, reports are published that summarise good and poor practice and give an opinion on how various education aspects are meeting expectations. The exact name of visits, arrangements, nature and description of outcomes vary in the different parts of the UK, but in all cases the quality code is used as the reference point of what is expected of UK higher education providers. In the four different administrations of the UK, there are different ways the QAA passes judgements on what it finds in each institution and different ways of dealing with poor practice.

The National Student Survey and information for students

The **National Student Survey** (NSS) for undergraduate courses started in 2005 and is now well established in virtually all publically funded institutions in the UK and is becoming more common in alternative providers, especially those with DAPs. It is a survey of student perception of satisfaction with their course. It has two main purposes, which have shifted in importance over the years, as has the balance between them.

One purpose is of being a **quality enhancement** tool to enable students to feedback their perceptions of their courses and for institutions to make consequent improvement and changes. Students have generally perceived assessment and the feedback they receive as the poorest elements of institutional teaching practices. Some improvement has occurred over the years in student participation and also their scores have gradually increased; scores in relation to assessment and feedback have particularly risen over recent years. The other purpose of the NSS is to give information about courses to existing and prospective students. In the next case study, the Pro Vice-Chancellor (Academic) from Sheffield Hallam University shows the influence the NSS has had.

Case study 2.4: Teaching at the heart of the university

There is little doubt that the NSS has rapidly become the largest single catalyst for change in universities like mine. This is not primarily because the NSS is seen as an ideal instrument to foster enhancement, but because it is the only means of benchmarking our student satisfaction across the sector and, further, it is the most dynamic single element in the major university league tables conducted by the national newspapers. While **Research Excellence Framework** results will contribute a stable score for six years, the NSS provides immediate movement on a tiny compressed scale annually. Because NSS is heavily weighted in such tables, a 1 per cent or 2 per cent move can have a disproportionately large effect in a university's placing. University managers and leaders therefore watch these results very closely.

Despite the shortcomings of NSS and the generally baleful effects of university league tables, the survey has been an important factor in rebalancing universities' missions towards a fuller recognition of teaching and learning. This means that those now entering the profession will discover close attention paid to teaching at the interview, and indeed, in annual appraisals that are likely to include evidence of teaching quality. Heightening awareness of good teaching and its value to the university is also profiled in our annual student-nominated 'Inspirational Teaching Awards' designed to celebrate the achievements of those colleagues whom students see as truly inspirational. These awards form part of a group of initiatives and policies supporting the recognition of teaching, including a Postgraduate Certificate in Teaching and Learning for new staff without teaching experience, continuing professional development (CPD) programmes in teaching, peer supported review and observation, and the university's HEA accreditation scheme. Importantly, much of our support here is 'peer-to-peer' to share and develop expertise. We do not believe that such initiatives separately automatically 'make good teachers', but they do contribute to the building of a participative culture in which reflection, experimentation and analysis of teaching form part of the vocational lives of higher education academics.

One of the biggest challenges of the teaching and learning agenda however is something that sits largely outside the classroom – the virtual learning environment (VLE) and the use of electronic resources more generally. While technological change forges ahead, established academics increasingly find that the pace of their electronic skills is outstripped by that of their students. New or younger staff therefore often find that they may be quickly identified as likely 'digital natives' capable of leading their more venerable colleagues through the intimidating world of digital innovation. Student expectations run high and at my university we recognise that the importance attached by students to the ready availability of digital resources through mobile devices, remotely or on campus, is a powerful driver of change (see Chapter 10). As we consider another pressure – student and government concerns around 'contact time' – we recognise that online contact, in its many forms, has a large role to play in what Graham Gibbs calls 'time on task' (simply the amount of time students spend working, in and out of class – the most powerful determinant of educational gain and student success (see Chapter 14).

One striking feature of the NSS everywhere is that the generally high levels of student satisfaction for teaching are not reflected in assessment scores. Like many other universities, mine has introduced a new assessment framework that limits the amounts of assessment set in relation to credit values to ensure consistency, scheduling of assessments to avoid bunching as far as possible, and a speeding up of assessment returns to students so that they can make the most of the feedback provided in their next assessment task. Research clearly shows that quick feedback is more effective than slow and over-elaborate commentary, and that clear and simple assessment criteria are more effectively communicated and implemented than those encumbered by a plethora of learning outcomes (see also Chapter 8).

(Philip Martin, Pro Vice-Chancellor (Academic) Sheffield Hallam University)

In the last few years there has also been an increase in other data published about teaching and courses, some in league tables (which often draw on the NSS) and some through more informal social media sites. At a UK level, there has been a focus on providing robust data in a comparable format though a **Key Information Set** for each course, and wider information published on institutions or the **Unistats** website (see references for the web address). Such data have become a considerable driver of institutional behaviour, generally with a positive impact, but with negative overtones where such a focus has been to the detriment of other important features of education that are not so easily measured or presentable in a robust comparable format. It is important that students know what they can and should expect from the institution they attend and what they can do when this is not forthcoming. At the time this book was written, a wide-ranging review of the information nationally available for students was being conducted and further changes in this are to be anticipated.

Interrogating practice

When have some of these issues, such as a QAA visit, a departmental teaching committee, the views of an external examiner come to your attention? How have these affected your practice?

CONCLUSION AND OVERVIEW

This chapter has described some of the main features operating at UK, national, institutional and more local levels that academics in the UK need to be aware of and work within with regard to their teaching. Many of these operate well to create the context for effective learning and teaching, but improvements are always possible in national arrangements, in institutions and among staff that are already doing an excellent job to create effective learning environments. Subsequent chapters in Parts 2 and 3 of this book elaborate on the underlying theory and practice of teaching to elucidate the rationale and actions that teachers should consider to maximise learning gain.

REFERENCES

The web addresses of various organisations mentioned in the chapter are provided.

Department for Business, Innovation and Skills (BIS) (2011) *Putting Students at the Heart of the System*. London: BIS https://www.gov.uk/government/news/putting-students-at-the-heart-of-higher-education (accessed 12 December 2013).

Department for Employment and Learning, Northern Ireland http://www.delni.gov.uk/ (accessed 12 December 2013).

Higher Education Statistics Agency (HESA) (2013) All statistics taken from http://www.hesa.ac.uk/index.php?option=com_content&task=view&id=1897&Itemid=706 (accessed 13 September 2013).

Higher Education Academy (HEA) http://www.heacademy.ac.uk/ (accessed 12 December 2013).

Higher Education Funding Council for England (HEFCE) http://www.hefce.ac.uk/ (accessed 12 December 2013).

Higher Education Funding Council for Wales (HEFW) http://www.hefcw.ac.uk/ (accessed 12 December 2013).

National Union of Students (NUS) http://www.nus.org.uk/ (accessed 12 December 2013).

Office for Fair Access (Offa) http://www.offa.org.uk/ (accessed 12 December 2013).

Office of the Independent Adjudicator http://www.oiahe.org.uk/ (accessed 12 December 2013).

Quality Assurance Agency for Higher Education (QAA) http://www.qaa.ac.uk/Pages/default.aspx (accessed 12 December 2013).

Quality Assurance Agency for Higher Education (QAA) *The UK Quality Code for Higher Education* http://www.qaa.ac.uk/AssuringStandardsAndQuality/quality-code/Pages/default.aspx (accessed 30 December 2013).

Scottish Funding Council http://www.sfc.ac.uk/ (accessed 12 December 2013).

Shattock, M (2012) *Making Policy in British Higher Education 1945–2011.* Maidenhead: McGraw Hill, Open University Press.

Unistats http://unistats.direct.gov.uk/ (accessed 29 October 2013).

Universities and Colleges Admission Service (UCAS) http://www.ucas.com/ (accessed 12 December 2013).

Vitae http://www.vitae.ac.uk/researchers (accessed 12 December 2013).

<table>
<tr><td>3</td><td></td></tr>
</table>

3	# UK higher education
	## An international context

Stephanie Marshall, Heather Fry
and Steve Ketteridge

INTRODUCTION

This chapter presents a brief overview of the changing character of teaching and learning in UK universities with respect to its position and operation in an international market for higher education. Since the 1970s, UK higher education has moved beyond an elite system to one that is more accessible and inclusive, has expanded enormously and widened its offer with respect to the diversity of subjects offered at degree level, mode of study and range of providers. Not only have the numbers of UK students increased, but also those from outside the UK. The growth in numbers of non-EU students has been particularly significant and important over the past twenty years. This chapter explores some of the main drivers for this growth in non-EU ('international') students and the associated implications for academic staff working in UK universities and colleges. These include *where* staff teach because some have a requirement to teach at an overseas campus; *who* they teach, recognising the rising proportions of international students in their classes; *how* they teach to meet the needs of international learners; and *what* they teach.

But apart from students coming to the UK, it is also apparent that for students in England, Wales and Northern Ireland, the change in first degree funding towards payment of higher fees (currently up to £9,000 per annum) has meant that countries in mainland Europe, such as the Netherlands, that offer programmes taught in English may present an attractive alternative to higher education in the UK. Consequently, some students will seriously consider and take up undergraduate studies in Europe. Also, it should not be overlooked that the large number of international students coming to the UK contributes significantly to the UK economy and education sector.

In reading this chapter, it will become apparent that the UK higher education system should now be viewed not just as a means of delivering the greater good (Collini, 2012) but also as a successful UK business providing high quality graduates to the labour market across the modern world. Competition between the UK and overseas universities to attract international students is intensifying, as is the competition for 'high flying' staff.

In this chapter, we present a brief overview of different approaches taken by UK higher education institutions to actively engage with internationalisation and present some selected quantitative information to illustrate the scale of international operations and the main players on the global stage. We use case studies to illustrate successful aspects of international operations, drawn from three universities, but recognise that there is much good practice in the UK and that we could have referred to many other examples from elsewhere. However, we first briefly consider one aspect of the European dimension that has an impact on higher education within the UK.

THE EUROPEAN DIMENSION

There are approximately 4,000 higher education institutions across Europe (including the UK), with wide ranging missions and motivations, including new universities of technology and arts colleges, ancient seats of learning and research, metropolitan universities and small, specialised institutions.

In 1988, the 'Bologna process' (**Bologna Magna Charta Universitatum**) (European Universities Association, 1988) started with an emphasis being placed on institutional autonomy, but became increasingly directed to ensure common frameworks for undergraduate and postgraduate taught and research degrees ensuring parity of length of study. The consequence of this has been to draw attention to UK taught Masters programmes that are distinctive, typically one-year full-time – shorter than similar programmes in Europe. This debate continues.

In 2012–13, the European Commission conducted an exploration of the current state of teaching and learning across the European States. This led the Commission to reinforce the principles of the Bologna agreement, but also to highlight that **employability** had become a growing concern:

> …the quality of teaching and learning should be at the core of the higher education reform agenda in our Member States – with a focus on curricula that deliver relevant, up-to-date knowledge and skills, knowledge which is globally connected, which is useable in the labour market, and which forms a basis for graduates' on-going learning.
>
> (European Commission, 2013: 5)

COMPETITION FOR MARKET SHARE

All UK universities and many other HE providers seek to recruit students who arrive in the UK from a non-EU country for their higher education, be it a first degree, Masters or postgraduate qualification.

Over the last twenty years and in various ways there have been restrictions set by governments in the UK on the number of undergraduate EU (including UK) students that an institution can recruit, thereby limiting inward cash flow through fees and government funding to universities for teaching. No such restrictions have been placed on postgraduate students because they are funded in different ways and universities have been free to recruit such students on a full-cost fee basis. Universities have actively marketed postgraduate taught programmes in the international market for many years, offering specialist courses of one to two years duration that are often vocationally based, providing routes into high level careers in engineering, technology, business, medical specialities, law, etc. There has been fierce competition between nations, such as the United States, Australia and Canada to attract international students to these countries, with Germany recently announcing that it wants to increase its share of the international student market (by 25 per cent) over the years running up to 2020 (Mechan-Schmidt, 2014). The numbers of non-EU first degree students and postgraduate taught student enrolments has almost doubled in UK institutions over the decade to 2012, as shown in Figure 3.1. There have been many effects from this expansion, not least that as UK demand for taught postgraduate courses has tailed off, international students have assumed extreme importance to the financial well-being and viability of this type of provision.

UK universities have taken a number of approaches to recruiting international first degree and postgraduate students. Many UK universities have set themselves strategic ambitions of becoming global universities and to extend their reach and impact beyond UK shores, using the quality of their research and teaching to underpin that ambition. They argue that they provide staff and students with a range of study and travel opportunities that help position them for success within the global employment market. The different approaches to internationalisation are set out in international strategies and the implementation of these and plans for growth will be the responsibility of a member of the institutional executive leadership team, usually a Pro Vice-Chancellor International. The international strategy is not regarded as an add-on activity (see Case study 3.4) but as in the example of the University of Nottingham, 'is embedded in and driven by all university activities'.

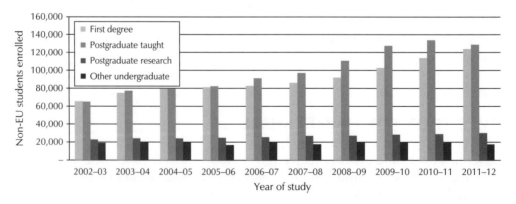

Figure 3.1 Trends in non-EU student enrolments by level of study,
2002–03 to 2011–12
Source: adapted from International Unit (2013a)

International strategies may include a number of different elements:

1   International branch campuses. These are operations located in a country other than that of the home campus, with a physical presence in the host country, at least partly owned by the home institution, and from which the students can earn degrees in the name of the home institution. Research can also be a significant driver of such partnerships. Investment in the development of such overseas campuses has been successfully achieved, for example, by the University of Nottingham in Malaysia (http://www.nottingham.edu.my/index.aspx), Ningbo China (http://www.nottingham.edu.cn/en/index.aspx) and the Heriot-Watt University campus in Dubai (http://www.hw.ac.uk/documents/heriot-watt-international-strategy.pdf). Heriot-Watt describes itself as Scotland's most international university.

2   Developing academic international partnerships and relationships in teaching and research with suitable overseas university partners. There are many examples involving UK universities. These include teaching partnerships with joint under-graduate and postgraduate academic awards, off-campus delivery and split-site PhD schemes. There are many examples, including the partnership between the University of the West of England (UWE), Bristol and Northshore College of Business and Technology in Sri Lanka, that delivers Computing and Engineering degrees awarded by UWE, Bristol and the Queen Mary, University of London – Beijing University of Posts and Telecommunications described in Case study 3.1.

    Such relationships include a wide variety of arrangements from full jointly awarded programmes, through **franchising arrangements** to validation.

    Relationships of types 1 and 2 above are also referred to later as **transnational education** (TNE).

3   Study abroad schemes for students (and staff) with the possibility of scholarships to help provide financial support in an overseas work placement of some kind. Such schemes are long established in many universities and go beyond the Language Assistant scheme (British Council, 2014a) that may be part of many language degree programmes. Study periods abroad provide the opportunity for a different cultural experience and to add an international dimension to the curriculum vitae of the student. They are well established in many universities. Similarly, other countries are encouraging their students to go abroad for language courses, internships or university exchanges, such as Germany where about one-third of students starting courses each year spend part of their studies abroad (Mechan-Schmidt, 2014).

    The Erasmus Programme is part of the European Union (EU)-funded Lifelong Learning Programme 2007–14 and aims to enhance the European dimension of higher education and promote mobility within the EU. Many UK universities have been awarded the Erasmus University Charter (Extended) for the period 2007–14 and so have been able to participate in the scheme to send students and staff members to and from higher education institutions in 33 European countries on study, training, teaching or work experience placements (British Council, 2014b).

With employers demanding more globally aware graduates, there is more atten-tion on the outward mobility of UK students – in 2013 the UK higher education International Unit (2013b) published its first strategy for outward mobility. The strategy seeks to increase the proportion of UK students benefiting from an inter-national experience as part of their studies to 20 per cent by 2020. The strategy sets out clear benefits for UK students, institutions and businesses.

4   Internationalising the curriculum implies developing integrated and inclusive curricula, relevant to the disciplinary, cultural and learning needs of all students in the university (Welikala, 2011). It means equipping them with an education that will be relevant to them and their future employers working in a global economy.

Whilst the UK has sought such partnerships to expand opportunities and hori-zons for students and staff to enhance reputation and contribute to financial sus-tainability, there have been reciprocal beneficial drivers from the host or target countries. For example, joint research collaborations have promoted the ambitions of both partners and, as in Case study 3.1, both partners have benefited from curric-ulum innovation that draws on different strengths from each of them.

TRANSNATIONAL EDUCATION

Many countries in the Far East have focused on attracting high profile research uni-versities from Europe, the United States and Australia to work locally in international branch campuses or as academic partners in order to build research strengths and col-laborations and offer high quality degree programmes to local students. This has been the case particularly in science, technology, engineering and medical subjects to help support their economic growth and development. Many UK institutions have embarked on transnational programmes and Case study 3.1 provides a good example of the approach used by Queen Mary, University of London working in partnership with Beijing University of Posts and Telecommunications (BUPT). This partnership is built around a small group of specialist degree programmes involving telecommunications engineering and building on the considerable research strengths within the Queen Mary School of Electronic Engineering and Computer Science and BUPT. Of particular note are Professor Cuthbert's comments on teaching Chinese students at BUPT and the gender bias in the degree classification of cohorts of graduating students.

> ### Case study 3.1: The Queen Mary model for transnational education

In 2004, Queen Mary (QM) teamed up with Beijing University of Posts and Tele-communications (BUPT) to offer a set of jointly run degree programmes in tele-communications, systems and networks using a new model. The partnership is genuinely equal – students graduate with two degrees, one from BUPT and one from the University of London, with teaching split between the universities. Students graduate with a unique blend of skills, valued in China and around the world. Of the annual crop of almost 500 graduates, a high proportion (65 per cent) go on to postgraduate education outside China at good universities including Cambridge, Oxford, Stanford, Carnegie Mellon and many others – evidence that the programme is highly valued by universities around the world.

Before the planning of the joint programme in China, Queen Mary had been actively expanding its international profile, but this programme was a new model, very different from existing forms of cooperation. China was an attractive proposition because the quality of university education in China is very good, but tends to be narrowly focused on scientific and mathematical detail, rather than the broader approach that young engineers need to understand the context in which the science is applied. BUPT was also particularly attractive as a partner because the two universities already had links and the then president of BUPT obtained his PhD in the UK followed by post-doctorate experience in London, and so understood the differences between the two systems.

The Joint Degree Programme (JP) between QM and BUPT is a genuinely equal partnership. Launched in 2004, it has been an outstanding success, winning the 'Right Partner' category in the 2009 British Business Awards and the 'New Horizons' category in the 2011 Cathay Pacific Business Awards. It is the only professionally accredited engineering degree in mainland China that is accredited by the UK Institution of Engineering and Technology.

The programme draws on the best aspects from both systems – the mathematical and scientific rigour from China and the engineering and creative problem-solving skills from the UK. The syllabus and teaching materials are based on the curricula of both institutions, and are subject to the quality assurance systems of both universities and countries. All teaching takes place in China, in English, with 50 per cent of the teaching from each university. The first five cohorts have now graduated and the programme reached its initial steady state with 2,000 students, but the addition of a new programme is now leading to a growth of 2,800 students. The addition of a new personal development component brings out creativity and communication abilities, enabling graduates to fit into Masters programmes around the world. The number going on to postgraduate education has increased annually, from 70 per cent in 2008 to 85 per cent in 2011, with 65 per cent studying abroad at some of the best universities in the world.

Quality is ensured by using the same staff who are teaching in QM or BUPT to teach on the JP. UK-based staff (who also teach in London) fly regularly to Beijing to teach in 'block' mode so that one module is covered by four 10-hour blocks, each delivered across five days. While this results in a lot of flying, it is more environmentally friendly than recruiting the same number of students to come to the UK. It is also unlike most other Sino–British programmes, which do not use core teaching staff in this way (and which do not award double degrees from the parent universities).

The quality of the student intake is extremely good: the programmes are recognised as 'national key programmes' and JP students must score significantly above the top national line in the Chinese national university entrance examination (the GaoKao) to meet not only the criterion for key universities but also the criterion for BUPT. Coupled with the high level of Mathematics and Basic Science taught at school in China, this means that the average capability level of the cohort is very high. As the content is more than in a UK degree and students have to pass everything, the results are even more impressive than the basic statistics.

Teaching on the JP has been an interesting experience for QM staff, who have had to learn to adapt and interact in a different way:

- Chinese students are passive in the class and it is really difficult to get them to interact, even when bribing with chocolates; however, after class or in the break between consecutive lectures, they crowd around asking questions.
- The good students will go through the lecture material in fine detail and compare with past examination questions and textbooks – they will want to know the reason behind the slightest discrepancy so staff have to be really on top of their subject and sometimes simplifying a topic to 'make it more understandable' actually makes it less so!

For an engineering degree the proportion of female students is remarkably high – around 40 per cent of an entry cohort of over 600. They also do extraordinarily well, with 80 per cent of the women in the 2010 Telecoms Engineering cohort obtaining a First Class Honours degree; regularly no more than 20 per cent of the top 20 students are male. We have no real understanding of why this is.

We believe that this is the best Sino–British joint educational programme in existence because of the model of making it a genuine partnership and in using core staff. By combining the best and the most stringent requirements from each side, the programme pushes its students to reach their potential. The rigour associated with a Chinese degree makes it demonstrably more demanding than a normal British degree, and at the same time the programme develops transferable skills in a way that does not generally happen in a Chinese degree. Combining different aspects such as these simply would not have been possible without the partnership.

Academic staff members from UK and China are exposed to teaching methods from the other country and this is beneficial in spreading good practice within and between the two countries. In addition, access to BUPT has opened up new research opportunities for colleagues at Queen Mary.

Overall, the JP has shown unequivocally that a British and a Chinese university can work hand-in-glove together, and this model of cooperation and friendship sets a pattern for others to follow. The model is sustainable, embedded in the Chinese system and is not an 'add-on'.

(Laurie Cuthbert, Queen Mary, University of London)

The recent growth in TNE provision has seen a shift in the centre of gravity from the Middle East, where in 2009, the United Arab Emirates had a quarter of the 162 branch campuses worldwide. The trend is to move eastwards, notably with China seeking more ties with European institutions. A potentially significant development is the likely increase in intra-regional TNE arrangements and 'south-to-south' activity in Asia through the rise of the Association of Southeast Asian Nations, which is looking to develop a credit transfer system between a network of member universities by 2015 (Lawton et al., 2013).

The UK is a major supplier of TNE worldwide, teaching more students (on a simple head count) in their own (or a third) country than those who come to the UK. Statistics for 2011–12 from the Higher Education Statistics Agency (HESA) show that there were 575,000 TNE students registered on UK courses, with a further 435,000 studying in the UK. Table 3.1 shows the ten countries that have the highest numbers of students studying for a UK qualification but not coming to reside in the UK.

There is some need for caution in these headline figures because they are head-count numbers (with over half registered for an Association of Certified Chartered

Table 3.1 Top 10 countries with UK-registered TNE students 2011–12

Country of origin	Number of students
Malaysia	66,920
Singapore	51,770
Pakistan	39,080
China	38,275
Hong Kong, China	30,100
Nigeria	24,000
Ghana	17,225
Ireland	15,715
Trinidad and Tobago	13,565
United Arab Emirates	13,460

Source: Adapted from International Unit (2013a)

Accountants qualification, which students have up to ten years to complete and because some students are studying part-time); nonetheless the volume is considerable.

Questions may be raised about the quality of TNE, given the range of types of provision and location of delivery. It is the responsibility of the awarding institution to ensure that the same standards apply to all UK degrees whether delivered in the UK, overseas or through online or distance learning. At the time of writing, QAA (with the International Unit and the Higher Education Funding Council for England) is re-examining quality assurance for TNE to ensure it is robust and remains fit for purpose.

INTERNATIONAL STUDENTS

Around the world the number of students studying overseas has increased, from 0.8 million in 1975, to 2.1 million in 2000, and more than doubling to 4.3 million in 2011. Asian countries account for 53 per cent of all international students, and the vast majority of overseas students are enrolled on courses in **G20 countries**, of which nearly half (48 per cent) are in Europe. Significant changes in market share between 2000 and 2011 have seen the United States losing out to the UK and Russia (Organisation for Economic Co-operation and Development [OECD] 2013), as shown in Table 3.2.

Like most G20 countries, the UK is a significant net importer of students. The OECD considers key factors in the choice of location of study to include language of study, quality of programmes, tuition fee levels and immigration policy (OECD, 2013). The first two may explain why the UK is such a popular destination for overseas students;

Table 3.2 Changing shares of the international student market, 2000 and 2011

Country	Market share		
	2000 (%)	2011 (%)	Net movement
United States	22.9	16.5	Down
United Kingdom	10.8	13.0	Up
Germany	9.0	6.3	Down
France	6.6	6.2	Down
Australia	5.1	6.1	Up
Canada	4.6	4.7	Up
Russian Federation	2.0	4.0	Up
Japan	3.2	3.5	Up
Spain	1.2	2.5	Up
China	1.8	1.8	

Source: Adapted from Organisation for Economic Co-operation and Development (2013)

Table 3.3 Non-UK student enrolments by location of institution, 2011–12

UK country of institution	Number of EU students	Number of non-EU students	% Of all students in region
England	105,185	251,908	12
Scotland	17,475	28,500	13
Wales	6,020	19,250	15
Northern Ireland	3,875	2,950	6

Source: Adapted from International Unit (2013a)

however, recent changes to immigration policy in the UK have demonstrated how sensitive the international student market is to changes.

For the UK, by far the greatest number of overseas students studying on undergraduate and postgraduate taught and research degrees come from China; however, what is significant is the importance of postgraduate taught provision in attracting overseas students to the UK – particularly from outside the European Union – as shown in Figure 3.1.

While the United States holds the largest market share, international students make up less than 5 per cent of their total student population. This contrasts markedly with the UK where international students make up around 17 per cent of all students in higher education (in a significant minority of UK institutions, this percentage exceeds 30 per cent). Only Australia, at 19 per cent, has a higher percentage of its student population made up of international students (OECD, 2013). Table 3.3 shows a fairly even spread of non-UK students across three of the UK nations and a lesser proportion in Northern Ireland.

Interrogating practice

- What are the proportions of UK, EU and non-EU students enrolled for undergraduate, taught postgraduate and research degrees at your institution?
- How easy was it for you to find this information?

INTERNATIONALISATION AND LEARNING AND TEACHING

Beyond the importance of international students to the financial health of the UK higher education sector, particularly those studying on postgraduate taught courses, international students are recognised as beneficial for UK domiciled students. For example, the Welsh Government (2013) Policy Statement on Higher Education considers that international students add value by 'enriching learning and teaching, and helping to make Welsh graduates better prepared for an international labour market and a variety of cultural settings.'

Curricula too are influenced by internationalisation. Case study 3.1 has shown how UK and Chinese strengths have been blended in the creation of the curriculum. Curricula have become more inclusive in terms of content, use of case studies and examples. Lecturers are more aware, with students from diverse backgrounds and cultures in their classrooms, of taking an inclusive approach and making fewer assumptions about cultural norms and reference points. They also need to appreciate the different educational experiences that form the background for many of their learners who started their education in different traditions. Thus, the transition to a UK approach to higher education has to be something not assumed but explained and sensitively approached (see also Case study 3.4). Diverse learners (see Chapter 11) need lecturers who are prepared to take diverse approaches. Iannelli and Huang (2013) draw attention to a number of these features and argue that universities often underestimate the challenges and costs of properly supporting students new to the UK higher education system. They particularly mention language issues, the need for strong pastoral support, academic guidance and explanation to non-UK students of what is expected from them.

Case study 3.2 demonstrates the educational enrichment to be derived from internationalisation – even when the students and staff concerned do not physically meet.

Case study 3.2: Responding to the global challenge through innovative three-way collaboration

Students become engaged in learning when the experience is authentic and challenging. For this reason, they often use technology to engage with their peers globally to develop their skills and knowledge. In Music Technology (as with many other subjects), students often share work with their peers digitally, comment on the work of others and work at collective development tasks. This aspect, though valuable, is not always applied in the formal curriculum and is sometimes seen as slightly subversive by higher education institutions.

Similarly, organisations use new technology to engage in peer-production and collaborators can be in different continents. This concept is proving particularly useful for the production of digitally orientated services and products, such as software, music, film and design, etc. Acquiring the skills of peer-production is therefore useful for students in order to become global practitioners in the future. Despite its potential in education to create deeper and broader understanding, peer-production is, however, not always used to its full potential in academic circles.

Furthermore, digital technology can be used to share student work with potential employers. This has obvious benefits to the student and the employer but is not particularly common.

To address the potential of these concepts, a three-way collaboration between Coventry University, New York University (NYU) and an industry organisation called **JAMES (Joint Audio Media Education Support)** was formulated. JAMES accredits courses and creates and maintains supportive links between education and the media industries. The project focused on audio recording techniques modules taught independently by the two institutions. Emerging technology was used to join activities between the two institutions and JAMES. Learning materials were shared across the two institutions, peer-assessment took place and collaborative projects emerged from the interaction.

The project achieved **student engagement** through a number of key principles. First, it facilitated active and collaborative learning in the manner in which the two cohorts of students needed to share their work, commit to working collaboratively on tasks and to assess each other's work. These all focused on common learning goals. Second, the academic challenges were unusual. Working with peers in a different continent or with high-level industry professionals is not commonplace in undergraduate studies. The project approach therefore presented technical, logistical and cultural challenges and the engagement with professionals brought an authenticity that could cause students to 'raise their game'. These aspects were grounded in the wider opportunity that the project presented to enrich the educational experience of the students. Third, it brought the opportunity for **formative assessment** from academics in both institutions and the industry professionals. In this way, students became self-regulated learners. Lastly, the project legitimised the kind of learning that students often engage in outside the formal curriculum, using technology and networks. This was an effective learning strategy not only in this context but also in the way in which it can be applied to continued professional development beyond graduation.

(Mark Thorley, Head of Music Technology,
Coventry University)

POSITIONING IN THE GLOBAL MARKET

Global league tables, where the measures predominantly relate to research, influence the recruitment of international staff and students. Such tables have received great attention in the press, as well as from executive leadership teams, particularly in research-led universities. They have undoubtedly resulted from and contributed to even greater competitiveness amongst higher education providers. Case study 3.3 explores the growth of such league tables.

Case study 3.3: Global league tables

In the last decade, the world higher education environment has been transformed by the advent of global league tables, which have enhanced competition within national systems and across borders. University rankings shape a university's reputation and increase the performance pressures on universities, especially in relation to the quantity and quality of research. For many university leaders, the chief performance indicator is now to improve the global ranking of their institutions. One effect of league table competition has been expansion of the global labour market in mobile, high-quality personnel working in universities. The climate of comparison has also encouraged a growing investment in higher education in many countries, most notably in the Far East.

As well as global rankings, the rapid growth of international education has highlighted comparisons between countries as sites of teaching and learning. In the absence of sound comparative data on the teaching performance of the different institutions and countries, judgments about where to enrol tend to be based on an institution's reputation. In university ranking, research is by far the most important aspect of performance. Research paper outputs and citations are relatively easy to measure, and research capacity tells us something about the capacity for innovation in the global knowledge economy.

In 2003, the Shanghai Jiao Tong University issued its first Academic Ranking of World Universities (ARWU), focusing on research performance. In 2004, the *Times Higher Education* (THE) followed, with a broader comparison that included surveys of reputation and of global employability of graduates, and data on research performance, staffing resources and internationalisation. The ARWU ranking is the best known and most credible of the mainstream global university rankings. Its indicators include Nobel Prizes and Field Medals in mathematics (the most controversial of the indicators), number of high citation researchers in the institution, number of articles in *Nature* and *Science*, number of citations to papers published and aggregate performance on these indicators on a per staff member basis.

It shows that the English-speaking universities continue to dominate world research university rankings. Of the leading 200 institutions, 85 are located in the United States, 19 in the United Kingdom and 7 each in Canada and Australia. Harvard is overwhelmingly ahead of the rest of the world, followed by Stanford, Berkeley and MIT, and the United States has 17 of the top 20. The only non-American universities are Cambridge (5), Oxford (10) and the Swiss Federal Institute of Technology in Zurich (20). Germany and France each have just four universities in the top 100 and this has prompted both governments to concentrate higher levels of investment in selected research institutions to improve their global position. The University of Tokyo, equal with University College London in 21st position, is the leading Asian university. These patterns have altered little over the ten years of ARWU league tables.

The most obvious change has been the rise of China's research universities. The number of ARWU top 500 universities in mainland China increased from 8 to 28 between 2005 and 2013. There were five more in Hong Kong. In 2011, Tsinghua was the only top 200 university from China; in 2013 there were five: Tsinghua, Peking, Zhejiang, Fudan and Shanghai Jiao Tong. It is likely that by 2025–2030, the leading universities in China, South Korea, Taiwan and Singapore will be highly ranked with many more in the top 200.

The rise of higher education and research science in East Asia and Singapore has been spectacular. From 2000 to 2010 the Gross Tertiary Enrolment Ratio (GTER), i.e. participation rate, in East Asia and the Pacific rose from 16 to 29 per cent. Apart from China, all systems are pushing beyond 50 per cent participation rates towards near universal levels and China's target is 40 per cent by 2020.

South Korea invested 3.74 per cent of GDP in 2010 and Taiwan 2.90 per cent compared with 3.96 per cent in Finland and 2.88 per cent in the United States. China's investment was 1.70 per cent of GDP. China is increasing investment by 0.1 per cent a year and if spending continues to grow at this rate, it will pass that of the world leader, the United States, in the next decade.

(Simon Marginson, Professor of International Higher Education, Institute of Education, University of London)

Interrogating practice

- How does your institution position itself globally?
- In terms of staff and students, how international is your institution (or discipline)? What are the recognised social and economic benefits? What outward opportunities are there for staff and students internationally?
- What types of collaborative relationships does your institution or department have with overseas institutions?

Much of this chapter has demonstrated the growth and multifaceted nature of the internationalisation of higher education (even though it has barely touched on research activities). Huddersfield University, the Times Higher Education University of the Year 2012, has an approach to internationalisation that reflects its predominantly educational mission and regional commitment. In Case study 3.4, the university's Deputy Vice-Chancellor, Professor Peter Slee, talks about this in conversation with the authors.

Case study 3.4: The significance of internationalisation at the University of Huddersfield

What are the main components of your international strategy?

There are three main components of Huddersfield's international strategy: first, to develop an international reputation through teaching and research partnerships; second, to achieve a balanced income generation through recruitment; and third, to develop a genuine international experience for home and international students.

What sorts of overseas activities is the University of Huddersfield engaged in (i.e. overseas campuses, joint programmes, student recruitment)?

Our international activity focuses on areas that are aligned to our international strategy – research partnership, student recruitment, student exchange and study abroad.

What percentage of your students are classified as overseas or EU?

Fifteen per cent of our total student population are overseas students, with a further 5 per cent from the EU (non-UK).

What facilities does Huddersfield offer for overseas students?

Over a five-year period, the University of Huddersfield invested over £100m into a remodelled campus. Overseas students enjoy the same excellent academic and social facilities as home students. Specialist facilities for overseas students include timetabled language and cultural support for all students every week, visa services, financial support, a **buddying scheme** where existing students offer support to new students. And our multi-faith worship facility came out top in the International Student Barometer (ISB) survey (a survey that elicits student feedback on a range of aspects of the student experience which include academic structure and student services). We have used the ISB to steadily improve the international student experience, focusing on areas that initially achieved low scores.

How has Huddersfield internationalised its curriculum?

As our international population has grown, our curriculum has been internationalised to the benefit of both international and home students. Thankfully, the learning sections of the ISB survey produced results that correlated well with our NSS scores and our own experience, with good scores for Performance and Feedback, the Library and Work Experience. So we had confidence that the scores were likely to reflect very accurately the overall experience of our students.

Anything else that you feel staff 'new to teaching' should think about with respect to the internationalisation agenda?

They need to learn to understand the pedagogic habits of their international students and help them learn to adapt to the UK approaches. This is easier if the students are joining the early stages of a programme and more difficult if they are 'top-up' students. They need to be aware of obvious language adjustment issues and work closely with support services if these are problematic. Both of these issues can be addressed effectively through a progressive approach to feedback and assessment. Staff should be self-aware when using colloquial language. For example, many use familiar terms (at least to them) such as 'bob back to see me' (colloquial version of 'come and see me'), and are amazed when an overseas student looks perplexed. They also need to find ways to allow international students to share their own perspectives on the key issues under discussion. All new staff should be aware that, with at least one-in-seven jobs dependent on international student fees, learning to support learning across a wide range of different cultures is now a core part of their job.

(Peter Slee, Deputy Vice-Chancellor, University of Huddersfield)

Interrogating practice

- Are you aware of the international strategy of your institution?
- What implications does it have for you and your educational practice?

OVERVIEW

This chapter considers the importance of the international agenda and focuses on some of the impact that internationalisation may have on UK HE – at both institutional and national levels. The chapter also aims to raise awareness of the impact of internationalisation on educational practice. It is an important part of the context of academic practice in the twenty-first century. Three of the case studies demonstrate institutional approaches to working with international students, and the fourth comments authoritatively on positioning in a global market through international rankings.

REFERENCES

British Council (2014a) *Language Assistants*. Available from http://www.britishcouncil.org/languageassistants-ela.htm (accessed 7 February 2014).

British Council (2014b) *Erasmus + Traineeships*. Available from http://www.britishcouncil.org/study-work-create/work-volunteer/erasmus-work (accessed 7 February 2014).

Collini, S (2012) *What are universities for?* Milton Keynes, UK: Penguin.

European Commission (2013) *Improving the quality of teaching and learning in Europe's higher education institutions*. Brussels: European Commission. Available from http://ec.europa.eu/education/higher-education/doc/modernisation_en.pdf (accessed 9 December 2013).

European Universities Association (1988) *Bologna Magna Charta Universitatum*. Pizza: University of Bologna. Available from http://www.magna-charta.org/library/userfiles/file/mc_english.pdf (accessed 7 February 2014).

Iannelli, C and Huang, J (2013) 'Trends in participation and attainment of Chinese students in UK higher education', *Studies in Higher Education*, 34: 1–18.

International Unit (2013a). *International Higher Education in Facts and Figures, Autumn*. Available from http://www.international.ac.uk/media/2416084/intfacts2013.pdf (accessed 14 February 2014).

International Unit (2013b) *Press Release: 6 December. Outward Mobility Strategy launched*. See more at http://www.international.ac.uk/news-centre/press-releases/press-release-6-december-outward-mobility-strategy-launched.aspx#sthash.9jKynpRe.dpuf (accessed 7 February 2014).

Lawton, W, Ahmed, M, Angulo, T, Axel-Berg, A, Burrow, A and Katsomitros, A (2013) *Horizon scanning: what will higher education look like in 2020?* Available from http://www.obhe.ac.uk/documents/view_details?id=934 (accessed 7 February 2014).

Mechan-Schmidt, F (2014) 'Germany lays out the welcome mat for foreign students', *Times Higher Education*, 2(135): 18–19.

Organisation for Economic Co-operation and Development (OECD) (2013) *Education at a Glance 2013*. Paris: OECD. Available from http://www.obhe.ac.uk/documents/search?region_id=&theme_id=&year=All+Years&keywords=&author=&document_type_id=1&search=Search (accessed 7 February 2014).

Welikala, T (2011) *Rethinking international higher education curriculum: mapping the research landscape – Universitas 21: Teaching and Learning Position Paper*. Available from http://www.universitas21.com/relatedfile/download/217 (accessed 7 February 2014).

Welsh Government, Llywodraeth Cymru (2013) *Policy Statement on Higher Education*. Available from http://wales.gov.uk/docs/dcells/publications/130611-statement-en.pdf (accessed 7 February 2014).

4 Success as a university teacher

Steve Ketteridge, Heather Fry and
Stephanie Marshall

INTRODUCTION

This chapter is aimed primarily at those who have recently entered the world of higher education in the UK as members of academic staff, although it will also be highly relevant to others joining in professional services roles. It will consider, in particular, the role of the university teacher, recognising that in different institutions this will vary according to mission and that it will be part of a complex and variable range of responsibilities that are best collectively described as **academic practice**. The chapter will also have much to offer more experienced staff coming back into the world of higher education having worked in industry, public service or the professions.

All academic staff starting their careers will have previously experienced life as students, researchers, part-time teachers, etc. and may well have a thorough understanding of the complexities of working in a UK university. They bring with them experience gained, perhaps in teaching as postgraduate students and, in many cases, as postdoctoral workers where it may have included research supervision. As part of the selection process, institutions commonly make formal and informal judgements on applicants' potential as university teachers through a presentation of some type given at interview and judgements are made on candidates' ability to communicate enthusiasm for their specialist disciplines to others. What this chapter sets out to do is to identify the aspects of your performance and achievements once in post that may subsequently be used to demonstrate your success as a university teacher and in facilitating student learning.

Embedded in this chapter are case studies from three university leaders in different types of institutions in the UK higher education sector in which they share thoughts about being successful in their own universities. In Case study 4.1, Professor Evelyn Welch of King's College London talks about a number of things, including the importance of managing your time, getting involved and understanding what the university expects from you.

Case study 4.1: Success at King's College London

Congratulations. If you are reading this book, it's because you are well on your way to a successful academic career. If you are working at an institution such as King's College London, founded in 1829, you will be balancing your teaching, research, administration and innovation activities. Learning how to be excellent across all aspects can seem challenging but is increasingly important to your future.

King's is one of 24 so-called '**Russell Group**' universities in the UK, a term that comes from the name of the hotel in London where the Vice-Chancellors who had to manage medical schools met in the 1990s. These universities are by no means the only elite research-led institutions in the UK but they are able to act together and share some common values and approaches. If you have joined a 'Russell Group' university, or one like it, you might be tempted to think that the only way to succeed is through a ruthless focus on research. But success in a research-intensive university in the UK has many components, some spoken and some unspoken. Here are some tips for when you arrive and as you progress.

- You will probably be on probation. Make sure that you have a mentor and that both of you clearly understand what is required. Does successful teaching delivery mean getting a Masters level teaching qualification? Is there an expectation that you will start to bring in PhD students or be trained as a supervisor? This may seem obvious but it is surprising how often you are just told to publish and to teach well without specific criteria – get this information in writing.
- Unless you are on a fully paid research grant with high overheads, your students pay your salary because, importantly, they are the next generation of citizens and scholars who will look after you in your old age. Remember this when you are tempted to complain about your teaching load and marking getting in the way of your research.
- Online learning is your best friend when balancing teaching with finishing overdue publications; an online platform forces you to put all your teaching materials together well in advance of the start of term. When done well, it means that you should be able to balance your time once the students arrive.
- 'Old lags' at your institution may talk about training with derision but do sign up. A good session on time-management, another that helps you to identify your own strengths and weaknesses and those that provide shared insights into how to manage complex teaching situations can be worth their weight in gold.
- Put your hand up. Once you have settled in, look for opportunities to connect to other parts of the organisation. Administrative meetings are actually the best way to meet colleagues outside your field.

But above all, while academia is changing fast, it is still great fun and offers intellectual challenges and autonomy. There is a reason why you spent so long on your PhD, work long nights to finish your publications, develop new ideas for teaching and feel delight when your students do well. Remember what brought you here and enjoy your new role.

(Evelyn Welch, Vice-Principal for
Arts and Sciences, King's College London)

STRATEGY TO INFORM LEARNING AND TEACHING

All universities will have a strategic plan, approved by its council, court or governing body, and probationary staff may be presented with this at their induction into the university (and rarely see it again). The plan sets out the broad strategic goals or themes for the institution over the planning horizon, usually over three to five years, and describes how it is going to achieve these, how it is going to measure progress and who will be responsible for delivery. The strategic plan helps new staff to understand the type of organisation in which they work and the strategic priorities in the organisation which will impact widely, even down to reward and recognition systems for all staff. Strategic plans often include statements committing to 'excellence in learning and teaching', 'delivering an exceptional student experience' and 'inspirational learning and teaching', and many refer to teaching in an environment enriched by research and engaging students (see Chapter 2). Most strategic plans also define values that set out the principles of how people in the organisation will work together. For example, the University of Leeds defines five values: academic excellence (which is at the heart of everything it does), community, integrity, inclusiveness and professionalism (University of Leeds, 2009). Aligned to this top-level plan are sets of subsidiary strategies that may include the university **learning and teaching strategy**, along with others such as the research strategy, estates strategy, and so on. The learning and teaching strategy defines strategic aims and objectives for learning, teaching and assessment, and provides staff with a framework that should be used to inform the development of curricula (for example, a requirement to integrate employability skills or work experience) and how it is to be delivered (for example, through the use of technology, by research-led teaching). Learning and teaching strategies may set strategic ambitions for all stages of the undergraduate student journey from before entry to graduation and beyond to equipping students for the world of work.

Institutional learning and teaching strategies should include specific targets or measures of success (key performance indicators, KPIs) to be reviewed annually at school, faculty or institutional levels. Often, learning and teaching strategies make reference to the training of staff who teach with the aim of increasing the percentage of staff with teaching qualifications on a year-by-year basis. It is noteworthy that the 2011 UK Coalition Government's Higher Education White Paper recommended that universities publish 'anonymised information for prospective and existing students about the teaching qualifications, fellowships and expertise of their teaching staff at all levels' (Department for Business, Innovation & Skills [BIS], 2011). This could be included in institutional **Key Information Set (KIS)** data and the **Higher Education Statistics Agency (HESA)** now states that it is 'compulsory' for all institutions to complete data returns on staff teaching qualifications (Grove, 2013a).

Interrogating practice

- Have you read your university's Learning and Teaching Strategy?
- Does it have KPIs?
- How does your school ensure it meets these KPIs and how does the strategy influence your practice?

In the UK, statistical data for 2011–12 on the make-up of staff delivering teaching in universities shows that about two-thirds (65 per cent) of all academic staff are employed by higher education institutions on full-time contracts of some type (HESA, 2013). There are significant numbers of part-time teachers in academic roles (35 per cent) with different job titles, apart from teaching assistants and demonstrators. All academic staff will have the responsibilities of their role set out in job descriptions and these should give an outline of expectations on appointment.

Over the past few years, the diversity of staff working in UK universities has increased as institutions strive to recruit the best staff in a global market. In English universities, 75 per cent of academic staff are UK nationals, 13 per cent come from EU countries and 12 per cent from non-EU (Higher Education Funding Council for England [**HEFCE**], 2012). The science, technology, engineering, medicine and mathematics (STEMM) disciplines have probably experienced this change more than others, and in engineering subjects, for example, 35 per cent of all academic staff are non-UK nationals, with the greatest proportion coming from China.

The attention given to specifying the requirements for teaching and learning in job descriptions varies considerably. For experienced applicants coming into more senior roles, 'evidence of relevant teaching experience at tertiary level' might be prescribed. Most universities have now moved towards a requirement for less experienced academic staff entering the profession to have, or to achieve as part of their period of probation, some type of accreditation and/or teaching qualification. Often the requirement in the person specification is for 'a Postgraduate Certificate in Education, Certificate of Education, Postgraduate Certificate in Academic Practice or Fellowship of the Higher Education Academy (HEA), or willingness to obtain a University-approved qualification within three years of appointment'.

There are obviously distinct differences in academic roles according to the mission of the university. These relate to the balance between teaching and supporting learning, research and other duties, such as administration, management, contribution to the community and professional service, as in medicine and dentistry. A recent change, although this is less likely to affect probationary staff, has been the differentiation of some contracts of employment for academic staff according to their contribution to research and teaching. In more research-led universities, this has been driven by preparations leading up to the **Research Excellence Framework** (REF, 2014) in 2014 and involved moving academic staff, who will not be submitted to the REF, to roles designated as 'Teaching and Scholarship' roles. This might apply to academic staff if they do not have sufficient papers thought to be of at least 3-star quality for the REF. Staff on 'Teaching and Scholarship' type contracts would be allocated a significantly larger weekly teaching load than those judged as more 'research active' in 'Teaching and Research' roles.

To help staff manage their time, many universities across the sector have now developed and put into place academic workload allocation models that recognise the different activities undertaken by members of staff and allocate an agreed time allowance to each of these. These cover all members of academic staff in schools, faculties or institutions and all work-related time. Academic staff and their heads of schools should have a clear picture of who is doing what and what proportion of time they should give to it (Perks, 2013). Workload models are meant to ensure activities are distributed equitably, taking account of different types of contribution and including part-time staff. For new staff, an academic workload model should add to clarity of expectations and, importantly, help them regulate time on tasks. To be successful it is important to keep a watchful eye on the outputs that you are going to need to demonstrate success in whatever your chosen career route.

STARTING OUT IN YOUR FIRST ACADEMIC POST

Academic posts are usually offered subject to a probationary period, which is commonly three years for those taking up their first university appointments. In a few institutions, probation may be for five years. Staff on **probation** are usually set targets at an early stage in the probationary period by a senior colleague in their discipline or line manager, as agreed with the head of school. Their performance in meeting these targets is monitored and part of regular discussions on progress. The probationary targets set out expectations for the probationary period and will be shaped according to the needs of the job, the probationer and the institution. They specify outputs from teaching activities, research and other scholarly activities, professional service, as relevant, to demonstrate successful completion of probation. To support the probationer in meeting probationary targets, it is usual to assign the probationer a probationary adviser or **mentor** to act as a 'critical friend' and ensure that she or he knows what has to be done to complete the probation successfully and offer support through the process.

It is usual for universities to specify a programme of continuing professional development (CPD) to be completed as part of probation, and for those with no accredited training in teaching and supporting student learning, this may well be an essential requirement for successful completion of probation. Most universities have learning and development programmes targeted at probationary staff and offered from Human Resources (HR) and/or specialist academic professional development units, such as the King's Learning Institute in London (http://www.kcl.ac.uk/study/learningteaching/kli/index.aspx) and the Oxford Centre for Staff and Learning Development at Oxford Brookes University (http://www.brookes.ac.uk/services/ocsld/). Within institutions, it is often still the case that there seem to be inconsistencies between schools over the teaching load allocated to probationary academic staff. Some schools give greater remission from teaching duties than others to take account of the CPD requirements and allow research outcomes to be completed in probation.

Universities in the UK may require probationary staff to undertake a teaching qualification (if they do not have one) and the programme of choice will be one accredited by the **Higher Education Academy (HEA)**. Depending on your university and their policy, a more flexible CPD route, such as the ASPIRE framework at the University of Exeter (http://as.exeter.ac.uk/aspire/about/) or the AcceleRATE/CPD approach at Glasgow Caledonian University (http://www.gcu.ac.uk/lead/leadthemes/acceleratecpd/) may be offered. Both provide staff at different stages in their careers with a means of gaining a Fellowship at one of the four levels offered by the HEA: Associate, Fellow, Senior Fellow or Principal Fellow. There has been much debate over the years about the need for professional accreditation of teachers in higher education and the framework developed. The **UK Professional Standards Framework (UKPSF)** for teaching and supporting learning (HEA, 2013a) is used to accredit recognised programmes in institutions and for individuals. Evidence to show successful achievement of one of the dimensions of practice associated with a particular descriptor in the standards framework brings with it Fellowship of the HEA at a level commensurate with the descriptor achieved (as shown in Table 4.1). Achievement of 'Fellow' status of the HEA (Descriptor 2) may commonly be set for new academic staff as a probationary requirement in their first university appointment. This can be automatically achieved after successful

Table 4.1 UK Professional Standards Framework: descriptors, 2011

	Category of HEA recognition	Target groups
Descriptor 1	Associate Fellow (AFHEA)	Graduate Teaching Assistants Early career researcher with some teaching responsibilities
Descriptor 2	Fellow (FHEA)	Lecturers Experienced academic staff with substantive teaching and learning responsibilities
Descriptor 3	Senior Fellow (SFHEA)	Middle management staff with academic leadership role
Descriptor 4	Principal Fellow (PHEA)	Senior academic staff with leadership responsibilities making demonstrable impact

Source: Higher Education Academy (2013a)

completion of an accredited Postgraduate Certificate programme. The descriptors in the UKPSF form a useful hierarchy for those seeking progression along a career route with a learning and teaching focus in mind, and as such may be a useful tool for planning future CPD.

At the end of probationary period, the progress made by probationary staff against targets set will normally be reviewed by a panel at faculty or institutional level. The panel will make a decision on whether to confirm the probationer in post or to extend the probationer period if there are concerns about progress. Some staff may fail to meet the performance targets expected of them, even after an extension of the probation period. It is a harsh reality that the small numbers of individuals in this position may find themselves 'managed out' of the institution or come to realise that it is necessary to find opportunities elsewhere if they are to progress.

Recent research commissioned by the HEA (2013b) has investigated the impact made by the UKPSF. Whilst it has shaped institutional curricula for professional development courses and the development for institutional frameworks for CPD, it has made less of an impact on institutional strategies and policies, and reward and recognition schemes. Of the teaching staff surveyed in this research, a third had knowingly engaged with the framework, but a larger proportion reported not being aware of the framework prior to the survey.

BUILDING YOUR CAREER AFTER PROBATION

Understanding promotion routes

Once past your probationary period, you should have a much clearer view on where you wish your career to take you in the university and perhaps beyond your first academic appointment.

Careers may be built around a teaching and learning focused route, research focused route, an academic management route, or, for some staff, a mixture of two or three of these, plus for some building in professional service. Institutional promotions criteria should allow staff to see what they have to demonstrate for advancement. Whilst there are some differences across the sector, promotions beyond the grade of Lecturer lead to Senior or Principal Lecturer, Reader or Associate Professor, and on to full Professor. (Universities all have single salary spines and different levels of job grades map at different points and ranges onto these.) The detailed criteria differ greatly, but there will be some mechanism for the assessment of different types of contribution made by academic staff. At Queen Mary, University of London, there are three major categories for assessing the contribution of academic staff:

- Knowledge creation: research publications, research grants and income
- Knowledge dissemination: teaching, supporting learning and associated scholarship
- Enabling activities: activities at group, school, faculty or institutional level that facilitate and support knowledge creation and dissemination

Queen Mary's promotion criteria (http://www.hr.qmul.ac.uk/acadreview/index. html) give details of the level and scope of requirements at the level of Lecturer, Senior Lecturer, Reader and Professor, setting out indicative evidence needed to make a claim for promotion to a higher grade. Usually a feature of the criteria for the award of a professorial title is a requirement for impact or standing at an international level. The criteria for appointment to a University of London chair speak of 'the person's national/international standing in the relevant subject or profession as established by outstanding contributions to its advancement through publications, creative work or other appropriate forms of scholarship or performance, and through teaching and administration' (University of London, 2008).

However, the playing field may not be perfectly level. Across the higher education sector there is some gender imbalance when considering all categories of academic staffing, with the overall ratio of 44.5 per cent to 55.5 per cent, women to men (HESA, 2013). The greatest gender gaps seem to be at the professorial level where women make up 20.5 per cent of the total professoriate, suggesting that women lack progression through the academic ranks. The proportion of women professors varies in different institutions, with Aberystwyth (7.9 per cent) at the bottom of the list in the year surveyed. Only at the University of the Arts London, Courtauld Institute, University of Roehampton and the Institute of Education London (out of 129 surveyed in 2011–12) did the proportion exceed 50 per cent. There are disciplinary differences, with arts and humanities subjects showing highest representation of women at professorial level (Grove, 2013b). Progression of women to top leadership positions in UK universities is even worse, with just 14 per cent women Vice-Chancellors. Recognising such imbalances, the Athena SWAN Charter (http://www.athenaswan.org.uk/content/athena-swan) was originally established to support women in developing their careers in academia in STEMM disciplines. It has expanded to cover the arts, humanities and social sciences. There are three levels of award recognising commitment to equality in career progression in institutions. Athena SWAN really can make a difference, such as the School of Biological Sciences at Queen's University, Belfast where since 2006–07 the proportion of female lecturers has risen from 22 per cent to 40 per cent and it has received a gold award, which goes to 'beacons' for gender equality (Gibney, 2013).

Reviewing your performance as a university teacher

Personal review and development

While we can all think about how well we might be doing in our careers and what we have achieved over the past year, other processes might help to give a reality check and confirm that we are on course. All universities require staff to engage at least annually in some type of staff/personal review and development scheme, performance assessment or **appraisal** process. Whatever the scheme is called, this should give you the opportunity, working with an independent reviewer, to assess objectively your progress in post, your own strengths and weaknesses, to gain clearer insight into your institution, and understand what you need to do to succeed along your preferred career path. At the centre of the process is the review meeting in which:

- performance against objectives set last time is reviewed;
- any learning and development undertaken is reviewed and evaluated;
- the one being reviewed receives feedback on performance from the reviewer;
- personal work objectives are set for the year ahead; and
- any learning and development needs identified for the year ahead.

The personal objectives set must align to school or faculty objectives or service plans set for the year ahead and ultimately to strategic objectives.

The meeting should be a positive and constructive discussion of performance and achievements. This discussion should be built around the expected performance standards for the member of staff at the current level, and objectives set for the year should take account of any academic workload model. These review meetings should allow you the opportunity to explore potential for progression and, if relevant, how to meet promotion criteria. The success of the personal review process relies on the spirit of openness in discussion between the reviewee and reviewer, mutual trust and confidentiality. Your HR department will have guidance notes on the operation of your scheme.

Setting measureable objectives on teaching and learning during personal review may be challenging. Appropriate types of quantitative information in objectives might include targets for your own delivery of teaching activities, for example mean scores from the next run of the university student evaluation of teaching scheme. If there is a peer observation of teaching scheme (see next section) in which you receive a summative judgement on your performance, then that may allow setting of a grade as a target. Experience has shown that objective setting around student assessment needs care and sensitivity. Setting a target such as 'a normal distribution of marks among students' in overall module assessment might be appropriate and protect from any possibility of grade inflation (Grove, 2013c). For those seeking a career route with emphasis on a teaching role, relevant objectives for personal review might certainly include plans for progression up the UKPSF (see Table 4.1) from your current level.

Interrogating practice

- How do you see your academic career developing in the next five years?
- What do you want to achieve by then? Who is going to help you get there? What is going to hinder your progression?
- How can you use your performance reviews to help you achieve this outcome?

In Case study 4.2, David Llewellyn from Harper Adams University talks about being successful in a small institution, specialising in subjects related to the agri-food business and rural studies. He considers the personal attributes needed to be a successful in an institution with a strong student focus.

Case study 4.2: Success at Harper Adams University

As a university specialising in agri-food and rural subjects, we have strong connections with the wide range of businesses in the agri-food and rural sectors. Our founder wished to create an institution focused on practical and theoretical education, an approach to which we still adhere. We offer sandwich degrees across our course portfolio; conduct applied research that feeds back into our curriculum; and, as a smaller-scale academic community, try to provide a supportive learning environment for our students, many of whom come from a rural background and want to study in that setting rather than in a large city.

So, what makes a successful university lecturer in this sort of institution? I believe there are six factors, each of which is essential, but which, in combination, can make a lecturer really stand out.

1   Show passion for the subject, consistently, but with the sensitivity to know that not everyone feels the way you do about your chosen field. Find ways to bring reluctant learners on board – they could react positively to the attention, and you could be surprised by the results.
2   Remain connected to the 'real world' through research, collaboration with industry, the professions or the wider community, depending on the subject area. Students appreciate a lecturer who is able to translate practice into theory, and vice versa, as long as their 'real-world' experience is up-to-date. This is particularly important when courses involve an industry placement because students may be quick to tell you that their experience 'out there' was different.
3   Be available to students, not just immediately after lectures, but at other times when they need advice or support. We are all busy, but the ability to spend a few moments really finding out how a student is doing will reap rewards for you and for them.
4   Show willingness to keep learning about the practice of teaching, not just in relation to new technology, but also in trying out new methods to interact with students in the classroom or in approaches to assessment. Making use of institutional groups, training activities or seeking opportunities to learn from colleagues in other institutions will all help.
5   Listen and respond to student feedback. You may have to learn to not fear the inevitable comment that is less than positive, but to change your approach where necessary.

6 Finally, make sure that you are equipping your students to handle change by encouraging independent learning and their ability to reason and question. The challenges they will face over their lifetime will require these skills, not just a sound base of knowledge.

To address the above points, talk to other lecturers and find out where you can access help and support. It is often available within the institution but you may simply need to be pointed in the right direction. Lecturers who work with their colleagues in this way get to know their students and investing in their practice makes a real difference to their institution. Their success may not be guaranteed, but at least they will be laying the right foundations to get themselves noticed as someone who cares about their teaching and the difference it can make to their students.

(David Llewellyn, Vice-Chancellor,
Harper Adams University)

Information on your teaching practice

Usually staff can expect to receive information on their teaching practice at module level through undergraduate students' evaluation of teaching, organised at school or university level. Such student surveys may be administered online or involve students completing paper questionnaires. Whatever the system, these usually give responses to a standard question set, but often more importantly provide free text boxes for students to write on the best aspects of teaching and the things that could be improved. These sections can provide the most useful information on your teaching.

Peer observation of teaching is well established across the HE sector and staff at all levels will be required to engage, both as observer and the one being observed. The real value of this process is the opportunity for feedback and discussion on teaching, which is of benefit to both sides, but especially the observed. All types of teaching can be considered, from the lecture to group teaching, practical work and teaching in professional settings, such as bedside (in medicine) and chairside (dentistry). Universities have their own peer observation schemes and a good example is that at Leeds Metropolitan University (Race et al., 2009). Academic staff can expect to have at least one session observed yearly. Schemes vary, but usually an observation takes place after the observer and the person to be observed agree a time and date for the class to be attended.

Engaging in observation of teaching is a requirement of probationary staff in most institutions and is an integral part of Postgraduate Certificate type initial training programmes for new teachers. In these cases, there are detailed forms to be completed by both the observer and the observed, often with a grade being given for the session, such as 'good', 'pass' or 'unsatisfactory'. The quite-detailed records of observed teaching sessions will become part of your **teaching portfolio**. As you become more experienced, you may well start to observe the teaching of your colleagues and that too can be a rewarding experience and a powerful stimulus for reflection on your own practice.

For all staff, information from students or from peers should be a valuable resource for enhancing personal teaching practice, provided they are prepared to listen to what they are being told, reflect upon it and take action. Remember such information might also be included in personal applications to university reward schemes or for promotion as independent evidence of the quality of your teaching and/or supporting student learning.

Awards for excellence in teaching

University awards for teachers

Most universities have schemes to recognise, reward and celebrate excellent teaching and the efforts staff make to create an excellent student experience and bring innovation to teaching and learning. These are often run by student unions, but can also have input and advice from expert staff in the university. A really good example of such a scheme is the Strathclyde Teaching Excellence Awards run by the University of Strathclyde Students' Association (http://www.strathstudents.com/tea). Students are invited to nominate university staff teaching them in one of three categories – most supportive, most enthusiastic or most innovative teacher – and include quotes as to why they are nominating that person. The scheme has some broad criteria that students are asked to say what makes them 'so excellent' when making a nomination. Nominations submitted in these categories are considered for awards of Teacher of the Faculty or Best Overall awards. The awards are judged by a panel of students and staff and the winners presented with their Teaching Excellence Awards at a ceremony. What is interesting about this scheme is an annual Best Practice Report is created using students' supporting statements and this captures comments from over 500 student nominations from over 300 different students from all faculties. The report says a lot about what students perceive to be excellent teaching and goes on to make suggestions for staff as Dos and Don'ts. Keele University has the Keele Excellence Awards in Learning and Teaching (http://www.keele.ac.uk/lpdc/learningteaching/keeleexcellenceawards/) in which nominations may come from students or colleagues for those who have inspired or been outstanding in their support for student learning. The four annual awards take the form of certificates awarded at a Graduation Ceremony, but there is further recognition by the award of a £1,000 prize.

Nomination for an award that recognises excellent teaching and support of student learning provides powerful evidence of success in a claim for promotion or reward on the basis of high quality teaching and could form part of a future application for another job.

In Case study 4.3, Professor Geoff Layer from the University of Wolverhampton talks about the needs of the local community, a diverse student population, inclusivity in designing teaching and learning, and the skill set needed to be successful.

Case study 4.3: Success at the University of Wolverhampton

The University of Wolverhampton has a high proportion of local students, many of whom are the first in their family to be in higher education and a significant proportion of whom are from minority ethnic groups. We offer a multi-campus and local experience and have a significant range of part-time programmes. Having been in existence for over 180 years, our approach still focuses on our original ambition of providing opportunity within the industrial heartlands, based on the economic needs of the area with a recognition that many of our students will want to work locally after graduating.

Our broad mix of undergraduate level programmes and the diversity of the student body create a particular set of requirements. We seek for all staff to engage with this position by developing degree outcomes that deliver digital literacy, graduate employment and a recognition of the impact of diversity. We focus very much on implementing a student lifecycle model in which we aim to engage with learners at all stages of their journey, including aspiration raising, progression, attainment raising and securing graduate employment. We encourage all staff to address inclusive learning through securing a social model of higher education in which we try to alleviate the barriers that traditionally exist.

To be a successful lecturer in our University, we would look for the following factors:

- A demonstrative passion for learning in which the teacher is able to embody that enthusiasm for their subject and their research in the classroom.
- To be innovative and challenging, recognising the need to pilot, take risks and evaluate with students as partners in the process.
- To be fully committed to their own professional development and to engage in peer review of pedagogical processes and classroom engagement.
- To recognise and be aware of the very different cultural approaches to learning amongst our students and to develop methods that get the best out of them, which is best achieved by working in teams and sharing developments and experiences. This means recognising that equality and diversity does not mean treating everyone the same, but that we need to recognise and celebrate differences.
- To be up-to-date in the developments in their profession or industry through professional networks, subject groups and the regional economic needs.
- To be aware of work experience opportunities, the changing economic landscape for that area of study and the approaches to supporting innovation and entrepreneurship.

- To be a creative and innovative user of blended learning with time spent generating and empowering successful learning.

As well as all of these factors, we want all our staff to be full and active members of the University community.

(Geoff Layer, Vice Chancellor, University of Wolverhampton)

Interrogating practice

- Start thinking now about your own career progression.
- Identify the different types of information you will need to collect as evidence of your own successful practice.

National Teaching Fellowship Scheme

These are national awards for recognising excellence in teaching and/or supporting the learning experience of students in higher education. The **National Teaching Fellowship Scheme (NTFS)** is run by the HEA (http://www.heacademy.ac.uk/ntfs) and the scheme is open to staff in universities in England, Wales and Northern Ireland that subscribe to the HEA. Each year, up to 55 awards of £10,000 each are made to recognise winners on the basis of individual excellence. The intention is that the award will be used for the National Teaching Fellow's professional development in learning and teaching or aspects of pedagogy. Nominations for the NTFS are submitted to the HEA by the institutions and not the individual; the number of nominations any one institution can submit is currently three each year. Both full-time and part-time academic staff and others in professional roles who support the student learning experience can be submitted. The NTFS area of the HEA's website has full details of what is required. The individual member of staff must write a personal statement showing how he or she demonstrates excellence in relation to each of the three headline award criteria. These are:

1. Individual excellence: evidence of enhancing and transforming the student learning experience commensurate with the individual's context and opportunities afforded by it.
2. Raising the profile of excellence: evidence of supporting colleagues and influencing support for student learning; demonstrating impact and engagement beyond the nominee's immediate academic or professional role.
3. Developing excellence: evidence of the nominee's commitment to his/her ongoing professional development with regard to teaching and learning and/or learning support.

The personal statement must include reflection on current practice. It needs to show critical evaluation of practice from different perspectives. Also the nominee needs to show how their practice has had impact in the institution. Nominations must be accompanied by a statement from a senior manager confirming institutional support, which also helps to put the submission in context.

National Teaching Fellowships are regarded as prestige teaching awards and institutions often like to note how many such Fellows they have in promotional material. Some learning and teaching strategies even set targets for the number of NTFS winners that they aim to secure during the tenure of that strategy. Clearly, winning such a Fellowship represents national recognition of your high standing as a university teacher and should be an asset in future career progression.

Continuing Professional Development (CPD)

All academic and professional staff must expect to engage in continuing professional development activities throughout their careers, which can take many different forms, and there are differences between disciplines and professions as to what this involves. CPD means more than going to courses (face-to-face or online), although that will be a component. In terms of keeping updated in developments in learning and teaching, generally or specifically in your own discipline, there are a number of providers, including:

- Your own institution will have learning and development professionals to offer events and activities, such as learning and teaching days for all staff and specific workshops to roll out new systems.
- The HEA has regular conferences showcasing recent pedagogical research and developments in teaching, learning and assessment, often organised at the level of thematic and disciplinary area.
- Professional bodies and learned societies at conferences often have educational events sharing best practice in teaching and learning in specific disciplinary areas. Many professional bodies have CPD requirements to maintain professional standing, which include updating practice in learning, teaching and assessment.
- For those with a mainstream interest in the pedagogy of learning and teaching, conferences and events organised by the Society for Research into Higher Education (http://www.srhe.ac.uk) and the Staff and Educational Development Association (http://www.seda.ac.uk) may be of interest, as well as the HEA.

CONCLUSIONS AND OVERVIEW

This chapter has sought to help academic and professional staff, at early stages in their careers, to gain a better understanding of opportunities for developing their understanding and expertise as university teachers. The expectations placed on academic staff in different UK universities vary considerably with respect to emphasis placed on supporting learning, teaching, research, scholarship, supervision, professional service, etc. However, there may be choices that can be made about the direction of travel in your career and the extent of engagement in the types of schemes outlined in this chapter. You will also need to be aware in your institution of any differences in 'parity of esteem' in the way that different aspects of practice (teaching and learning, research and scholarship, etc.) are recognised and rewarded. It is a reality that more than two-thirds of university staff report that they have never been recognised or rewarded for their teaching (Grove, 2013d). Your key to success is likely to be an understanding of the expectations of your institution, being able to deliver on time and with high quality outcomes. As we have seen, apart from promotion and progression up salary scales, there can be other rewards or marks of distinction to confer success, such as the teaching prizes and fellowships, study leave, one-off bonus payments or access to quality CPD activities. Understanding your institution and being able to respond to their requirements should also give you greater job satisfaction.

REFERENCES

Department for Business, Innovation & Skills (BIS) (2011) *Higher Education White Paper: Students at the Heart of the System*. Norwich: The Stationary Office. Available from: https://www.gov.uk/government/uploads/system/uploads/attachment_data/file/31384/11-944-higher-education-students-at-heart-of-system.pdf (accessed 14 December 2013).

Gibney, E (2013) 'With cash on the line, Athena SWANs take wing', *Times Higher Education*, 25 April 2012, 10.

Grove, J (2013a) 'State puts weight behind teaching qualification data', *Times Higher Education*, 29 August 2013, 6–7.

Grove, J (2013b) 'Gender survey of UK professoriate', *Times Higher Education*, 13 June 2013, 6.

Grove, J (2013c) 'Surrey considered grade targets for staff appraisal', *Times Higher Education*, 18 July 2013, 6–7.

Grove, J (2013d) 'Apple for teacher, but few promotions or pay rises', *Times Higher Education*, 4 July 2013, 5–6.

Higher Education Academy (HEA) (2013a) *UK Professional Standards Framework*. York, HEA. Available from: http://www.heacademy.ac.uk/ukpsf (accessed 14 December 2013).

Higher Education Academy (HEA) (2013b) *Measuring the Impact of the UK Professional Standards Framework for Teaching and Supporting Learning (UKPSF)*. York, HEA. Available from: http://www.heacademy.ac.uk/assets/documents/ukpsf/UKPSF_Impact_Study_Report.pdf (accessed 14 December 2013).

Higher Education Funding Council for England (HEFCE) (2012) *Staff employed at HEFCE-funded HEIs Trends and profiles 1995–96 to 2010–11*. Available from: http://www.hefce.ac.uk/pubs/year/2012/201214/name,73612,en.html (accessed 14 December 2013).

Higher Education Statistics Agency (2013) *Staff in Higher Education Institutions 2011/12*. Available from: http://www.hesa.ac.uk/content/view/2694/393/ (accessed 14 December 2013).

Perks, S (2013) *Academic workload: a model approach.* Available from: http://www.theguardian.com/higher-education-network/blog/2013/apr/15/academic-workload-modelling-management (accessed 14 December 2013).

Race, P, *et al.* (2009) *Using peer observation to enhance teaching.* Leeds Met Press. Available from: https://www.leedsmet.ac.uk/publications/files/090505-36477_PeerObsTeaching_LoRes.pdf (accessed 14 December 2013).

Research Excellence Framework (REF) (2014) *Research Excellence Framework.* Available from: http://www.ref.ac.uk/ (accessed 14 December 2013).

University of Leeds (2009) *Strategic Plan 2009.* Available from: http://www.leeds.ac.uk/downloads/file/276/ (accessed 14 December 2013).

University of London (2008) *Regulation 3: Professors and Readers.* Available from: http://www.london.ac.uk/fileadmin/documents/about/governance/ordinances/New_Ordinances/Regulation_3_Professors_and_Readers.pdf (accessed 14 December 2013).

FACULTY OF HEALTH + SOCIAL CARE
Library
27 NOV 2014
Virtual Campus
Clatterbridge
UNIVERSITY OF CHESTER

Part 2
Learning, teaching and supervising in higher education

5

Student learning

Sue Mathieson

INTRODUCTION

Teaching is about engendering learning. This chapter looks at some of the common learning theories that have been applied to higher education, starting with the **'approaches to learning'** research described next. This has been the most influential theoretical approach in changing learning and teaching in higher education over the last thirty years. This chapter then looks at socio-cultural approaches to student learning, which explore the interaction between learning and the social and cultural environment, focusing in particular on learning as a process of induction into a **'community of practice'** (Wenger, 1998).

The focus on student learning in higher education has emerged along with the changes taking place in higher education, in particular the shift from an elite to a mass higher education system in which, along with larger class sizes, there is an increasing diversity of students. Student learning can no longer be assumed to result automatically from exposure to disciplinary experts, if it ever could; academics need to have a basic understanding of the processes of learning in higher education if they are to create an environment in which the expected learning can be attained by a diverse range of students (see also Chapter 11).

However, there is no direct line between teaching and learning. New academics often feel baffled and frustrated by their students, wondering why they don't learn in the ways academics expect them to learn. The aim of this chapter is to offer some ideas and concepts to help you to understand what might be happening as you seek to facilitate your students' learning through your teaching. This is one of the great intellectual and imaginative challenges of teaching in higher education. As Ramsden (2003) argues, it is a challenge many academics seek to avoid by blaming their students as poor learners. However, he argues that a more effective way of facilitating student learning is to constantly reflect on what is happening in the interaction between teaching and learning in order to improve the quality of student learning. This chapter will provide you with an entry point to some of the key theoretical tools that you can use in that reflection, together with some references you can follow up.

SO WHAT IS IT THAT WE WANT OUR STUDENTS TO LEARN?

There is a developing consensus about our expectations of graduates for the twenty-first century. Many of these expectations have a long tradition in higher education: **critical thinking** and problem solving in the disciplines; the ability to understand and the relationships between concepts and how these can be applied appropriately to address real-world problems and issues; the ability to approach problems analytically, creatively and imaginatively, applying independent judgement; the ability to understand (some?) knowledge as relative rather than absolute, and to locate one's own point of view within a variety of perspectives.

However, along with these traditional disciplinary capabilities, there is an increasing expectation that graduates will be equipped with the **life skills** expected by employers. Graduates are expected to be able to use abstract academic knowledge in real-life settings through participating competently in the social practices of their chosen profession or workplace; they are expected to have developed appropriate leadership, communication, teamworking and ICT skills in putting their knowledge into practice.

In addition to these **employability** capabilities, graduates are expected to have developed the personal qualities to enable them to deal with a world of uncertainty and change (Barnett, 1997), and to act as responsible and ethical citizens in a complex and changing democracy.

BUT, MIND THE GAP

Although there is a broad consensus that these are the attributes expected of twenty-first century graduates, there is no clear link between these outcomes and the approaches to teaching in higher education. In fact, some common teaching practices in higher education are likely to achieve the opposite of the learning that is intended, such as passive individualised attendance at mass lectures focused on covering an ever-expanding syllabus, with a short end-of-term exam used to test student learning. Such approaches may work with well-prepared students who have a good understanding of the expectations of them in developing graduate attributes; however, with the increasingly diverse student intake into higher education, including international students, there will be many more students who have not internalised these expectations of them as learners through their previous educational experiences, and who need more active guidance to develop the expected **graduate attributes**.

Addressing this gap between the intended outcomes for our students, and the teaching practices used to achieve them, has been the focus of most of the recent research and writing about learning and teaching in higher education.

> ### Interrogating practice
>
> Before you begin the next section, take a few minutes to write down your answers to the follow questions:
>
> - How do you think students learn?
> - Teaching is…
> - Graduates in my subject should be able to…
> - The main challenge I face in helping students to learn is…
>
> As you read this chapter, think about how the different theories support and challenge your existing theories of learning and teaching, and how you might adapt and change your initial statements.

THE 'APPROACHES TO LEARNING' RESEARCH

The 'approaches to learning' research highlighted the challenges for student learning in contemporary higher education, as outlined earlier, that higher education was changing, bringing in a far more diverse student body, and that a more student-learning focused approach to teaching was required to bridge the gap from the diversity of knowledge and understanding of students at the beginning of their university journey to develop the attributes expected of graduates.

It aimed to bring about a shift in teachers from focusing on what they were going to teach in the syllabus, and how, to a learner-focused approach, critically reflecting on how their students were learning, and adjusting their teaching to bring about the intended **learning outcomes** (see Chapter 6).

THE INFLUENCE OF CONSTRUCTIVISM

The 'approaches to learning' research draws upon **constructivist theories** of learning to shape this learner-centred approach. Constructivism challenges the idea that students are a 'blank slate' to be filled with content knowledge; instead, it views learning as a process of building and adjusting the structures in the mind through which we hold knowledge. These structures are known as 'schemata' and need to be amended in order to incorporate new knowledge. Learning is thus not simply about adding new knowledge, but about making changes to existing knowledge in order to accommodate new ways of understanding; so teachers need to engage with and challenge the existing conceptions of students in order to bring about learning. Learning is thus an active process of individual transformation and changes in understanding.

Piaget (1950) and Bruner (1960) are the key educationists associated with constructivism. Bruner argued that teaching should focus on structure, to penetrate a subject, not to cover it. He argued that you did this by 'spiralling' into it, first by gaining an intuitive sense of it, and then going over the same material more deeply and formally (Bruner, 1960: 20).

This approach of understanding and working on existing schemata and developing them in order to bring about conceptual change is useful in thinking about how diverse students learn: rather than seeing students through a deficit lens as simply having an absence of knowledge that needs to be filled, teachers need to engage with the existing understandings of their students and find ways of developing and challenging these. For example, international students may have learnt certain approaches to understanding that need to be understood by teachers in order to build upon them, and also to challenge students to think in new ways. Unless teaching helps students to adjust their existing schemata, the facts that they learn will be disjointed and will not be retained effectively. This focus on developing understanding suggests the sorts of activities teachers need to encourage to lead students to the desired learning outcomes. Teaching is not a matter of transmitting knowledge, but of engaging students in **active learning**, building their knowledge in terms of what they already understand.

Surface and deep approaches to learning

The initial **approaches to learning** research was undertaken by Marton and Säljö (1984/1997). They focused on how students experienced the learning process using qualitative, open-ended interviews to identify different categories of approach to learning by students. They found that students adopted different approaches to learning related to their intentions for learning and their understanding of what the task required. The two main approaches identified in students were a **'surface' approach** and a **'deep' approach**.

In the surface approach, students' intention is to get the task done with the minimum of effort by concentrating on facts and details, but with no comprehension of the underlying themes. It involves rote learning of content instead of understanding, so students approach learning with low levels of cognitive capacity. Students may apply a surface approach to their learning if they misunderstand the depth of learning expected, if they are anxious or overloaded with work, or have not prioritised their learning. Teaching can encourage a surface approach where isolated topics are taught without drawing out the links between topics by overloading the curriculum with content or by having low expectations of students.

In the deep approach, students' intention is to engage meaningfully with the task, with the appropriate background knowledge and the ability to focus at a high conceptual level. It involves students focusing on meaning and is based on a desire to understand. It involves building up the big picture through the details and by relating concepts to existing understandings. Teaching can encourage a deep approach to learning by explicitly bringing out the structure of the topic, by teaching to elicit an active response from students, by building on what students already know and confronting their misconceptions. Assessments should focus on the overall structure rather than independent facts, and there should be opportunities for students to learn from their mistakes throughout the learning process. Students need to be motivated and encouraged to apply a deep approach to their learning by teachers setting high expectations and valuing students, by making learning meaningful for students and showing them how they can improve.

The links to constructivist theory are clear here, with the deep approach being the one that is going to bring about the quality of learning expected of graduates.

A key element of the findings of this research was that the intentions of students were not a fixed and innate characteristic of learners, but a response to an educational context (Prosser and Trigwell, 1999). The approach to learning is in part influenced by the way learners perceive teaching and the requirements of a course of study. It is thus possible for teachers to influence the approach to learning of their students by making it clear to the students what the expectations are, providing a learning environment that leads students into taking a deep approach and by discouraging students from adopting a surface approach. Those researching approaches to learning argue that the task of the teacher is to change the perspective of the learner so that they take a deep approach to their learning.

Teaching for deep learning – constructive alignment

Biggs (Biggs and Tang, 2009) developed upon and popularised the approaches to learning research by showing how it could be used to fundamentally rethink how teachers organised the learning environment. Biggs argues that since it is the learner's perspective that determines what is learned, the learning outcomes of the course need to be fully understood by students. Teachers need to focus on changing the learner's perspective on their learning so they fully understand and engage with the learning at the appropriate level. He argues that in order to encourage students to take a deep approach to their learning, teachers need to develop a '**constructively aligned**' curriculum, that is, using a constructivist approach where students are seen as constructing knowledge based on their existing schemata, in an aligned curriculum, by which he means that the intended learning outcomes of the course are aligned with the teaching environment, and with the modes of assessment. He argues that in a constructively aligned curriculum students have little opportunity for learning in a surface way because the teaching and assessment are all designed to lead to the development of the learning outcomes for the course; in such a curriculum it is much more likely that **student engagement** with their learning will be exhibited. The focus in a constructively aligned curriculum is on the whole range of learning activities students are engaged in, not just classroom teaching. The chapters on curriculum design, teaching methods and assessment (Chapters 6, 7 and 8) consider how to bring about a constructively aligned curriculum from each of these perspectives.

Case study 5.1: Using the principles of constructive alignment to develop the project-based BA Architecture Programme at Northumbria University

Constructive alignment in project-based learning provides the opportunity to 'entrap students in a web of consistency' (Biggs and Tang, 2009). The architecture programmes at Northumbria University employ and extend constructive alignment beyond the coordination of learning outcomes, taught content, delivery, feedback and assessment within individual modules by establishing explicit and meaningful connections between the individual modules in any academic year. The use of the architectural design project as the vehicle and focus of supporting modules (history and theory, technology and environment, communications methods, and practice, management and law) provides relevance and meaning to student learning. Advanced scheduling of module delivery ensures that student engagement with design projects is supported by timely taught content, which directly relates to the student's intended level of performance and development. The alignment of the taught syllabus contributes to a holistic consideration of the curriculum as the 'totality of the experiences the pupil has as a result of the provision made' (Kelly, 2009) whereby the pace and timing of content delivery, assessment and learning opportunities can enhance student engagement and satisfaction. The provision of academic space (Barnett and Coate, 2005) within the curriculum – intentional gaps for reflection and distance – facilitates the construction of meaningful knowledge, enables differentiated learning, and encourages experimentation and creativity. In short, advanced and coordinated planning of the curriculum contributes to the satisfaction and well-being of students (as well as academics) by design to ensure engagement, variety and manageability, and to avoid student burn-out, disengagement and overburden, for example through the congestion of assignment submission deadlines.

(Peter Holgate, Department of Architecture and Built Environment, Northumbria University)

Developing levels of understanding through the learning journey – the SOLO taxonomy

Biggs (Biggs and Tang, 2009) argues that a constructively aligned curriculum needs to focus on clarifying the learning outcomes so that they make explicit the levels of understanding to be achieved by students. He argues that if teachers and students have a shared understanding of the expectations of a course, students are more likely to approach learning at the appropriate cognitive level. Biggs developed the SOLO taxonomy as a way of articulating the development of learning over a programme of study based on these principles of constructive alignment. It defines five levels of progressive understanding:

- *Pre-structural:* misses the point
- *Unistructural:* identifies only part of the knowledge, missing out important attributes (identify and carry out simple procedures)
- *Multistructural:* many facts are present, but they are not structured and do not address the key issue(s) (describe or list)
- *Relational:* the development of understanding by making sense of key facts in relation to the topic as a whole (compare/contrast, explain causes, analyse, relate, apply)
- *Extended abstract:* a coherent whole is conceptualised at a high level of abstraction, and knowledge is applied to develop new understandings (theorise, generalise, hypothesise, reflect)

The words in brackets indicate the kinds of verbs that can be used to define learning tasks at the different levels. While the first three levels involve a quantitative increase in knowledge (associated with a surface approach), it is at the 'relational' and 'extended abstract' levels that the qualitative changes in knowledge take place, involving the conceptual restructuring of schemata and the critical thinking expected of graduates (deep approach). A key challenge of undergraduate courses is to move students from the multistructural, where they accumulate knowledge, to the relational, where that knowledge is put to use in the ways expected in the discipline. SOLO is similar to Bloom's Taxonomy (Bloom, 1956), which also defines a hierarchy of knowledge with associated verbs that can be used in developing learning outcomes.

Limitations of the 'approaches to learning' research

While the 'approaches to learning' research provides some powerful tools that can be used by academics in designing curricula, it does have some limitations. The terms 'surface' and 'deep' learning have at times been used to propose a simplistic and reductionist account of student learning into just two types. Haggis (2003) argues that this is inadequate in accounting for how students approach learning, and that closer attention needs to be paid to the diversity of approaches adopted by learners, with more complex social explanations of the variety of approaches to learning. She also questions the assumption that learners can be easily shifted from a surface to a deep approach, arguing that learners' approaches to learning are deeply embedded in identities, and students may resist, or find extremely difficult, efforts to change their learning approach. In place of the reductionist dichotomies of surface and deep learners, she proposes a more complex social understanding of student learning that moves beyond educational psychology to engage with developments in the social sciences.

In particular, she proposes engaging with the 'academic literacies' research (Lea and Street, 1998), which highlights the discourses involved in academic learning. This research argues for a more explicit focus on what is involved in academic approaches to study, and the need to provide opportunities for students to model and explore the expected learning behaviours over an extended period of time in the context of specific disciplinary learning, for example opportunities to explore what is meant by abstract concepts like 'critical thinking', 'argument' and 'evidence' through engaging with exemplars (Lea and Street, 1998). Many such discourses are explored in Part 3.

Case study 5.2: Using writing exemplars to develop academic literacy in the 'Society' Joint Honours Programme at Northumbria University

Learners value the opportunity to spend some class-time working collaboratively and formatively on exemplars that illustrate different approaches to a specified task because it gives them genuine insight into what their tutors are really looking for. Accordingly, on our courses we have designed workshops in which students are invited to make evaluative judgments about the relative merits, and aspects to improve, in a range of exemplars. These take the form of very brief examples of student writing that demonstrate good, 'sound standard' and unsatisfactory responses to a subject-specific task. First, students are asked to evaluate each piece using appropriate criteria and to try placing them in rank order. This is followed by dialogue with tutors, who explain their views of how effectively each exemplar approaches the task and respond to any questions the students may have. Finally, students are invited to generate feedback statements that would help to improve each exemplar, and we discuss these as a whole group.

Our workshops are designed to involve students in thinking proactively about assessment from the assessor's point of view, and we have discovered they work best if the exemplars are brief and blatantly illustrate different ways of seeing an important **threshold concept** (this term is explained later in this chapter). To this end, we've found it's worth spending time selecting or carefully writing exemplars that encourage students to move beyond a view of the (admittedly important) *technical* features of the writing, to focus squarely on the meaning-making and *conceptual* aspects, which, from tutors' viewpoints, typify understanding and represent deep approaches to learning.

(Kay Sambell, Childhood Studies, Northumbria University)

SOCIOCULTURAL APPROACHES TO STUDENT LEARNING

Socio-cultural approaches to learning focus on the interaction between learning and the social and cultural environment, and in particular how participation in social activity influences learning.

It marks a shift away from the abstractions of 'surface' and 'deep' to see students as people who learn by actively engaging in specific practices, and who develop new social identities through their participation in **learning communities**. Teaching should therefore focus on giving students opportunities to engage collaboratively in activities where they can practice using the concepts and tools that are used by the appropriate community (for example, scientists, mathematicians, historians, engineers). This can be seen as a further development of constructivist ideas of learning, with the shift away from seeing learning as the transmission of fixed knowledge to the idea of learning as an active process of individual transformation and changes in understanding. However, social practice approaches focus on the social, or community dimension of learning, more than on learners as individuals.

Lev Vygotsky (1978) was key to the development of socio-cultural approaches to learning. He developed the concept of the Zone of Proximal Development (ZPD). He argued that you need to understand two levels of development: the level that a learner can perform independently, as well as the potential learning that a learner can perform with assistance (i.e. ZPD). He argued that teachers should create opportunities for students to practice in the ZPD, where learning is **'scaffolded'** by the teacher in order to stretch students to higher levels of learning.

Lave and Wenger built on these ideas to develop a framework for understanding learning as participation in social practices through **'communities of practice'** (Lave and Wenger, 1991; Chaiklin and Lave, 1993; Wenger, 1998). 'Communities of practice' are understood as communities that emerge spontaneously whenever people come together to engage in any activity, and learning is seen as central to that process. They should be understood to include the informal communities that develop around any activity, and not just the formal structures. Learning in 'communities of practice' depends on opportunities for 'mutual engagement' with other members of the community, on access to information about what counts as competence in a particular community, and to the shared ways of doing things that have been developed over time within the community.

Lave and Wenger (1991) developed the concept of **Legitimate peripheral participation** (LPP) to describe the process by which novice members of a community are given opportunities to become competent participants of the community of practice. This involves creating opportunities for learning at the periphery of a community by providing newcomers with plenty of access to engagement both with other newcomers and with more established members of the community, and providing access to the 'shared repertoire' and ways of knowing within the community. LPP creates the space for newcomers to develop an inbound journey to become competent members of the community, developing new identities of participation. Lave and Wenger also point out the potential for communities of practice to exclude novice members at the periphery, or to selectively discriminate by denying access to engagement and to the knowledge and repertoires of the community.

This approach to learning can be applied to the curriculum of any higher education programme. It has been enthusiastically taken up in higher education as a means of designing curricula that actively engage students in the practices of a community of learning, with opportunities for engaging in real-life experiences, such as **work-based** and **project-based** learning. LPP is a useful metaphor for understanding the student journey from first year of undergraduate studies as a novice learner on an inbound journey to become a competent member of the discipline or profession through graduation and beyond. It suggests the kinds of activities that would encourage students to engage in that learning journey, by providing multiple opportunities for formal and informal learning, for example the mentoring of junior students by more senior students, disciplinary societies and work-based experiences through which students could gain access to a broader experience of participation in the practices of the disciplinary or professional community and access to established members of the community. Such learning spaces can provide students with access not just to the formal knowledge of a community, but also to the informal rules and practices, for example appropriate language and behaviour, and for developing a more holistic sense of the identity of becoming a member of the community of practice.

Communities of practice theory also provides a means for thinking through how practices of exclusion might be embedded in the practices of a learning community, some of which may be unintended. Since it is argued that activity and learning cannot be separated, the social nature of learning is foregrounded, including the emotional aspects. For first-year students, the dissonance between their understandings of how to participate, and the expectations of academics, are likely to be at their widest. Depending on the level of dissonance between students' expectations and those of the university, students will experience varying levels of discomfort, which in extreme cases may lead them to drop out. As Lea (2005) has argued, communities of practice theory can be used to focus on how learners can become excluded or marginalised, how power works to enable participation and to exclude, and how membership might be difficult for non-traditional learners due to hidden repertoires of a community, and how access might be denied to newcomers.

Induction processes need to be managed in a way that *all* students are given spaces to participate legitimately in the practices of the disciplinary and wider university community, so that new students can begin on an inward-bound trajectory, feeling comfortable and confident, with multiple opportunities for learning what they need to learn in order to become full members of the university community. Communities of practice theory provides a means for understanding why large classes might be bad for student learning if they limit the opportunities for engagement with competent members of the community. It also offers us tools for thinking about how we might ameliorate such negative effects, for example by creating opportunities for learning between novice and more experienced members of the community through mentoring and through clubs and societies. The use of online and virtual learning spaces has been enthusiastically explored from a communities of practice perspective. Communities of practice theory also provides a conceptual framework for understanding the whole network of communities to which students might belong, not just the formal curriculum but the informal learning spaces offered by a university. It provides a framework for thinking about what these informal learning spaces offer, and how these can be optimised to give the widest range of students the opportunities to develop graduate attributes.

> ## Case study 5.3: Using ideas of induction into a 'community of practice' to teach health care professionals on a Masters Health Care Programme
>
> The focus on induction into a 'community of practice' through a process of 'legitimate peripheral participation' has influenced the delivery of a three-year part-time Masters programme that prepares health care professionals to become teachers in health care and higher education contexts in the north of England. Within this programme, a number of collaborative learning groups are formed each year. Each group of five or six individuals work together to provide a series of health-related learning sessions to groups of sixth form and further education students. The health care student teachers negotiate the focus of this learning with the educational institution that they are functioning in. They then assess the needs of the learning groups and plan teaching sessions that are delivered in line with the requirements of the prescribed curriculum. As this unfolds, the small groups of health care student teachers engage in a continuous process of feedback and discussion to evaluate the efficacy of their educational practice. All of this takes place within a real-world context with real school and college students working to a real curriculum. At every stage of the collaborative learning activity, the student teachers are supported by a member of the teaching team from the health care teacher preparation programme, who observes and offers feedback on their teaching practice and the educational theory that might be used to inform this.
>
> Through this real-world experience, student teachers are exposed to the 'community of practice' of teaching and are enabled to further develop their identities as members of the teaching profession through engaging in a social learning activity. The reality of the experience and the immediacy of the constructive feedback received helps students to link theory to practice and to critically scrutinise the efficacy of such theory.
>
> (Stephen Tawse, Department of Education and Lifelong Learning,
> Northumbria University)

THRESHOLD CONCEPTS

Another development from constructivist approaches to learning is the idea of **'threshold concepts'** in the disciplines (Meyer and Land, 2003). Like the constructivists, the focus is on learning as transformation, with a focus on learning as changing existing 'schemata' or knowledge structures, rather than seeing knowledge as the accumulation of facts. Threshold concepts are defined as key concepts held in the disciplines that are central to the mastery of their subject; however, not every key concept is a threshold concept, which are those concepts that change the way you understand key elements of the discipline. Threshold concepts are transformative, like a portal, or gateway through which students have to pass before they can understand further parts of the subject, and can thus be conceptually challenging for students. Rather than focusing on stuffing the curriculum with more and more content, this research argues that teaching should identify the threshold concepts in the disciplines, and focus teaching on challenging students to engage with these concepts and gain mastery over them.

The research into threshold concepts has focused on how to identify threshold concepts across the different disciplines. Threshold concepts are:

- *Transformative:* once understood they have the potential to effect significant learning. They often involve changes in identity and may have an affective element with changes in feeling or attitude.
- *Irreversible:* like Adam and Eve who were expelled from Eden once they had eaten from the Tree of Knowledge, threshold concepts are unlikely to be unlearned, and there may be no going back to a previous state of innocence. They may also involve a sense of loss and may be resisted by students.
- *Integrative:* threshold concepts can expose the previously hidden interrelatedness of things. They are like a key to open knowledge.
- *Troublesome:* threshold concepts may be troublesome for a range of reasons: they may be conceptually challenging, or counterintuitive, challenging previously held beliefs about the nature of things. Students may experience a sense of loss on internalising a threshold concept, in giving up old familiar ways of knowing, hence students may get stuck, entering a liminal state from which they find it hard to move on, and in this state will be unable to progress in the discipline. Teaching needs to focus on helping students through these liminal states.

Threshold concepts can be a useful focus for developing the curriculum. Teachers can ask themselves what are the ways of understanding that are stopping students from making progress with their learning? What are the threshold concepts that need to be in place before they can get to the next stage? Are there misunderstandings by students that need to be challenged in order for them to progress to the next level of understanding? If teachers can identify these bottlenecks to learning, they can build the curriculum around addressing these. Teachers need to help students gain mastery over threshold concepts, understanding how students can get stuck and focusing learning around the changes in understanding th at students need to make. While mastery of threshold concepts can be sudden, students can also oscillate between old ways of knowing and new ways, and need help in moving through the portal.

> ## Interrogating practice
>
> - Have you ever considered what the threshold concepts are in your discipline?
> - It may be useful to get students to map the threshold concepts they have encountered, to talk about them, and in this way help to make explicit the journey students have taken in mastering threshold concepts.
>
> This will also help you identify for future teaching areas where students may need the most support to become 'unstuck'.

LEARNING STYLES

The **learning styles** research focuses on the diversity of preferred ways of learning, which are seen as due to innate differences between individual learners. The learning styles research does not make value judgements about these different learning styles, all of which are seen as valuable, and in this it differs from the 'approaches to learning' research, which sees a hierarchy of approaches from 'poor' surface approaches to 'good' deep approaches. The aim of the learning styles research is to make both teachers and learners aware of the diversity of preferred ways of learning of individual learners, and to ensure that the curriculum provides opportunities for all types of learners to fully engage with learning. Teachers and students should be encouraged to be aware of and value their own preferred learning styles, as well as recognising their less preferred styles of learning and developing these too.

There are a range of different ways of categorising learning styles, including multiple intelligences (Gardner, 1984), the Kolb **experiential learning** inventory (Kolb, 1984; Honey and Mumford, 1986), and the Myers Briggs inventory (Myers et al., 1998). This section will focus on Kolb's experiential learning inventory because it has influenced many ways of approaching learning and teaching in higher education, including work-based learning, action learning and reflective practice.

Experiential learning

Experiential learning theories (Kolb, 1984) argue that understanding is not fixed, and is influenced by experience. Experiential learning is viewed as a continuous process where students bring their own knowledge and previous experience to learning. In this, it draws upon constructivist approaches to learning. It views learning as a continuous cycle rather than as a fixed object, which is characterised by four phases, from concrete

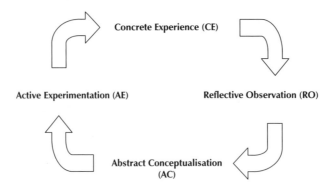

Figure 5.1 The Kolb Learning Cycle

experience to reflective observation on that experience; this is followed by abstract conceptualisation, drawing on theories where learners integrate their ideas and understanding with their existing knowledge; this revised understanding is then tested through active experimentation, leading to a new concrete experience in a new situation.

This **learning cycle** (see Figure 5.1) is repeated in a spiral process as a form of continuous reflection on practice, leading to increasing expertise. It is the quality of reflection and abstract conceptualisation by learners that will lead to improved understanding and hence of performance, so teachers need to focus in particular on the quality of support and feedback at these stages of the learning cycle. Experiential learning theory, and in particular theories of reflective learning (Schon, 1987; Boud et al., 1985), have been influential in shaping approaches to professional learning and development, including the professional development of teachers in higher education.

The experiential learning cycle has informed the development of Kolb's Learning Styles Inventory, which has also been developed by Honey and Mumford (1986). This inventory is based on a view that learners have preferences in the way they approach their learning through the learning cycle. Four learning styles are identified that relate to the different stages of the learning cycle:

1   Those who learn best by reflecting on concrete experience (*divergent*)
2   Those who learn best by developing abstract theories and theoretical models of their observations (*assimilation*)
3   Those who like to put theories into practice (*convergent*)
4   Those who like to experiment to plan new concrete experiences (*accommodator*)

*   *Divergent learners* are good at viewing concrete situations from a variety of perspectives. They are good at brainstorming and generating ideas with an open mind to different points of view, tend to be imaginative and like group work.
*   *Assimilating learners* can cope with a wide range of information and put it into a concise, logical form. They are more interested in ideas and concepts than people, and value concepts for their logical coherence more than their practical application.

- *Convergent learners* like to find practical uses for ideas and theories, and learning through experimentation. They are good at problem solving and prefer technical to social and interpersonal issues.
- *Accommodating learners* prefer hands-on action oriented learning, carrying out plans and engaging in challenging experiences.

When constructing curricula, teachers need to create learning opportunities that engage the learning preferences of all these types of learner.

Myers Briggs inventory

The Myers Briggs inventory is based on Jung's personality types, posing four sets of oppositions, or preferences, leading to sixteen different personality types that can be linked to preferences in learning. These oppositions/preferences are: extraversion/ introversion, sensing/intuition, thinking/feeling and judging/perceiving.

- *Extraversion:* focus on the outer world of people and activity
- *Introversion:* focus on the inner world of ideas and experiences
- *Sensing:* prefer to take information that is concrete and are observant about details and practical realities
- *Intuition:* like to see the big picture, focusing on patterns, relationships and connections between facts
- *Thinking:* focus on principles, and the logical consequences of a choice or action in decision-making
- *Feeling:* focus on what is important for all the people involved in decision-making, based on empathy and respect
- *Judging:* prefer to live in a planned, orderly way, sticking to a schedule and getting things done
- *Perceiving:* prefer to live in a flexible and spontaneous way, seeking to experience and understand life rather than control it

Accommodating learning styles in teaching

It is important as a teacher to be aware of your own preferences because these are likely to influence your preferred ways of teaching. It is worth reflecting on the curriculum and its teaching/learning and assessment activities to ensure that it enables all types of learner to fully engage. One can assume that any group of students will have a range of learners, covering all of the main learning styles identified earlier.

It can also be helpful for students to become more aware of their own learning preferences because this will empower them to take more responsibility for their learning, as well as giving them confidence in their strengths as learners. But they should also be encouraged to develop their less preferred approaches to learning.

CONCLUSION AND OVERVIEW

This chapter has provided an overview of key theories of student learning, showing why they are important for teachers in higher education. The key message of this chapter is that to be a good teacher in higher education you need to be constantly alert to how your students are learning, drawing on a range of theories to support your reflection. There is no one best theory, and you are likely to find different theories useful in different situations. You should consider what they might have to tell you about how to teach, how to design learning experiences and how to assess. You can use the theories in this chapter as a toolbox that can help you to 'diagnose' problems when learning is not happening as you expected. You might find some of the theories particularly interesting or useful, and use this chapter as a starting place for further research.

Interrogating practice

At this stage, I recommend that you answer again the questions that were posed at the beginning of this chapter. As you write your answers, reflect on how your initial statements may have developed or shifted through the process of engaging with the theories explored in this chapter, and by reflecting on the relevance of these theories to your own experiences of being a teacher in higher education.

1   How do you think students learn?
2   Teaching is...
3   Graduates in my subject should be able to...
4   I could use (which) theory to address the biggest challenge I face in facilitating my students' learning...

REFERENCES AND FURTHER READING

The asterisked references may be especially useful to follow up on to develop your understanding and practice further.

Barnett, R (1997) *Higher Education: A Critical Business*. London: Society for Research into Higher Education.

Barnett, R and Coate, K (2005) *Engaging the Curriculum in Higher Education*. Maidenhead: Open University Press.

*Biggs, J and Tang, C (2009) *Teaching for Quality Learning at University*. 3rd edn. Maidenhead: Open University Press.

Bloom, B (1956) *Taxonomy of Educational Objectives. Handbook I: The Cognitive Domain*. New York, NY: David McKay.

Boud, D, Keogh, R and Walker, D (1985) *Reflection: Turning Experience into Learning.* London: Kogan-Page.

Bruner, J (1960) *The Process of Education.* Cambridge, MA: Harvard University Press.

Chaiklin, S and Lave, J (eds) (1993) *Understanding Practice: Perspectives on Activity and Context.* Cambridge: Cambridge University Press.

Gardner, H (1984) *Frames of Mind.* London: Paladin.

Haggis, T (2003) 'Constructing images of ourselves? A critical investigation into "approaches to learning" research in higher education', *British Educational Research Journal*, 29(1): 89–104.

Honey, P and Mumford, A (1986) *A Manual of Learning Styles.* Maidenhead: Peter Honey.

Kelly, AV (2009) *The Curriculum: Theory and Practice.* 6th edn. London: Sage Publications.

Kolb, D (1984) *Experiential Learning.* Englewood Cliffs, NJ: Prentice Hall.

*Lave, J and Wenger, E (1991) *Situated Learning: Legitimate Peripheral Participation.* Cambridge: Cambridge University Press.

Lea, MR (2005) 'Communities of practice in higher education: useful heuristic or educational model'. In: D Barton and K Tusting (eds). *Beyond Communities of Practice: Language, Power and Social Context.* Cambridge: Cambridge University Press, 180–197.

Lea, MR and Street, BV (1998) Student writing in higher education: an academic literacies approach. *Studies in Higher Education*, 23(2): 157–171.

Marton, F and Säljö, R (1984/1997) 'Approaches to learning'. In: F. Marton et al. (eds). *The Experience of Learning.* Edinburgh: Scottish Academic Press, 36–55.

Meyer, JHF and Land, R (2003) 'Threshold concepts and troublesome knowledge: linkages to ways of thinking and practising'. Available from: http://www.etl.tla.ed.ac.uk/docs/ETLreport4.pdf (accessed 1 April 2014).

Myers, IB, McCaulley, M, Quenk, NL and Hammer, AL (1998) *MBTI Handbook: A Guide to the development and use of the Myers-Briggs Type Indicator.* 3rd edn. Washington, DC: Consulting Psychologists Press.

Piaget, J (1950) *The Psychology of Intelligence.* London: Routledge and Kegan Paul.

Prosser, M and Trigwell, K (1999) *Understanding Learning and Teaching. The Experience in Higher Education.* Buckingham: Society for Research into Higher Education and Open University Press.

Ramsden, P (2003) *Learning to Teach in Higher Education.* 2nd edn. London: RoutledgeFalmer.

Schon, D (1987) *Educating the Reflective Practitioner: Toward a New Design for Teaching and Learning in the Professions.* San Francisco, CA: Jossey-Bass.

Vygotsky, L (1978) *Mind and Society.* Cambridge, MA: Harvard University Press.

Wenger, E (1998) *Communities of Practice: Learning, Meaning and Identity.* Cambridge: Cambridge University Press.

6

Describing what students should learn

Chris Butcher

INTRODUCTION

Deciding and describing what students should be learning has taken on greater significance for many universities following investment in major curriculum reviews resulting
from the significant changes to the context in which we operate and work (see Chapters
2 and 3). The curriculum allows institutions to express their distinctiveness and focus
on issues such as internationalisation, employability (half of the top 100 world-ranking
universities mention their graduates' employability as part of their attractiveness) or
research-informed teaching. This chapter will explore some of the factors that should
inform curriculum design, as well as discuss the ways in which we can tell our students
about the expectations we have of them – the **intended learning outcomes**.

Whilst the taught curriculum and co-curricular (extra-curricular) opportunities
comprise the total student experience, this chapter will focus on the taught curriculum.

COHERENCE: PROGRESSION AND CURRICULUM MODELS

Many of us design (and deliver) a small part of the curriculum – our module or part of a
module – at a particular level in the course. When planning, it is important to consider
the whole course/programme: what comes before, what follows and what is happening at the same time. In this way, we take the students' perspective and ensure they
see a coherent, not fragmented, course. We build in the interconnections essential for
helping students develop a full understanding of the disciplinary concepts, skills and
attributes. We also ensure progression within the curriculum, with current learning
building on and taking account of what has been studied before, or building towards
the next stages of the course. Awareness of the shape of the curriculum, discussed next,
helps here.

Another essential aspect of coherence is neatly encapsulated by the idea of *constructive alignment* (Biggs and Tang, 2011). The aim is to ensure that the learning experience/

Table 6.1 An illustration of constructive alignment

Learning outcome	Teaching/learning	Assessment
Explain	Lectures, reading, videos of the content and tutorials to discuss ideas	*Formative* feedback helps students develop their ideas and abilities
Apply	Tutorials/**problem classes** – students work together using the ideas	*Summative* assessment, requiring explanation, application and formulation, tests ability
Formulate	Students co-create conclusions and meanings and see how others do this	*Criteria* differentiate how well students do these three things

teaching that is provided relates directly to the knowledge, attribute or skill that we expect the students to gain or achieve, and that assessment tests this accordingly. Table 6.1 illustrates this for the intended outcome that students are better able to explain an idea and apply it in order to formulate an explanation of an event or phenomenon.

Curriculum models

The shape of the curriculum illustrates the way in which modules, or components of the course, relate one to another. Do they stack one on another like a tower of Lego bricks? This is often called a *vertical* or *Lego* curriculum. If some of the modules are totally freestanding, then the term *satellite* is frequently used to describe them. If all of the modules provide component parts to a bigger picture that you do not see fully until the course is done, then the label *jigsaw* fits well here. Do several modules form the basis for a higher level module, building up like a *pyramid*? Do the students return to topics as they progress through the course and treat them in more complex and demanding ways on each occasion? This is usually termed a *spiral* curriculum.

Invariably the whole course or programme is not described by just one of these labels, but telling the students how the parts fit together helps them to gain an understanding of the bigger picture and why they are asked to learn this, in this way, at this stage of the course.

WHAT IS IN AND WHAT IS OUT?

When thinking about the taught curriculum – what students should learn – there are a number of useful reference points and ideas that should inform our thinking.

Subject benchmark statements

These are an essential reference point. The Quality Assurance Agency states that subject benchmark statements:

> set out expectations about standards of degrees in a range of subject areas. They describe what gives a discipline its coherence and identity, and define what can be expected of a graduate in terms of the abilities and skills needed to develop understanding or competence in the subject ... do not represent a national curriculum in a subject area. Rather, they allow for flexibility and innovation in programme design within an overall conceptual framework established by an academic subject community.
>
> (QAA, 2013a)

Benchmark statements, crafted by renowned academics within the discipline, provide an overview of what students should study, outline the necessary skills and attributes that students should develop and provide notions of progression and expected standards, usually at the threshold (pass/fail) and median (2i/2ii) levels with respect to honours classification. They are written for most subjects at undergraduate level and for some at Masters.

Level/qualification descriptors

One problem that many early career academics find when planning is the level – what makes this level 5 rather than level 4, 6 or even 7? The QAA provides qualification descriptors (QAA, 2011) and these can be further refined to give level descriptors within a qualification. Many institutions have their own versions. Like all generic statements they may, at first glance, lack specificity; however, comparing one level against another shows the progression and this is illustrated first for content:

- Level 4: demonstrate a familiarity with basic concepts, information, practical competencies and techniques that are standard features of the discipline;
- Level 5: demonstrate a broad understanding of concepts, information, practical competencies and techniques that are standard features in a range of aspects of the discipline;
- Level 6: understand and demonstrate coherent and detailed subject knowledge and professional competencies, some of which will be informed by recent research/scholarship in the discipline.

And then for intellectual demand:

- Level 4: predictable, providing a familiarisation with the discipline;
- Level 5: simple if unpredictable and complex if predictable;
- Level 6: includes the use of complex and unpredictable situations.

Graduate skills/graduateness

Several years ago higher education institutions were asked to justify the high cost (at that time to the tax payer) of studying at university and to explain the added value in terms of gaining a degree. More recently universities have been developing lists of attributes and skills that students should gain by fully engaging in the curriculum – taught and extra/co-curricula – as a means of demonstrating distinctiveness. You need to think about the contribution that your course/module makes to this bigger picture and inform your students of this expectation. For example, at the University of Leeds Graduate Skills are linked to the University's values (University of Leeds, 2009). The full list comprises 27 statements under the five values headings. An abbreviated version (one per value) is provided for illustration:

- *Academic excellence* e.g. ability to work autonomously, take the initiative and to be self-directed in undertaking tasks.
- *Community* e.g. responsible awareness of and respect for other perspectives and sensitivities, whether local, national or international and the implications for individual behaviour.
- *Integrity* e.g. honesty and openness and with a sense of academic and social responsibility.
- *Professionalism* e.g. articulate one's own skills and abilities confidently and convincingly, tailored to the target audience as appropriate.
- *Inclusiveness* e.g. engagement with society and individuals, acknowledging and managing preconceptions or prejudice.

Case study 6.1: The Leeds Curriculum

As a world-class, research-intensive, large, civic university, we want to develop 'outstanding graduates and scholars to make a major impact upon global society' (University of Leeds, 2009) by studying a curriculum that mirrors, and is distinctive to, the institution. We also want to ensure an equal student experience no matter what subject is studied. To achieve this, we embarked on an institution-wide project in 2010 to enhance the undergraduate curriculum for implementation by September 2015.

Continuing to place a research-based education at the heart of the Leeds Curriculum, the Project set out to ensure:

- Equity for our students in terms of skills development and preparedness for employment;
- Responsiveness to the changing HE landscape in which there is increased competition in attracting students from both home and overseas markets,

and in which students (and parents) seek a clear statement of the advantages of a research-based education and the opportunity provided by the breadth of disciplines available at Leeds; and

- Greater clarity around information and guidance to support student choice.

To meet these aims, staff defined the 'model' graduate – the abilities, attributes and skills that should be demonstrated by all graduates of any discipline, based on the University values. They defined our approach to research-based learning and mapped it across all programmes. Also, staff and students identified Core Programme Threads that we want incorporated in all programmes:

- Employability
- Ethics and responsibility
- Global and cultural insight

The expectation is that these Threads are interpreted by schools in ways that are specific and integral to their programmes, resulting in students who have an enhanced understanding of the relevance and intellectual position of their primary discipline.

In addition, we have thought in imaginative ways about how we organise our elective modules with the aims of:

- Ensuring our students have the opportunity to broaden their intellectual horizons and to explore interesting and socially relevant issues;
- Providing students with structured opportunities to develop skills beyond their core discipline that will be valuable in their future life/career; and
- Fostering the mental flexibility that employers say they want.

This has resulted in ten Discovery Themes ranging from *Power and Conflict* to *Creating Sustainable Futures*, which will have academic coherence, dedicated academic leaders and will allow students to broaden their studies, make connections between different subject areas and understand different disciplinary approaches to knowledge.

The Project has also evaluated assessment and feedback practice across the institution and is seeking to enhance how students experience assessment through adherence to a set of discipline-sensitive principles that have been developed from the evidence and good practice at this institution and elsewhere. The intention is, as the result of an assessment audit, to reflect on ways in which we assess students and give them feedback on their progress.

The Leeds Curriculum will afford the template for every undergraduate degree and provide a clear statement of what is distinctive about studying at the University of Leeds.

(Caroline Pearman, Project Manager)

Internationalising the curriculum

Graduates need to be international in their understanding and outlook; they need to be culturally sensitive and able to live and work in a diverse and multi-cultural world and workplace. This can be achieved in a number of ways, including:

- Exploiting the fact that staff and students themselves are from a number of different countries and cultures (University of Leeds has 103 different nationalities of staff and students from 141 countries [University of Leeds, 2013]);
- Opportunities to work and study abroad;
- International case studies to illustrate topics; and
- Ensuring diverse opinions and perspectives are considered within subject content.

The Higher Education Academy (HEA, 2013) notes the need for *cross-cultural capabilities* and provides a valuable range of resources to support you.

Digital literacy

The **Jisc** definition provides the starting point for thinking about the impact on the curriculum and the Jisc projects provide you with the resources and tools for the task.

> By digital literacy we mean those capabilities which fit an individual for living, learning and working in a digital society: for example, the skills to use digital tools to undertake academic research, writing and critical thinking; as part of personal development planning; and as a way of showcasing achievements.
>
> (Jisc, 2011)

Employability

Generic, sometimes transferable, skills may not fit well with our focus on specific, disciplinary content and skills. However, with 70 per cent of graduate employment opportunities now being subject blind, the notion of graduate skills discussed earlier relates directly to the employability agenda. Being more aware of the expectations of the job market for our graduates, and building these attributes and skills into the curriculum, has become a standard and vital part of the curriculum design narrative. The employer/industrial/alumni panels and committees that are an increasingly significant part of the landscape in higher education, both at institutional and disciplinary level, are an important source of critical information on this issue.

Including opportunities to develop these skills/attributes is important but we need to engage our learners in a dialogue about what they are gaining and developing from their courses and ensure they can, 'articulate (their) own skills and abilities confidently and convincingly'.

Case study 6.2: Employability at Leeds Trinity University

Leeds Trinity University has a long-established record of embedding employability skills in the undergraduate curriculum. Graduate employability forms a key part of the Leeds Trinity Strategic Plan and the following are listed as priorities:

1   Embed graduate employability skills at all levels in the curriculum.
2   Strengthen and broaden links with employers and alumni to inform the curriculum and expand student opportunities.
3   Provide an integrated careers and employability service showing best practice in the support of students and academic departments.

Students undertake two six-week work placements, one at the end of the first year of study, and a second mid-way through the second year. These are embedded within 20-credit Professional Development and Placement modules. At Levels 4 and 5, the curriculum is designed to support students in their preparation for their placements, and with their employability skills more generally. Students are provided with guidance on general employability issues, such as producing an effective CV, and are able to practice their interview skills, undertake evaluations of their own strengths and weaknesses, and gain experience of assessment centres. In addition, visiting speakers from a range of organisations give talks on their expectations of graduates and provide invaluable information about the best and worst things that students can do before and after graduation to make themselves a more attractive prospect to a potential employer.

The placement process itself often includes an interview with a potential placement provider and, in most cases, the onus is on the student to make contact with the provider and effectively introduce themselves and discuss the opportunity that is available to them. Students are also expected to communicate effectively and in a professional manner with the Placement Team in the Careers and Employability Office, and are required to provide copies of their CV and, if they have arranged their own placement, to provide details of this. For the majority of students, the Placement Team helps to arrange suitable placements for students, and so it is essential that students liaise with the Placement Team, as well as with their departmental placement coordinator.

The process of liaising with the Placement Team to make arrangements for a suitable placement is, in itself, an opportunity for students to develop skills of communicating and liaising with others.

The precise form that assessment takes is tailored to the subject area, but includes some form of portfolio and a placement report, in addition to satisfactory performance during the placement itself. The assessed work at Level 5 in psychology, for example, includes a portfolio in which students reflect upon a range of activities and tasks (e.g. experience of Graduate Assessment Centre tasks, psychology in the workplace) and a placement report, including a reflective learning diary, an analysis of the organisation from a psychological perspective and a career-path reflection. The intertwining of subject knowledge and employment experience in this way helps to embed employability firmly within the curriculum.

(Steve Jones, Department of Psychology)

Professional, Statutory and Regulatory Bodies

Professional, Statutory and Regulatory Bodies (PSRBs) are organisations that are authorised to accredit, approve or recognise courses and programmes. PSRBs are important because accredited courses are often the gateway to employment opportunities within a particular sector (QAA, 2013b). Accrediting bodies usually have a syllabus, including knowledge, skills and attitudes/values that must be included within the course in order for it to gain accreditation. For example, if you are an early-career academic, you may be on a course accredited by the HEA which incorporates the **UK Professional Standards Framework** (UKPSF) – the recognition for Fellowship of the HEA being one outcome (see Chapter 4).

PSRB accreditation is one way that universities ensure professional standards and quality are maintained and that students gain the skills and knowledge required by employers (you may need to know how your part of the course relates to any relevant professional requirement). Unfortunately, some see (and use) PSRB guidelines as limiting factors on the curriculum, rather than seeing the opportunities for dialogue and partnership with the professional association.

Ways of Thinking and Practising

Hounsell and Entwistle led the Enhancing Teaching-Learning Environments in Undergraduate Courses (ETL, 2001) project and coined the phrase 'Ways of Thinking and Practising in the Subject' to capture the particular thinking processes and subject skills that staff seek to develop in their students.

Interrogating practice

- What is particular and special in terms of skills needed for your discipline?
- Are there particular attitudes and approaches that are essential to study the discipline?
- What, if any, PSRB guidance do you need to be aware of?

Right of inclusion

Before looking at ways of making expectations explicit to our students, i.e. drafting learning outcomes, here are some thoughts about selecting content. Harden (1986) suggested content should satisfy one of four criteria, and these can be used to reduce the possible list of content into a more manageable and realistic syllabus.

1 *Mainstream*: directly contributes to a module/programme aim or learning outcome, e.g. students need to know x or how to use y in order to…
2 *Precursor*: core knowledge or skill that is needed for a later part of the course, e.g. knowledge of a mathematical process in order that the results of experimental work can be computed.
3 *Opportunistic*: allows students to develop necessary intellectual skills, e.g. conflicting evidence helps develop analytical and critical thinking skills in coming to terms with ambiguity.
4 *Supportive*: it contributes to other areas of the course, e.g. an industrial or commercial example that illustrates and clarifies.

INTENDED AIMS AND LEARNING OUTCOMES: DESCRIBING AND DRAFTING

Learners need to know where they are going in order to get there. This section of the chapter looks at the ways in which we can give learners the map, intended aims and learning outcomes.

Terminology

Allan (1996) coined a useful term 'educational intent', which provides the answer to the question often asked by students 'why are we doing this?' She also noted the long list of words that can clutter thinking about this topic, including aims, objectives, goals and outcomes. I do not mind what you call them, as long as you have the conversation with your students about *educational intent*. In this chapter, I will use *aims* and *learning outcomes* because they are the most frequently used and it is useful to have two ways in which to describe what we are trying to achieve.

Purposes – why are we doing this?

Aims and learning outcomes provide *guidelines and a common understanding* for students (and other stakeholders, e.g. employers) *of what is to be achieved*. They give guidelines to students of academic expectations and indicate standards.

Aims and learning outcomes – making the distinction

Aims are broad and tell students overall purposes and they are often written as actions for lecturers/tutors. Learning outcomes state what a student is expected to be able to do at points during and at the end of study, and include subject-specific content, concepts, skills, attributes and abilities. They work best when written in student terms and characterised as SMART (Butcher et al., 2006):

- **S**pecific: detail about particular aspects of expectations
- **M**eaningful: language that is understandable to all
- **A**ppropriate: 'fit for purpose' – suit learners and satisfy standards
- **R**ealistic: given time constraints, resources, etc.
- **T**estable: some measure of progress/achievement can be made

Writing aims and outcomes

Aims and outcomes should encompass the whole of the taught curriculum and the progression of demand within the subject, and could usefully recognise three areas or **domains** of outcomes. The Bloom taxonomy (Bloom, 1956) underpins this classification and the original terminology is included in brackets.

- **What students should know and can do with what they know**, comprehending knowledge and information (cognitive), e.g. calculate statistical power and required sample size for situations that can be analysed using one or two sample t-tests.
- **Expected attitudes, approaches and values** (affective), e.g. respect for patients and colleagues that encompasses, without prejudice, diversity of background and opportunity, language, culture and way of life.
- **Skills, both personal and motor** (psychomotor), e.g. communicate effectively taking account of the audience.

For each aspect, a hierarchy of intellectual demand and expectation can be defined. Table 6.2 illustrates this. Each stage is defined and verbs (*italicised*), which are useful for drafting cognitive learning outcomes, are provided.

Some colleagues regard this classification as incomplete because some planned outcomes, for example creativity, are not immediately apparent. Anderson and Krathwohl (2001) revised the taxonomy and included 'Create = putting elements together to form a novel, coherent whole or make an original product', suggesting verbs like 'generating, planning and producing'. In addition, they classified the knowledge that students should gain, which fits well with some disciplines:

- **Factual knowledge:** basic elements that students must know to be acquainted with a discipline or solve typical problems: *know terminology, know specific details and elements.*

Table 6.2 Hierarchy of verbs that can be useful in drafting cognitive learning outcomes

KNOWLEDGE = recalls	Able to recall information but not necessarily establish links between ideas or remember general principles or theories
	defines, describes, identifies, lists, matches, names, outlines, recalls, recognises
COMPREHENSION = understands	Ability to recall information, demonstrate links and meanings, manipulate ideas and re-represent
	classifies, converts, distinguishes between, explains, extends, generalises, paraphrases, predicts, summarises, transforms, translates
APPLICATION = uses in known or novel situations	Ability to apply abstract principles to particular and concrete known or novel situations
	arranges, classifies, computes, demonstrates, employs, extrapolates, modifies, operates, predicts, relates, solves, transfers, uses
ANALYSIS = breaking down	Deconstructs information, ideas and concepts by breaking into constituent parts and identifying relationships or patterns
	deduces, diagrams, differentiates, discriminates, distinguishes, estimates, experiments, identifies, infers, orders, separates, subdivides
SYNTHESIS = combining	Combines facts or ideas to create new patterns or structures derived from the original data
	combines, compiles, composes, constructs, creates, designs, formulates, generates, hypothesises, manages, rearranges, relates, summarises
EVALUATION = judging	Recognises the value of ideas, methods or principles
	appraises, assesses, compares, concludes, contrasts, criticises, discriminates, evaluates, judges, justifies, revises, supports

- **Conceptual knowledge:** know the inter-relationships amongst the basic elements within a large structure that enable them to function together: *know classification, know principles and generalisations, know theories, models and structures.*
- **Procedural knowledge:** know how to do something, the methods of inquiry and criteria for using skills, algorithms, techniques and methods: *know subject-specific skills and algorithms, know techniques and methods, know criteria for determining when to use appropriate procedures.*
- **Meta-cognitive knowledge:** knowledge of cognition in general, as well as awareness of one's own cognition: *strategic knowledge, cognitive tasks including appropriate contextual and conditional knowledge, self-knowledge.*

I suggest you use the Bloom *and* the revised taxonomy for the help they both provide rather than be limited by either – they are frameworks not cages.

Writing attitudinal and skill outcomes

Similar hierarchies have been identified for skills and attitudes/approaches that we need to include in outcome statements. I have described these elsewhere (Butcher et al., 2006) and provided two approaches to making expectations explicit. The steps to writing such outcomes are (1) to decide where the students are on the hierarchy and (2) where you want them to be at the end of their learning – the outcome is written as the transition.

Objection to outcomes and how to make them work

One problem with the Bloom-based classification is that the words can be used at all levels of education – early years in secondary and A-level syllabi use the terms. However, outcomes are used within a context, in this case higher education, and that sets the level. The balance between being specific without being too limiting or prescriptive is the ideal but very difficult target. Specificity can be achieved by writing outcomes that include *performance*, *condition* and *criterion*.

- **Performance:** a statement of what the learner should be able to do, which may relate to an intellectual skill, a practical skill or an attitude.
- **Condition:** the conditions under which the performance should occur.
- **Criterion:** the level of performance that is considered acceptable.

For example, 'By level six, students should be able to use secondary as well as primary sources to develop a critical argument, drawing relevant inferences from what they see, hear and read, working either in groups or individually'.

Interrogating practice

- Review the outcomes that you have for a module – are they SMART?
- Try using the performance/condition/criterion approach to clarify expectations.

Intended learning outcomes are of no value if they stay 'hidden' in course documentation, programme catalogues or module handbooks. They are most valuable when discussed and elaborated with students, and this can be achieved in a variety of ways:

- Discussed at the start of a module, linked to assessment expectations and teaching/learning methods and opportunities (constructive alignment);
- Included in session materials as guidance; and
- Made clear to students at the start of teaching (e.g. lecture tutorial or seminar) as long as you go back later to review progress.

OVERVIEW

This chapter has two distinct messages. First, be aware of the factors (both external and internal to the institution) that should guide thinking about the taught curriculum, in addition to the disciplinary content, to guarantee a coherent curriculum that ensures students are equipped for life and employment in a global and digital society. Second, on the ways in which we make the expected learning outcomes explicit to our students, remember the purpose is to provide a guideline and common understanding. As noted earlier, learning outcomes are a framework, not a cage, and allow us (staff and students) to share the map of the journey and important landmarks on the way.

REFERENCES

Allan, J (1996) 'Learning outcomes in higher education', *Studies in Higher Education*, 21(1): 93–108.

Anderson, LW and Krathwohl, DR (eds) (2001) *A Taxonomy for Learning, Teaching and Assessing: a Revision Of Bloom's Educational Objectives.* London: Longman.

Biggs, J and Tang, C (2011) *Teaching for Quality Learning at University. What the Student Does.* 4th edn. Maidenhead: Open University Press.

Bloom, BS (ed) (1956) *Taxonomy of Educational Objectives. Handbook 1: The Cognitive Domain.* London: Longman.

Butcher, C, Davies, C and Highton, M (2006) *Designing Learning: From Module Outline to Effective Teaching.* London: Routledge.

ETL (2001). *Enhancing Teaching-Learning Environments in Undergraduate Courses.* Available from: http://www.etl.tla.ed.ac.uk/project.html (accessed 8 December 2013).

Harden, RM (1986) Ten Questions To Ask When Planning a Course or Curriculum. *Medical Education*, 20(4): 356–365.

Higher Education Academy (HEA) (2013) *Internationalising the Curriculum.* Available from: http://www.heacademy.ac.uk/resources/detail/internationalisation/ISL_Internationalising_the_curriculum (accessed 8 December 2013).

Jisc (2011) *Developing Digital Literacies.* Available from: http://www.jisc.ac.uk/whatwedo/programmes/elearning/developingdigitalliteracies.aspx (accessed 8 December 2013).

Quality Assurance Agency (QAA) (2011) *Quality Code*. Available from: http://www.qaa.ac.uk/Publications/InformationAndGuidance/Pages/quality-code-A1.aspx (accessed December 2013).

Quality Assurance Agency (QAA) (2013a) *Subject Benchmark Statements*. Available from: http://www.qaa.ac.uk/AssuringStandardsAndQuality/subject-guidance/Pages/Subject-benchmark-statements.aspx (accessed December 2013).

Quality Assurance Agency (QAA) (2013b) *Professional Bodies*. Available from: http://www.qaa.ac.uk/Partners/PSRBs/Pages/default.aspx (accessed December 2013).

University of Leeds (2009) *University Values*. Available from: http://www.leeds.ac.uk/qat/tsg/02-values.html (accessed December 2013).

University of Leeds (2013) *Facts and Figures: Academic Excellence*. Available from: http://www.leeds.ac.uk/info/20014/about/234/facts_and_figures (accessed December 2013).

FURTHER READING

Moon, J (2002) *The Module & Programme Development Handbook*. London: Kogan Page.

Toohey, S (1999) *Designing Courses For Higher Education*. Buckingham: Society for Research into Higher Education and Open University Press.

Watson, P (2002) 'The role and integration of learning outcomes into the educational process', *Active Learning in Higher Education*, 3(3): 205–219.

7 Lecturing, working with groups and providing individual support

Ruth Ayres

INTRODUCTION

The primary consideration when designing/delivering any **module** or **programme of study**, is what you want your students to achieve by the end of their period of study: the **intended learning outcomes**. Biggs (1996) notes the need for curricula to be constructively aligned such that there is adoption of learning and teaching activities that best realise the intended learning outcomes and appropriate assessment tasks – formative and summative – designed to test whether students have met these intended learning outcomes.

The nature of the intended learning outcomes will determine your choice of learning and teaching method. The ensuing chapter can help you with this decision, providing a detailed discussion of two of the most commonly adopted teaching methods in higher education: lecturing and group work. Consideration is also given to supporting the diverse needs of learners, key for any module or programme.

LECTURING

Why lecture?

There has been much debate in the literature about the value of lecturing. Classically, Bligh (1972) noted that lectures were no more effective than other types of teaching method for transmitting information, and are less effective than discussions for promoting thought.

Despite this research and advances in technology, which have led to the development of many online courses including **MOOCs** (Massive Open Online Courses), the lecture is still one of the most commonly adopted teaching methods in higher education (e.g. Edwards et al., 2001). Many students continue to expect and value the lecture as a key facet of university education. From the academics' perspective, the lecture provides the opportunity to inspire and motivate students (e.g. Edwards et al., 2001; Dolnicar, 2005) whilst presenting consistent information to large groups in a cost effective manner. The best lectures engage, inspire and challenge students, promoting **active learning** to ensure a thorough, deep understanding and good retention of the topics covered. Having your teaching observed by a peer, or a more experienced colleague can be helpful in gaining constructive feedback on your teaching. You may also want to consider having your lecture filmed so that you can watch it back and review your practice.

Interrogating practice

- What are your strengths as a lecturer?
- What are the areas you need to improve on?
- How will you bring about the improvements you've identified as requiring attention?

How to give a good lecture

It is important to know your students' existing knowledge and prior experience so that you can build on this and make material relevant and meaningful (e.g. Dolnicar, 2005). Lectures with a clear structure, that stretch students while providing appropriate support (often referred to as 'scaffolding', based on the work of Vygotsky (1978)), enable students to progress and achieve their potential. If you are new to teaching, it is worth exploring the debate in the literature on learning styles (see Honey and Mumford, 2006; Fleming and Mills, 1992; Gardner, 1993; Coffield et al., 2004a, 2004b; Hall and Moseley, 2005; Rogers, 2009) as this will inform your lecture planning. Any student group is likely to consist of individuals who learn in a variety of different ways. For example, the **VARK** Model (Fleming and Mills, 1992) is based on the senses and suggests that **visual learners** learn most effectively by looking at visual information, for example diagrams, charts, graphs, photos, videos; **auditory learners** learn most effectively through listening/hearing information, for example listening in class or playing back lecture recordings, questioning and talking things through; **read/write learners** learn most effectively through text-based information, such as PowerPoint slides, lists and reports; and **kinesthetic learners** learn most effectively through undertaking activities that simulate reality, for example role play and demonstrations/videos of real-life examples and applications. Many learners adopt a combination of these learning styles and are known as **multimodal learners**. This clearly has an impact on the design of the lecture. By providing materials in a range of formats and including a variety of different learning activities in each lecture, you are meeting the diversity of learning styles that may exist in any group.

Enthusiastic, stimulating delivery, with a demonstrable passion for the subject matter, is key to motivating and inspiring your students. Student learning will be more effective if you are able to create a positive and relaxed atmosphere in your lectures. The lecture should contain relevant, research-informed content, supplemented with 'real-world' examples, illustrations and applications. Within the constraints of the subject matter, examples should also be multicultural and non-gender specific. Aim to be confident in your delivery, projecting your voice to the group and providing a steady pace. You will also need to give attention to the materials you present visually, such as slides and handouts, ensuring these are inclusive and accessible, complying with equality and disability legislation. They should have appropriate typeface, colours and backgrounds, but not be too cluttered or text-heavy, so that they can be easily read from all parts of the lecture theatre. You should ensure that any materials are provided in a variety of formats, preferably in advance of the lecture. This will be beneficial for all students, not just those with special educational needs and/or disabilities. Jisc TechDis (http://www.jisctechdis.ac.uk/techdis/home) provides advice and a range of resources for inclusive practice in learning and teaching and can provide guidance on how to produce accessible PowerPoint slides and other learning materials.

Check out the copyright for any images, brands, logos, etc. used in your materials and consider how you want students to use handouts in your lectures. Do you want students to have full copies of your lecture slides, or just 'gapped' or 'skeletal' handouts that only contain key information and which the students are required to annotate during the lecture? There is some evidence that notetaking enhances student achievement, with the use of skeletal handouts leading to higher student achievement scores for the same lecture than the use of full handouts (e.g. Annis, 1981; Russell et al., 1983). In a study by Titsworth (2001), students were found to retain information for longer when they took notes, but research by Hadwin et al. (1999) found listening, rather than notetaking, may result in higher student achievement for more challenging/complex lecture material. Either way, ensure you explain to the students how you expect them to use the handouts at the start of the lecture.

Good lectures are well structured, with clear **learning outcomes**, which specify what students are expected to learn and achieve from each session. There should be a 'beginning', a 'middle' and an 'end' to each lecture with appropriate **signposting** (Brown and Atkins, 1987; Moore et al., 2008) to indicate the structure and direction of the lecture. Material should be linked to topics covered previously and areas to be explored in future sessions. This requires careful planning to ensure that there is sufficient time available to address all learning outcomes, highlight key points and provide a clear 'ending' with conclusions and any recommended additional reading or follow-on activities.

At the start of the lecture, it is important to capture students' attention through a clear 'opening'. This can be achieved through a variety of means, including stating a topical and/or interesting/controversial fact relating to the subject of the lecture, posing a question/problem to the group, or answering a question/problem that you left with the group at the end of the previous session. Ensure that you are fully *au fait* with any technology you intend to use in the session and have a contingency plan in case the technology fails. It is always worth visiting the lecture room in advance of the lecture to check out the audio-visual facilities and get a feel for the room and how it is arranged.

Maintaining students' interest and attention through the lecture can be a challenge, particularly when attention levels are known to drop when listening passively over long periods of time (e.g. Lloyd, 1968). With this in mind, it is important to vary the pace, tone and nature of activity throughout the lecture to maintain your students' attention and keep them energised. You could, for example, introduce a multimedia clip, 'real-world example' or illustration, provide a short break, check understanding by asking the group some questions and/or taking their questions, set a problem/scenario to be discussed/solved by groups within the lecture, or simply give attention to sustaining a varied delivery style throughout the lecture. Humour and anecdotes can often be used to good effect when re-energising the group, but these are best avoided if they do not come naturally to you because they may fall flat with the group. It is also worth remembering that what works well with one group will not necessarily work well with another group – learners are all individuals.

In addition to retaining student attention, the introduction of active learning encourages higher-level thinking, such as analysis, application, problem-solving and evaluation in lectures, which is key to aiding student understanding and retention of information (e.g. Briggs, 2007). Technology can help with this. For example, 'clickers' (a type of **student response system** involving hand-held, wireless devices) can be used during lectures to encourage voting and/or check understanding through a series of multiple choice questions posed to the group. Dependent upon available technology, students vote/answer questions anonymously using either 'clickers' or their own mobile devices, such that they can see their peers' responses and determine whether their own answers are correct. This provides helpful feedback to students on their learning whilst also allowing the lecturer to gauge the degree of understanding amongst the group, and hence the effectiveness of their lecture. Over time, lecturers tend to develop a rapport with their student groups, making it easier to determine understanding from students' behaviour and reactions during the lecture.

A number of lecturers have abandoned the traditional lecture in favour of the **'flipped classroom'**. With lecture capture technology, the lecture is recorded and made available digitally to students (e.g. via websites or the institutional **Virtual Learning Environment** (VLE)). They are generally required to watch the online lecture prior to the timetabled session. The lecturer can then move away from real-time lecturing to using the timetabled session more creatively for discussion, application of content to real-life problems and exposition of material. The other advantage of the recorded lecture is that students can replay the whole lecture, or sections of the lecture, to aid their learning and understanding (e.g. Traphagan et al., 2010; von Konsky et al., 2009). This can be particularly valuable for revision purposes, for students for whom English is not their first language and for students with special educational needs and/or disabilities.

Interrogating practice

- What are you aiming to achieve in your lecture?
- How might this best be achieved?
- What 'new' approaches from the earlier information might you try?

GROUP WORK

What is the purpose of group work?

Group work can be a very effective way to motivate students, enhance their learning and develop their transferable or **employability** skills. It is built upon the **constructivism** model of learning (see Vygotsky, 1978; Bruner, 1983, 1986), where students construct their own knowledge and understanding through their experiences, building upon their existing knowledge. In the case of group work, constructivist learning is achieved through active learning (Bonwell and Eison, 1991), where students take responsibility for their own learning. By undertaking a variety of learning activities (e.g. problem-solving, experimentation, discussion, learning from others), students develop their higher-order thinking skills, such as analysis, synthesis and evaluation. Group members should be encouraged to reflect upon what they have learnt through the process and how their understanding has changed. This information could be logged in a reflective journal (either paper-based or online through a blog) and prepares students for future professional practice.

Most group work activities provide students with an element of choice in the topic/task and the activities to be undertaken. This provides a degree of motivation for students, by allowing them the opportunity to focus on an area of particular interest. In completing the task, students build upon the knowledge and skillset of the group. When group work is conducted well, students develop a range of valuable transferable/employability skills that include good communication and negotiation skills, critical thinking, analytical skills, effective teamworking, ability to project plan and meet deadlines, ability to manage conflict and a range of other important research and IT skills specific to the project undertaken.

While group work offers a number of benefits for student learning, it is a very different approach to lecturing. The tutor takes on more of a facilitator of learning role, prompting and encouraging independent learning and providing the necessary structure and support to enable successful completion of the task by the group. It is worth noting that while many students enjoy group work, there are others who find it challenging. This may be due to lack of experience of group work, a poor experience previously, cultural differences or specific learning difficulties. Before embarking on any group activities, thought should be given to what you are hoping to achieve with students and whether group work presents the best way to achieve desired outcomes.

Ensuring effective group work

For group work to be effective, it is important to outline the purpose and benefits of the activity, together with your intended learning outcomes. You should also explain how the work will be assessed. The next stage is to establish ground rules with the students to agree expectations of students and tutor, role and responsibilities of the tutor and group members, and the course of action to follow should any problems arise during the course of the group work. A good way to address this area is to ask students to think about factors that would cause the group task to fail and then get them to suggest ways to avoid or address each of these factors. Ideally, these ground rules should be negotiated, agreed and preferably documented with your students before commencing any group work. This should help to avoid any problems arising later on, and also ensure that there is a degree of ownership of the ground rules amongst the students themselves.

Whilst the establishment of group work and ground rules requires a significant investment of time from the tutor at the start of the activity, its benefits to the smooth and effective running of group work, and a better learning experience for students cannot be underestimated.

Selecting groups

For group work to be effective, it is important that there are good working relationships between members of the team. There are several ways to select teams, each presenting their own advantages and disadvantages.

Tutors can select student groups randomly (e.g. via student numbers/names out of a hat or via a computer programme which generates numbers randomly; or very simply in class by giving each student a number from 1–5 and then asking them to group with other students who have the same number as themselves). This random selection of student groups has gained popularity over recent years, given its relevance to real-life situations where you can't choose your work colleagues, but need to learn to work effectively with them as part of a team. In such situations, teams will consist of people who may not have worked together previously, and may not even know one another. In these situations, team members should be encouraged to spend some of their initial group work time getting to know one another and exploring the prior knowledge, skills and experience of the group members.

Alternatively, tutors may choose to select student groups based on their prior knowledge of the students to ensure each group has an equal mix of one or more of the following attributes: gender, race, nationality, ability, Belbin team roles (http://www.belbin.com/)/Myers Briggs Personality Types (Myers and Myers, 1995).

Another option is to allow students to self-select and choose their own groups. In such situations, students tend to select team members based on friendship/tutor groups. The advantage of building groups from existing friendship groups is that members already know one another really well and may additionally be aware of each other's strengths

Table 7.1 What problems might arise with group work and how do I address these?

Problem	Action
Non-attendance	Assess attendance and contribution
	Explain value of attendance
	Distribute additional materials in session
Quiet student	Ask questions by name
	Assign and rotate roles
	Use of rounds and buzz groups
	Ask why and try to support
Dominant student	Note or praise where appropriate and encourage others to contribute
	Ask questions by name
	Assign and rotate roles
	Use of rounds
Group messing about	Confront and refer to ground rules
	Break up group using 'cross-overs'
	Focus back on task
Freeloading	Refer to ground rules and agreed procedures for problems
	Grade contribution/process

and weaknesses. As such, the group can start work quickly, drawing upon individuals' strengths without the need to devote time to breaking the ice and getting to know one another. On the downside, however, friendship groups can present difficulties when one (or more) member of the team is not pulling their weight and/or completing tasks on time because individuals tend to be reluctant to expose problems involving friends.

Table 7.1 explores ways to address or prevent problems that may result from use of group work.

Group formation

Booth (1996) suggests five to eight members as the optimum size for small group teaching. Any more than this can result in some members 'freeloading', while smaller numbers can lead to divisions.

There can be some disagreement between group members before they establish an effective working relationship as a team. Tuckman (1965) termed the stages in group development as 'forming, storming, norming and performing'.

Assessing group work

With any assessment, it is important to consider what it is you want students to achieve on completion of your module/programme (the learning outcomes) and ensure that these are reliably tested by your assessment(s). Biggs (1996) and Biggs and Tang (2011) highlight the importance of ensuring that your curriculum is **constructively aligned**, i.e. does your learning and teaching strategy enable students to achieve the desired learning outcomes for the module/programme and are these learning outcomes reliably tested by the chosen assessment method? If the group work activity is designed to develop students' wider transferable/employability skills such as effective team-working, research skills, communication skills, etc. then these skills need to be assessed throughout the module/programme.

There are many different grading models available for group work: some assess end product only, while others assess both process and end product. The end product could be a report or presentation, a set of recommendations, the creation of a tool, resource or artefact or another entity. When assessing process, a mark could be awarded for individual contribution and/or individuals could be asked to reflect on their experiences of working in a team via individual reflective diaries (paper-based or online), or through individual/group blogs and/or portfolio(s) containing documentation associated with their group work, such as raw data, literature searches, logs, meeting notes and action sheets, etc.

The grading can be conducted entirely by tutors, or else students can be involved in the grading via a form of peer assessment. The benefits of peer assessment to student learning are well documented (e.g. Stefani, 1994; Falchikov, 1995). Students can be asked to contribute to the grading of the process, the end product or both components. It is important that all grading is undertaken against clear, well-publicised assessment criteria that align with the learning outcomes for the module/programme. Student marks may count for one or more elements of the assignment, a percentage of one or more elements of the assignment, or their marks may be weighted/scaled by the tutor. For example, individuals could be asked to assess their own contribution to the group work and the contribution of their peers. These marks may be taken as a percentage of the overall module/programme grade or they may be weighted/scaled by the tutor. Another option is for the tutor to award one overall grade for the end product where each individual group member has a scaled grade according to their level of contribution as determined by either their peers, or the tutor.

Some ideas for small group activities

In addition to group projects, there are opportunities to undertake some small-scale group activities during lectures and seminars to promote **active learning** and re-energise students. For example,

- Brainstorming: students generate and collate all ideas on a topic/problem without comment/intervention from the tutor or other students. Discussion and evaluation of all the ideas is the next stage. This can be a useful way to gather ideas on a topic/ project or to determine students' knowledge on a particular topic.

- **Buzz groups**: students discuss in pairs a topic/problem or series of questions posed by the tutor. This gives students confidence because they are able to rehearse their answers with another student before sharing more widely with the tutor and the group as a whole.
- Pyramiding/snowballing: students consider alone a topic/problem posed by the tutor, then discuss in pairs, then in fours, and so on. This provides a good forum for students to share ideas and perspectives, but may prove unpopular when students have to keep repeating points made at the start of the activity as new members join the group.
- Cross-overs: some members of the group are asked to 'cross-over' with members from another group. This can be useful where students are working on different aspects of a problem/topic and by crossing-over they can share findings between groups, leading to sharing of knowledge and group collaboration. The technique can also be useful when all groups are working on the same topic, but they are not performing well together and there is a need to split up some group members.
- Rounds: each student is asked to respond in turn to the question posed by the tutor. The question must clearly be one that can be answered in many different ways, such as examples, future learning plans, and reflections on learning. Given the time taken to collect responses from every student, rounds are best suited to smaller groups with no more than 15 or so members.
- Fishbowls: the group splits into an 'inner group', which conducts the work and is observed from the outside by an 'outer group'. The tutor can stop the inner group at any time to ask the outer group questions about what they have observed or to highlight key learning points.
- **Role play**: students play the part of someone else in an imaginary scenario (simulating a real-life situation or problem), using their knowledge or perception of that role to enact the part. This is a valuable way for students to understand attitudes and behaviours, in particular how it feels to be in the role and how others behave towards you when in that role. This technique is commonly used in medical, health, education and legal professions, but can be used to good effect in a variety of other disciplines.

HOW DOES ONLINE GROUP WORK DIFFER FROM FACE-TO-FACE GROUP WORK?

The principles for establishing effective group work outlined earlier in this chapter can also be applied to online group work. The key difference with online group work is that students only 'meet' online and hence there is a need for the tutor to ensure clear understanding of the task, learning outcomes, roles and responsibilities from the outset. Facilitation takes place online so mechanisms need to be established that allow effective **synchronous** and **asynchronous** communication between group members. This is particularly important when group members are working at different times, in different locations. Tutors also need to ensure that there are processes in place to monitor and assess each group's progress with the task and the contributions made by individual group members. As with face-to-face group work, there need to be clearly documented assessment criteria appropriate for the online task.

STUDENT SUPPORT

When designing and delivering any modules/programmes, it is important to consider the diversity of today's learners: students may be studying in their home country or internationally; may be full-time or part-time; school leavers or mature students; and may come into campus for formal teaching or study entirely online. This has important implications for our curricula and the support offered to students. The National Union of Students (NUS) has produced a Charter on Academic Support (available from http://www.worc.ac.uk/academictutor/documents/NUS_AcademicSupportCharter.pdf) and the UK Quality Code for Higher Education requires that all higher education institutions provide equal access for all to educational opportunities, irrespective of factors, which include age, nationality, gender, sexual orientation, race, ethnic origin, cultural/educational background, special educational needs and disability.

As a tutor, it is your responsibility to ensure that your module/programme is accessible and inclusive, i.e. you have taken into account the likely educational, cultural and social background and experience of your students, together with any potential special educational needs and/or disabilities amongst the group, irrespective of whether these have been disclosed by students. This is known as anticipatory needs and requires you to anticipate the likely needs of students and factor these into your course design, delivery and assessment. You should consider how your module/programme will be delivered and what materials and information are provided to students. When designing course materials, it is a good idea to provide learning materials in a variety of formats. **Jisc** provides guidance on making materials accessible (http://accessibilityessentials.jisctechdis.ac.uk/).

Assessment strategies should offer options such that there are alternative means of assessment that meet the same learning outcomes when students are unable to complete one particular type of assessment due to their special educational needs and/or disability. Are field trips/work placements essential for the module/programme, and if so, are sites accessible to all? How are special needs accommodated at external sites and venues? It is important to remember that one size does not fit all. Talk to students with disclosed special educational needs and/or disabilities to determine what they find most beneficial to aid their learning, and make use of the advice and guidance available from national groups and societies.

Disability legislation (http://www.legislation.gov.uk/ukpga/1995/50/part/IV/chapter/2) requires all higher education institutions to make reasonable adjustments for disabled people so as not to disadvantage them or set up unnecessary barriers for their study. This can relate to changes in the physical features of buildings, changes to policy and practice, or provision of support workers such as interpreters. The following factors should be considered when determining what constitutes reasonable adjustment: effectiveness of the proposed adjustment in avoiding the disadvantage that the student would face should this adjustment not be made; the practicality and cost of the proposed adjustment; and the institution's available resources.

Most tutors are required to act as personal tutors for their students, providing pastoral advice and guidance as appropriate. Whilst you are not expected to be an expert in all areas, you should be able to guide students to the professional service that best meets their needs. Within your institution, you should be familiar with the groups responsible for advising and guiding students in study skills, information and digital literacy, career development, finance, health and well-being. Similarly, you should be aware of the support available for international students.

Technology has enabled tutors to provide support to students outside formal teaching sessions through a variety of online resources. These include additional reading, tests and quizzes, glossaries of key words and phrases, study skills materials such as information searching and how to write an essay, and discussion boards and blogs to encourage discussion and debate outside the classroom. Support from peers and tutors can be particularly important for students during their transition to higher education (Thomas, 2012).

OVERVIEW

With any module, programme or session, it is important to consider what you want students to achieve at the end of their period of study and then choose the most appropriate learning and teaching methods to achieve this. Remember the diverse nature of learners in any group and provide a range of learning activities and resources to accommodate different needs and learning styles. Both lecturing and group work need to be clearly structured, well prepared and at an appropriate level for the module/programme in order to be effective. When students are motivated and inspired (there are a number of suggestions for how to achieve this in the chapter), their learning is generally enhanced. Lastly, try to promote active learning where possible because this leads to better student learning and retention of information.

REFERENCES AND FURTHER READING

Annis, LF (1981) 'Effect of preference for assigned lecture notes on student achievement', *Journal of Educational Research*, 74: 179–182.

Biggs, JB (1996) 'Enhancing teaching through constructive alignment', *Higher Education*, 32: 1–18.

Biggs, J and Tang, C (2011) *Teaching for Quality Learning at University. What the Student Does.* 4th edn. Maidenhead: Open University Press.

Billings-Gagliardi, S and Mazor, KM (2007) 'Student decisions about lecture attendance: do electronic course materials matter?', *Academic Medicine*, 82(10): 73–76.

Bligh, DA (1972) *What's the Use of Lectures?* Penguin Books.

Bonwell, C and Eison, J (1991) *Active Learning: Creating Excitement in the Classroom AEHE–ERIC Higher Education Report No. 1.* Washington, DC: Jossey-Bass.

Booth, A. (1996) *Assessing Group Work.* In: A Booth and P Hyland (eds). *History in Higher Education.* Oxford: Blackwell, 276–297.

Briggs, L (2007) *Can Classroom Capture Boost Retention Rates?* Available from: http://campustechnology.com/articles/2007/10/can-classroom-capture-boost-retention-rates.aspx (accessed 19 August 2013).

Brown, G and Atkins, M (1987) *Effective Teaching in Higher Education.* London and New York: Methuen.

Bruner, J (1983) *Child's Talk: Learning to Use Language.* New York, NY: Norton.

Bruner, J (1986) *Actual Minds, Possible Worlds.* Cambridge, MA: Harvard University Press.

Coffield, F, Moseley, D, Hall, E and Ecclestone, K (2004a) *Learning Styles and Pedagogy in Post-16 Learning: A Systematic and Critical Review.* London: Learning and Skills Research Centre. Available from: http://sxills.nl/lerenlerennu/bronnen/Learning%20styles%20by%20Coffield%20e.a..pdf (accessed 1 April 2014).

Coffield, F, Moseley, D, Hall, E and Ecclestone, K (2004b) *Should We Be Using Learning Styles? What Research Has to Say to Practice.* London: Learning and Skills Research Centre. Available from: http://www.itslifejimbutnotasweknowit.org.uk/files/LSRC_LearningStyles.pdf (accessed 1 April 2014).

Dolnicar, S (2005) 'Should we still lecture or just post examination questions on the web? The nature of the shift towards pragmatism in undergraduate lecture attendance', *Quality in Higher Education*, 11(2): 103–115.

Edwards, H, Smith, B and Webb, G (2001). Introduction. In: H Edwards, B Smith and G Webb (eds). *Lecturing: Case Studies, Experience and Practice.* London and Philadelphia: Kogan Page, 1–10.

Falchikov, N (1995) 'Peer feedback marking: developing peer assessment', *Innovations in Education and Teaching International*, 32(2): 175–187.

Fleming, ND and Mills, C (1992) 'Not another inventory, rather a catalyst for reflection', *To Improve the Academy*, 11: 137–155.

Gardner, H (1993) *Multiple Intelligences: The Theory in Practice.* New York, NY: Harper Collins.

Hadwin, AF, Kirby, JR and Woodhouse, RA (1999) 'Individual differences in notetaking, summarization, and learning from lectures', *The Alberta Journal of Educational Research*, XLV: 1–17.

Hall, E and Moseley, D (2005) 'Is there a role for learning styles in personalised education and training?', *International Journal of Lifelong Education*, 24(3): 243–255.

Honey, P and Mumford, A (2006) *The Learning Styles Questionnaire 80-item version.* Revised edn. Maidenhead: Peter Honey Publications.

Lloyd, DH (1968) 'A concept of improvement of learning response in the taught lesson', *Visual Education*, October: 23–25.

Moore, S, Armstrong, C and Pearson, J (2008) 'Lecture absenteeism among students in higher education: a valuable route to understanding student motivation', *Journal of Higher Education Policy & Management*, 30(1): 15–24.

Myers, IB and Myers, PB (1995) *Gifts Differing: Understanding Personality Type*. 2nd edn. London: Davies-Black Publishing-Nicholas Brealey Publishing.

Rogers, K (2009) 'A preliminary investigation & analysis of student learning style preferences in further & higher education', *Journal of Further & Higher Education*, 33(1): 13–21.

Russell, IJ, Caris, RN, Harris, GD and Hendricson, WD (1983) 'Effects of three types of lecture notes on medical student achievement', *The Journal of Medical Education*, 58: 627–636.

Stefani, LAJ (1994) 'Peer, self and tutor assessment: relative reliabilities', *Studies in Higher Education*, 19(1): 69–75.

Thomas, E. (2012) *Building Student Engagement and Belonging in Higher Education at a Time of Change: Final Report from the What Works? Student Retention & Success programme*. Available from: http://www.heacademy.ac.uk/assets/documents/retention/What_works_final_report.pdf (accessed 19 August 2013).

Titsworth, BS (2001) 'The effects of teacher immediacy, use of organisational lecture cues, and students' notetaking on cognitive learning', *Communication Education*, 50(4): 283–297.

Traphagan, T, Kucsera, JV and Kishi, K (2010) 'Impact of class lecture webcasting on attendance and learning', *Educational Technology Research and Development*, 58: 19–37.

Tuckman, B (1965) 'Developmental sequence in small groups', *Psychological Bulletin*, 63(6): 384–399.

Von Konsky, BR, Ivins, J and Gribble, SJ (2009) 'Lecture attendance and web based lecture technologies: a comparison of student perceptions and usage patterns', *Australasian Journal of Educational Technology*, 25(4): 581–595.

Vygotsky, LS (1978) *Mind in Society: The Development of Higher Psychological Processes*. Cambridge, MA: Harvard University Press.

8 Assessing assessment

New developments in assessment design, feedback practices and marking in higher education

Sue Bloxham

INTRODUCTION

The **assessment** that students undergo communicates to them what really matters in our courses; it strongly influences students' learning, including what they study, when they study, how much work they do and the approach they take to their learning. Consequently, if we want to improve students' learning, effort and achievement, assessment is a good place to start. This chapter provides an overview of key theories and issues in developing assessment as well as practical ideas for designing, managing and marking coursework and exams and engaging students with feedback on their assessment.

> ### Interrogating practice
>
> - What type of assessment do you use?
> - What is your rationale for their use?

PURPOSES OF ASSESSMENT

One of the challenging features of assessment is that, ideally, it fulfils several major functions within the educational process.

- Certification characterises how we traditionally view assessment. It involves assembling evidence of students' achievement through summative assignments, examinations and performances for purposes of selection and certification (gaining a degree or qualifying as a nurse, lawyer or engineer). This purpose constitutes Assessment *of* Learning.

- **Quality assurance** is a second key purpose of assessment. An institution's academic standards are demonstrated through students' assessed work and scrutiny of it forms a key accountability process. For example, external examiners, in their role in assuring standards, judge the quality of programmes largely through reviewing student assessment. This purpose also constitutes Assessment *of* Learning.
- Learning is a third purpose of assessment. It emphasises the formative and diagnostic function of engaging students in assessment, helping students learn through completing their assignments and gaining feedback. It provides information about student achievement to both teachers and learners, which enables the student to self-regulate their learning and the teacher to respond to the needs of the learner. This purpose constitutes Assessment *for* Learning.
- **Lifelong learning** sees student involvement in assessment as moments of learning in themselves. Its purpose is to develop students' ability to self-assess and self-regulate their learning as essential to being an effective independent learner beyond formal education (Boud 2000). This purpose constitutes Assessment *as* Learning and is an important subset of Assessment *for* Learning.

Each of these purposes is important if we wish to maximise the full potential of assessment. Sadly, much of higher education assessment emphasises 'certification' and 'quality assurance' at the expense of using it to support learning. This chapter aims to start your thinking about how the management of summative assessment and feedback methods can balance the different purposes of assessment, encouraging lecturers to fully integrate assessment into course design. In order to do this, it will discuss the validity of assessment and then explore aspects of 'learning oriented assessment', which encompasses both assessment *for* and *as* learning. The case studies will provide examples of the effective integration of the different purposes into individual module assessment strategies. The chapter concludes with a section on marking and academic judgement.

ASSESSMENT VALIDITY

In the higher education context, most assessment has a **summative** function; it is used to demonstrate the extent of a learner's success in meeting course requirements and contributes to the final mark given for the module or programme. Its role in 'certifying' student achievement means that the **validity** of summative assessments is extremely important. There are many descriptions and uses of the concept of validity but in this context we are focusing on 'intrinsic validity', that is assessment tasks are assessing the stated learning outcomes for the module. For example, it is questionable whether a diet of unseen examinations can validly assess the range of graduate and postgraduate knowledge and capabilities that students are now expected to acquire. Many programmes have diversified assessment tasks to capture learning beyond knowledge and understanding but, as Knight and Yorke (2003) argue, it is enormously difficult to reliably and validly warrant some areas of achievement, let alone attempt to grade them.

This principle of **valid** assessment design is clearly underpinned by the notion of **constructive alignment** in requiring lecturers to carefully check that assessment requirements are not only testing what they say they are testing, but are also directing students towards appropriate learning. Assessment tasks can vary hugely in what types of **learning outcome** they are capable of assessing, from simple recall of information (factual tests) through display of both professional knowledge and communication skills (**Objective Structured Clinical Examinations (OSCE)**) to demonstration of analysis and evaluation (reflective practice assignment). Well-designed assessment methods can also have the additional benefit of authenticity. For example, coursework can involve designing learning materials for others, presenting ideas, analysis of an industrial case study, evaluation of work-based learning, completion of small-scale research, and designing a web page. Such **authentic** tasks help to motivate students and contribute to their developing employability through encouraging **soft skills**, for example managing their workload, communicating well, learning independently, solving problems and working effectively with others. An enquiry-based team project may be much more successful at assessing this type of learning than an exam or essay. At heart, a fundamental condition of effective assessment is its validity in assessing the desired learning. For examples of many different assessment methods, beyond the scope of this chapter, see Bloxham and Boyd (2007) or Sambell et al. (2012).

LEARNING-ORIENTED ASSESSMENT (*FOR* AND *AS* LEARNING)

Whilst summative assessment has the potential to promote learning, its high stakes nature exerts pressure on students to behave strategically and focus on marks that may have a negative effect on their learning. For example, it may be easiest to memorise something quickly for a test, although the knowledge will soon be forgotten because there is little incentive to really try and understand the material. It is this backwash effect of poorly designed summative assessment that has prompted a new emphasis on interrogating the contribution of assessment methods to student learning, that is assessment *for* and *as* learning. Carless et al. (2006) characterise learning-oriented assessment as designing tasks that lead to learning – when students are involved in evaluating their own work and when feedback is forward-looking so that students can act upon it.

A review of significant studies of assessment indicates the following characteristics that promote learning-oriented assessment and employability:

- Assessment should have a **formative** function, providing **feedforward** for future learning that can be acted upon;
- Tasks should be challenging, demanding higher order learning and integration of learning from both the university and other contexts such as work-based settings;

- Learning and assessment should be integrated, assessment should not come at the end of learning but should be part of the learning process;
- Students are involved in self-assessment and reflection on their learning; they are involved in judging performance;
- Assessment should encourage **metacognition**, promoting thinking about the learning process not just the learning outcomes;
- Assessment expectations should be made visible to students as far as possible;
- Tasks should involve the active engagement of students developing the capacity to find things out for themselves and learn independently;
- Tasks should be authentic, worthwhile, relevant and offering students some level of control over their work;
- Tasks are fit for purpose and align with important learning outcomes; and
- Assessment should be used to evaluate teaching as well as student learning.

Similarly, Sambell et al. (2012) have a model that argues that assessment *for* learning:

- Is rich in formal feedback (e.g. tutor comment);
- Uses high stakes summative assessment rigorously but sparingly;
- Develops students' abilities to evaluate their own progress and direct their own learning;
- Offers extensive 'low stakes' confidence-building opportunities and practice;
- Emphasises authentic and complex assessment tasks; and
- Is rich in informal feedback (e.g. peer review of draft writing, collaborative project writing).

There is sufficient commonality in these catalogues of characteristics to provide the lecturer with key principles that can be used to review existing assessment methods. The next step is to find practical, sustainable and acceptable (to students, staff and regulations!) ideas for turning such principles into action. Sambell et al. (2012) offer much detailed assistance both generically and across a range of disciplines. In the room available here, the focus will be on the crucial themes of formative assessment, including feedback and involving students in assessment.

FEEDBACK

Feedback is arguably the most important aspect of the assessment process in raising achievement (Black et al. 2003, Gibbs and Simpson 2004–5) because of its formative potential. It helps students understand what they need to do to improve and provides them with the confidence that they can control their achievement. It is also important to remember the importance of peer and self-assessment in creating feedback opportunities for students. Every time a student has to examine another student's piece of work, they gain feedback through comparison with their own performance.

Research indicates that students value feedback (Weaver 2006), although they often fail to engage with it (Gibbs and Simpson 2004–5) and it is not always perceived as useful by students. University initiatives and quality assurance in the UK following successive years of poor student satisfaction ratings for feedback in the **National Student Survey** have undoubtedly prompted improvement in some of the worst problems such as minimal, incomprehensible or illegible coursework feedback, but dissatisfaction continues. This on-going dissatisfaction is often accompanied, from the lecturer's perspective, with a lack of engagement by students who seem disinterested in collecting marked assignments or reading and acting on the feedback. Studies suggest that lack of engagement and dissatisfaction with feedback are the result of how and when it is 'delivered':

- It is one-way communication whereas students seek a dialogue about their work in order to really understand how to improve;
- Students often find it difficult to act upon;
- It does not come at a time when students can easily use it;
- It looks back at the work they have done rather than forward to how they can improve; and
- Students recognise that tutors may value different features of course work and therefore one tutor's feedback is not always seen as useful guidance for future assignments.

How can we tackle these shortcomings?

Making written feedback more useful and timely

Recent studies have placed great importance on the notion of feedforward (Hounsell 2007), which focuses on what a student should pay attention to in future assessment tasks. For example, it may be more useful to students if feedback states three clear ways in which they can improve future assignments rather than providing copious detail on the assignment. General praise is not useful; whereas comments on something a student has done well and why it is good helps students build on that successful strategy in future assessments and may be more helpful than negative feedback (Hattie and Timperley 2007). Word-processing of feedback means that it is easy to read, comments can be returned to students online, which can save time, and it also allows the use of comment banks, which can create the core of effective feedback quickly and allow more time for individualised comment.

The language of feedback is an important consideration. Unfortunately, it is often difficult to explain complex academic ideas in short feedback comments that can be understood easily by novices to the discipline. You may have a good understanding of 'critical analysis', but it is remarkably difficult to explain simply in written feedback. This is why the opportunity for dialogue about feedback is so important to enable students to really understand what they are doing well and how they can improve. Sadly, it is often easier to give feedback on simple technical errors, such as referencing and grammar, but this can lead students to think such features are more important in gaining grades than they really are. Feedback language should match the mark; writing 'very good, 63 per cent' is confusing to students and doesn't help them understand how they can improve. It is just as important to provide constructive feedback to students who are doing well.

A useful way to provide prompt feedback is to note the general strengths and weaknesses that emerge in marking the work. This group feedback is then emailed to the students providing very prompt generalised feedback, which avoids the delay which can be caused by second marking and moderation. This feedback can also be used as guidance for future cohorts.

Integrating feedback into teaching and learning: formative assessment

A key characteristic of learning-oriented assessment is the integration of assessment into the learning process and formative assessment opportunities are at the heart of this. Tutors are often anxious that students will not engage with formative assessment because it doesn't 'count' and that providing formative assessment will increase their workload. Let us tackle the first challenge – getting students to engage with formative assessment. Interestingly, when students leave school or college they are used to the habit of completing regular low stake tasks, such as homework. They will have been set exercises, practice essays, questions from past papers or required to do early drafts of assignments for vocational qualifications. They recognise this as part of the preparation process for summative assessment and we can learn from this in terms of the necessary conditions needed to encourage students to continue completing formative tasks once they enter higher education. Formative assessment should therefore:

- Explicitly help students complete summative assessment tasks;
- Require the students to submit it in some way (bring to class, post online, hand it in) and action is taken if they fail to do this;
- Lead to students receiving useful feedback; and
- Not be contaminated by summative purposes. If tasks contribute to summative grades, then students will be reluctant to admit that they don't understand something or need more help. A fundamental purpose of formative assessment is to provide a safe context for students to expose problems with their study and obtain help.

There is a range of ways in which formative tasks can meet these conditions, for example online tests giving immediate feedback on topics that feature in the final examination; writing summative assignments and receiving peer feedback on the draft online or in class; completing 'sub' tasks for the summative assessment for in-class discussion and feedback (as in Case study 8.2); and in lecture multiple choice or true/false questions using personal response systems or a show of hands if the technology is not available. Peer, self- and automated marking, and in-class feedback are all ways in which this formative assessment can receive useful and fast feedback without increasing the marking load for staff. Case study 8.2 is an example of a tutor significantly reducing her marking load whilst increasing student engagement through regular formative assessment and peer discussion. It is worth noting that peer assessment in this formative context avoids concern about unfair marking, a common complaint even though it is not supported by the evidence (Falchikov 2005).

It is important to encourage students to recognise and use all sources of feedback, including one-to-one studio discussions, seeing or hearing about other students' work and comparing their own with it, feedback from work-based supervisors and mentors, and in-class informal feedback. Students are most likely to take note of feedback if they receive it at a point when they perceive that they can really use it. Lecturers can provide this, as mentioned earlier, by sharing feedback on the common mistakes or weaknesses evident in the last cohort. Alternative methods involve asking students to peer assess draft assignments or providing opportunities for students to practice assessment such as practical presentations and mock exams. Formative feedback can be provided informally or through model answers, which students can self-assess against, as in Case study 8.1. Alternative approaches involve giving students feedback at the draft stage when they are much more likely to read and act on it (this is what we typically do for PhD students) and encouraging drafting and redrafting work just as we do in writing for publication (O'Donovan et al. 2008). Tutors can then provide a short global comment and grade on the final item. Keep copies of your comments on the drafts to demonstrate to students, examiners and assessors that you have given feedback appropriately.

ASSESSMENT AS LEARNING AND SELF-REGULATION

Recent developments in the field of feedback are focusing on the importance of the student as self-assessor – someone who is able to provide their own feedback because they understand the standard they are aiming for and can judge and change their own performance in relation to that standard. This is self-regulation (Nicol and Macfarlane-Dick 2006). Systematic reviews of research (Black and Wiliam, 1998; Falchikov, 2005) indicate strong positive benefits to students being involved in their own assessment. The theoretical basis for this is Sadler's (1989) seminal exposition of three essential conditions for improvement (paraphrasing):

1   Students must know what the standard or goal is that they are trying to achieve;
2   They should know how their current achievement compares to those goals; and
3   They should have strategies to reduce the gap between the first two.

Unfortunately, such conditions are not easily met. In relation to the first condition, it is very difficult to make the tacit knowledge (things we know but find it difficult to express) involved in judging the quality of academic work explicit (O'Donovan et al., 2008). However, involving students in assessment provides an authentic opportunity for them to learn what 'quality' is in a given context and apply that judgement to their own work (Black et al., 2003). Peer assessment is particularly useful in this context. Research shows that it can help students understand the expected standards of their discipline more effectively than anything else (Black et al., 2003) as they review others' attempts at the same task. It is important that students understand this purpose of peer assessment with the main benefit gained through the experience of being a peer assessor rather than being peer assessed.

Group assignments also provide the opportunity for students to see how others think about and tackle academic tasks, and this can be another important source of feedback on expected standards, their own performance and what action they might take to achieve those standards. This is particularly the case if they are helped to recognise the learning opportunity of involvement in assessment and working with others.

Feedback studies have also emphasised the need for more dialogic approaches to allow the tacit assumptions of teachers to be made more visible (Sadler's first condition); students value dialogue, seeing it as crucial to their understanding of both assessment tasks and feedback and to identify the particular expectations of individual teachers (Bloxham and West, 2007). Student-to-student dialogue alone may be insufficient (Northedge, 2003), principally because it is not dialogue in the company of someone with 'expertise' – a key component of learning tacit knowledge. Therefore, dialogue should involve engagement with those who already have a grasp of the standards (teachers, peer advisers, postgraduates) and comprise opportunities to ask questions to make guidance, feedback and judgements clearer. Some possible ways to do this at the guidance stage include outlining expectations for an assignment in class or online where students have the opportunity to ask questions. Alternatively, Rust et al.'s (2003) intervention used a combination of students discussing exemplar assignments coupled with input from the teacher to explain the criteria used. In general, there is a growing emphasis on dialogue regarding exemplars as a useful form of guidance (Handley and Williams, 2011). In these approaches, the dialogue about real work is informed by an expert view.

In relation to feedback dialogue, it can be inbuilt in seminar sessions. A useful method suitable for small and medium-sized seminar groups is that work is returned to students and they are asked to read the feedback and bring it to the next seminar. During the seminar, students work in groups on a prepared task whilst the teacher meets each student for 3–5 minutes to check their understanding of feedback on the returned work and clarify or emphasise the main elements they need to pay attention to in further work. Alternatively, students can be asked to peer review each other's draft work in the context of the teacher's explanation of the requirements. The students are encouraged to give each other feedback and to ask questions that are generated by looking at the drafts. A further method is to pass copies of feedback to personal tutors and ask them to use existing personal tutorials to encourage students to identify the changes they need to make to improve their assessed work.

CASE STUDIES

Two case studies provide concrete examples of learning-oriented assessment embedded in actual modules. In both cases, they use formative assessment techniques but have successfully engaged the students by linking them to the summative assessment, providing incentives to complete the tasks, offering useful feedback and not contaminating the formative tasks with summative purposes. In relation to Sadler's conditions, Mark's example (Case study 8.1) creates an excellent opportunity for the students to develop an understanding of the required standards and their own performance in relation to them. Georgia's module (Case study 8.2) describes a useful method of thoroughly integrating the assessment with the teaching to increase student learning and engagement.

> ## Case study 8.1: 'Tell me how you did' – model answers with an honours class

This case study describes combining model answers with self-critique followed by teacher–student dialogue. It can cut down on marking time, encourage engagement by students with feedback and ensures that the formative elements of your assessment are not lost in the glare of a summative mark.

This assessment involves a class of about 30 honours students writing a 2,000 word critique of a published scientific paper. We discuss an example paper and critique in class to show the kinds of topics (relevant research design, appropriate sample size, correct use of statistics, logical arguments, etc.) I am looking for. Students then choose one of two papers and produce their critique, which should include positive as well as negative comments. As soon as the work is submitted, I release a model answer for each paper and then mark the assignments. I explain to the students at the start of the module that in order to receive a summative mark back, they need to email me a short appraisal of their own work, drawing on the model answer provided. This cannot influence the grade (the marking is done) but does require them to engage with the model answer and to reflect on their own attempt. I respond to their email emphasizing the points they correctly identify and adding any they miss. An additional feature is that the final assessment for this module includes an elective examination question that does the same thing – critiques a published paper – hence students know that this coursework feeds forward into another assessment.

Only 2 per cent of more than 150 students have failed to send a self-assessment email over the past five years, perhaps because I am careful to explain to students *why* I use this approach (drawing on the research about the 'blinding' effect of summative marks). I have never had a complaint about 'hiding' marks, and student self-critiques are often thorough and thoughtful, making lengthy feedback from me unnecessary.

(Mark Huxham, Napier University)

Case study 8.2: Improving the learning, reducing the marking

A Level 4 undergraduate module in teacher education, assessed through a 4,000 word 'portfolio', was redesigned to increase the involvement of students throughout the module and spread the student workload whilst reducing the marking. Students completed a Professional Development Activity (PDA) in their own time after each taught session in preparation for the following week. The PDAs were an extension or application of topics covered in the session. The following week, the PDAs were used in various ways, for example peer reviewing, collating or applying research, or sharing of work. For example, one week, students in groups of four peer reviewed a mini essay, commenting in turn on content, academic conventions and writing, and the use of description/ analysis. At the end, they wrote how they would improve their writing in the final assignment. They found this formative assessment very useful.

At the end of the module, they had to submit a final summative assignment of 1,500 words and include all eight PDAs as appendices. The PDAs were not marked as such, but had to be assimilated into the main assignment and referred to explicitly.

In evaluating this approach, a number of points emerged. The students tended to engage fully in completing the formative PDAs because they were always used in the following session. This created a real purpose for doing it. If they didn't do it, they were letting people down or squandering an opportunity for formative feedback.

In module evaluations, the students overwhelmingly commented very favourably about the module and its approach to assessment. They liked the spread of workload and the formative assessment feedback they received. The PDA follow-up activities brought them closer together as a group because they involved sharing personal perspectives, or because they had to work collaboratively to create a joint product. I felt they were more involved and engaged in their learning because they had made a greater investment into the sessions.

My marking load was reduced. I did look through the PDAs but did not use them to grade the assignment. I looked particularly to see if they had used the feedback from the peer-reviewed PDA described earlier. I commented explicitly when they had clearly improved their final piece of work in response to this, which many of them had. The follow-up activities could also be developed further to include greater higher order thinking skills. Overall, it was an approach that benefitted both me and the students greatly, and which I will continue to use in future modules.

(Georgia Prescott, University of Cumbria)

MARKING AND ACADEMIC JUDGEMENT

Marking is often considered one of the most tedious elements of a teaching role. However, following the earlier discussion, we can see that marking and the associated feedback generated can make an important contribution to student learning and satisfaction. In the UK, the **Quality Assurance Agency (QAA)** expects institutions to have transparent and fair mechanisms for marking and moderation, and you will find that your institution has quality assurance processes to check marking and moderation and to protect its academic standards. Nevertheless, university-level marking is notably less systematic than typical public and professional examinations, such as 'A' levels, and there is nothing like the infrastructure to support and scrutinise reliability between markers and subjects. With the exception of the Open University, the scale is small in comparison and rigorous processes of testing the marking reliability are largely absent because tutors generally set and mark their own papers checked by the limited safeguards of second marking, moderation and external examining. Consequently, in a period of high student fees and potential appeals and complaints about grades, it is not surprising if new lecturers feel anxious about marking and a lack of confidence in their judgements.

Delivering fairness, consistency and reliability in higher education marking is a significant challenge (Yorke, 2011). **Reliability** means that assessment tasks should be generating comparable marks across time, across markers and across methods. Whilst assessment criteria have been developed to improve marking reliability, there is growing evidence that academic judgement cannot easily be represented by a short set of explicit criteria however carefully formulated. The 'hidden' and inexpressible nature of the tacit knowledge used in tutors' judgement is compounded by the complex nature of work being assessed at higher education level, which allows for a wide range of satisfactory student responses. For example, students may respond to an essay question or design brief in very different, but equally effective, ways. In addition, the language of criteria always needs an element of interpretation. This means that most marking is a matter of 'judgement', not 'measurement' (Yorke, 2011).

Nevertheless, providing guidance on the essential requirements of an assignment assists new markers in making assessment decisions if they are supported by discussion (see later). In addition, they may help students focus their efforts in the right direction but only if they are helped to understand the criteria. Given the need for interpretation, it is wise to encourage students to see assessment criteria as broad guidelines, rather than the basis for systematic measurement of achievement. In particular, specifying too much detail in criteria encourages dependent, rather than independent learning, with students focusing on meeting individual criteria, rather than gaining a holistic overview of the purpose of the assignment.

Lecturers generally learn to mark and use appropriate standards through an informal process of marking alongside departmental colleagues (Shay, 2005). It is difficult to learn tacit knowledge in any other way. However, the differentiated and socially situated nature of this learning creates the potential for individual differences in marking judgement because standards are influenced by a host of factors, including lecturer's values, specialist knowledge, socialisation processes, relationships with students and their previous experience (Bloxham, 2012). Shay (2005: 664) suggests that 'differences between markers are not "error", but rather the inescapable outcome of the multiplicity of perspectives that assessors bring with them'. As a result, it is argued that lecturers construct their own Standards Frameworks (Ashworth et al., 2010). Such highly complex frameworks represent how various influences combine to create a unique lens through which each tutor reads and judges student performance. Standards Frameworks are dynamic, constructed and reconstructed through involvement in communities and practices including engagement with student work, moderation and examiners' feedback (Crisp, 2008). However, as a result, lecturers can focus on different aspects of student work, for example their first impressions or presentational features (Hartley et al., 2006) leading to different judgement about the quality of a student's work. It is also important to be aware that 'assessors' grading behaviour is tacitly influenced by norm referencing (Yorke, 2009) and that tutors draw on their knowledge of different students' work in order to make their judgement.

Consequently, tutors should not be unduly worried or surprised if their marks do not align closely with their colleagues. What is important are the processes undertaken to align marks with broader standards and to ensure that students get as fair and as accurate a mark as possible. Likewise, marking research (Sadler, 2009) indicates that we should not be surprised if we find ourselves making holistic judgements about the quality of student work, rather than judging assignments criterion by criterion. This holistic approach is common to professional decision-making in general. Post-hoc checking of a holistic judgement against a marking scheme is a method used by lecturers to check or confirm judgement (Bloxham et al., 2011) and to frame feedback against the stated criteria.

The following paragraphs outline some methods that can be used to develop and safeguard marking standards in this difficult context.

Pre-moderation and discussion

Consistency can be improved for new (and experienced) markers if they have an opportunity to discuss the criteria and establish common meanings, making use of marking schemes and real examples of student work. This is the best way to calibrate your personal standards against those of your colleagues. A useful way to do this is pre-moderation, which refers to assessors all pre-marking the same small sample of scripts and discussing the marks before marking the main batch. For example, Price (2005) reports an approach where staff all mark the same sample work and meet to agree the mark as an approach to improving consistency.

Maintaining your own consistency and standards in marking

It is important for each of us to be aware of the influences on our marking. For example, marks can be affected by varying the amount of time spent marking individual items. When good work is marked after poor work, it is easy to inflate the marks, and levels of tiredness can impact on decision-making. Tutors should also be alert to their own standards framework and academic prejudices, which may unfairly sway marking too far up or down, giving weighting to factors you particularly care about. Some lecturers will 'punish' poor grammar or inconsistent referencing particularly harshly and beyond the agreed criteria. Hartley et al. (2006) found that tutors gave significantly higher marks on average to essays typed in 12-point font rather than 10-point font!

Deciding what mark to award

A student's work will not typically fit one grade descriptor (e.g. 2.i.). One approach to take is a 'best fit' approach for individual criterion. This involves identifying which of the statements in the grade descriptor or marking scheme is nearest to the student's performance for any criterion. Once the best fit has been identified for each individual criterion, it will be easier to identify the overall band for the work by examining where the majority of criteria lie or by compensating strong performance in one area with weak performance elsewhere. It then remains to decide whether the work should be placed in the upper or lower level within that overall grade band.

Interrogating practice

As a result of reading this chapter have your ideas about assessment changed? If so, what changes are you considering making to your practice?

CONCLUSION

Assessment in higher education is a very significant area of endeavour and this chapter has only been able to touch on a number of key aspects. Readers are encouraged to make use of the suggestions for further reading in order to pursue the topics introduced here and to find other practical ideas and solutions. There are a number of key areas that are beyond the scope of this chapter, including the design of programme level assessment strategies, technology-enhanced assessment, equality and diversity in assessment practices, preparing students for assessment, plagiarism and many more. On the other hand, the chapter has provided a starting point for thinking about assessment, arguing that a good balance between the different purposes of assessment creates a strong foundation for upholding academic standards within a learning-oriented environment.

REFERENCES

Ashworth, M, Bloxham, S and Pearce, L (2010) 'Examining the tension between academic standards and inclusion for disabled students: the impact on marking of individual academics' frameworks for assessment', *Studies in Higher Education*, 35(2): 209–223.

Boud, D (2000) 'Sustainable Assessment: rethinking assessment for the learning society', *Studies in Continuing Education*, 22(2): 151–167.

Black, P. and Wiliam, D (1998) 'Assessment and classroom learning', *Assessment in Education*, 5 (1): 7–74.

Black, P, Harrison, C, Lee, C, Marshall, B and Wiliam, D (2003) *Assessment for Learning: Putting it into Practice*. 1st edn. Maidenhead: Open University Press.

Bloxham, S (2012) '"You can see the quality in front of your eyes": grounding academic standards between rationality and interpretation', *Quality in Higher Education*, 18(2): 185–204.

Bloxham, S and Boyd, P (2007) *Developing Effective Assessment in Higher Education: a Practical Guide*. Maidenhead: Open University Press.

Bloxham, S and West, A (2007) 'Learning to write in higher education: students' perceptions of an intervention in developing understanding of assessment criteria', *Teaching in Higher Education*, 12(1): 77–89.

Bloxham, S, Boyd, P and Orr, S (2011) 'Mark my words: the role of assessment criteria in UK higher education grading practices', *Studies in Higher Education*, 36(6): 655–670.

Carless, D, Joughin, G, Liu, N and Associates (2006) *How Assessment Supports Learning: Learning-oriented Assessment in Action*. Hong Kong: Hong Kong University Press.

Crisp, V (2008) 'Exploring the nature of examiner thinking during the process of examination marking', *Cambridge Journal of Education*, 38(2): 247–264.

Falchikov, N (2005) *Improving Assessment Through Student Involvement*. London: RoutledgeFalmer.

Gibbs, G and Simpson, C (2004–5) 'Conditions under which assessment supports student learning', *Learning and Teaching in Higher Education*, 1(1): 3–31.

Handley, K and Williams, L (2011) 'From copying to learning: using exemplars to engage students with assessment criteria and feedback', *Assessment & Evaluation in Higher Education*, 36(1): 95–108.

Hartley, J, Trueman, M, Betts, L and Brodie, L (2006) 'What Price Presentation? The effects of typographic variables on essay grades', *Assessment & Evaluation in Higher Education*, 31(5): 523–534.

Hattie, J and Timperley, H (2007) 'The Power of Feedback', *Review of Educational Research*, 77(1): 81–112.

Hounsell, D (2007) 'Towards more sustainable feedback to students', in D Boud and N Falchikov (eds.) *Rethinking Assessment in Higher Education*. London: Routledge, 101–113.

Knight, PT and Yorke, M (2003) *Assessment, Learning and Employability*. Maidenhead: Open University Press.

Nicol, D and Macfarlane-Dick, D (2006) 'Formative assessment and self-regulated learning: a model and seven principles of good feedback practice', *Studies in Higher Education*, 31(2): 199–218.

Northedge, A (2003) 'Enabling participation in academic discourse', *Teaching in Higher Education*, 8(1): 17–32.

O'Donovan, B, Price, M and Rust, C (2008) 'Developing student understanding of assessment standards: a nested hierarchy of approaches', *Teaching in Higher Education*, 13(2): 205–217.

Price, M (2005) 'Assessment standards: the role of communities of practice and the scholarship of assessment', *Assessment & Evaluation in Higher Education*, 30(3): 215–230.

Rust, C, O'Donovan, B and Price, M (2003) 'Improving students' learning by developing their understanding of assessment criteria and processes', *Assessment & Evaluation in Higher Education*, 28(2): 147–164.

Sadler, DR (1989) 'Formative assessment and the design of instructional systems', *Instructional Science*, 18(2): 119–144.

Sadler, DR (2009) 'Indeterminacy in the use of preset criteria for assessment and grading', *Assessment and Evaluation in Higher Education*, 34(2): 159–179.

Sambell, K, McDowell, L and Montgomery, C (2012) *Assessment for Learning in Higher Education*. London: Routledge.

Shay, S (2005) 'The assessment of complex tasks: a double reading', *Studies in Higher Education*, 30(6): 663–679.

Weaver, MR (2006) 'Do students value feedback? Student perceptions of tutors' written responses', *Assessment & Evaluation in Higher Education*, 31(3): 379–394.

Yorke, M (2009) 'Faulty signals? Inadequacies of grading systems and a possible response', in G Joughin (ed.) *Assessment, Learning and Judgement in Higher Education*. New York, NY: Springer.

Yorke, M (2011) 'Summative assessment: dealing with the 'measurement fallacy'', *Studies in Higher Education*, 36(3): 251–273.

FURTHER READING

There is a growing number of useful publications on assessment in higher education and the following selection is offered as a gateway to valuable material. Readers are also encouraged to follow up discipline specific assessment literature.

Bloxham, S and Boyd, P (2007) *Developing Effective Assessment in Higher Education: a Practical Guide*. Maidenhead: Open University Press.

Boud, D and Falchikov, N (2007) *Rethinking Assessment in Higher Education*. London: Routledge.

Merry, S, Price, M, Carless, D and Taras, M (2013) *Reconceptualising Feedback in Higher Education*. London: Routledge.

Price, M, Rust, C, O'Donovan, B, Handley, K and Bryant, R (2012) *Assessment Literacy, The Foundation for Improving Student Learning*. Oxford: OCSLD.

Quality Assurance Agency (QAA) (2012) *Understanding assessment: its role in safeguarding academic standards and quality in higher education*. 2nd edn. Gloucester: QAA. Available from: http://www.qaa.ac.uk (accessed 26 September 2013).

Sambell, K, McDowell, L and Montgomery, C (2012) *Assessment for Learning in Higher Education*. London: Routledge.

Feedback to and from students

Building an ethos of student and staff engagement in teaching and learning

Camille B. Kandiko Howson

INTRODUCTION

Feedback is essential to improving and enhancing teaching and learning. Building upon Chapter 8 about **assessment** and the importance of entering into dialogue with students about **feedback** on their assessed work, this chapter looks at the role of feedback to and from students about teaching, learning and the student experience. The aim of this chapter is to go beyond only using student **evaluations** and to show how engaging *with* students can enhance students' learning and provide feedback to staff on how teaching can be improved.

Recent changes in higher education, including shifts in funding across higher education, have led to a repositioning of students in higher education. A negative view of this is to see students as customers and student feedback as criticism and complaint. However, such changes can also be seen as an opportunity to engage with students in the processes and practices of teaching and learning. This is seen in current trends in the literature on feedback, which includes self-regulation, dialogue, social learning and active **student engagement** (Orsmond et al., 2013; Hattie and Timperley, 2007; Nicol and Macfarlane-Dick, 2006).

This chapter on feedback to and from students focuses on using feedback to build a culture of engagement and partnership. First, the notion of engaging students in teaching and learning is explored. This is used as the basis for three principles of feedback to and from students: first, that students have opportunities to feedback on their learning experience; second, that students' feedback is listened to and valued; and third, communicating on how student feedback has been acted upon. The dialogic role of feedback to and from students can help lecturers develop as teachers and students to develop as learners (Nicol, 2010; Yang and Carless, 2013). The notion of student engagement is developed and used to show how groups of staff and students can use feedback to create sustainable partnerships that enhance teaching and learning.

Why is student feedback important?

- Student feedback can provide insight for modifying, planning or redesigning a module or teaching session.
- When feedback is collected during the term, it provides the opportunity to address issues regarding student learning whilst the module is in progress.
- Students may appreciate that their experiences on a module matter, and they respond well when they feel that their feedback is valued.
- Student feedback and evaluations of teaching are important ways to measure teaching effectiveness and document development for a teaching portfolio and peer review processes.

FROM EVALUATION TO ENGAGEMENT

Gathering feedback from students is generally done as part of national and institutional **quality assurance** and enhancement efforts and for local academic development purposes. Student feedback has been most commonly done through end-of-module evaluations and satisfaction surveys sent at the end of a student's course. Whilst providing information for evaluation, these are passive forms of gathering feedback that focus on improvements for the next cohort of students, not current students, and position students as consumers of education. To move beyond 'customer satisfaction' approaches to evaluating the student experience, a more holistic, socially embedded conceptualisation of feedback is needed (Price et al., 2011). A sharing of values and approaches to learning and teaching between staff and students is key to engaging students in the learning process. The ethos of student voice work and a principle of student engagement is to bring students into a **learning community** as active agents of their learning experience. Engaging with feedback to and from students in a meaningful way goes beyond simply hearing students, to listening and responding to students, and may involve reconceptualising students' role.

Student voice work therefore is seen as involving some or all of the following **meta-cognitive** activities:

- Asking questions about student experiences;
- Seeing and understanding the student perspective;
- Reflecting on implications for practice;
- Hearing or listening to previously inaudible or ignored voices.

(Seale, 2010: 997–998)

ENGAGING STUDENTS IN TEACHING AND LEARNING

Including student perspectives of their experience has become a key higher education policy initiative (Browne, 2010). In institutions, this involves both gathering feedback from and providing feedback to students. This can be in terms of teaching, assessments and the wider student experience. In addition to dialogue about students' assessments, this also involves feedback on teaching from individual students and through collective representation systems.

Staff attitudes towards students and student feedback play a significant role in empowering students and in promoting a culture of student engagement rather than passive student evaluation. A key principle is that 'student engagement is a process rather than a product' (McFadden and Munns, 2002: 362), which is strongly influenced by relationships between staff and students. Student engagement can be enhanced through a culture where students feel that the teaching staff on their course are attentive to their perspectives, willing to listen to concerns about the course and use feedback they have received for continual improvement.

Case study 9.1: A student perspective

In an Arts and Humanities subject like Theology, students are constantly reminded that university is where they become **independent learners**. As essential as this is, it can occasionally cause lecturers to give minimal or brief feedback lacking detail, perhaps in hope that students will 'work it out for themselves'. It is invaluable to students when a lecturer finds the balance between encouraging them to self-critique and offering clear and helpful feedback on assignments.

One particular personal example of this can be seen in my dramatically improved results in my history modules. One particular lecturer feared that one-to-one feedback would be seen as showing special attention to students. As a result of this fear of 'spoon feeding', I did not receive any clear direction and struggled to improve. This lecturer's attitude made it impossible to communicate that I was struggling in the class.

I was eventually able to meet with a PhD history student who was helping in my class for a one-to-one tutorial to get some more detailed feedback on my work. She provided the opportunity for me to talk about how I was understanding the subject. She briefly but clearly gave me three very useful pointers for my work. The direction she gave me was not something I could independently discover and such guidance was invaluable. As a result of clear feedback and her willingness to meet with me, in my last three history papers I have dramatically improved my results.

(Katherine Jarman, Second-year Undergraduate Student, Theology, King's College London)

Interrogating practice

- Do you present students with an attitude that welcomes and encourages feedback?
- Could your approach be improved/enhanced?

OPPORTUNITIES FOR STUDENTS TO FEEDBACK

To engage students, the first stage is in creating opportunities for students to provide feedback. This can start with developing a culture showing students that staff do encourage feedback. This can happen at a variety of levels within an institution and includes professional services and administrative staff, those in student support roles and senior management. Much of this is beyond the control of an individual lecturer, but feedback at the module level has the most impact on students' learning experiences.

INFORMAL FEEDBACK

A basic form of feedback from individual students is informal verbal feedback, which may be during lectures and teaching sessions, following class sessions or through office hours. There can also be informal written feedback opportunities through letter drop-boxes, providing an email address to students or using **virtual learning environment** (VLE) communications. Structured informal feedback, such as having students respond verbally or in writing to the following types of questions, can also be collected during sessions:

- What was the main point of today's lecture?
- What is the one thing you have still have a question about?
- What was unclear about the lecture today?
- What do you like about the course? What is working well?
- What do you not like about the course and what changes would you suggest?
- What aspects of the module would you like to start, stop doing or continue?

Discussions can also be structured that allow a small number of students to discuss issues that require improvements and have a representative from each group submit a summary. Further options include writing up a brief questionnaire (around five to ten questions) that targets specific areas of interest, such as a new technique, a new textbook or a new lecture style, using a five-point scale.

An advantage of informal feedback is that the lecturer has control of the questions and they can be specified to the learning context. It also allows for changes to be made that affect the students being asked, as well as future students taking the module. Whilst informal options can be very productive for basic feedback, such as voice volume, lighting and presentation clarity, it can be challenging for more substantive issues and difficult to manage with large groups, and many students do not feel comfortable approaching lecturers directly with their comments.

MODULE AND COURSE EVALUATIONS

Module and **course evaluations** provide information on students' perceptions of their satisfaction, engagement, learning outcomes, instructors' behaviour and course activities. Such feedback helps guide changes in future iterations of the course and the instructor's teaching. It is now largely standard to collect module evaluations at the end of term. In some institutions and faculties, these are standardised forms whilst others allow for bespoke evaluations. Also, some institutions have policies for online evaluations and others for specified class time to allow students to fill them out. There are generally higher response rates for in-class evaluations.

Evaluation feedback is usually anonymous, but students may be sceptical about the degree of anonymity, so it is useful to explain the data collection and analysis procedures to students. This includes who sees the data and how it is presented, for example if the data are collated and if student comments are typed up before being presented to lecturers. Anonymous feedback opportunities can help gather wider student opinion and allow students the space to ask potentially 'dumb' questions without fear of judgement. However, this can provide students with a space to post brutally honest or offensive comments, so it may provide a learning opportunity about appropriate feedback.

It is good practice to explain to students what happens with the data from their feedback, including who reads it and where it goes. This builds in responsibility for the feedback, and it is useful to say who will respond (e.g. the lecturer, departmental staff, or a staff–student liaison committee), through what means (e.g. a class announcement, a committee report, or through student representatives) and in what timeframe. It can also be useful to explain to students why they are being asked to provide their feedback. You can encourage them by suggesting ways in which this feedback will be useful, with prompts such as:

- This is your opportunity to shape the development of modules;
- You can affect change that students after you will benefit from;
- As part of this cycle, you benefit from feedback because changes are made on the basis of feedback from students taking modules before you; and
- Your feedback will help improve the course and this in turn can add value to your degree.

Most institutions have a standardised course representative system. These may be elected or voluntary student positions and often last for one year. Developing a relationship with the student representative for a course can be another way to gain student feedback. This can lead to engaging in dialogue about issues that may have come to his or her attention about the course. Representatives can also be useful in collecting feedback on certain issues that may be of concern, such as the pacing of lectures or the assigned reading load, and helpful for disseminating responses to student comments.

In general, year-end course evaluations follow similar patterns to module evaluations, although they may be coordinated by a senior member of the course team or department, or be part of national standardised evaluation schemes.

INSTITUTIONAL SURVEYS AND DATA COLLECTION

Institutionally collected data provides another way to ascertain feedback from students. Such data can come from customised institutional evaluations, commonly done when there have been major curricular changes or new initiatives. Some institutions choose to use standardised international surveys, such as the iGrad Survey, the **International Student Barometer (ISB)** survey and student engagement surveys (e.g. **National Survey of Student Engagement, NSSE**), which usually provide the benefit of comparative data from other institutions and/or countries.

In the UK, there are also national student evaluations, which have included the **National Student Survey (NSS)** sent to final year undergraduate students, the **Postgraduate Taught Experience Survey (PTES)** and the **Postgraduate Research Experience Survey (PRES)**. Data from these surveys provides important information on how students experience their course and can be useful for course teaching teams. For individual lecturers, since the data is only available at the course level, it can be challenging to use it to evaluate specific teaching practices.

Some national surveys provide data that is made publically available, such as the NSS, which is used in government-sponsored information websites and media league tables of institutions. This means that data from such surveys can have a strong influence on departmental and institutional policies. It can be useful to review findings from national surveys with incoming students and discuss how such feedback is used and any changes that have been made in response. Some institutions use a hybrid approach to surveys to collect student feedback that can be compared with other institutions and address local initiatives at the same time.

Additional data, which is useful for enhancing teaching and learning, may also be collected by the institution, such as data on library usage, activity on Virtual Learning Environments (VLEs) and feedback from virtual comment boxes. Further sources of feedback from students may include course-related Facebook pages, Twitter and other external social media platforms. Care should be taken to engage in all social media activity with students in an ethical and professional fashion.

> ### Case study 9.2: An institutional approach to collecting feedback on student engagement at Oxford Brookes University

Oxford Brookes is committed to enhancing its student experience based on evidence, and consequently pays close attention to student responses to 'satisfaction' surveys such as the NSS and PTES. However, we are also interested in asking students to consider their own behaviours and the role that these play in their university experience. Accordingly, Brookes is keen to use a UK 'student engagement' survey. At Brookes, four core scales (course challenge, critical thinking, academic integration, collaborative learning) are augmented by further items that evaluate engagement opportunities and student behaviours in response to a range of institutional initiatives that come together to form an integrated enhancement strategy towards a valuable and distinctive 'Brookes' student experience. The Brookes Student Engagement Survey is an opportunity for students to give feedback on their experience and provides a rich set of data, some of which is particular to the teaching and learning experience at Brookes and some that can be compared across other institutions.

Aims and objectives

The case for another survey has to be a strong one in an era of survey fatigue and consequent decreasing response rates. Brookes' motivation for using such a survey is threefold. First, concern over the almost exclusive dominance of student satisfaction ratings as valid measures of the student experience and the quality of their education. Second, born from an understanding that surveys alter behaviours, encapsulated in the old adage 'what gets counted gets done', the desire to further consider, measure and thereby encourage the type of educational opportunities, practices and student behaviours from which students draw benefit. Finally, the need to measure the educational impact of a suite of evidence-based institutional initiatives that form a coherent programme to enhance the Brookes student experience. These include a proactive framework for academic advice and guidance; the implementation of five graduate attributes as core outcomes of a Brookes' education; and an assessment compact detailing good assessment and feedback practices and responsibilities.

Outcomes and impact

Results from the survey are not about rankings or publicity, but provide us with additional evidence to gauge the educational quality of our offering, the impact of our current enhancement initiatives, and to drive future improvements. Such information informs all lecturers, but particularly those new to Oxford Brookes. New lecturers face a steep learning curve when they first start to teach. There is a lot to know and sometimes it can be hard to focus on what really matters in student learning. The Brookes Engagement Survey provides evidence to underpin focused enhancement and guide new staff towards the educational practices that energise student learning and enhance student retention and success, including the particular curriculum characteristics that make up a distinctive 'Brookes experience'. For example, questions evaluating the opportunities for, and behaviours engendered by, particular assessment and feedback practices known to underpin student achievement, already embedded in Brookes' policy, can encourage further good practice, both guiding student behaviour and staff effort. The national comparative data can show how students in specific subjects engage with their learning compared to their peers in other institutions.

(Berry O'Donovan, Principal Lecturer for Student Experience, Academic Lead Business and Management, Oxford Brookes University)

Interrogating practice

• What data do you use to reflect on your teaching practice?
• What other sources could you consider?

MAKING SURE FEEDBACK IS LISTENED TO AND VALUED

Part of encouraging students to provide feedback is showing students that their feedback is listened to and valued. One way to help do this is to inform students about the audience for the feedback and how it can be used to assist them. For example, feedback can be used by:

• Lecturers to modify and improve the approach, pedagogy and content of the module for the future;
• Postgraduate students to apply for teaching posts and lectureships;
• Departments to evaluate staff for promotion, gather data for accreditation and make curricular changes to the course;
• Other students to guide them in their course and module choices; and
• Institutional committees to provide data for teaching awards.

For informal feedback, lecturers' attitudes towards students are the main way to let students know their feedback is listened to and valued. This includes acknowledging receipt of feedback, listening attentively, taking notes and thanking the student for their comments, whether they were positive or negative. For students, such an attitude is described by the 'approachability' of the lecturer.

As noted earlier, an explanation of the process, importance and use of feedback can show how it is valued. In class, this can include a discussion of how feedback is collected throughout the course and module, both formally and informally. Outside of class, this includes responding promptly to emails, being available to meet with students and having scheduled office hours. It is important to acknowledge that students are giving some of their time and effort to help and inform lecturers, staff and other students to enhance the student experience.

Interrogating practice

- In your department, what happens to data collected from student questionnaires?
- How are students involved?

HOW IS FEEDBACK ACTED UPON AND DISSEMINATED

The key to 'closing the feedback loop' is to make it clear to students how their feedback has been acted upon through a clear dissemination process. This can include engaging students in an ongoing dialogue about why feedback was sought, how it was collected and analysed, and what is being done as a result. Part of good feedback practice includes providing feedback to those students who were questioned, even if they have graduated or the module has finished. A key element in building a culture of good feedback practice is at the beginning of a new course or module announcing the changes that have been made based on previous feedback from students.

Mechanisms for responding back to students can include:

- Acknowledgement to individual student(s)
- Verbal report back to students
- Report back to class by a student representative
- Posting on course notice board
- Posting on a departmental website or module VLE
- Report to relevant committees with student representatives
- Report in a department or student newsletter
- General email to all involved

With students' feedback, some key issues identified by students can be acted upon straight away. Others may take time to implement, and so may result in actions for future years, but it is good practice to explain this process to students. Some issues may not be acted upon for particular reasons and, although it may be difficult, it is useful to explain this to students and also provide additional vehicles for students to comment. Ideally, the mechanism for feeding actions back to students is planned prior to the evaluation so that students can be informed about how and where they can access information about the response to their feedback. This is particularly important for module evaluations and large-scale surveys because it can help present them in a positive light and encourage a higher rate of participation. Educating students about the purpose, process and value of feedback is an important part of inducting students into a learning community.

Interrogating practice

- How do you share feedback you have received from students?
- Do you respond to students who have completed questionnaires?

STUDENT ENGAGEMENT

Working with students to develop an active and mutually beneficial feedback cycle can empower students to become more involved in their learning experience. Student involvement or engagement provides an instructive focus for working with students to enhance teaching, learning and the student experience. This may be a role some students are unfamiliar with because they need to have developed capabilities to be able to understand, process and engage with feedback (Sadler, 2010). For feedback to be effective, the content, focus and processes must be appropriate, but also the environment for engagement must be supported. The work of Lea and Street (1998) complements the notion of feedback as a social practice. The importance of the wider environment is part of reframing engagement as a process in which students have choices of action (Chinn and Brewer, 1993), and are not passive consumers of their education.

Focusing on the earlier discussion of feedback to and from students, there are three main aspects of student engagement that are important. The first is the amount of time and effort students put into academic pursuits and other activities that decades of research show are associated with high levels of learning and personal development (Chickering and Gamson, 1987; Pascarella and Terenzini, 2005). Chickering and Gamson (1987) outline a variety of educational practices that are associated with high levels of student engagement: student–staff contact, cooperation among students, active learning, prompt feedback, time on task and high expectations. The importance and resilience of these has been reiterated in recent literature (Gibbs, 2010, 2012).

The second key aspect of student engagement is how institutions allocate their resources and organise their curriculum, other learning opportunities and support services (Kuh, 2003). These areas measure how institutions provide the environments for students that lead to the experiences and outcomes that constitute student success, broadly defined as persistence, learning and degree attainment (Kuh, 2001). This definition of student engagement is based on developing each individual student's involvement in his or her own learning within the context of opportunities provided by the institution. Such activities that promote student engagement are grouped into broad indicators of effective educational practice:

- Academic Challenge – including Higher-Order Learning, Reflective and Integrative Learning, Quantitative Reasoning, and Learning Strategies;

- Learning with Peers – including Collaborative Learning and Discussions with Diverse Others;
- Experiences with Staff – including Student–Staff Interaction and Effective Teaching Practices;
- Campus Environment – including Quality of Interactions and Supportive Environment; and
- High-Impact Practices – incorporating undergraduate opportunities such as Study Abroad, Research with Staff, and Internships that have substantial positive effects on student learning.

(McCormick et al., 2013)

There are specific examples of these indicators in practice, and survey items that relate to them, such as how often have you asked a question in class or have you worked with staff on a research project, which are part of some national student engagement surveys (Coates, 2005; Hanbury, 2007; McCormick et al., 2013).

The third key aspect of student engagement is the participation of students in quality enhancement and quality assurance processes, resulting in the improvement of their educational experience (Quality Assurance Agency (QAA), 2012). This approach to student engagement draws heavily on decades of work in collaboration with students' unions and other representational bodies. Taken together, this tripartite model provides multiple ways for students and staff, individually and collectively, to work in partnership to enhance the student experience.

Interrogating practice

- How do you gauge the means by which students are engaging with the subject matter?

PARTNERSHIP

Engaging students as active agents in their learning is the basis of a partnership approach. This can be done through representational structures, teaching and learning enhancement initiatives and work with individual students. Baxter Magolda and King (2004) have developed the Learning Partnerships Model, which portrays 'learning as a complex process in which learners bring their own perspectives to bear on deciding what to believe and simultaneously share responsibility with others to construct knowledge' (2004: xviii). This individual student approach highlights how partnership can engage each student and not be limited to representational structures. Partnership can transform students' learning experience through giving them the opportunity to have a role in shaping their experience. When this is fully realised, it goes beyond providing passive feedback, or membership of committees, to creating real opportunities for enhancement of the student experience and for students' own personal and professional development.

Case study 9.3: Staff engaging with student engagement at the University of Bath

The University of Bath has a longstanding and successful tradition of engaging students in developing, innovating and inspiring teaching. Building on an ethos of strongly felt democratic principles, the University and Students' Union have over many years created a culture of engaging students at all levels as co-owners of the learning and teaching process and wider student experience. This success has been achieved by engaging its own staff effectively first and foremost.

New staff that join the University are introduced to our reciprocal engagement ethos from the start. For probationary lecturers participating in the institution's academic practice programme in the early years of their careers, this means that they encounter the University's approach to student engagement throughout, in workshops and assessment alike. The Students' Union Sabbatical Officers, with responsibility for education, contribute to this programme as part of induction, and highlight the importance of their role and that of the wider student community in informing institutional learning and teaching policy development. Staff delivering different aspects of the programme will explore the many ways in which they can involve students in developing teaching, revising curriculum and agreeing feedback mechanisms. Within the programme, lecturers and teaching fellows are asked to consider existing policies, for example on feedback, and review how this is implemented in their department, and what the student feedback on assessment and feedback practices is. In their essays, they are then invited to comment on how to bring student interests and policy in practice, closer together.

Colleagues joining the University in more senior roles with considerable prior experience of working in higher education are also introduced to our values regarding student engagement. During staff inductions, the University's values around student engagement are highlighted and all new professorial staff (recruited or promoted from within) meet with senior teaching leaders to discuss teaching values and priorities within their roles. Admittedly, this is made easier by being part of an institution that receives very high praise from its students on teaching quality and satisfaction with the student learning experience. It is clear that academic colleagues have an obvious interest in keeping it that way, and have been found consistently eager to embrace the University of Bath's ethos.

In other efforts to enhance teaching and the student learning experience, the University acknowledges and recognises the importance of ensuring its ethos is borne out in practice. When funding is made available for teaching development, project proposals must include students on the project team, who co-develop or inform the project and its outcomes. Furthermore, students can bid in their own right through the Students' Union, in which case they are expected to work with relevant staff on their projects. All centrally run development projects or within faculties are also set up with substantial student representation.

By working in these ways, the University believes it is best able to connect teaching efforts as closely as possible with learning interests, thereby creating the highest quality of learning and teaching.

(Gwen van der Velden, Director of Learning and
Teaching Enhancement, University of Bath)

There are many ways to provide enhanced partnership roles for students through work with lecturers, in addition to other opportunities that may be available through and beyond the institution. The level of participation and partnership with students varies, and may develop over time (*sensu* Arnstein, 1969). One is through developing students as **peer tutors**. This can be done with students in one module or with students who have completed a module working with current students taking it. Students can also be brought in as project team members, researchers and scholarly authors in disciplinary and pedagogical research projects (Bovill, 2013; Cook-Sather, 2010). Such activities require that staff adopt varying roles, including acting as learning **facilitators** or becoming co-producers, co-researchers or co-authors with students.

Partnering with students in the enhancement of teaching and learning is an increasing area of work and of particular interest to students when it is framed as helping them build **employability** and professional skills. Such partnership activities include working with students as pedagogical consultants, where they conduct teaching observations or provide comments on the design of assessments and internships focused on enhancing teaching and learning. Students can also be engaged as co-developers and co-designers of the curriculum and teaching and learning enhancements (Bovill et al., 2011). Partnership work can facilitate students' entry into the academic community (Lave and Wenger, 1991; Wenger, 1998). Such efforts can position students as change agents and active contributors to the learning experience and the institutional community.

The new relationships and positions adopted through partnership work make it important to consider the impact of power relations (Ramsden, 2003). Open dialogue throughout can help facilitate transitions and create further learning opportunities for students.

> ### Interrogating practice
>
> - Do you give students the opportunity to have a role in shaping their learning experience?
> - How could your approach be improved/enhanced?

CONCLUSIONS AND OVERVIEW

Student engagement begins before a student enrols, through the development of the environment for learning and lecturers' attitudes towards students. Engagement approaches to teaching and learning can move students beyond simply being present and passive to becoming involved and active learners. A vital part of this is informing and encouraging students that they have a shared responsibility with the institution for their own learning. It is important to share expectations of students, even though they may seem obvious. Entering dialogue with students is the first stage, and a brief summary of activities and approaches to promote student engagement include:

- Encouraging study groups within a class, which may instil a sense of belonging and shared identity;
- Reminding students to take advantage of academic and personal advising services for career and course planning;
- Incorporating local engagement with the community and bringing in global perspectives where possible;
- Bringing students on to research projects;
- Asking for and valuing student input;
- Seeking student comment on syllabi, reading lists and assessment tasks;
- Developing a relationship with student representatives; and
- Sharing feedback from students with relevant teaching and learning committees.

REFERENCES

Arnstein, SR (1969) 'A ladder of citizen participation', *Journal of the American Planning Association*, 35(4): 216–224.

Baxter Magolda, MB and King, PM (2004) *Learning Partnerships: Theory and Models of Practice to Educate for Self-Authorship.* Sterling, VA: Stylus.

Bovill, C (2013) 'An investigation of co-created curricula within higher education in the UK, Ireland and the USA', *Innovations in Education and Teaching International*, DOI:10.1080/147 03297.2013.770264.

Bovill, C, Cook-Sather, A and Felten, P (2011) 'Students as co-creators of teaching approaches, course design, and curricula: implications for academic developers', *International Journal for Academic Development*, 16(2): 133–145.

Browne, J (2010) Securing a Sustainable Future for Higher Education: An Independent Review of Higher Education Funding and Student Finance. London: Department for Business, Innovation and Skills.

Chickering, AW and Gamson, ZF (1987) 'Seven principles for good practice in undergraduate education', *American Association for Health Education Bulletin*, 39(7): 37.

Chinn, C and Brewer, W (1993) 'The role of anomalous data in knowledge acquisition: a theoretical framework and implications for science instruction', *Review of Educational Research*, 63(1): 1–49.

Coates, H (2005) 'The value of student engagement for higher education quality assurance', *Quality in Higher Education*, 11(1): 25–36.

Cook-Sather, A (2010) 'Students as learners and teachers: taking responsibility, transforming education, and redefining accountability', *Curriculum Inquiry*, 40(4): 555–575.

Gibbs, G (2010) *Dimensions of Quality*. York: Higher Education Academy.

Gibbs, G (2012) *Implications of 'Dimensions of Quality' in a Market Environment*. York: Higher Education Academy.

Hanbury, A (2007) *Comparative Review of British, American and Australian National Surveys of Undergraduate Students*. York: Higher Education Academy.

Hattie, J and Timperley, H (2007) 'The power of feedback', *Review of Educational Research*, 77(1): 81–112.

Kuh, GD (2001) 'Assessing what really matters to student learning: inside the National Survey of Student Engagement', *Change*, 33(3): 10–17, 66.

Kuh, GD (2003) 'What we're learning about student engagement from NSSE: benchmarks for effective educational practices', *Change*, 35(2): 24–32.

Lave, J and Wenger, E (1991) *Situated Learning: Legitimate Peripheral Participation*. Cambridge: Cambridge University Press.

Lea, MR and Street, BV (1998) 'Student writing in higher education: an academic literacies approach', *Studies in Higher Education*, 23(2): 157–172.

McCormick, AC, Gonyea, RM and Kinzie, J (2013) 'Refreshing engagement: NSSE at 13', *Change: The Magazine of Higher Learning*, 45(3): 6–15.

McFadden, M and Munns, G (2002) 'Student engagement and the social relations of pedagogy', *British Journal of Sociology of Education*, 23(3): 357–366.

Nicol, D (2010) 'From monologue to dialogue: Improving written feedback in mass higher education', *Assessment & Evaluation in Higher Education*, 35(5): 501–517.

Nicol, DJ and Macfarlane-Dick, D (2006) 'Formative assessment and self-regulated learning: a model and seven principles of good feedback practice', *Studies in Higher Education*, 31(2): 199–218.

Orsmond, P, Maw, SJ, Park, JR, Gomez, S and Crook, AC (2013) 'Moving feedback forward: theory to practice', *Assessment & Evaluation in Higher Education*, 38(2): 240–252.

Pascarella, ET and Terenzini, PT (2005) *How College Affects Students: A Third Decade of Research*. San Francisco, CA: Jossey-Bass.

Price, M, Handley, K and Millar, J (2011) 'Feedback – focussing attention on engagement', *Studies in Higher Education*, 36(8): 879–896.

Quality Assurance Agency (QAA) (2012) *UK Quality Code for Higher Education – Chapter B5: Student Engagement.* Available from http://www.qaa.ac.uk/Publications/Information AndGuidance/Pages/quality-code-B5.aspx (accessed 26 September 2013).

Ramsden, P (2003) *Learning to Teach in Higher Education.* London: Routledge Farmer.

Sadler, DR (2010) 'Beyond feedback: developing student capability in complex appraisal', *Assessment & Evaluation in Higher Education,* 35(5): 535–550.

Seale, J (2010) 'Doing student voice work in higher education: an exploration of the value of participatory methods', *British Educational Research Journal,* 36(6): 995–1015.

Wenger, E (1998) *Communities of Practice: Learning, Meaning and Identity.* Cambridge: Cambridge University Press.

Yang, M and Carless, D (2013) 'The feedback triangle and the enhancement of dialogic feedback processes', *Teaching in Higher Education,* 18(3): 285–297.

FURTHER READING

Cook-Sather, A, Bovill, C and Felten, P (2014) *Engaging Students as Partners in Teaching & Learning: A Guide for Faculty.* San Francisco, CA: Jossey-Bass.

Dunne, E and Owen, D (eds) (2013) *The Student Engagement Handbook, Practice in Higher Education.* Bingley: Emerald.

Little, S (ed) (2011) *Staff–Student Partnerships in Higher Education.* London: Continuum.

10 | Effective online teaching and learning

Sam Brenton

INTRODUCTION

This chapter offers a practical route into thinking about how to teach online. It argues that the principles of effective online teaching are not so different from those of other modes, and that the medium itself offers opportunities to build on these principles to increase student engagement in beneficial ways.

In the five years since the previous edition of this Handbook, online learning has matured and is now a normal rather than exceptional part of most students' experience of higher education, as is evidenced by some of the case studies and examples of online and digital learning throughout this book. Though application remains patchy, all institutions now use software to enable students to learn online, whether through the basic provision of materials, or by online assessments, feedback, communications, activities and routine course management.

More students than ever are also learning entirely online: in the US, 6.7 million students took at least one course online in the fall 2011 term (Sloan-C, 2012) and 261,990 people were registered as distance learning students with UK institutions in 2011/12 (Higher Education Statistics Agency, 2013). The **Massive Open Online Course (MOOC)** phenomenon of the last couple of years has proved that there is a huge untapped appetite for access to online learning. Whether or not the end-logic of these developments spells the creative destruction (e.g. Christensen and Eyring, 2011) or transformation (e.g. Barber et al., 2013) of higher education as we know it, is a question for elsewhere, but it is clear that online learning is here to stay.

The web itself, and the learning technologies it supports, has now developed to a point where some of the distinctions between campus-taught 'face-to-face' provision and online teaching and learning have blurred and are slowly collapsing. The online medium now supports a range of human interactions, which can be as rich as – or at times richer than – face-to-face communications, and with thoughtful design and application, we can create the conditions for engaging educational experiences in a way that simply was not possible even a few years ago, whether we are teaching fully online or weaving online tools and techniques into the learning design of largely campus-based programmes.

It is therefore now vital for academic practitioners to have an understanding, not just of how to use the tools at our disposal, but also of how to use them to teach effectively.

LEARNING DESIGN

We don't jettison all the things we know help to make learning successful when we start teaching online. Indeed, it is useful to resist the temptation to rush in with particular tools and start podcasting or screencasting or building online assessments, and think first about *how* we are going to teach and by the same token *how* we are going to ask students to learn.

This is a *learning design* approach, where we think first about the purpose of our teaching (what we want students to learn, achieve or demonstrate) and then design strategies and approaches to realise those outcomes. If we follow this approach for online teaching and learning, we can ensure that the substance and detail of a course or module or other unit of teaching will be geared tightly towards student learning and engagement, and we can avoid some of the pitfalls of technology for its own sake, or arbitrary or misapplied uses of tools (for example, the empty discussion forums or hour-long lecture videos of too many attempts at online delivery).

The following list reflects a kind of current consensus about sound educational practice in learning design. Wherever such a list appears, there is debate about whether it is applicable for all subjects and all teaching situations, and it starts to look less like a consensus and more like a position. This chapter does not argue the merits of each, but provides this summary list to show that, where a course may apply these principles in its face-to-face incarnation, they can be retained with positive effect in the design of an equivalent online course.

Principles of effective learning design (for online and face to face teaching)

- Clear aims and learning outcomes, which are then aligned to the materials, activities and assessment (see Figure 10.1).
- Opportunities for students to apply their learning as they study, thus building knowledge through experience.
- Assessment that is paced through the course so that students can learn from their assessments, as well as their learning being measured through them.
- An inclusive approach to learning where there is a variety of ways for students to engage with the topic, giving flexibility for students who have different educational needs, dispositions and tendencies in the way they learn.
- Opportunities for deeper engagement with each topic, further self-directed learning, critical analysis and reflection.
- Clear signposting so that students know what they are studying, why and the context of their learning at each point within the wider context of a programme.

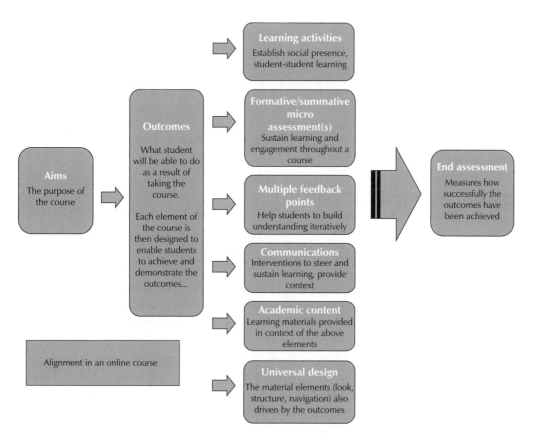

Figure 10.1 Alignment in an online course

- Multiple points of prompt feedback, which allow the students to build their understanding iteratively. This might be feedback from the lecturer, but may also include self-evaluation or peer feedback.
- The chance to learn collaboratively, as well as directly from the lecturer and materials, so that understanding is built up as a cohort or learning community.
- A coherent approach to the assurance and enhancement of quality, so that the teaching and learning is reviewed and refined as it progresses, for example through the use of evaluation.
- Opportunities for students to participate in the direction of a course, to create and apply their own strategies for learning and to realise their own personal goals.

If we keep these principles in mind when we are thinking about how to teach online, we can start to define a sequenced structure where the building blocks of teaching and learning – the materials, learning activities, feedback points, formative and summative assessments, and so forth – all complement each other and combine to help students realise the course's learning outcomes.

Interrogating practice

Try sketching out a learning design. Start with the learning outcomes, then break the course or module into topics and fill in the detail under these headings: learning activities, content, feedback points, assessment(s).

FROM DESIGN TO PRACTICE

There is a good deal of theory about online learning, although one can also say, as this chapter argues, that 'there are no models of e-learning *per se*, only e-enhancements of models of learning' (Mayes and de Freitas, 2004). How we design for our students' online learning, and what philosophical traditions we are acting within or making anew when we do so, is a fascinating and complex question which we don't have the space to give further consideration in this chapter. The interested reader is directed to excellent books that include overviews of learning models as applied to e-learning and useful checklists for the practitioner (e.g. Beetham and Sharpe, 2007) and online studies about mapping theory to practice in e-learning design (e.g. Fowler and Mayes, 2004).

Whether you are an avid constructivist or an ardent behaviourist, or not by nature a theoretician of learning, you may find that in practice your educational choices about how you teach a campus-based course are constrained. The teaching schedule, high student numbers, the practicalities of workload, and even the nature of the estate in which you are teaching often limit the choices you can make about how a course can be taught and assessed.

Online, you have much more freedom to design a course with the educational strategies that you think will work best. You can build in rich student–student interaction, experiential learning, peer feedback, small group learning, short writing tasks that build towards an essay, multiple modes of assessment … the choice is liberated by freedom from the constraints of time, distance and physical space.

Having looked at those elements of learning design that online courses share with face-to-face teaching, we can turn to areas of practice where the online medium can enrich the learning opportunities afforded to students. The following summaries provide an outline of how some of these elements can help you as an online teacher in the areas of assessment, academic content, learning activities, feedback and the role of the teacher.

ASSESSMENT

If **assessment** drives, as well as simply measures, student learning and is 'the most powerful lever teachers have to influence the way students respond to courses and behave as learners' (Gibbs, 1999: 41), so it follows that by carefully integrating assessed elements into the learning design of an online course we can maintain engagement and help learners to shape their learning as they go.

For this reason, effective assessment in online programmes tends to move away from end-point examinations and towards a modular or continuous assessment model, deploying an appropriate selection of **formative** and **summative** assessment types, always aligned tightly with the learning outcomes, which provide multiple touch points for students to gauge and refine their progress.

Anxiety about security and validity in assessment is sometimes seen as one of the main barriers to bringing programmes online, though this need not be the case. The topic may be approached from a learning design perspective by starting with three fundamental questions:

1   Does the assessment measure the students' success in meeting the learning outcomes?
2   Does the course prepare students for the assessment and equip them with the skills needed to undertake it?
3   Does the assessment act as a learning tool in itself, providing useful and timely feedback and sustaining student engagement?

These questions can help us think about how to design assessments that are woven into the fabric of a module or unit of teaching. Online, we therefore have available to us a variety of possible assessment techniques, which may work well within an online programme. These include:

- Written coursework assignments or essays;
- Shorter, frequent written assignments;
- Online tests or quizzes with automated feedback (formative or summative);
- Assessed contributions to online discussions (as part of guided activities);
- Group exercises;
- Digital artefacts (for example, an assessed blog or video presentation);
- Interactions with or within simulated environments (such as a virtual lab);
- Peer assessment within collaborative online spaces;
- e-Portfolios where students reflect on their learning or assemble a collection of artefacts for presentation and review (can be especially useful in professional or work-based learning where students need to demonstrate the practical application of their learning in professional contexts);
- Oral assessments by web conference;
- Open book assessments (between coursework and examinations);
- Examinations under invigilated conditions or their online equivalents (using locked-down browsers, webcam identification, or third-party proctoring services).

Finally, quality or security is not assured by deploying a plethora of assessment methods. There is a danger of over-assessment online, precisely because the medium lends itself so well to various opportunities for assessing student learning. A high quality online programme will use assessment judiciously and at appropriate points to measure and stimulate student learning.

LEARNING MATERIALS/ACADEMIC CONTENT

Only a decade or so ago, content was still commonly regarded as the cornerstone of most online distance learning courses. The correspondence course model still influenced their design, using the web as a publishing vehicle for detailed materials for students to work through at their own pace.

Accordingly, various estimates were made of the high cost of developing online learning. A 1998 Open University estimate reported that 120 hours of development time might be needed to create just one hour's worth of learning (Bingham and Drew, 1998). These kinds of ratios persist in the popular consciousness, though in reality online distance learning courses do not any longer need to develop large amounts of bespoke expensive multimedia learning content for students to work through. The multimedia CD-ROM approach to learning (with its information-transfer model and high cost of development) is outdated and need not be emulated by an online programme today.

The web has since evolved into a collaborative design space and means for global human communication and interaction, rather than simply a mass networked publishing system. This means that there is now space for a greater range of human interaction, and the content-led information–transmission model needn't be the template for online teaching and learning today.

As we have shown, an effective course stems from the learning design, and content is one supporting element in this. It is sometimes possible to create a series of rich learning opportunities from a relatively small seed of designed content.

Today, online teachers can produce web-based learning materials relatively quickly, and indeed it is increasingly common to re-use and share educational materials, or use third-party materials from educational publishers. As access to high quality educational content becomes widespread, our students can also seek out content from beyond the walls of their particular course, and sometimes our role may be to steer them through this journey, helping them to navigate, source and evaluate information, rather than being original content-producers ourselves.

Recordings of teaching events, or any other digital learning objects, can be re-used, and of course can be shared across programmes and even institutions. The Open Educational Resources (OER) movement has grown over the last few years (e.g. UKOER Programme, 2009–13, see Higher Education Academy, n.d.), and, while **reusable learning objects** and their repositories have not perhaps becomes as widespread a currency as some have predicted, it is nevertheless the case that there is a wealth of online content available for you to use as teachers within your course, and indeed for your students to discover, share, critique and use to complement their studies.

Interrogating practice

Try searching for open educational resources for your discipline. You could start at http://www.jorum.ac.uk also try http://www.oercommons.org

Search the web for other resources, for example to see if the Higher Education Academy and JISC UKOER programme ran any projects with outputs relevant to you.

All this is to reassure practitioners that we don't need to become individual publishing houses when we move online. Where you do need to create content, such as short narrated presentations or videos, these things can now often be done cheaply and quickly on computers or even on the phone you carry in your pocket. Students want to know that you are an active, guiding presence in an online course, and often a quick intervention (by say, audio feedback, or a media recording of yourself summarising a learning activity) will be as or more valued than an expensively produced video broadcast. Beyond multimedia, readings, images, links to e-journal articles and so forth all have their place in an online course, so long as they are in service of the learning outcomes and integrated into the course's learning design so that students can engage with content purposefully.

SOCIAL LEARNING ACTIVITIES

Learning activities are structured exercises that advance a course's learning outcomes by asking students to learn together in a guided, collaborative way. They are an essential component of online courses today, where we need to do more than merely provide academic content and then measure how well students have learned from it. They also help to build **social presence** (e.g. Kear 2010), which creates a sense of an active learning community and encourages students to engage with each other.

Online, it is easy to dream up all sorts of ideas for learning activities, and there is always a danger that you end up creating activities for the sake of it.

Here are some guiding questions to bear in mind before designing an activity, which can help to focus your learning design:

1   People (WHO?)
    Who is the exercise for? Is it appropriate for your students? Is it inclusive to all students?
2   Shared purpose (WHY?)
    What is the aim of the exercise? Which of the course's learning outcomes does it help to advance? Does it help students to learn at the required levels?

3   Locating framework/social conditions (WHERE?)
     Where in the course does the exercise occur? Have students been prepared for
     working together in this way? Is it sequenced with other content, feedback points,
     assessed elements and activities in a way that advances the course and develops
     understanding of the topic?
4   Method (HOW?)
     How will this exercise help students to learn? Make sure you are not asking stu-
     dents to do things for the sake of it, and that the method is developed at each step
     to allow for deepening engagement.
5   Activity (WHAT?)
     You are now well placed to design the detail of the exercise. Remember to produce
     it so it is addressed directly to your students, and think about whether the detail is
     clear to them as they approach it.

By asking yourself these questions at the outset, you can design social learning activities that are more likely to unlock and harness the potential pedagogic energy of the
social web.

There are many good sources of examples of online activities (e.g. Salmon, 2002) and
some of the case studies in this book also provide practical examples of ways to embed
online elements into teaching.

The following case study shows some ways in which you can increase choice, social
presence and **instructor presence** by using simple online tools.

> ## Case study 10.1: Application of knowledge and choice in formative evaluation

It has been my experience, working in education for many years, that learners
perform at their best level when they are given assignments that allow them
to immediately apply the knowledge they acquire. Students have indicated to
me that they enjoy performing tasks when they are given a choice of topics and
technology tools to complete the assignment. This desire for choice is not different in the face-to-face classroom.

Example: While teaching future educators at an institution in Las Vegas, Nevada,
I required my students to engage with various technology tools in order to create their assignments. I took this route so that these future educators had the
opportunity to become more digitally literate. Some of the tools I advocated that
my students use for content creation included blogs and video.

My expectation was that my students should blog regularly. They were asked to
be bold, be courageous and take a stand in their writing. Students were to find

relevant news articles related to their future teaching practice or content area and write a brief synopsis of the article. Students would then stake out positions on their article of choice and defend or promote them based on cited evidence. The inclusion of recent articles made the work more current and relevant to the students and allowed them to be viewed as thought leaders as they interviewed for positions in the local school district.

A number of the traditional face-to-face course assignments were written tasks. As I transitioned the course to be delivered in a blended format (meeting face-to-face only three times in a term), it was necessary for these assignments to be submitted electronically. The assignments themselves were formative evaluation tools that allowed for students to practice application of concepts and theory.

One example of this was the students' identification of their own teaching philosophy. This assignment was typically a two-page written paper, but when considering modifications for a blended modality, the assignment was modified to allow students to either submit a blog post or a video.

Example: In my current role, I work with faculty to assist them in the development of high quality online programs. With this in mind, my colleagues and I have developed a series of professional development MOOCs. One such course is focused on helping faculty improve instructor and social presence in online courses.

The participants in this MOOC created introduction videos for their own online courses. The objective of the video was to introduce themselves to their students, and welcome the students to the course. Each participant also created their own action plan for incorporating social presence into their future teaching. The top three actions that faculty wish to incorporate into their own courses are the use of audio and video feedback on assignments, using peer reviews to increase collaboration and critical thinking, and having students start blogging about their learning.

(Whitney Kilgore, Senior Vice President for Learning Technologies,
Academic Partnerships)

FEEDBACK

Offline, **feedback** is usually either given live in group settings, by written responses to assessed work or in one-to-one tutorials.

Online, you have the option to replicate these approaches (e.g. by moderated discussions or virtual classroom seminars, by graded work received and replied to online, or by web conference) or one can use the medium itself in web-native ways. (e.g. by sophisticated annotation of work, where you insert audio or graphical feedback into submissions, by modelling-back approaches in simulations, by immediate automated feedback to formative assessments, by building in peer-feedback points to online learning activities or by giving students access to learning analytics data about their performance).

THE ACADEMIC ROLE

There is more fluidity to the academic role online. In an online learning course, you might see the traditional academic role broken down in interesting ways. The lecturer-as-oracle might be retained, but you may also see that role supplemented by online moderators or tutors who can work with students in more personalised ways to guide their learning. The lecturer may also become more of a facilitator, directing students to online sources, helping them to evaluate, critique and share them. With the constraints of live physical events lifted, one can bring in 'guests' more readily from far flung locations (e.g. for pod-casts on a particular topic or virtual seminars), or you can use extant materials on the web (a terrific lecture from another institution posted on iTunes U, for example, or a clip on YouTube which illustrates a point). One can choose the extent to which you wish to bend the academic role depending on your levels of comfort, the number of students on the course and the nature of what you are teaching, but you have the option of using the lead academic to give high quality (perhaps research-led) pedagogic input, and employing different strategies for providing learning opportunities alongside that.

EXEMPLAR: A UNIT OF ONLINE TEACHING

What follows is a hypothetical and generic exemplar of a unit of online teaching, which weaves together the elements discussed to create a simple, sequenced structure, as shown in Table 10.1. There are many other ways of doing such a thing, but it is provided to show how each element supports others, and can in combination provide a cohesive and varied experience for students.

Interrogating practice

Find out what educational support and development is available in your institution.

There is likely to be a learning technologies or online learning support team somewhere who can provide pedagogic and practical guidance, as well as a range of institutionally supported learning technologies.

Table 10.1 Sequencing a unit of online line teaching

	What	Features
1	Publish a short video presentation to introduce the topic. Explicitly link it to the learning outcomes and assessment criteria.	Instructor presence Alignment
2	Provide links to further background materials (e-journals, your own content, or third-party found resources).	Information transfer Open Educational Resources
3	Release a learning activity around the content (for example, asking students in groups to critique the content by asking and answering questions about it between themselves, perhaps supported by moderators).	Social learning Social presence Peer feedback
4	Summarise the learning across the groups by recording a short audio summary. Publish any further information that may clarify particular ideas that students may find difficult.	Provides context for the social learning Instructor presence Feedback point
5	Release a short online formative assessment to allow students to gauge their understanding and get quick feedback.	Feedback point
6	Conclusion: revisit learning outcomes; invite students to reflect (e.g. in e-portfolio) on their learning, make notes-to-self on how well they feel they have engaged with the topic. Signposting to conclude the unit of learning, pointing forward to the next topic and relating this topic to the assessment criteria.	Reflective learning

CONCLUSIONS AND OVERVIEW

Rather than dwelling on the functionality of different tools and media, this chapter has sought to offer a way to approach online teaching and learning from a learning design perspective. If you do this, starting from the learning outcomes and then working through what learning activities, content, feedback points and assessments are appropriate, then ideas for using different tools – a discussion board, a web conference, short videos or student blogs or what have you – will follow naturally from the educational strategies you pursue. This approach also means that you are less likely to become bogged down in – or dazzled by – the latest technologies for their own sake.

Online learning tools and fashions date quickly. Back around the turn of the century, large projects were in progress to revolutionise education through electronic media. Grand claims were made, and much money spent, for example on the ambitious and ill-fated UK e-University project (House of Commons Education and Skills Committee, 2005). There was also something of a gold rush to repurpose learning materials and launch large-scale, content-led, broadly self-study distance learning programmes, only a handful of which still exist in an ever more crowded market.

Today, the rise of MOOCs has generated still greater cycles of hype and enthusiasm. They may indeed prove to be higher education's 'Napster moment' (Bean, 2013), or they may be the latest innovation that suffers from 'apocalyptic predictions that ignore the history of earlier educational technology fads' (Daniel, 2012).

MOOCs aside, the focus for taught online credit-bearing programmes is returning to what makes good teaching, and thus encourages successful learning, whatever tools and media are being used. In an era of widespread, free access to high quality materials, a successful course – distance or blended – has to be about much more than high quality electronic content. Rather, it will be distinguished by the quality of the learning design and the richness of the learning opportunities it offers: how students work alone and with each other to make pertinent, visible contributions; how the teacher stimulates collaborative learning and chooses appropriate uses of technologies for key activities; how assessed elements keep the students learning and engaged in discourse; and how well the teaching team (whether module conveners, lecturers, online moderators or teaching assistants) can use the media and tools available to instruct, guide, interest and inspire their students.

Far from being automated or purely self-directed learning, it is clear that where effective online learning takes place today, it does so with the guidance and presence of a thoughtful practitioner making judicious learning design choices about how they teach and how their students will engage with the various elements that comprise an online course in order to construct knowledge and understanding successfully.

REFERENCES

Barber, M, Donnelly, K and Rizvi, S (2013) *An Avalanche is Coming: Higher Education and the Revolution Ahead*. London: IPPR. Available from: http://www.ippr.org/publication/55/10432/an-avalanche-is-coming-higher-education-and-the-revolution-ahead (accessed 23 December 2013).

Bean, M (2013) *MOOCs, Napster and the Tyranny of Conventional Wisdom: Where's the Next Giant Leap for Higher Education?* Speech at Queen Mary, University of London. Available from: http://ess.q-review.qmul.ac.uk:8080/ess/echo/presentation/151cc759-8613-4ff3-9581-09d61e303693 (accessed 23 December 2013).

Beetham, H and Sharpe, R (eds) (2007) *Rethinking Pedagogy for a Digital Age: Designing and Delivering E-learning*. Oxford: Routledge.

Bingham, R and Drew, S (1998) *Costing and Resources: Open, Flexible and Distance Learning Pack 3*. Learning and Teaching Institute, Sheffield Hallam University, 5.

Christensen, C and Eyring, H (2011) *The Innovative University: Changing the DNA of Higher Education from the Inside Out*. Chichester: John Wiley & Sons.

Daniel, J (2012) *Making Sense of MOOCs: Musings in a Maze of Myth, Paradox and Possibility*. Available from: http://www.academicpartnerships.com/sites/default/files/Making%20Sense%20of%20MOOCs.pdf (accessed 2 January 2014).

Fowler, C and Mayes, T (2004) *Stage 2: Mapping Theory to Practice and Practice to Tool Functionality Based on the Practitioners' Perspective*. Available from: http://www.jisc.

ac.uk/uploaded_documents/Stage%202%20Mapping%20(Version%201).pdf (accessed 23 December 2013).

Gibbs, G (1999) 'Using Assessment Strategically to Change the Way Students Learn', in S Brown and A Glasner (eds), *Assessment Matters in Higher Education*. Buckingham: Society for Research into Higher Education and Open University Press, 41–53.

Higher Education Academy (HEA) (n.d.) *Open Education Resources (OER)*. Available from: http://www.heacademy.ac.uk/oer (accessed 2 January 2014).

Higher Education Statistics Agency (2013) *Student and Qualifiers Data for 2011–12*. Available from: http://www.hesa.ac.uk/index.php/content/view/1897/239/ (accessed 2 January 2014).

House of Commons Education and Skills Committee (2005) *UK e-University. Third Report of Session 2005–05*. London: The Stationery Office. Available from: http://www.publications.parliament.uk/pa/cm200405/cmselect/cmeduski/205/205.pdf (accessed 23 December 2013).

Kear, K (2010) *Social Presence in Online Learning Communities*. Proceedings of the 7th International Conference on Networked Learning 2010. Available from: http://www.lancaster.ac.uk/fss/organisations/netlc/past/nlc2010/abstracts/PDFs/Kear.pdf (accessed 2 January 2014).

Mayes, T and de Freitas, S (2004) *Review of E-learning Theories, Frameworks and Models*. Available from: http://www.jisc.ac.uk/uploaded_documents/Stage%202%20Learning%20Models%20(Version%201).pdf (accessed 23 December 2013).

Salmon, G (2002) *E-Tivities: The Key to Active Online Learning*. London: Routledge.

Sloan-C (2012) *Changing Course: Ten Years of Tracking Online Education in the United States*. Available from: http://sloanconsortium.org/publications/survey/changing_course_2012 (accessed 2 January 2014).

FURTHER RESOURCES ONLINE

Links to various resources and practical guides about online teaching and learning: Higher Education Academy (HEA). http://www.heacademy.ac.uk/resources/detail/cll/Online_resources (accessed 2 January 2014).

A host of resources about the use of digital technologies for teaching and learning: JISC. http://www.jisc.ac.uk/ (accessed 2 January 2014).

A repository of free open educational resources: JORUM. http://www.jorum.ac.uk (accessed 2 January 2014).

The advisory service for UK Higher Education on technologies for inclusion: TECHDIS. http://www.jisctechdis.ac.uk (accessed 2 January 2014).

11 Challenging students

Enabling inclusive learning

Veronica Bamber and Anna Jones

INTRODUCTION

Our chapter is entitled 'Challenging students: enabling inclusive learning' because we consider the idea of challenge from three perspectives: first, the diversity of the student population and how we might deal with the challenges this brings; second, how we as teachers can challenge students to be active and to engage with their learning; and, finally, how we can enable students to challenge us, themselves and the world beyond university, and to be thoughtful, independent, critical thinkers.

With a move to mass higher education, the demographics of the student population has changed. There are now many more students, larger classes and a much greater range of students attending university. This diversity brings with it great opportunities, both for teachers and students, and also challenges. In a very diverse classroom, a teacher can no longer assume that something will work or be understood and accepted. Students bring with them a wide range of assumptions, expectations, formative previous experiences and patterns of learning. This chapter considers how engagement can help students succeed in a diverse higher education setting and how teachers can help to facilitate that engagement. We do not set out to consider specific approaches for each particular group of students because we argue that good teaching (facilitating good learning) puts both the student and the intellectual experience at the centre, and is good teaching for all students.

DEALING WITH THE CHALLENGES OF DIVERSITY

In the contemporary university, diversity encompasses language, background, ethnicity, class and financial background, age, sexuality, religion, disability, gender, previous educational experience, part-time/full-time, and so on. With this comes a range of abilities, aspirations, motivations and behaviours. It also brings with it a range of expectations about the process and purpose of a university education. The combined factors of an increasing number of non-traditional students accessing higher education and an increase in fee-paying international students has changed the student population. There are now many students in each classroom who are the first in their family to attend higher education, many for whom English is not their first language and many who were not schooled in the same country in which they are attending university. For these reasons, those of us responsible for teaching in higher education cannot make assumptions about the previous experiences and expectations of our students.

Diversity in context

Hussey and Smith (2010) argue that the most appropriate response to diversity is a flexible approach that enables transition from dependent to autonomous learning. They suggest that it is only through designing programmes that encourage the type of learning considered to be desirable, through clear expectations, course planning and assessment, that we can adequately teach for a diverse student population.

The 3P (Presage, Process, Product) model (Biggs 1993) is one way of understanding student learning that can be helpful. The 3P model is useful because it takes account of what the student brings to the classroom (their prior knowledge, ability, ways of learning and so on); this is part of Presage. The educational setting (the course structure, curriculum, teaching and assessment) is part of Process. The importance of what students bring to the classroom is not new, and a great deal of research has already been done into, inter alia, the influence of socio-economic context, expectations of success (Duffy and Jonassen, 1992), ways of thinking (Gardner, 1993), emotional intelligence (Goleman, 1995) and teaching in higher education (Prosser and Trigwell, 1999; Ramsden, 2002; Ballard and Clanchy, 1997). But what is important is that it is a dynamic system. The student and the teaching environment interact together and with the task (the process) to create a product (the learning outcome). It is not a one-way system because there is interaction and negotiation between the presage elements. Thus, if a student has a particular set of expectations, motivations and ways of learning, and these react with a particular set of teaching and assessment practices, the final product or learning outcome may be a superficial or strategic understanding of the subject matter in question. What is important is not that teachers cater minutely to each individual student in each moment but rather that the teacher is aware that the learning environment (the teaching element of Process) is the part they (to some extent) can control or shape through planning their teaching. For example, staff can have conversations with students regarding expectations. They can articulate their own expectations to their students, explaining what is required in their learning and how this can be achieved. They can also listen to student expectations, and this conversation may uncover disparities between the student and teacher views, which can be negotiated.

One criticism levelled at some of the literature on diversity in higher education is that it can be cast in terms of deficit, hinging around the view that students are lacking in ability or motivation. Rather than viewing students as deficient, we see difference as valuable and learning as a transition or a 'becoming' (Barnett, 2007).

Student diversity: international students

As an example of student diversity, we can consider international students, although it is very important to recognise that they are a far from homogeneous group and vary in their exposure to Western education, English language ability, previous educational experiences and cultural beliefs and practices. Jones (2005) has pointed out that there is a tendency to define some cultures, for example Chinese, in terms of deviation from Western norms and to view them as less independent as learners (Carson, 1992; Dunbar, 1988; Samuelowicz, 1987). However, as Jones suggests, while there may be some differences, the ways in which teaching and assessment tasks are set up, explained and **scaffolded** is more significant than cultural differences.

One important consideration when teaching international students is the clarity of explanations. This means providing a clear outline of what is required, providing models of successful practice, and aligning objectives with teaching and assessment. The Higher Education Academy (2013) outlines the international student 'life cycle' of pre-arrival, induction, the classroom, outside the classroom and employability and transition out. They point to some clear areas in which international students will need particular support, such as **critical thinking**, academic writing, avoiding plagiarism, reading and note taking, and **independent learning**. What is important to note here is that making expectations about such things transparent and explicit is helpful for *all* students.

Interrogating practice

Consider an instance where international students in your class appeared to be disengaged – perhaps not participating. What was your reaction? Why? How did you address the situation?

CHALLENGING STUDENTS TO ENGAGE WITH THEIR LEARNING

What is student engagement?

A great deal has been written about **student engagement** in the light of data from the **National Survey of Student Engagement** (NSSE) in the US, and its Australian equivalent, AUSSE, which defines engagement as 'Students' involvement with activities and conditions likely to generate high-quality learning' (AUSSE, 2010: 3).

Despite reservations about student surveys (e.g. Kahu, 2013), the thinking and research derived from them can help us address the challenge of student diversity, and to tackle a range of issues which will be familiar to many of us, such as level of academic challenge, encouraging active learning, enriching educational experiences and developing a supportive learning environment. For Kuh et al. (2007), helping students to engage fully with learning and to persist to graduation requires a combination of:

1   The time and energy students invest in educationally purposeful activities; and
2   The efforts institutions put into ensuring effective educational practices (both inside the classroom and beyond).

Cuseo (2007) advocates 'intrusive intervention' (i.e. intentional, proactive provision of support brought *to* the student), and a strong emphasis on partnership and a culture of collaboration, whether with students or between institutional services – very much in line with the current thrust towards partnership working. So engagement involves the student, the teacher, the institution and the learning context. It is a 'meta-construct' that brings together various threads of research on student success (Kahu, 2013: 758) – reminiscent of the 3Ps concept. In Table 11.1, 'Aspects of Engagement', we have summarised the key factors that a number of writers link with engagement. Given this complex mix, it is not surprising that there are many interpretations of student engagement; nonetheless, there are common strands and widespread interest in the potential educational gains. In England, the Higher Education Funding Council, with the National Union of Students and others, has even set up a specific unit 'to involve students more fully as partners in their own higher education' (HEFCE, 2013).

The common strands around student engagement are:

*   Institutional characteristics
*   Student characteristics
*   Setting high expectations
*   Identity, belonging and social interaction
*   Students managing their learning
*   Feedback and assessment, and
*   Teaching.

These different strands don't operate in isolation; it is the interplay between them that matters (Kahu, 2013). Bryson et al. (2009) say engagement is both process and outcome: institutions do the former ('engaging students') and students do the latter ('students engaging'). We have combined Bryson et al.'s two perspectives with the strands in Figure 11.1.

In Figure 11.1, we outline the continuum of student and institutional efforts to improve engagement, from clear institutional responsibilities at one end and, importantly, student responsibilities at the other, and joint engagement in the middle. The relationships between the different factors are complex, but certain factors stand out as being particularly important, such as relationships with staff and peers, and feeling part of a learning community. The purpose of the scale is to illustrate joint ownership of, but different responsibilities for, aspects of engagement: it is not all down to the teacher, or to the student, or to the institution.

Table 11.1 Aspects of engagement

Type of factor	Chickering and Gamson (1987)	Kuh et al. (2007)	Pascarella et al. (2004)	Krause (2005)	Gazeley and Aynsley (2012)	Cuseo (2003)	Coates (2010) / AUSSE (2010)
Institutional characteristics		Institutions' structural characteristics (e.g. mission, size, supportive campus environment)			Access to additional support to meet specific needs		Supportive learning environment
Student characteristics	Respect for diverse students and diverse ways of knowing	Student background (e.g. demographics) and pre-university experiences		Monitoring and responding to subgroup differences	Academic preparedness, and a good fit between the young person's prior expectations and the institutional context	Student's cognitive, social and emotional needs: the whole person	
Setting high expectations	High expectations	Student perceptions of the learning environment, including level of academic challenge	High expectations	Creating a stimulating intellectual environment, with high academic standards and explicit expectations. Acknowledging the complexity of engaging with learning.		Sense of purpose	Academic challenge

Table 11.1 (Continued)

Type of factor	Chickering and Gamson (1987)	Kuh et al. (2007)	Pascarella et al. (2004)	Krause (2005)	Gazeley and Aynsley (2012)	Cuseo (2003)	Coates (2010) / AUSSE (2010)
Identity, belonging and social interaction	Cooperation among students, and student-staff contact	Interactions with staff and peers	Student–staff contact, cooperation among students and influential interactions with other students	Fostering social connections, including in online learning	Development of a robust learner identity. Social integration	Personal validation. Active involvement and social integration.	Student and staff interactions
Students managing their learning	Active learning and time on task	The quality of effort students put into purposeful educational activities	Active learning and time on task	Providing targeted self-management strategies and acknowledging the challenges		Self-awareness, self-efficacy and reflective thinking	Active learning
Feedback and assessment	Prompt feedback to students		Prompt feedback	Using assessment and feedback to shape the student experience			
Teaching			Quality of teaching				Enriching educational experiences
Other							Work-integrated learning

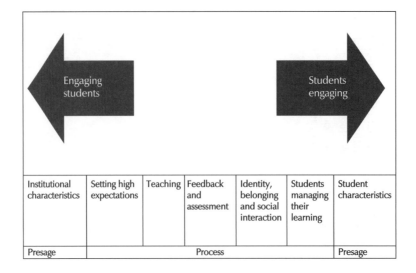

Figure 11.1 Engaging students

What the scale does not show is the cumulative effect: engagement breeds engagement (Kahu, 2013: 767). The other missing element is the wider **socio-cultural** influences that affect every student differently, but this chapter will focus on what we, as academics, can do to enable inclusive learning, rather than considering, for example, the impact of high tuition fees. In terms of the 3Ps, Figure 11.1 gives us an interesting sandwich: what the institution and the student each bring to the engagement scenario is Presage, and the activities that both contribute are Process. Responsibility for engagement is shared (Trowler and Trowler, 2010) and 'student engagement is a function of the interaction of student and institutional characteristics' (Hu and Kuh, 2002: 571). Some aspects of this are difficult to change (such as student background), but students can be helped to understand what is required, and taught how to meet those high expectations. The combination leads, hopefully, to the Product of successful student retention and graduation. For the teacher, this means being clear about aims, objectives and expectations and communicating this to students in ways they will understand, such as actually talking to them rather than putting an oblique statement in the course handbook.

We will not attempt to cover all these aspects of engagement in this chapter, and you will find that several aspects are discussed in other chapters. Two presage factors that we will briefly address are institutional and student characteristics.

INSTITUTIONAL CHARACTERISTICS

Institutional characteristics (including institutional size and mission; institutional/disciplinary cultures; and expectations of curriculum and assessment) are presage factors that are difficult to change in the short term. For example, Pascarella et al. (2004) found that students attending liberal arts colleges reported significantly higher levels of good practice than students in research or regional institutions. And some institutions seem to add more value than others, in terms of converting engagement into better student results (Carini et al., 2006). This might be attributable to a combination of factors, which, according to Pascarella et al. (2004: 70–71) include:

- First year socialisation processes;
- Smaller institutional size (with 'a more manageable social–psychological environment');
- Academic sub-environments, which include learning communities, and non-classroom interactions with staff; and
- Cultures that value teaching.

The National Survey of Student Engagement (2012) in the US and Canada found deep engagement with learning was more likely when six institutional characteristics were in place:

1 A 'living' mission and a 'lived' educational philosophy;
2 An unshakeable focus on student learning;
3 Clearly marked pathways to student success;
4 Environments adapted for educational enrichment;
5 An improvement-oriented campus culture; and
6 Shared responsibility for educational quality and student success. (2012: 14).

Interrogating practice

What is the learning culture at your institution? Are there things that you can reasonably do to create a positive learning environment?

This may mean that staff in some institutions have to work harder to counteract factors that make student engagement especially challenging. There is no one right solution for all contexts, although the principles and practices of engagement do offer some helpful ideas.

Student characteristics, and challenging students

The intentional learner

The Association of American Colleges and Universities (2002: xi) describes the 'intentional learner' as someone who, amongst other qualities, can communicate effectively, tackle quantitative and qualitative problems, embrace the idea of global communities and take some responsibility for society.

Student characteristics are Presage factors – so there is not a lot you can do to affect what a student brings into the learning situation. Once they are with us, however, there is a symbiotic relationship between what we do as staff, and student engagement (Kuh et al., 2004). If we expect students to write, they will, generally, write. If we expect students to work in diverse groups, they will. Where staff use 'effective educational practices' (Kuh et al., 2004: 28), students are more likely to act like intentional learners. These effective educational practices particularly include active and collaborative learning (Kuh et al., 2004: 29). So, while you can't change student characteristics on entry, you can teach them to engage.

The reluctant learner

In considering student characteristics, it would be remiss of us not to acknowledge the stressful 'anti-factors', such as worries about money and pressure from family commitments. No matter how hard we work to engage students with effective teaching and learning practices, these 'lifeload' factors (the combination of pressures in each student's life (Kahu, 2013: 767) can militate against effective learning.

So perhaps the other side of the 'intentional learner' is the 'reluctant learner', who comes in many guises (Wells et al., 2013), and the following Case study 11.1 ('Lecturers' views') suggests a few scenarios. Their recommendation for dealing with these is to take a positive, collaborative approach, rather than a judgemental one, because the latter is likely to further alienate students. Of course, this is no simple matter. A difficult situation can either be escalated or it can be defused, and defusing problems can require great patience and skill. One response to students who are reluctant or resistant is the use of 'motivational interviewing'. Its use is outlined in more detail in the literature (Wells et al., 2013) but it is a technique that seeks not to apportion blame but rather to negotiate a constructive approach that takes account of structural constraints that cannot easily be changed (for example, timetables, assessment requirements, deadlines, and so on). It is a collaborative technique that is focused on the process of change.

Interrogating practice

Can you recall a 'reluctant learner'? How did you respond and why? What was the result? Would you do it differently now?

In Case study 11.1, which takes the form of mini-examples, we consider some of the varieties of reluctant learning that you may come across, and later how reluctance might be overcome.

Case study 11.1: Lecturers' views

The following views have been collected from lecturers within the HE sector:

Lecturer's view 1: students not preparing for classes

'My students drive me mad: every week I give them work to prepare for tutorials, and usually about a third of them do it. It makes the classes meaningless, because I just have to explain the ideas to them, rather than getting them to apply the ideas on their own. I tell them they'll get more out of it if they do the work, but it doesn't seem to help.'

Lecturer's view 2: they don't turn up

'At the start of term, most students attended classes. But within a few weeks, classes were getting smaller and smaller. I'm now left with a core of 'good' students. I've asked for their help in encouraging their peers to attend, but with little effect. My colleagues tell me this is normal: the students have lots of commitments, and as long as they pass the assessment I shouldn't worry too much.'

Lecturer's view 3: students using social media in class

'I really don't know what to do about students using their phones and laptops in class. I've asked them not to do it, but they give lots of reasons as to why they're doing it: they're accessing their notes, looking up a definition, typing up notes of what I'm saying. I'm really uncomfortable because I think that most of the time they're on Facebook. I have colleagues who advocate using social media (e.g. Twitter for teaching), but I'm not sure.'

Lecturer's view 4: what's it all about?

Mary, a first generation university attendee from an underprivileged inner city area, said:

'This isn't what I expected university to be like. I'm working 20 hours a week in a supermarket, I'm living at home and helping out in the house, and I'm just not managing to get through the work. It feels like I've got the worst of all worlds. As if that wasn't bad enough, I have no idea what lecturers are talking about half the time – I get a D, and they write 'Be more critical in your approach to the literature'. What do they mean? They tell us to do these things, but they don't show us how.'

WHAT CAN YOU DO?

There are many reasons for students experiencing difficulty, and for difficult behaviour. While we cannot control student motivations, we are responsible for managing their learning experience. So what can you do, in order to challenge your students to engage, persist, learn and graduate? In this section, we offer some possible strategies.

Of course, using a specific teaching technique does not guarantee student engagement. Neither does 'what works' in one context necessarily translate to another. But improving engagement in the classroom does seem to help both general and specific student outcomes (Trowler and Trowler, 2010).

Strategy 1 – reality check

Dealing with the earlier lecturers' views starts with checking the realities of what is going on: are students not turning up because they are bored by classes? Or because many of them are working 20 hours a week in supermarkets? Are they failing to prepare because they have not yet been taught that universities expect them to study autonomously? Or because they just don't understand what to do? Are the classes so teacher-centred that they have nothing active to do? Or because they are, seriously, studying the topic in parallel with what you are doing? And could you use social media to your advantage? Asking yourself and the students these questions, and running ideas past colleagues, might help.

Strategy 2 – utilise stages of assimilation

The Scottish Enhancement Themes (Quality Assurance Agency, 2013) outline four stages of the student life cycle: getting there, being there, staying there and leaving there. While all of these stages are vital, it could be argued that the initial culture shock is a make or break experience: 'becoming' is more difficult than 'being' part of a university community. Transitions matter, especially transitions into HE.

Supporting student engagement is vital during the critical first year and especially the first few weeks of higher level study. In fact, academic habits established at this early stage can have long-term impact for the rest of the student life cycle (Cuseo, 2003: 4).

Tinto's (2004) research into student retention and engagement asks us to support students at three stages of their assimilation into higher education:

1 Entry into HE – especially important for first generation students, who may find it difficult to decode what is expected at university. You can make expectations very explicit from the start of their course, for example with pre-entry information, either in paper or social media format; by orientation activities during induction; and by discussing with students their learning approaches regularly throughout

the year. One option is peer support schemes. These can be highly formalised like **Supplemental Instruction (SI)** or PASS (McCarthy et al., 1997) or more fluid. Some focus on induction whereas others are content learning focused. However, they provide valuable peer mentoring and collaborative learning opportunities (Boud, Cohen and Sampson, 2001; Falchikov, 2002; Whitman and Fife 1988).

2   Integration into the university's academic and social systems (affecting subsequent commitment to the learning experience). Academically, this might involve specific tasks focused on helping students to plan, implement and control their own learning strategies; to understand the language we speak in universities ('critical thinking', 'analytical approach'), as well as the norms and language of the disciplines; and to grasp what higher level learning is. This support is often provided in targeted activities during the critical induction phase, e.g. for international students or those coming direct from further education college. But longitudinal induction, such as briefing sessions about learning approaches throughout the academic year, will be more effective. Socially, this means fostering a sense of belonging to the academic community. Belonging needs to start before induction, and will involve providing information, informing expectations, developing academic skills, building social capital (e.g. links with peers and staff) and nurturing a sense of belonging (Thomas, 2012: 22).

3   Structural integration, to meet academic standards.

Strategy 3 – build community

The one engagement factor that all the writers in Table 11.1 share is that of building community, identity, belonging and social interaction. Quite apart from making the most of social learning, belonging is a key factor in student retention:

> Students who are actively involved with peers, faculty and staff – especially in learning activities – are more likely to learn, persist, and graduate.
>
> (Tinto, 2004: 8)

And:

> Peers substantially influence how students spend their time and the meaning they make of their experiences including their personal satisfaction with college.
>
> (Hu and Kuh, 2002: 570)

Helping all students build relationships with staff and students and get actively involved in a community of learners is vital. We can do this by introducing group work early, by talking with students outside of class, through peer tutoring and mentoring, or simply by learning their names. The quality of student interaction with staff is key; rather than frequency of interaction, students gain most from staff responding to their individual needs, with a broad intellectual focus, and from contact outside of formal instructional settings. This can happen, for example, when discussing grades, talking about career plans, or discussing ideas from class (Coates, 2010: 7).

Cuseo (2003) reminds us that university education needs to be holistic, e.g. addressing emotional, social and intellectual development. Most students who leave early do so for non-academic reasons, and 'some of the most creative, highly able students leave before earning a degree' (Kuh et al., 2008: 557). So the student *experience* is an important concept, and looking after the student's academic well-being is only one part of the picture.

Strategy 4 – set high expectations

In Table 11.1, you will see the importance of 'setting high expectations' so that students understand the quality of what is expected of them, and its purpose. These processes need to be threaded through all of Tinto's (2004) stages. Yes, acknowledge the challenges of working at a high level, and support students in meeting these challenges, but create a stimulating intellectual environment for them to learn in. Tinto (2004: 11) also recommends monitoring student progress over time, to help identify students at risk of low engagement. An interesting development in this respect is electronic tracking of student participation in online learning, as a proxy for assessing engagement. It is perhaps contentious to track student hits on the **Virtual Learning Environment (VLE)**, but the benefit of using such early warning systems is that students with different needs or from different backgrounds can be offered support before it is too late to help them.

Students who are required to work harder have been found to be more satisfied with their student experience, as are students who develop high quality relationships with staff, while the contrary applies to students working long hours off campus (Belcheir, 2001: 8).

Strategy 5 – help students manage their learning

Table 11.1 suggests a number of elements involved in helping students understand and manage their learning. It is vital to help them develop self-management strategies, and come to terms with the quality, quantity and timing of effort needed.

A key aspect of managing their learning is students spending time on their studies. In Hayek and Kuh's (2002) study of this, they found that first-year students spent about half the time that staff estimated preparing for classes and many students turned up for classes unprepared (Hayek and Kuh, 2002: 60). Many students felt that their institution placed little emphasis on studying and spending time on academic work, and almost half of first-years never discussed ideas from classes with staff outside of class (Hayek and Kuh, 2002: 61). NSSE (2012), however, indicates that senior students spend more time on preparing for classes than staff anticipate.

How can we ensure students are clear about 'time on task'? It helps to give students a clear (written) outline of what they need to do, by when and how long it will take them. They also need to understand how this 'directed independent learning' fits into their overall study behaviours, and the role of their own meta-cognition (i.e. their awareness of and ability to manage their own learning). In many universities, tutors use Personal/ Professional Development Planning to do this. Unfortunately, some of the terminology used when discussing this is off-putting for both staff and students: 'self-awareness', 'self-assessment', 'reflective thinking', 'learning logs' and especially 'personal development planning' are high level, abstract terms, which may be counter-productive.

Interrogating Practice

How do you help students to manage their learning? Why do you use this approach? Are there other approaches that might be helpful?

HOW CAN WE ENABLE STUDENTS TO CHALLENGE US, THEMSELVES AND THE WORLD BEYOND UNIVERSITY

Students, who are active in their learning, take responsibility for their progress and think for themselves, are better able to challenge us, themselves and the wider world. So if we use the strategies listed earlier to empower students to take responsibility for their learning, they will know how to think critically and present appropriate challenges to their own thinking and that of others. Currently, the concept of 'partnership' is being used to describe a level of engagement that goes beyond students participating actively in their own learning, to significant contributions to curriculum design and institutional decision-making. There are many institutional examples, such as the 'Student as Producer' project (University of Lincoln, 2011).

CONCLUSIONS AND OVERVIEW

This chapter has looked at how we use challenge and engagement to positive effect. Kuh et al. (2008) talk about 'high impact practices' (including involving students in learning communities and doing research with staff), and there appears to be a correlation between these high impact teaching practices and student engagement. What characterises these high impact practices is that they match the factors suggested by the writers in Table 11.1. We have outlined a number of strategies and practices that can help with this.

Ahlfeldt et al. (2005) talk about 'engaged teaching practices' not just 'student engagement', and note that this approach correlates with student stage of study: the higher the level of class, the higher the student engagement. A key challenge is how to obtain engagement with students who are perhaps in larger classes. It may also be more challenging in mathematics and the sciences than in arts and humanities (Ahlfeldt et al., 2005) – but there is no get-out clause. No matter what our context or who makes up our diverse student groups, the old paradigm of the teacher delivering large quantities of information to receptive students has been replaced by a new conceptualisation of what university education is about: students engaging with their own learning. Hake (1998) characterises teaching for engagement as heads-on (always) and hands-on (usually). This was the case in 1998, but is still true today. It requires us to challenge our students, and be challenged in turn.

How these variables interact with demographics like gender, race, income level and ethnicity is complex. Pre-college achievements are important, but the importance of these diminishes considerably once the effects of college experiences are taken into account.

What is clear is that student engagement matters and is especially important for students with 'two or more risk factors' (Kuh et al., 2008: 555). While teachers cannot control the presage factors, they can create an environment that will enhance the educational experience of their students and enable as many as possible to stay, to learn and to thrive.

REFERENCES

Ahlfeldt, S, Mehta, S and Sellnow, T (2005) 'Measurement and analysis of student engagement in university classes where varying levels of PBL methods of instruction are in use', *Higher Education Research & Development*, 24(1): 5–20.

Association of American Colleges and Universities (AAC&U) (2002) *Great Expectations: A New vision for Learning as a Nation Goes to College*. Washington, DC: AAC&U.

AUSSE (2010) *Doing More for Learning: Enhancing Engagement and Outcomes. Australasian Survey of Student Engagement, Australasian Student Engagement Report*. Victoria: ACER.

Ballard, B and Clanchy, J (1997) *Teaching International Students: A Brief Guide for Lecturers and Supervisors*. Canberra: IDP Education Australia.

Barnett, R (2007) *A Will to Learn: Being a Student in an Age of Uncertainty*. Buckingham: SRHE and Open University Press.

Belcheir, MJ (2001) *What Predicts Perceived Gains in Learning and in Satisfaction?* Report No. BSU-RR-2001-02. Boise, ID: Office of Institutional Advancement (ERIC Document Reproduction Service No. ED480921).

Biggs, J (1993) 'From theory to practice: a cognitive system approach', *Higher Education Research and Development*, 12(1): 73–85.

Boud, D, Cohen, R and Sampson, J (2001) *Peer Learning in Higher Education: Learning from & with Each Other*. Abingdon: Psychology Press.

Bryson, C, Hardy, C and Hand, L (2009) *An in depth investigation of student engagement throughout their first year in university*. UK National Transition Conference, University College London, 24 April.

Carini, RM, Kuh, GD and Klein, SP (2006) 'Student engagement and student learning: Testing the linkages', *Research in Higher Education*, 47: 1.

Carson, J (1992) 'Becoming biliterate: first language influences', *Journal of Second Language Writing*, 1(1): 37–60.

Chickering, A and Gamson, Z (1987) 'Seven principles for good practice in undergraduate education', *American Association for Health Education Bulletin*, 39(7): 3–7.

Coates, H (2010) 'Development of the Australasian survey of student engagement (AUSSE)', *Higher Education*, 660: 1–17.

Cuseo, J (2003) *Academic-Support Strategies for Promoting Student Retention and Achievement During the First Year of College*. University of Ulster, Student Transition and Retention. Available from: http://www.ulster.ac.uk/star/resources/acdemic_support_strat_first_years.pdf (accessed 1 November 2013).

Cuseo, J (2007) 'The big picture', *E-source for College Transitions*, 5(1): 2–3.

Duffy, TM and Jonassen, DH (eds.) (1992) *Constructivism and the Technology of Instruction*. Hillside, NJ: Lawrence Erlbaum Associates.

Dunbar, R (1988) 'Culture-based learning problems of Asian students: some implications for Australian distance educators', *ASPESA Papers*, 5: 10–21.

Falchikov, N (2002) 'Unpacking peer assessment', in P Schwartz and G Webb (eds.), *Assessment (Case Studies of Teaching in Higher Education Series): Case Studies, Experience and Practice from Higher Education*. London: Kogan Page Stylus Publishing, 70–77.

Gardner, H (1993) *Frames of Mind: The Theory of Multiple Intelligences*. New York, NY: Basic Books.

Gazeley, L and Aynsley, S (2012) *The contribution of pre-entry interventions to student retention and success. A literature synthesis of the Widening Access, Student Retention and Success National Programmes Archive*. York: Higher Education Academy.

Goleman, D (1995) *Emotional Intelligence*. New York, NY: Bantam Books.

Hake, RR (1998) 'Interactive-engagement vs traditional methods: a six-thousand student survey of mechanics test data for introductory physics courses', *American Journal of Physics*, 66: 64–74.

Hayek, J and Kuh, G (2002) 'Insights into effective educational practices', *EDUCAUSE Quarterly*, 25(1): 60–61.

HEFCE (2013) *New Student Engagement Unit to be Launched*. Available from: http://www.hefce.ac.uk/news/newsarchive/2013/name,82620,en.html (accessed 1 November 2013).

Higher Education Academy (HEA) (2013) *International Student Lifecycle Resources Bank*. York: Higher Education Academy. Available from: http://www.heacademy.ac.uk/international-student-lifecycle (accessed 1 November 2013).

Hu, S and Kuh, GD (2002) 'Being (dis)engaged in educationally purposeful activities: the influences of student and institutional characteristics', *Research in Higher Education*, 43: 5.

Hussey, T and Smith, P (2010) *The Trouble with Higher Education: A Critical Examination of our Universities*. New York and London: Routledge.

Jones, A (2005) 'Culture and context: critical thinking and student learning in introductory macroeconomics', *Studies in Higher Education*, 30(3): 339–354.

Kahu, ER (2013) 'Framing student engagement in higher education', *Studies in Higher Education*, 38(5): 758–773.

Krause, K-L (2005) *Engaged, inert or otherwise occupied? Deconstructing the 21st century undergraduate student*. Sharing Scholarship in Learning and Teaching: Engaging Students, James Cook University, Queensland, 21–22 September 2005.

Kuh, GD, Cruce, TM, Shoup, R, Kinzie, J and Gonyea, RM (2008) 'Unmasking the effects of student engagement on first-year college grades and persistence', *The Journal of Higher Education*, 79(5): 540–563.

Kuh, GD, Kinzie, J, Cruce, T, Shoup, R and Gonyea, RM (2007) *Connecting the Dots: Multi-Faceted Analyses of the Relationships between Student Engagement Results from the NSSE, and the Institutional Practices and Conditions that Foster Student Success*. Bloomington, IN: Center for Postsecondary Research.

Kuh, GD, Nelson Laird, TF and Umbach, PD (2004) 'Aligning faculty activities and student behavior', *Liberal Education*, Fall: 30.

McCarthy, A, Smuts, B and Cosser, M (1997) 'Assessing the effectiveness of supplemental instruction: a critique and a case study', *Studies in Higher Education*, 22(2): 221–231.

National Survey of Student Engagement (NSSE) (2012) *Promoting Student Learning and Institutional Improvement: Lessons from NSSE at 13*. Bloomington, IN: Indiana University Center for Postsecondary Research.

Pascarella, ET, Wolniak, GC, Cruce, TM and Blaich, CF (2004) 'Do liberal arts colleges really foster good practices in undergraduate education?', *Journal of College Student Development*, 45(1): 57–74.

Prosser, M and Trigwell, K (1999) *Understanding Learning and Teaching: The Experience in Higher Education*. Buckingham: Open University Press.

Quality Assurance Agency (QAA) (2013) *Enhancement Themes: Guide to the Outcomes of the Themes*. Quality Assurance Agency for Higher Education. Available from: http://www.enhancementthemes.ac.uk/themes-outcomes-guide (accessed 1 November 2013).

Ramsden, P (2002) *Learning to Teach in Higher Education*. 2nd edn. London: RoutledgeFalmer.

Samuelowicz, K (1987) 'Learning problems of overseas students: two sides of a story', *Higher Education Research and Development*, 6: 121–134.

Thomas, L (2012) *Building Student Engagement and Belonging in Higher Education at a Time of Change. Final Report from the What Works? Student Retention & Success programme*. Paul Hamlyn Foundation. Available from: http://www.heacademy.ac.uk/assets/documents/retention/What_works_final_report.pdf (accessed 1 November 2013).

Tinto, V (2004) *Student Retention and Graduation: Facing the Truth, Living with the Consequences*. Occasional Paper 1. Washington, DC: The Pell Institute.

Trowler, V and Trowler, P (2010) *Student Engagement Evidence Summary*. York: Higher Education Academy.

University of Lincoln (2011) *Student as Producer*. Available from: http://www.lincoln.ac.uk/home/studyatlincoln/discoverlincoln/teachingandlearning/studentasproducer/ (accessed 1 November 2013).

Wells, H, Jones, A and Jones, SC (2013) 'Teaching reluctant students: using the principles and techniques of motivational interviewing to foster better student–teacher interactions', *Innovations in Education and Teaching International*. DOI: 10.1080/14703297.2013.778066.

Whitman, NA and Fife, JD (1988) *Peer Teaching: To Teach Is To Learn Twice*. ASHE-ERIC Higher Education Report No. 4. Washington, DC: ERIC Clearinghouse on Higher Education (ERIC Document No: ED 305016).

12 Encouraging independent learning

Martyn Kingsbury

FACULTY OF HE... + SOC...

27 NOV 2014

Wirral Campus
Clatterbridge

UNIVERSITY OF CHESTER

INTRODUCTION

This chapter focuses on independent learning and how a teacher may best facilitate it. Independent learning is widely regarded as vital in higher education, where there is a need for students to learn independently of direct teacher support and a desire to produce learners who are capable of **lifelong learning**. It is also increasingly clear that employers require graduates who are self-motivated independent learners. In order to achieve this, an ability and confidence in independent learning are vital to equip students to transfer their understanding, and the strategies they successfully employ to achieve it, into different contexts.

While there is apparent consensus on the need for students to become independent learners, and this has become an accepted aim of higher education, there is no clear definition of independent learning. This chapter explores these issues and highlights two case studies that show different ways of supporting independent learning.

WHAT DO WE MEAN BY INDEPENDENT LEARNING?

Although there is agreement on the importance of **independent learning**, there is no real consensus as to the definition, and there is an inconsistency of terminology with terms such as 'independent learning', 'self-regulated learning' and **self-directed learning (SDL)** used almost synonymously and interchangeably at times.

Self-regulated learning comes from Albert Bandura's work on social cognitive theory, which argues that human behaviour, including learning, is significantly motivated and regulated by self-influence (Bandura, 1994). Self-regulated learning in an academic sense can be defined as an 'active, constructive process whereby learners set goals for their learning and then attempt to monitor, regulate, and control their cognition, motivation, and behaviour, guided and constrained by their goals and the contextual features in the environment' (Pintrich, 2000: 453). Self-regulation relies on the learners' self-generated beliefs and feelings about their ability to engage with academic tasks; it is reflective, strategic and is influenced by their motivation and the learning environment as they progress towards achieving the desired goal. Self-regulated learning can usefully be considered as having cyclical phases (Zusho and Edwards, 2011). This starts with a 'forethought phase', a perception and planning stage when the learner recognises and analyses the learning task, sets goals and strategically plans their approach. Self-efficacy, the learner's belief in their ability to produce the necessary performance to complete the task, is critical at this stage (Bandura, 1994). This pre-learning phase is followed by a 'performance phase' when the learner follows their strategies and learning processes. This includes aspects of self-control, as the learner manages themself and their performance so that they can complete the learning task, and self-observation – a reflective and iterative examination of performance that links the learner's self-control and learning. In this context, self-control is linked to self-efficacy and motivation and is the learner's ability to stick to the learning task in the face of distracting alternatives. Finally, there is a 'self-reflection phase' when the learner reflects on their performance and adjusts their goals, processes and strategies. This **reflection** also informs and adjusts the learner's self-efficacy. Successful learning, particularly when challenging, tends to increase self-efficacy and enhance motivation. Self-regulated learning is where the learner takes responsibility for and control over the process of learning; it does not imply that this is done without direction or advice from others.

Self-directed learning has its origins in the ideas of **andragogy** and adult education developed by Malcolm Knowles. Knowles himself defined self-directed learning as 'a process in which individuals take the initiative, with or without the help of others, in diagnosing their learning needs, formulating learning goals, identifying human and material resources for learning, choosing and implementing appropriate learning strategies and evaluating learning outcomes' (Knowles, 1975: 18). Self-directed learning may incorporate self-regulatory learning skills and approaches; motivation and self-efficacy are also important. While there is significant overlap with self-regulation, in self-directed learning the learner sets the learning goals or desired outcomes, decides on the approach and direction to take, and the strategies and resources to use. They therefore take responsibility for the direction of the learning and not just for the process of learning; again this does not imply this is done in isolation.

Independent learning is 'learning in which the direction, control and regulation of the learning process is solely guided and managed by the learner' (Balapumi and Aitken, 2012: 2), implying that, for independent learning, the learner takes sole control of both the process and direction of the learning. While this does not necessarily mean this process happens in isolation, it does seem to suggest that the student be autonomous and independent of teacher, curricula and other learners. However, 'independent learning' is often used more loosely with a spectrum of meanings, which has this strict definition at one end and merely suggests the promotion of self-motivated learning with only key inputs from the teacher at the other.

For this chapter, I adopt the broad definition of self-directed learning suggested by Garrison as an 'approach where learners are motivated to assume personal responsibility and collaborative control of the cognitive (self-monitoring) and contextual (self-management) processes in constructing and confirming meaningful and worthwhile learning outcomes' (Garrison, 1997: 18). I believe that this is a more workable definition that extends aspects of both self-regulation and self-direction and is less likely to result in more dependent learners being labelled 'deficient'. To label the dependent learner as somehow deficient risks reducing self-efficacy and, consequently, decreasing the likelihood of future independent learning, and ignores the idea that learners may take different approaches at different times, depending upon context.

So in terms of this chapter, independent learning is learning in which the learner takes responsibility for setting the learning goals and managing the learning process and direction. While they take responsibility for their cognition and direction, this may be collaborative, with teachers (and others) offering advice and guidance.

WHAT IS EFFECTIVE INDEPENDENT LEARNING AND WHAT LEARNING BEHAVIOURS SUPPORT IT?

To some extent the answer to this question is contextual. Independent learning can be any work that students do by themselves or in groups with minimal teacher support. This can range from tasks such as researching information for an individual tutorial, presentation or essay, to **problem-based learning (PBL)**, distance learning or to research and other project work. Importantly, it also includes the independent self-study students carry out as an adjunct to formal teaching to make sense of their subject and develop their thinking and a **deeper approach to learning** (see Chapter 5).

Interrogating practice

- What independent learning tasks do you employ in your teaching?
- Is there potential for more/other self-directed, independent learning?

While independent learning strategies will depend on the learner (their knowledge, motivation and self-efficacy), their context (for example, the time and resources available), and the learning task they face, it is useful to consider it in a general sense. In this broader sense, independent learning involves three overlapping and interrelated dimensions (Garrison, 1997):

1 Self-management and control of the learning task
2 Self-monitoring and cognitive control and responsibility
3 Motivation and self-efficacy

Self-management is the management of the learning, the resources and processes associated with the implementation of that learning. It is how the learner attempts to shape the contextual conditions in the performance of goal-directed learning, and is linked to setting learning goals and to the strategies employed to achieve them.

Task management involves balancing proficiency (the learner's abilities, skills and knowledge) with the available resources, including those added by a tutor, facilitator or peers, in order to achieve the desired learning. There is also a need to consider 'what counts' as worthwhile knowledge in the given context. At its simplest, self-management is the relationship between what the student knows and what they can do with the learning resources available in order to achieve the desired learning. This may involve aspects that are specific to individual learning tasks, such as the use of particular software or library systems to retrieve information, or experimental methods to generate data. General strategies, such as knowing when and where to ask questions and when the task can be achieved without assistance, are often equally important.

Self-monitoring involves the cognitive and meta-cognitive processes of marshalling and monitoring a repertoire of learning strategies, together with an awareness of and an ability to plan and modify thinking according to the learning task at hand. This is the process whereby the learner takes responsibility for integrating new ideas and concepts with previous knowledge and constructing new personal meaning to create understanding. The learner's performance depends on their cognitive abilities, their learning strategies and how these are applied to the contextual and cognitive demands. Can the learner recognise the gap in knowledge and employ appropriate strategies to build on their existing understanding to bridge that gap? Can they achieve this within the contextual limitations of, for example, time and resources? And are they reflective and critical so they may adjust their strategies and efforts appropriately as the task progresses? Self-monitoring often requires both internal and external feedback. Internal feedback and self-evaluation are important in this process, but may lack accuracy and fidelity. The challenge is often to integrate external information and feedback from teachers and/or peers without losing control or independence.

Motivation and self-efficacy are critical to self-directed learning. In the pre-implementation phase 'entering motivation' is key; this is the motivation that drives the desire to commit to the goal and start the learning task. Students will likely have a higher entering motivation if they think the learning goals are achievable and will meet their needs and match their interests and expectations. The learner's perceptions of their ability influences entering motivation and relates to contextual factors and the perceived cognitive demand. Following the decision to start a particular learning task, maintenance of intention during learning depends on 'task motivation'. Entering and task motivations can be extrinsic, external to the individual and linked, for example, to the rewards associated with exam grades, or intrinsic, personal inner rewards or enjoyment of the task.

The connections between motivation, cognition and performance are complex and much discussed in the literature. Whilst not appropriate to discuss this too deeply, it is perhaps useful to briefly consider 'achievement goal' theory (Pintrich, 2000) as a way of linking the complexities of motivation with independent learning. Achievement goal theory suggests two main types of underlying purposes that motivate learning: 'mastery goals' where learners engage with learning to develop competence, skill or ability, and 'performance goals' where learners engage in a learning task to demonstrate ability or competence. Both mastery and performance goals can be positive, aiming at success, or negative, aiming at avoiding the possibility of failure. Thus positive mastery goals ('mastery-approach goals') are engagement in order to develop competence, while negative mastery goals ('master-avoidance goals') are engagement in order to avoid a possible decline in performance or missing an opportunity for learning. Similarly, positive performance goals ('performance-approach goals') are engagement in order to demonstrate good performance, while negative performance goals ('performance-avoidance goals') are engagement in order to avoid demonstrating poor performance (Lichtinger and Kaplan, 2011). Mastery approach goals are positively associated with initiation of independent deep approaches to learning, while performance-avoidance goals are negatively associated with independent learning, but relate positively to avoidance and students' self-handicapping strategies (Pintrich, 2000; Lichtinger and Kaplan, 2011).

Case study 12.1: Independent learning in history

In history, self-directed, independent learning is important. This subject does not require acquisition of a set body of knowledge, but rather the development of certain skills and qualities of mind. History has to be discovered, interpreted and contextualised and can't simply be delivered as fact. Independent learning is also important when teaching history to students from other disciplinary backgrounds because it allows them to use their experience and interest to discover history that is relevant to them and their context. **Research-led teaching** of history is desirable at higher level, and in order to prepare the students to benefit from and participate effectively in this approach, the skills of self-regulation and independent learning are important. Initially, this might be through relatively bounded and supported reading of original historical sources, identification and interpretation of existing historical accounts, writing of essays and delivery of oral presentations, with feedback given on content, approach, critical thinking and reflection, and quality of analysis. This then builds through more extended essay tasks, to less directly supported and more open-ended project work, towards works that are more research-like and can, in the extreme, end-up being collaborative research. This approach builds the students' knowledge of the content of history, its concepts and theories, and also their qualities of perception and judgement. This, in turn, results in independent learning skills and strategies, and the motivation and capacity to work as an historian.

As teachers and course organisers, the difficulties are: how do we promote and encourage student responsibility for independent learning through research-led teaching whilst maintaining parity of level, quality and consistency of student experience, and the overall coherence of the degree programme? Giving students responsibility for their learning does not mean abdicating our own role as teachers; the goal should be to facilitate from a distance. We need to ensure that the individual student's desired independent learning goals and interests fit the broader course' intended learning outcomes and appropriate levels. It is also important to make this process explicit, so that students are aware of the value of various tasks and assignments in building their meta-cognitive skills and capacities for learning and self-evaluation.

(Abigail Woods, King's College, London)

WHY IS INDEPENDENT LEARNING IMPORTANT IN HIGHER EDUCATION?

While students may be successful as dependent learners in secondary education, academic success in tertiary education requires proactive, disciplined, creative self-regulated learners who engage with independent academic tasks. Independent self-regulated study is crucial to students developing the deeper approach to learning that is a prerequisite for handling the range and complexity of disciplinary content at this level. There is some evidence for a positive association between undergraduate self-regulated learning and academic achievement.

Independent self-regulated learning is also effective at helping students to integrate disciplinary content with existing understanding and apply it in a contextually relevant way. The skills involved in achieving this and the increased self-efficacy that often results from rising to the challenge of the learning are often transferable between contexts, relevant to 'life-long' learning and prized by graduate employers and society in general. This interweaving of disciplinary subject knowledge and the cognitive and metacognitive skills of successful independent learning is valuable.

The integration of disciplinary knowledge and the skills and strategies associated with self-regulated independent learning, together with self-efficacy and motivation are also important in developing future researchers. This is especially true when students are given the opportunity for independent learning with experimental or research projects when they can develop disciplinary research skills, cognitive skills and self-efficacy in research. The opportunity to pursue truly independent research within an undergraduate course is not commonplace, but represents the essence of the elusive research teaching nexus.

However, many students enter higher education lacking the skills essential for independent learning and have difficulty in setting academic goals and identifying and employing appropriate learning strategies. This can handicap students despite their intelligence, prior knowledge and academic ability. It seems that although some self-regulatory skills may be transferable, self-efficacy and at least some aspects of independent learning are contextual and may be problematic during transition. It is not hard to imagine that a student new to higher education, even one who proved a skilled and effective independent learner at school, might initially struggle when faced with very different expectations, cognitive load and available resources.

The ability to learn independently is not automatic; it needs to be encouraged and supported, especially as changing context and academic load may reduce self-efficacy and limit the effectiveness of established strategies even in confident, self-directed learners.

WHAT IS THE ROLE OF THE TEACHER IN INDEPENDENT LEARNING?

Grow (1991) suggested that the self-directed aspect of independent learning could be considered as staged, with the learner progressing from being dependent to being independent in four steps: dependent learner; interested learner; involved learner; and independent, self-directed learner. He suggests the role of the teacher should be adjusted to match these stages. For the dependent learner he thinks the teacher should be an authority, an expert dispensing information, coaching and providing direct feedback. They should try and provide praise, external motivation and help the learner overcome their deficiencies and any resistance to learning. In doing this, the learners may become more motivated, better skilled, interested learners. For the interested learner he argues the teacher should be a motivator and guide with inspirational teaching, guided discussion, and help with goal setting and learning strategies, working closely with students providing them with the skills, motivation and encouragement to become more involved, but directing and supporting them when needed. For the involved learner, he considers the teacher as a facilitator, guiding discussion and participation in project work on a more collaborative footing. Perhaps this is the key stage – the teacher facilitating group learning of disciplinary content and cultivating empowering skills such as communication, critical thinking, problem-solving and goal setting, and providing opportunity for students to develop learning strategies, self-evaluation and project management skills, and increase their confidence, motivation, self-efficacy and independence. When the learner is independent, the teacher becomes a consultant, delegating, advising, suggesting and guiding from a distance.

One must also remember that, depending on context and motivation, the learner may be independent in some areas of their studies whilst simultaneously being dependent in others. Any group may include students at different stages, and not all will be equally ready or able to pursue independent learning. Grow (1991) suggests that a course, or even a particular session, should be based around the teaching style of a particular stage of learning with the teacher iteratively using approaches for other stages with students as appropriate. So in a degree level course, the teaching may be based around the facilitated group learning best suited to the motivated, 'involved learner', but for those ready and able to learn independently there could be the possibility of independent project work, perhaps used to inform and motivate the rest of the group. While for the more dependent learners the teacher, either directly or perhaps via peer support, coaches in the basics and encourages towards greater independence. Teachers therefore need to consider the students and attempt to match the desired independent learning to their motivations and capabilities. The teacher also has to try and ensure that the available resource is appropriate for the desired learning needs and encourage self-regulatory strategies.

The teacher should explicitly define the purpose of the learning and indicate why an independent learning strategy would be beneficial. They should also prepare the path to independent learning, without being too directive or assuming control by, for example, liaising with the library to make sure they are aware of the topic and likely student needs, and that critical resources are available and perhaps in short-term loan.

Interrogating practice

Do you have a topic suitable for independent learning?

- Is it of appropriate level and scope; is it possible for the student(s) to complete it with the available time and resources?
- Does it 'fit'; is it flexible enough to suit the range of learners?
- Is it well resourced with multiple, easily accessed sources of information?
- Do the students know why/how the topic is of value to them; is it contextually relevant and interesting?
- Are you going to explain to students the nature and value of this type of learning?

Annotated resource lists to get things started are useful, as is encouraging 'study groups' to help students support each other. Providing information and signposts or links for further self-directed research, perhaps in a **VLE**, and referring to this in taught material can also be a useful strategy. However, simply providing supplementary material is sometimes not enough, and students' use of such material is variable. Consider how to scaffold effective use of such material and encourage independent learning without the direct intervention that might inhibit independence. Perhaps, for example, podcasting or other social media may provide such opportunities (see also Chapter 10).

Developing students' skills and strategies, perhaps by providing staged tasks that build from less to more challenging and independent, is vital. It is helpful, at least initially, to not only suggest approaches, but to include intermediate steps with explicit opportunities to check and review both learning content and strategy. Including opportunities for peer- and self-evaluation and making the evaluative process both visible and 'rewarded' can also help develop the self-reflection that is vital to successful independent learning. Specific training on self-regulation and meta-cognition (learners' awareness of their personal resources, processes and strategies in relation to their engagement with learning tasks) can also be very useful, especially when students are transitioning to a new stage or environment where the need for independent learning may be different from what they have been previously used to.

Case study 12.2: Supporting explicit reflection to facilitate the transition to independent learning

In a traditional undergraduate medical degree, the first two years of study often rely on largely **didactic teaching** of 'basic' information. In the third year, students are taught more in the clinical environment where organised didactic teaching is rare. Students have to adapt to a less familiar and controllable learning environment. (Similar transitions occur in other subjects, for example when students start project work or industry placements.)

During this time, tutorial support is less direct and directive, and students must recognise opportunistic learning and transition efficiently to a more self-directed, independent learning approach to maximise their learning potential.

As part of a Master's research study, students were taught explicit reflection skills based on Kolb (see Chapter 5). This teaching happened at the start of their clinical attachment and was linked to tutorials on taking a patient's history, a fundamental clinical skill and important for engagement and learning in the clinical environment. The impact of this approach was evaluated using sequential questionnaires and group interviews. Initially students reported feeling unsupported and did not feel confident. By the end of the teaching, self-assessed confidence, capability and effectiveness had all increased, and all students passed their assessment. While students initially found the reflection difficult and hard to fit in to their hectic schedule, they subsequently reported it a very helpful strategy that they would continue using. They liked the 'comfort' of having a process to follow that helped them make 'sense' of the unfamiliar situation. By the end of the attachment their reflection had progressed to the point where they reported using it to help them integrate information, evaluate their own skills, attitudes and feelings and set future learning goals.

Making the self-evaluation explicit, and supporting it as a skill in parallel with the skills required on the attachment, seems to have helped medical students successfully negotiate the transition into independent learning in the clinical environment.

(Varunika Lecamwasam, Consultant, Ealing NHS Trust)

While as teachers, there is a lot one can do to encourage independent student learning, students have to be prepared to accept the **autonomy** that independent learning requires of them. Often this is dependent on their personal motivation and self-efficacy with regard to the learning task they face.

While student motivation is difficult to influence, keeping independent learning tasks interesting, open and contextually relevant will certainly help. Frequent, high-stakes assessment tends to encourage students to focus on performance goals (passing the tests) rather than mastery goals and should be avoided to encourage independent learning.

Authentic mastery experiences are the most effective way of creating self-efficacy, that is experience (direct or indirect if there is a high degree of assumed personal similarity) of achieving success in a similar task. Tasks should be challenging enough to stimulate and motivate, but not so hard as to paralyse a student. Experience of 'easy success' and undemanding tasks is counter-productive because students may come to expect quick success and become easily discouraged by failure (Bandura, 1994). Self-efficacy is not so much learning how to succeed; it is learning from one's mistakes and how to persevere when one does not succeed. Effective teachers build self-efficacy by helping students see mistakes as positive contributions towards subsequent achievement.

In this sense, feedback both regulates and is regulated by students' motivation and self-efficacy; feedback not only influences motivation and self-efficacy, its interpretation is influenced by student motivation and self-efficacy. In independent learning, feedback is required to clarify what 'good performance' is and to align independent learning with course requirements. The challenge is to provide specific feedback that makes the requirements and standards clear, bridges any gap between the students' independent learning goals and those of the course, informs meta-cognition and builds motivation and self-efficacy without inhibiting independence. Providing opportunities for self-monitoring with structured tasks containing early and regular feedback is useful to develop the required student skills. Providing feedback on work in progress and drafts before final submission allows students to make changes and close the feedback loop, helping them develop their own evaluative skills, particularly if peer and/or self feedback play a part in this process (see Chapter 8). Perhaps using a two-stage process where feedback from stage one (e.g. a plan or learning strategy) can be used to close any performance gap and inform the second stage (e.g. the actual project). It is important to involve students in assessment and feedback so that feedback becomes a dialogue between teacher and student and, wherever possible, between peers.

Peer feedback is especially useful because often somebody who has just learnt the material is more aware of issues and strategies for learning. More importantly, for independent learning this develops evaluative skills and strategies and builds confidence, motivation and self-efficacy and keeps the responsibility for the learning with the student. The teacher's role is to facilitate this from a distance and to guard against potential misunderstanding.

CONCLUSIONS

Effective independent learning is a challenge for both teacher and student, but in many ways it is the essence of 'higher' education and the key to life-long and professional learning and personal development. The benefits of encouraging this approach in students therefore more than outweighs the effort involved.

REFERENCES

Balapumi, R and Aitken, A (2012) 'Concepts and factors influencing independent learning in IS higher education'. In *ACIS 2012: Location, location, location*. Proceedings of the 23rd Australasian Conference on Information Systems, 1–10.

Bandura, A (1994) 'Self-efficacy'. In VS Ramachdran (ed), *Encyclopaedia of human behaviour*, Vol. 4. Cambridge: Academic Press, 71–81.

Garrison, DR (1997) 'Self-directed learning: toward a comprehensive model', *Adult Education Quarterly*, 48(1): 18–33.

Grow, GO (1991) 'Teaching learners to be self-directed', *Adult Education Quarterly*, 41(3): 125–149.

Knowles, MS (1975) *Self-Directed Learning: a Guide for Learners and Teachers*. Englewood Cliffs, New Jersey: Prentice Hall/Cambridge.

Lichtinger, E and Kaplan, A (2011) 'Purpose of engagement in academic self-regulation', *New Directions for Teaching and Learning*, 126: 9–19.

Pintrich, PR (2000) 'Multiple goals, multiple pathways: the role of goal orientation in learning and achievement', *Journal of Educational Psychology*, 92: 544–555.

Zusho, A and Edwards, K (2011) 'Self-regulation and achievement goals in the college classroom', *New Directions for Teaching and Learning*, 126: 21–31.

FURTHER READING

Boud, D (1988) Developing student autonomy in learning. 2nd edn. London: Kogan Page.

Leese, M (2010) 'Bridging the gap: Supporting student transitions into higher education', *Journal of Further and Higher education*, 34(2): 239–251.

13 Supervising research degrees

Stan Taylor and Margaret Kiley

INTRODUCTION

Research degrees are the highest qualifications awarded by universities. Candidates are required to undertake a research project that makes an original contribution to knowledge and understanding in their subject(s) and present the results in a thesis. In this endeavour, the most important source of support for candidates is their supervisory team, and the quality of supervision has a major impact upon their learning experiences and upon their chances of timely completion. The aim of this chapter therefore is to highlight some of the practices that underpin high-quality supervision. The chapter includes sections on the context of supervision, recruitment and selection, establishing relationships, academic guidance and support, encouraging writing and giving feedback, personal, professional and career support, monitoring progress, supporting completion, supporting examination and reflecting upon and enhancing practice.

THE CONTEXT

Historically, very little attention was paid to doctoral supervision. As Park (2008: 2) has written:

> Traditionally, a 'secret garden' model prevailed, in which student and supervisor engaged together as consenting adults, behind closed doors, away from the public gaze, and with little accountability to others.

However, in the past few years, doctoral supervision has become subject to external scrutiny and governments and research sponsors in many countries have introduced codes of practice covering the quality of doctoral supervision and have acted to penalise non- or late completion of degrees. In consequence, institutions have begun taking a much greater interest in supervision and have introduced policies designed to meet external requirements, with which **supervisors** need to be familiar. Such policies are often outlined at training sessions for new supervisors, but there is also a need for established supervisors to be aware of them and align their practice accordingly.

> ## Case study 13.1: The UK Quality Code for Higher Education – research degrees
>
> In the UK, and many other counties, there is a **quality code** for research degree programmes which covers:
>
> - The research environment;
> - Selection, admission and induction of research students;
> - Supervision including:
>   ○ Skills and knowledge of supervisors;
>   ○ Main supervisors and supervisory teams;
>   ○ The responsibilities of research supervisors;
>   ○ Time allocations for supervision.
> - Progress and review arrangements;
> - Development of research and other skills;
> - Evaluation mechanisms;
> - Assessment;
> - Complaints and appeals procedures.
>
> The Code requires that institutions develop their own internal codes of practice to help them meet the national code, and that these are readily available to all candidates and staff involved in research degrees, including supervisors. Adherence to the national code forms part of institutional review by the **Quality Assurance Agency**.
>
> (Quality Assurance Agency, 2012)

RECRUITMENT AND SELECTION

In recruitment, the aim is, as Grasso et al. (2009: 23) have put it, to ensure that the 'right candidates apply' for research degrees. As Golde (2005) has pointed out, intending applicants are often ill-informed about what they are letting themselves in for because the data that they need is not available. Therefore, one of the keys to selection is ensuring that applicants know beforehand what is involved in undertaking a research degree and about the time in which they will be expected to complete it. Many higher education systems set a limit of three or four years for full-time candidates and six for part-time ones.

In selection, the key aim is that, as Grasso et al. (2009: 26) again have put it, that 'the right candidates are admitted' to the programme. Doctoral programmes obviously demand that candidates are capable of undertaking research. But, as Lovitts (2008) has shown, candidates who excel in taught programmes may not necessarily have the qualities to make successfully the transition to independent researchers. In view of this, Seigal (2005: 6) has argued that, as well as degree results, selection should also take into account 'demonstrated research experience' to maximise the chances that candidates can make the transition. Furthermore, in many universities now it is commonplace to interview applicants, in person or via Skype.

Additionally, in those disciplines where candidates themselves choose their topics, selectors also have to take into account whether the school or department has the skills and resources to support the candidate's topic. There is evidence that candidates are more likely not to complete or to delay completion where supervisors have little expertise in the topic (see Bair and Haworth, 2004) or a personal interest (McAlpine et al., 2012) or are 'pushed' to spend time with the student (Cohen, 2011). So, as well as the 'right' candidates, the selection process also needs to ensure the 'right' supervisors.

ESTABLISHING RELATIONSHIPS WITH CANDIDATES

Traditionally, the relationship between supervisors and candidates has been described in terms of a 'craft' model of master and apprentice. But this implies largely passive roles for supervisors in demonstrating and candidates in emulating, which does not correspond to the reality of doctoral supervision. Instead, supervision is increasingly being cast as a specialist form of teaching and supported learning with a focus upon supervisors' predominant styles of supervision and how far they meet candidates' needs.

One of the best known models of supervisory styles is that of Gatfield (2005) who extracted two key dimensions, namely 'structure' and 'support' (see Figure 13.1).

'Structure' refers primarily to the way in which supervisors perceive their roles in the organisation and management of the research project:

- At one extreme, supervisors conceive of their role as one of organising and managing the research project;
- At the other, supervisors conceive of their role as offering minimal intervention and giving candidates the maximum autonomy in organising and managing the research project.

'Support' refers to the way in which supervisors perceive their roles in personally supporting candidates through the ups and downs of life as a researcher:

- At one extreme, supervisors see it as the responsibility of candidates to manage themselves;

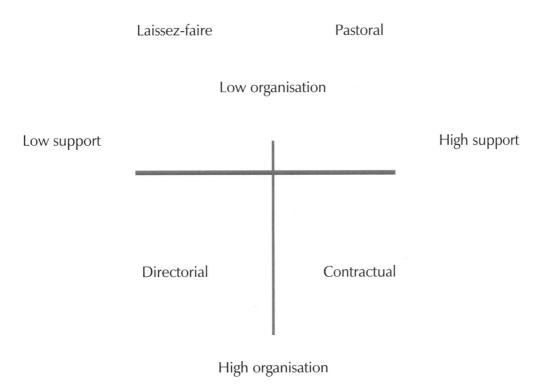

Figure 13.1 Perceptions of supervisory roles
Source: adapted from Gatfield (2005)

- At the other, supervisors conceive of their role as offering a full pastoral support service.

These two dimensions were dichotomised into 'low' and 'high' to yield four paradigms of supervisor styles.

1   The laissez-faire style, which assumes that candidates are capable of managing both the research project and themselves;
2   The pastoral style in which candidates are capable of managing the former but need personal support;
3   The directorial, which assumes that candidates need support in managing the research project but not in managing themselves; and
4   The contractual style, which assumes that candidates need support in both.

As Malfoy and Webb (2000) have suggested, generally as long as there is congruence between the supervisory style, the associated assumptions about the needs of candidates, and their actual needs, there should be no difficulties. But if there is discongruence, candidates' needs may not be met by their supervisors and problems can occur in the relationship.

Until comparatively recently, the answer to any mismatch would be that adjustment was up to the candidate, who would swim or sink as a result. However, in recent years, it has become unacceptable for supervisors to have one set style and they have been expected to deploy a repertoire to meet the different individual needs of candidates. This has become particularly important given the growth in the numbers of international candidates who may have very different expectations of the supervisory relationship (see Ryan and Carroll, 2005) and/or part-time ones who have very different priorities and needs from full-time candidates (see McCulloch and Stokes, 2008).

Additionally, as Gurr (2001) pointed out, supervisors need such a repertoire to meet the changing needs of candidates over the stages of the research project.

Interrogating practice

- Looking back on your own experience when you started as a research student, did your supervisor have a particular style of supervision?
- To what extent was his/her preferred style congruent with your needs?
- Over the course of your candidature, were you aware of your supervisor varying his/her style as you developed as an independent researcher? If so in, what ways did he or she adapt?

ESTABLISHING RELATIONSHIPS WITH CO-SUPERVISORS

At least outside the US, doctoral candidates have been supervised traditionally by a single supervisor. There can be benefits to the student from having one main source of advice and guidance to support their research projects; however, if that one person is negligent or the relationship doesn't work or if something happens to the supervisor, then serious problems can occur. So the argument runs that, with a supervisory team, there is a safety net for the student and for the research project.

Primarily for this reason, research sponsors and quality assurance agencies across the globe have been requiring or encouraging team supervision with each student having two or more supervisors. While this can have benefits, it can also lead to issues, including conflicts of standpoints, roles, interests and styles (see Taylor and Beasley, 2005). For that reason, the relationship needs to be actively managed by agreeing roles and expectations at the start of the candidateship and reviewing them during its course to ensure that the supervisory team remains fit for purpose.

ACADEMIC GUIDANCE AND SUPPORT

Research by Kiley (2009), Kiley and Wisker (2009), and Trafford and Lesham (2009) has identified at least six key **threshold concepts** that have troubled research degree candidates and inhibited their academic progress. These are the concept of research itself, what constitutes originality, the role of theory in informing research (and vice versa), setting research in its wider context, selecting among competing methodologies and methods, and producing a thesis/argument.

Kiley (2009) has suggested that supervisors need to support their candidates to acquire these concepts by explicitly discussing them, or organising mentoring by more advanced peers and by giving feedback, as well as referring candidates to examples, such as completed theses.

ENCOURAGING CANDIDATES TO WRITE AND GIVING FEEDBACK

In the past, particularly in the sciences, research degrees were seen as 'doing' the project, following which the student 'wrote it up'. In recent years, however, there has been a shift towards incorporating academic writing and feedback as an integral part of the research process from the start (see, for example, Wolff, 2010). Such a strategy:

- Encourages candidates to reflect upon what they have done to date;
- Builds a foundation for the future;
- Gives supervisors the chance to see what has been done and to advise on how to proceed; and
- Develops skills in academic writing early in candidature.

One way of doing this is to encourage candidates to keep a research diary, which is a daily record of what they have done towards their thesis. It includes a record of time spent on the work, activities, analysis and speculation. By keeping it, candidates get into the habit of writing every day, recording what they are doing and reflecting upon it. Further, as Murray (2006) has argued, it gives them a basis upon which to write larger pieces of work.

Of course when candidates do present larger pieces of work, they need to be given feedback. This can be a cause of apprehension among research degree candidates because their work is their own and criticism is often taken personally (see Wang and Li, 2011; McAlpine et al., 2012). It is therefore vital that supervisors think carefully about how and when they give feedback. Taylor and Beasley (2005) have suggested that this should involve ensuring that the setting is appropriate; setting out expectations; summarising what the supervisor thinks the student has written to check understanding; praising the successful parts; identifying the less successful ones; inviting comment from candidates; summarising the discussion; and maintaining a record. As importantly, candidates need to know when they can expect to receive feedback and this needs to be in good time for them to progress their projects.

PERSONAL, PROFESSIONAL AND CAREER SUPPORT

Research is difficult in itself as, by definition, there are always risks, and candidates have to cope with uncertainty, which may be compounded by social isolation and personal issues (see McAlpine et al., 2012). While supervisors are not, of course, trained counsellors, they need to be able to offer personal support to candidates in navigating the research journey.

As well as personal support, supervisors need to provide professional support in terms of:

- Facilitating networking;
- Advising on presentations;
- Encouraging and facilitating publication of candidates' work.

The last is particularly crucial if candidates are contemplating an academic career. As Casanave (2010) has argued, academic selection committees are no longer just looking for experts with PhDs, but for publications as well, and these are needed to be short-listed for academic posts.

In recent years, doctoral graduates have increasingly looked elsewhere for employment; however, employers have deemed doctoral training as poor preparation for non-academic jobs (see Akay, 2008), and in consequence there have been numerous initiatives designed to support candidates to acquire the wider skills necessary for the labour market (Phillips, 2010). In this, as Craswell (2007: 382) has argued:

> …supervisors are vital in developing candidates' awareness of the importance of skills development, in helping them to identify any skills gaps that might exist, and in encouraging them to address these systematically.

Of course, there are other sources of personal, professional and employment support available to candidates, including peer networks, research groups, graduate schools and student services, including welfare and careers. Supervisors need to be aware of these sources, which are often detailed in candidate or supervisor handbooks, and where appropriate direct candidates to them.

MONITORING PROGRESS

While, in practice, many of the reasons why candidates may leave programmes or delay completion lie beyond the influence of supervisors, the latter have come under considerable pressure to monitor candidates' progress and ensure timely completion.

In order to do this, supervisors need to be aware of the signs that candidates are falling behind. Manathunga (2002) has identified four key sets of indicative behaviours, namely candidates:

- Constantly changing the topic or planned work;
- Avoiding communication with their supervisor;

- Isolating themselves from their department and peers; and
- Avoiding submitting work.

Ahern and Manathunga (2004) sought to classify procrastination as lying in one or more of three domains – the cognitive, affective and the social, and suggested a range of measures that supervisors might adopt, depending upon the cause. For procrastination that arises from:

- Cognitive causes, they suggest that supervisors should broach the matter with the student and identify appropriate opportunities to improve knowledge and skills;
- Affective causes, they suggest helping the student to re-plan the research project as a series of small steps could be effective;
- Lack of academic and social integration, they offer the solutions of establishing research or reading groups or seminars as a way of incorporating their candidates into a supportive research culture.

As well as being aware of the informal signs of whether or not candidates are on track, supervisors also need to be fully informed about formal university systems for monitoring student progress. As Kiley (2011) has pointed out, in recent years institutions have tightened up and extended their monitoring systems with, usually, a 'make or break' initial review during the first year of the programme and regular reviews thereafter to ensure that they are keeping up to the mark. Supervisors have to be aware of these milestones and of the implications for their candidates.

Interrogating practice

- Does your institution have policies and procedure for monitoring the progress of doctoral candidates?
- What are the main milestones?
- Are you involved in judging whether the candidates' initial progress is satisfactory or is this undertaken by independent assessors?
- What is your role in monitoring subsequent progress through to completion?

SUPPORTING WRITING THE THESIS

Once they have completed the research project, candidates need to produce their theses. As Kiley (2009) pointed out, candidates often struggle to understand that a thesis is more than an account of what they have done during their period of research. So it can be helpful for supervisors to remind candidates that a thesis must present a case or point of view, support this with reasoned argument and evidence based upon original scholarship and contain materials that are new to the research community in the subject and are worthy of publication.

A further part of writing which candidates often find difficult is structuring, i.e. deciding what goes where in the thesis. In this context, one possible strategy identified (see Cryer 2006) is to ask candidates to think of themselves as explorers who have undertaken a journey and who are writing a guidebook to where they have been, and what they discovered in the process. This can be translated readily into the key features of the thesis.

Writing also has to be planned in terms of the balance of words. Many institutions have word limits on the total permissible length, of which candidates should be aware. But, given that the thesis will be examined primarily on the original contribution made to knowledge and understanding in the subject, candidates would be foolish to aim for half of their thesis to be taken up by the literature review, a further quarter by the methodology and only a quarter for the original scholarship. Supervisors then may need to advise candidates to allocate at least rough targets for each part of the thesis (see, for example, Dunleavy, 2003).

A further area where candidates may need advice is in relation to presentation, in particular about meeting any disciplinary style conventions or particular institutional requirements. Candidates then need to be directed towards appropriate sources of information about these matters, e.g. exemplar theses in the discipline or the institution's requirements for the form in which theses are submitted.

Finally, supervisors and candidates need to agree a timetable for writing. This should start by agreeing a target date for the production of the thesis in its final form. Bearing in mind that candidates often seriously underestimate the time required to develop the final version, it is then possible to work backwards and include the time to be allowed for re-drafting, a hand-in date for the first complete draft and hand-in dates for individual chapters.

SUPPORTING SUBMISSION AND EXAMINATION

Usually after several iterations, candidates produce a complete draft and, inevitably, ask their supervisors if it will pass. Once supervisors have acted as examiners a few times themselves, this becomes an easy question, but it can be more difficult for those who have no experience of examination. Here it can be useful to look at the formal and informal criteria used by experienced examiners (see Mullins and Kiley, 2002; Lovitts, 2007) and apply them to the draft, as well as to ask colleagues who are experienced examiners for their opinions.

Examiners then have to be found. Usually, it is the supervisory team which is asked to put forward the names of potential examiners, for which purpose they need to be aware of the formal criteria in the institution to examine a doctorate (see, for example, Tinkler and Jackson, 2004). In choosing examiners, supervisors will normally consult the student, but the latter does not have a power of veto.

In a few countries, most notably Australia and South Africa, it is only the thesis that is examined, but elsewhere there is also an oral examination of the candidate, the viva. This can cause apprehension in the best of candidates, and it is important that supervisors support their preparation for what will be the final hurdle. Suggestions include explaining what happens in the viva, going through institutional guidelines on the conduct of the examination, pointing candidates towards the relevant literature (see, for example, Murray, 2009), and organising a 'mock' viva to enable them to practice responding to questions about their work.

Examiners may make a range of recommendations that can vary from outright pass, pass subject to minor corrections, pass subject to major corrections/fail but with chance for re-submission, the award of a lesser degree, or the award of no degree at all. In practice, a very high proportion of candidates pass outright or with minor corrections, but there are some who are asked to undertake major corrections and re-submit. In such cases, supervisors have a role to play in supporting candidates to make corrections to the satisfaction of the examiners.

EVALUATING AND ENHANCING PRACTICE

Evidence suggests that new supervisors either emulate their own supervisor (if they were satisfied with their supervision) or react strongly against them (if they were not), neither of which necessarily affords a good basis for supervising doctoral candidates from other backgrounds and with other needs (see, for example, Barnes and Austin, 2009). So, as Hill (2011) has argued, supervisors need to evaluate their practice and, where appropriate, enhance it. A useful resource from the Oxford Learning Institute is given in the section 'Where to find more support'.

OVERVIEW AND CONCLUSIONS

Historically, the necessary and sufficient condition to be a supervisor was to be research active. The logic underpinning this was summarised over twenty years ago by Rudd (1985: 79–80) in that 'if one can do research then one presumably can supervise it'. But, while being a researcher is still a necessary condition for being a supervisor, it is no longer a sufficient one, and supervisors need to have a knowledge and understanding of good practice in supervision itself in order to succeed. While the authors have sought to include the key elements of such practice in this chapter, they are conscious that this is only part of a much broader picture. In particular, as one of the authors (Taylor, 2012) has argued elsewhere, developments in research education over the past three decades have meant that supervisors need to have a wide range of additional knowledge and skills – particularly the ability to respond effectively to cultural and social diversity among the student population – if they are going to offer research candidates the high quality learning experiences that they need and deserve.

WHERE TO FIND MORE SUPPORT

The Oxford Learning Institute at the University of Oxford has established a website dedicated to 'Improving your supervisory practice'. Available from: http://www.learning.ox.ac.uk/supervision/supervisor/improving/ (accessed 24 September 2013).

You may also find some useful ideas in the Vitae Database of Practice, originally developed by UK GRAD. The database is a searchable store of practice posted by universities and research institutes. While the majority of items submitted to the database focus on skill development for research candidates, it also includes support for supervisors.

REFERENCES

Ahern, K and Manathunga, C (2004) 'Clutch-starting stalled research students', *Innovative Higher Education*, 28(4): 237–254.

Akay, A (2008) 'A renaissance in engineering PhD education', *European Journal of Engineering Education*, 33(4): 401–413.

Bair, CR and Haworth, JG (2004) 'Doctoral student attrition and persistence: a meta-synthesis of research', in JC Smart (ed.) *Higher Education Handbook of Theory and Research X1X*. Dordrecht: Kluwer Academic Publishers, 481–533.

Barnes, BJ and Austin, AE (2009) 'The role of doctoral advisors: a look at advising from the advisor's perspective', *Innovative Higher Education*, 33: 297–315.

Casanave, C (2010) 'Dovetailing under impossible circumstances', in C Aitchison, B Kamler and A Lee (eds.) *Publishing Pedagogies for the Doctorate and Beyond*. London: Routledge.

Cohen, SM (2011) 'Doctoral persistence and doctoral program completion among nurses', *Nursing Forum*, 46(2): 64–70.

Craswell, G (2007) 'Deconstructing the skills training debate in doctoral education', *Higher Education Research and Development*, 26(4): 377–391.

Cryer, P (2006) *The Research Student's Guide to Success*. 2nd edn. Buckingham: Open University Press.

Dunleavy, P (2003) *Authoring a PhD*. Basingstoke: Palgrave Macmillan.

Gatfield, T (2005) An Investigation into PhD Supervisory Management Styles: Development of a dynamic conceptual model and its managerial implications. *Journal of Higher Education Policy and Management*, 27(3): 311–325.

Golde, C (2005) 'The role of the department and discipline in doctoral student attrition: lessons from four departments', *Journal of Higher Education*, 76(6): 669–700.

Grasso, M, Barry, M and Valentine, T (2009) *A Data-Driven Approach to Improving Doctoral Completion*. Washington, DC: Council of Graduate Schools. Available from: http://www.cgsnet.org/cgs-occasional-paper-series/university-georgia (accessed 24 September 2013).

Gurr, G (2001) 'Negotiating the "Rackety Bridge" – a dynamic model for aligning supervisory style with research student development', *Higher Education Research and Development*, 20(1): 81–92.

Hill, G (2011) 'Diffracting the practices of research supervision', in V Kumar and A Lee (eds.) *Doctoral Education in International Context: Connecting Local, Regional and Global Perspectives*. Malaysia: Universiti Putra Malaysia Press.

Kiley, M (2009) 'Identifying threshold concepts and proposing strategies to support doctoral students', *Innovations in Education and Teaching International*, 46(3): 293–304.

Kiley, M (2011) 'Government policy and research degree higher education', *Journal of Higher Education Policy and Management*, 33(6): 629–640.

Kiley, M and Wisker, G (2009) 'Threshold concepts in research education and evidence of threshold crossing', *Higher Education Research and Development*, 28(4): 431–441.

Lovitts, BE (2007) *Making the Implicit Explicit: Creating Performance Expectations for the Dissertation*. Sterling, VA: Stylus.

Lovitts, BE (2008) 'The transition to independent research: who makes it, who doesn't and why', *The Journal of Higher Education*, 79(3): 296–325.

Malfoy, J and Webb, C (2000) 'Congruent and incongruent views of postgraduate supervision', in M Kiley and G Mullins (eds.) *Quality in Postgraduate Research: Making Ends Meet*. Adelaide: Advisory Centre for University Education, the University of Adelaide.

Manathunga, C (2002) 'Early warning signs in postgraduate research education: a different approach to ensuring timely completions', *Teaching in Higher Education*, 10(2): 219–233.

McAlpine, L, Paulson, J, Gonslaves, A and Jazvac-Martek M (2012) '"Untold" doctoral stories: can we move beyond cultural narratives of neglect? *Higher Education Research and Development*, 31(4): 511–523.

McCulloch, A and Stokes, P (2008) *The Silent Majority: Meeting the Needs of Part-time Research Students*. London: Society for Research into Higher Education.

Mullins, G and Kiley, M (2002) 'It's a PhD, not a Nobel Prize: how experienced examiners assess research degrees', *Studies in Higher Education*, 27(4): 369–386.

Murray, R (2006). *How to Write a Thesis*. 2nd edn. Buckingham: Open University Press.

Murray, R (2009) *How to Survive Your Viva*. 2nd edn. Buckingham: Open University Press.

Park, C (2008) 'The end of the secret garden: reframing postgraduate supervision', *Research Supervision: an online journal*. Available from: http://www.lancs.ac.uk/celt/celtweb/files/ChrisPark.pdf (accessed 24 September 2013).

Phillips, R (2010) 'Encouraging a more enterprising researcher: the implementation of an integrated training programme of enterprise for PhD and postdoctoral researchers', *Research in Post-Compulsory Education*, 15(3): 289–299.

Quality Assurance Agency (QAA) (2012) *UK Quality Code for Higher Education – Chapter B11: Research Degrees*. Gloucester, Quality Assurance Agency.

Rudd, E (1985) *A New Look at Postgraduate Failure*. London: Society for Research into Higher Education and National Foundation for Educational Research. London: Nelson.

Ryan, J and Carroll, J (2005) '"Canaries in the coalmine' International Students in Western universities", in J Ryan and J Carroll (eds.) *Teaching International Students: Improving Learning for All*. London: Routledge, 3–10.

Seigal, L (2005) A Study of PhD Completion at Duke University. *Communicator*, XXXV111 (1). Washington, DC: Council of Graduate Schools.

Taylor, S (2012) 'Changes in doctoral education: implications for supervisors in developing early career researchers', *International Journal of Researcher Development*, 3(2): 118–138.

Taylor, S and Beasley, N (2005) *A Handbook for Doctoral Supervisors*. London: RoutledgeFalmer.

Tinkler, P and Jackson, C (2004) *The Doctoral Examination Process: A Handbook for Students, Examiners and Supervisors*. Buckingham: Open University Press and Society for Research into Higher Education.

Trafford, V and Lesham, S (2009) 'Doctorateness as a threshold concept', *Innovations in Education and Teaching International*, 46(3): 305–316.

Wang, T and Li, L (2011) 'Tell me what to do vs. 'guide me through it'. Feedback experiences of international doctoral students', *Active Learning in Higher Education*, 12: 101–112.

Wolff, L (2010) 'Learning through Writing: Reconceptualising the Research Supervision Process', *International Journal of Teaching and Learning in Higher Education*, 22(3): 229–237.

FURTHER READING

Boud, D and Lee A (eds.) (2009) *Changing Practices of Doctoral Education*. London: Routledge.

Lee, A (2012) *Successful Research Supervision*. London: Routledge.

14 Maximising student learning gain

Graham Gibbs

INTRODUCTION BY THE EDITORS

Professor Graham Gibbs has been an influential figure in the development of learning and teaching in UK higher education over the past twenty years or so. His research, publications and active engagement with learning and teaching at a wide range of institutions across the sectors have placed him in a unique position to offer a view of how to maximise student learning gain. Professor Gibbs' work is internationally followed and widely respected. In this chapter, to end Part 2 of the Handbook, the editors have invited him to provide our readers with an overview of key aspects of the learning experience that are crucial to ensure that students derive maximum learning gain from their university education. The three case studies he presents are from universities that are particularly well known to him.

(Heather Fry, Steve Ketteridge and Stephanie Marshall)

STARTING POINT

This chapter assumes that the purpose of all the guidance in other chapters about how to enhance those aspects of academic practice that are something to do with teaching is to increase how much students learn while they are at university: their learning gains. I emphasise *gains* here because learning *performance* is substantially determined by things out of teachers' control, particularly the grades of students entering your classes. The students who perform best at school also tend to perform best at university, even when university educational processes are not especially effective. If you teach in a high status, highly selective university, then your students will probably perform reasonably well, however well or badly you teach. But what determines learning gains, the difference between what students know and can do when they enter and when they leave, is largely determined by educational processes – by aspects of teaching, learning and assessment that teachers have choices about. This chapter considers what research evidence teachers should pay attention to (and, by implication, what not to bother paying so much attention to).

What follows is based on empirical evidence – on what the vast quantity of educational research tells us about the educational practices that lead to greater learning gains. A convenient summary of this evidence, written for policy formers, can be found in Gibbs (2010) and that report's detailed referencing will not be repeated here. The Further Reading at the end of the chapter identifies readable sources that provide a quick window on to the otherwise dispersed and technical educational research evidence.

The three case studies in this chapter have been chosen to illustrate pedagogic practices that operate across degree programmes and that are known to improve student learning gain.

WHAT DOESN'T MAKE A DIFFERENCE, OR IS OUT OF TEACHERS' CONTROL

I'll start by considering those aspects of universities that appear to make little or no difference to learning gains, or that are in any case beyond your control as a teacher, so that I can then move on to more worthwhile topics.

The funding available to spend on each student varies widely between institutions in the US, though less so in the UK. These funding differences make less difference than you might imagine. Additional funding could be used to do all kinds of things that are known to improve learning gains, such as reduce class sizes, increase close contact with teachers, increase feedback on assignments, and so on. In the UK, higher investment in learning resources (such as libraries) is associated with higher study hours. However, better funded institutions often do not actually use their funds to do these things to any greater extent than others, and teaching practices that are known to engage students best are no more prevalent in the better funded institutions than in less well-funded institutions. For example, in the UK, students experience small group classes taught by inexperienced postgraduates most frequently in the best funded universities, even though it is known that being taught by anyone other than full-time faculty reduces learning gains as well as retention and performance. And in some of the wealthy Ivy League universities in the US, it is uncommon for students to receive any feedback on their assignments from faculty until the later years of their study. I work at a small university that arranges small classes taught by academics despite its limited income, because small classes are known to improve learning.

Despite these idiosyncratic institutional practices there is still, on average, a positive impact of greater funding per student on student learning gains. However, institutions with very different levels of funding have been found to produce similar learning gains, meaning that additional funding does not always bring benefits. In the US, fees have increased enormously in recent decades while class sizes and other crucial variables have not improved. There is clearly scope to make much better use of funding than is currently common, and especially for better-funded universities to use their financial advantages to students' advantage. As teachers are not usually able to change the level of funding available to teach their students, this might not be of concern, but, to avoid despair, it is important to understand that much of the leverage lies elsewhere.

Next, does research strength make any difference? At the level of either individual teachers or individual academic departments, no one has managed to find any measure of research that consistently relates to any measure of teaching. Despite commonly held views, there are some perfectly sound measures of teaching that predict how much students learn, so the lack of a relationship is not a result of poor measurement tools. Some strong researchers are good teachers and some are weak. Some strong research departments are also strong as teaching departments, but some are weak. And many more are mediocre at both research and teaching. The perceived teaching strengths of research-intensive universities, in that their students perform better, are due almost entirely to their reputation, which attracts the higher entry grade students who then perform well. Neither reputation nor research strengths predict these students' learning gains. There may be educational processes that make good use of teachers' research prowess, but if so, they are clearly not used consistently enough for any overall pattern to emerge.

Nor does a PhD make you a better teacher, or the proportion of teachers with PhDs make a department or university better at producing learning gains. However, training in teaching (as opposed to training in research) does make teachers better and more effective as teachers. Training in how to teach improves students' ratings of teachers (using valid and reliable questionnaires), it develops teachers' understanding of teaching and learning and makes them more 'learning focused' in their decisions about teaching, and this enhances how their students go about their learning and their understanding. To achieve these benefits, training needs to be reasonably substantial (such as the 200 hours or so common in 'Postgraduate Certificates in Teaching in HE' in the UK).

In the UK, there is probably an *inverse* relationship between a university's proportion of trained researchers (holding PhDs) and its proportion of trained teachers. In the US, there is a strong *inverse* relationship between a university's research ranking and student satisfaction and even students' cognitive and affective learning gains. The department highlighted in Case study 14.3 is practically bottom of the research rankings in the UK in the discipline considered, but top of the discipline's teaching rankings, based on the **National Student Survey** (NSS).

If we want to understand where variation in students' learning gains comes from, we need to look not at pre-existing conditions in the universities (such as their reputation, selectivity, funding or research achievements), but at educational processes: what universities do with whatever resources, teachers and students they have.

The extent to which students are taught by part-time teachers, hourly-paid teachers and graduate teaching assistants usually negatively predicts student retention and performance. At the University of Oxford, the proportion of tutorials taught by anyone other than College Fellows (tenured full-time academics) negatively predicts students' degree classifications. In the UK, more than half of all small group teaching in the research elite **Russell Group** universities is now taught by doctoral students, and in institutions where there are fewer doctoral students, the proportion of teaching undertaken by what in the US are called 'adjunct faculty' has increased enormously.

Employing the right people as teachers is one of the biggest challenges to educational quality. This is not necessarily because part-time teachers are worse teachers (though graduate teaching assistants are often much worse) but because it is very difficult for them to understand how the programmes they are teaching and how their feedback on assignments contributes in order for them to align their efforts with that of others, to get to know students and support them outside of class, and so on. Being effective as a teacher involves a great deal more than classroom practice, and part-time teachers are often paid only for their class contact. I have encountered a course 'team' for a degree programme that consisted of four full-time academics, nine part-time teachers and 19 hourly-paid teachers. They had never all been in the same room together. Unsurprisingly, their students reported that they didn't understand what they were supposed to be doing and that marking standards were all over the place. In contrast, the University described in Case study 14.2 makes extensive use of part-time teachers but uses a range of mechanisms to ensure that this does not cause quality problems. There is clearly scope for other universities to use part-time teachers more cautiously than they currently do.

> ## Case study 14.1: The University of Oxford pedagogic system
>
> Everyone has heard of the Oxford tutorial system, but fewer understand what makes the overall pedagogic system work. Despite having less class contact than any other face-to-face university, and deliberately limited oversight of what teachers get up to, Oxford regularly stands alongside the Open University at the top of NSS rankings on questions about teaching, about assessment, about everything. How do they manage this?
>
> It might be argued that the very high level of research activity and achievement at Oxford (they are currently ranked third in the world) has something to do with it, but within Oxford, the research performance of departments is unrelated to their teaching performance in terms either of student grades or the extent to which students take a **deep approach** to learning.
>
> Tutorials obviously provide the 'close contact' that most students in higher education lack: an average of about an hour and a half per week one-to-one, -two or -three, and the equivalent of about 50 hours one-to-one over three years. What is more, almost all these tutorials are undertaken by academics, not by graduate teaching assistants.
>
> But it is what tutorials achieve out of class that is most important. Each hour of tutorial time generates on average about ten hours of out of class studying. That

is much more than lectures or seminars at other kinds of institution achieve, and results in Oxford having the hardest working students in the UK. There is more 'time on task' than anywhere else. And tutorials also generate huge quantities of feedback on assignments (that students undertake weekly, as preparation for each tutorial), most of it immediate, oral and highly personalised feedback. All of this assessment is '**formative** only' – for learning and most assuredly not for marks. Tutors are not supposed to even know what exams might contain, so they can concentrate on their tutee's learning. Oxford has far less **summative** assessment than anyone else. The ratio of formative-only to summative assessment at Oxford is about 10:1, whereas even at other elite universities it is usually about 1:10.

Oxford University spends more per student per year on their libraries and other learning resources than anyone else (and as much as ten times more than at some institutions), and students have easy access to whatever they need to read, including primary sources and archives. In England, funding on libraries predicts student effort and, again, Oxford students study more than anywhere else.

Finally, although they rely heavily on exams, they do so only after extended periods for 'revision' – often two or more months. Students describe the process of 'getting it all together' that revision for finals consists of as crucial to their learning, and they perceive exam demands as comprehensive and integrative, rather than involving selective question spotting for facts. This is very different to the last minute cramming that characterises most examination systems and that so corrupts the preceding learning.

However, such a pedagogic system inevitably costs more than conventional systems.

IMPROVING HOW STUDENTS LEARN

A crucial finding from the research literature is that what students do makes more difference to learning than what teachers do, and if you want to improve learning gains then it makes more difference to improve students and how students go about learning, than it does to improve teachers and how they go about teaching. The most obvious way to improve students is to recruit students with better grades. And universities who attract students with better school leaving grades also have the best performing students when they leave university. In the US, high school grades account for the lion's share of all variance in college grade point averages and have far more impact than teaching, class size, resources or anything else. However, recruiting better students does not, on its own, improve learning gains, which are not higher in selective institutions.

Improving the learning of students that you have recruited is not just an issue for central university student services that run 'study skills' courses. Improving students and what students do is best achieved within the curriculum, within classes, within assignments, within the feedback you give on assignments, and so on. It is the kinds of things teachers ask students to do, and how students are prompted to reflect on and develop how they do these things that determines how sophisticated and effective they become as learners, and hence how much they learn.

Students learn more when they have high 'self-efficacy'. This is similar to self-confidence but is domain specific: a student with high self-efficacy might say, 'This particular assignment looks challenging, but I am confident that, given my experience, provided I knuckle down I'll be able to tackle it well'. Students with low self-efficacy give up when faced with challenging tasks, or when they receive low marks. They assume they do not have the capacity to succeed. Students' self-efficacy can be built up by teachers and by pedagogic systems. For example, at the Open University (OU), many new science students gave up and dropped out early on, sometimes as soon as they got a low mark on their first assignment. By making the first four assignments easier, gradually building up to the previous standard by the fifth assignment; by making the first four pass/fail, with no marks; and by concentrating tutor's feedback on encouragement and building self-efficacy, the OU succeeded in improving student retention and also increased average marks in the end of course exam, even though more weak students took the exam.

Students who learn most have greater 'metacognitive awareness and control'. Successful students have a repertoire of ways of tackling reading, essays or problems and can explain to you why particular study demands are best met by doing things one way rather than another. They reflect on their effectiveness, use feedback more purposefully, improving themselves as students and becoming 'self-supervising'. Unsuccessful students have little or no self-awareness about how they study and use habitual methods in all contexts, without noticing whether they work well or not. Improving 'metacognitive awareness and control' involves encouraging students to be **reflective**, for example self-assessing their own assignments, keeping a log of how they spend their time, keeping a **learning journal** about how they tackle assignments, and discussing the learning process (and not just its content) in class and with other students, noticing that others do things differently and gradually understanding why.

A good example of the difference of emphasis between trying to improve teachers and trying to improve students concerns the efficacy of feedback. Teachers often spend more time writing feedback on assignments than they do teaching, yet the effectiveness of this feedback depends crucially on what students do with it. Successful students do quite different things with feedback than unsuccessful students. Changing what students do with your feedback can make more difference than changing your feedback. It is changing what students do in order to learn where the greatest leverage lies.

And most of all, students learn more when they work harder. While it is the case that some able students can succeed without working very hard, and some weaker students can work very hard without succeeding, overall if individual students work harder they will learn more and gain higher marks. And if whole cohorts work harder, then whole cohorts learn more and gain higher marks. This is the *'time on task'* principle. If students spend more time on the right learning tasks then they learn more. And possibly the most important thing a teacher does is to arrange things (and especially the way assessment works) so that students spend enough time on the right tasks.

This is especially important in the UK because its students currently do not work hard enough – in fact many work about half as many hours a week as they are supposed to and fewer hours a week than anywhere else in Europe – and the UK's semesters are shorter than elsewhere as well. In some subjects, the average number of hours students study per week is so low that full-time students study even fewer hours than part-time students should, and it would take them nine years to clock up the hours that the **Bologna Agreement** specifies for what is meant to be in a three-year Bachelor's degree programme.

Working against teachers' efforts to increase their students' time on task is the need today for many students to undertake paid work in parallel with their studies. In the US, students tend to 'work their way through college' by taking credits over an extended period, and often from more than one institution, while working to pay their way. In the UK, students seem to assume that they can complete a Bachelors' degree in three years while signed on as a full-time student, but only studying the hours of a part-time student while they work at a supermarket or in other casual employment. The research evidence is complex, but suggests that parallel work for pay reduces marks, progression and retention pretty much in proportion to the extent of that work. It also reduces academic and social integration (see the following).

CLASS CONTACT

While we have not seen students take to the streets demanding to be worked harder, they have argued vociferously for more class contact hours; however, evidence suggests that class contact hours, within quite a wide range, have no impact on student learning. One study found that if class contact hours were low, then students would study more out of class, and if class contact hours were high, then students would study less out of class, making total weekly hours pretty much exactly the same regardless of the amount of teaching. This relationship seems to hold up, except at very low levels of class contact hours. Once you are down below about six hours a week there is a danger of insufficient stimulation, structure, checking on learning and so on, and out of class study hours often drop as a consequence. However, the University of Oxford has class contact of less than six hours a week, in many subjects, and still has the highest total weekly study effort in the UK. Its use of tutorials works wonderfully well to generate enormous amounts of out of class studying. Lectures seem very unlikely to generate time on task to the same extent. But what matters is the way class contact is used and the way it generates students' engagement with their studies. There is currently a good deal of interest in designing courses in which the focus is on the design of out of class learning activity, with class contact designed specifically to support it. In contrast much conventional course design tends to revolve around the lectures, in the hope that students will do something or other out of class. Current evidence makes it clear that this is, at best, unrealistically optimistic.

Case study 14.2: The Open University pedagogic system

This case study is included here because this institution in the UK has very little of what is normally assumed to be crucial – class contact – but their pedagogic system still works very well. The Open University, a **distance learning** institution, has better NSS scores than most prestigious research universities and often tops the national rankings for teaching.

They have a number of characteristics that should actually make it very difficult for them to perform well pedagogically. Their 'cohort size' in terms of the number of students they enrol on a course can be over 10,000 and is seldom under 500. They have very little face-to-face teaching and on some courses, none at all. Their 7,000 tutors, who interact with students, are all part-time and are mostly not active researchers or even well qualified. Students are not on a campus, students are not well qualified educationally, they are almost all part-time, and so on. So how do they manage to teach so effectively?

The OU's class sizes, as students experience it in a tutor group, are actually small – usually 20 or smaller. Each tutor usually has only one class to teach, and so gets to know all students well. The fact that there may be 10,000 students enrolled on the same course does not impinge much on their experience except that the income generated by such numbers provides resources to produce outstanding quality learning materials, in print in their hands, or online. Enormous funds are allocated to learning materials production, infinitely more than is available to a conventional lecturer preparing lectures and handouts, and all of it produced by experienced academics working in collaborative teams, with external reviewers ensuring high standards. Open University students' access to the resources they need to study is often far better than that of face-to-face students competing for limited library resources or flinching at the cost of textbooks over and above the cost of their fees and their living expenses.

But the crucial component of their pedagogic system is their assessment. Students usually undertake five to eight assignments on a course – substantial assignments requiring a good deal of effort. And each assignment is allocated a good deal of tutor time in providing feedback. Over the course of a degree programme, OU students may receive ten times as much written feedback as students at many conventional institutions. And OU students have been found to make more use of that feedback than at conventional institutions. It is part of tutors' contracts to attend briefing and training sessions on topics such as giving useful feedback, and their pay covers training hours. The turn-round time of feedback is monitored, and the quality of the feedback is monitored by experienced senior tutors, who intervene and provide training and advice to tutors individually if they fall below the University's high standards.

The assignments are often linked in a long sequence so that all this feedback can **feedforward** to subsequent assignments over a ten month period, rather than there being one or two assignments over a much shorter course at conventional institutions. There has been very widespread exploitation of information technology, especially to engage students in interacting with each other and with tutors, and to produce and make available wonderful learning resources. But in essence, the Open University is a 'correspondence college' with most student effort devoted to undertaking sequences of assignments and much of the 'teacher' resource is allocated to providing quick and useful feedback on those assignments. And this pedagogic system works.

CLASS SIZE

Class size is such an important variable in understanding educational effectiveness in schools that it is used, in the form of a national average, to indicate the relative health of a country's educational system. By the 1980s, it was abundantly clear that in higher education, class size has a substantial impact on student performance, and in the UK often greater than the effect of students' school grades. Since then, class sizes have soared, especially in first-year courses when they are capable of doing most damage.

'Class size' effects are of different kinds for courses than for classes. Cohort sizes on courses affect social cohesion among students, the type of assessment methods used (that may reduce effort or the intellectual level required), and competition for learning resources (such as library books, computers and laboratory facilities) that may reduce effort and engagement. They often lead to fragmented staffing, with different teachers involved in lectures, seminars and marking, leading to incoherence – students may be less clear what they are supposed to be doing when in large courses. Large cohorts have also been found to lead to students adopting a **surface approach** to a greater extent – attempting only to memorise rather than understand course content. All kinds of things go wrong with large cohorts, and they markedly reduce student performance and retention.

For subjects that use specialist learning facilities such as laboratories and studios, increased cohort size reduces access – science students simply spend less time in the lab and arts students no longer have their own corner of the studio, but visit a shared space occasionally. This can dramatically alter the overall experience of studying a discipline and the educational goals that are achievable.

At the level of individual classroom experience, larger classes also cause problems. As discussion classes get larger the teacher may be tempted to speak for more of the time and students less. There is a risk that fewer students join in at all. The few students who do speak tend to ask for factual clarification rather than discuss ideas. It is easy to 'hide' so students prepare less well, and so on. If the demonstrable educational benefits of discussion groups are to be realised, they have to be small enough for all students to actually discuss.

There are exceptions to negative large class effects and it is possible to increase student performance despite large classes by adopting certain non-standard methods. But if class size increases without changes, the consequences are pretty predictable. Simply 'scaling up and thinning out' is not a successful strategy. In practice, it is more common for courses to change how they operate, as enrolment increases, in ways that maintain marks but reduce quality, for example by adopting multiple choice questions tests instead of essays. Learning gains may be reduced even if marks remain the same. In the past two decades in the UK, class sizes have doubled and doubled again and yet the proportion of students gaining good degrees has increased markedly.

As cohort size increases, there are some economies of scale with teaching, but not with assessment. Assessment costs increase in direct proportion to the number of students. So either assessment has to be trivialised or mechanised, to cut down marking time, or teachers end up spending more time on marking than on teaching. Either way, assessment and feedback problems then kick in.

ASSESSMENT AND FEEDBACK

Assessment usually has more impact than teaching does on what students study as well as how hard they study and how they go about their studying. There is enormous scope to improve learning gains by changing aspects of assessment, as demonstrated in Case study 14.3.

First, assessment demands generate time on task: students are very strategic nowadays and allocate their time very carefully. If work is not required, then it tends not to be done. A course with two assignments might generate work in the week leading up to the two submission deadlines, but little work in other weeks or on topics other than those addressed in the essays selected by the students, or the problems selected by the teacher on the problem sheets. And as noted earlier, time on task predicts learning gains. Examinations or tests with predictable and narrow questions also fail to elicit time on task or a reasonable spread of effort across topics as students make strategic decisions about what to risk not studying in depth, or at all.

Second, students learn more when they have a clear understanding of 'goals and standards' – what they are supposed to be learning and what their work would have to look like in order to achieve a pass or a top grade. Simply being explicit by stating **learning outcomes** or marking criteria in course documentation may not help students much. They need to see exemplars of good (and bad) work, and perhaps try marking it so they can calibrate their standards against those of their examiners. Self and **peer**

Table 14.1 Impact of TESTA

NSS question	NSS score		Improvement
	2011	2012	
Criteria clear	37%	96%	+59%
Assessment fair	50%	87%	+37%
Feedback prompt	73%	96%	+23%
Received detailed comments	56%	79%	+23%
Feedback helped	42%	79%	+37%
Overall satisfaction	48%	96%	+48%

Source: TESTA (2010)

assessment help. Seeing final year students' projects, and talking to them, can clarify what, after three years, students ought to be able to achieve. Quality assurance, whether in the form of institutions' own requirements for course documentation or external bodies' codes of practice and expectations, tends to emphasise clarity of goals and standards, especially the drafting of learning outcomes for both modules and degree programmes. But at least as important as clarity is the actual standard of these expectations. Students need to be challenged and stretched, and the standards need to be perceived by students as high. Clear but low standards achieve only a narrowing of focus and a limiting of effort.

Third, students learn more when they receive plenty of prompt feedback on their learning and on their assignments. 'Good practice emphasises prompt feedback' is one of the evidence-based 'Seven Principles of Good Practice in Higher Education' (see Table 14.1). In the UK, ratings on the NSS, which all graduating students complete, show that it is feedback that receives the lowest ratings of all aspects of their education – and also that it is usually difficult to improve. Case study 14.3, in contrast, offers an example of dramatically improved NSS ratings for assessment and feedback.

Case study 14.3: The University of Winchester: improving assessment and feedback through the TESTA project

It is known that assessment and feedback has a big impact on student learning, but is it possible to make changes to assessment that result in improvements to student learning? TESTA (Transforming the Experience of Students through Assessment) is a Higher Education Academy (HEA)-funded national project that helps degree programmes to diagnose problems with how their assessment regime supports students' learning. For example, despite many assignments, students may not work hard. Despite thorough documentation about learning outcomes and assessment criteria, students may be confused about what they are supposed to be doing. Despite teachers spending a long time marking and writing feedback on assignments, students may not find the feedback helpful – or even read it. And NSS scores for assessment and feedback questions might be very poor despite teachers feeling that they take these issues seriously. Nationally, NSS scores for assessment and feedback have been low and there is often resistance to attempts to improve them.

TESTA is based on an account of how assessment shapes how students respond to their courses, based on empirical and theoretical literature. It identifies conditions under which assessment supports student learning (see 'Principles of assessment', TESTA 2010). For example, 'Assessment supports student learning when it captures sufficient student time and effort and distributes that effort reasonably evenly across topics and weeks'. One assignment in week seven is likely to meet this condition poorly, but six assignments, one every two weeks, only one of which will be marked, at random, will probably achieve this condition quite well.

TESTA employs evaluation tools to reveal how well these conditions are met and how students behave in response to their perceptions of assessment demands. For example, how many assignments did students have to tackle, how hard did students actually work, how did they distribute their time and did they think it was possible to do well without working regularly? This data is discussed by all the teachers involved in the degree programme. TESTA then provides a repertoire of assessment strategies and tactics that can address identified weakness in courses and it uses the evaluation tools a year later to measure the impact of the changes made.

The most impressive evidence of the impact of TESTA comes from NSS scores. The first three degree programmes that used TESTA all ended up ranked top of the national rankings in their discipline. The data in Table 14.1 come from a Law degree programme and illustrate the scale of change that is possible.

Overall satisfaction increased further to 100 per cent in 2013 when this Law degree was ranked top in the UK. The average improvement in these NSS scores over this period, nationally, was about 1 per cent.

Over 20 Universities in the UK were using the TESTA approach to improving assessment at the time of publication, including a consortium of Russell Group research-intensive universities. TESTA is also used in Australia, India and elsewhere. The crucial point here is that it is possible to use 'evidence-based' approaches, based on the research literature about what exactly makes a difference to student learning, to make dramatic improvements in degree programmes in contexts where 'common sense' approaches to teaching and its improvement have failed.

STUDENT ENGAGEMENT

The crucial outcome of efforts to improve teaching is not just that students think the teaching is better (though that is nice to know), but that they are more engaged with their studies, both in terms of the quantity and quality of that engagement. For example, it makes a good deal of difference if the quality of engagement is characterised by students attempting to understand the course content and relate it to experience or other content, rather than only trying to memorise it for a test: taking a 'deep approach' rather than a 'surface approach'. In the US, a questionnaire called the **National Survey of Student Engagement** (NSSE) is used by over 800 institutions because it tells them exactly what they need to know in order to improve their education provision. Not only does it measure **engagement** so well that it predicts learning gains, but it also measures the extent to which students experience the pedagogic practices that are known to increase engagement, such as close contact with teachers, prompt feedback on assignments, and so on. Additional practices that also increase engagement, not already mentioned in this chapter, include the extent of collaborative learning (as contrasted with solitary competitive learning). The NSSE is starting to be used in the UK using a specially adapted version (for further information, see Buckley, 2013). Unlike questionnaires based around satisfaction or ratings of aspects of provision, the NSSE tells you which practices students do not get enough of, and therefore which practices to work on. In the US, there is abundant evidence that using the NSSE improves student engagement and hence learning gains.

THE SEVEN PRINCIPLES OF GOOD PRACTICE IN UNDERGRADUATE EDUCATION

These principles are underpinned by extensive research evidence and provide a convenient summary of much of what is known about how to improve student learning:

1   Good practice encourages student–faculty contact;
2   Good practice encourages cooperation among students;
3   Good practice encourages active learning;
4   Good practice gives prompt feedback;
5   Good practice emphasises time on task;
6   Good practice communicates high expectations; and
7   Good practice respects diverse talents and ways of learning (Chickering and Gamson, 1987).

SOCIAL AND ACADEMIC INTEGRATION AND RETENTION

In the US, student retention has hovered at around 50 per cent in higher education for several decades, and significant progress in understanding how to improve retention has developed at roughly the same pace that the problems faced have become worse. In the UK, retention varies from a steady 98 per cent at the University of Oxford to around 60 per cent at some institutions: much lower than two decades ago. The best predictor of likelihood of staying the course is students' past educational achievement. National university completion rates correspond roughly with the proportion of the age group entering that nation's higher education system – when 10 per cent of 18-year-olds enter university, retention tends to be very much higher than when 50 per cent enter. As participation widens, average educational achievement on entry (commonly demonstrated by A-level grades) drops and retention drops. But there are a whole range of things that are known to make a difference to retention that concern the way institutions operate and how students are taught and assessed. Institutions that adopt methods that are known to work have succeeded in improving retention.

The most important underlying concept here is 'academic and social integration'. It is what is missing in large anonymous classes, in huge cohorts where students do not know anyone, and in modular courses where students do not have a stable group of students (of which they feel they are a member) around them as they study. To illustrate what is often missing, one of the most effective ways to improve retention is to get students to form study groups, of perhaps eight, that agree among themselves which modules they will all study next, so that they progress through the university as a stable group. They trade off freedom of choice for a form of social integration that they create themselves, and it works.

Close contact with teachers, or a special teacher, also has an impact. Students who make it all the way through despite their background often attribute this to an individual teacher acting as a kind of mentor who took an interest in their progress. Part-time students' retention is worse than full-time students' retention, even when educational background is taken into account. Students on residential campuses have better retention than those who live at home and commute to urban universities with dispersed buildings. But urban universities can simulate some of the effects of residential campuses by employing collaborative learning, engineering social contacts, developing their Students' Union, and so on. There are currently a range of initiatives, concerned with **students as partners** and active involvement in the life of universities that are attempting to increase engagement, retention and learning.

COLLABORATIVE LEARNING AND STUDENTS PERFORMING TEACHING ROLES

The vast majority of learning I undertook as an undergraduate was solitary and competitive. The literature makes it clear that social and collaborative learning leads to much better learning gains. Peer tutoring, peer assessment, group projects, independent study groups, peer supervision and mentoring – all kinds of mechanisms have been developed and evaluated, and in the main they improve student learning. Specific practices with detailed specifications as to how they should operate, such as Supplemental

Instruction (SI, in which students who performed well last year help students this year), have been evaluated hundreds of times and almost always increase student performance by one grade. Such social and collaborative practices engage students well and make them active in their learning roles, taking more responsibility for their learning. In fact, these roles often resemble teaching roles. When students do for themselves and each other what teachers might previously have done for them, this tends to work rather well (as well as being very cheap!). As teachers, we tend to assume we are indispensable. Not only is this not the case, but in fact students themselves are, in these cash-strapped times, the main untapped educational resource.

CONCLUSIONS AND OVERVIEW

If university teachers and degree programme directors wish to improve how much their students learn from their studies, then they should pay more attention to:

- Improving students as learners so that they undertake their studies in more sophisticated and effective ways;
- Engaging those students in more study hours (time on task) and at a deeper level (rather than encouraging or allowing a 'surface approach');
- Making learning resources more easily accessible;
- Increasing the extent to which students understand educational goals, what they should be doing, and to what standard, so they can supervise themselves, and setting these goals high, so as to challenge and engage students;
- Arranging for more studying to be undertaken collaboratively, instead of privately and competitively;
- Increasing 'close' contact with teachers;
- Providing more frequent, prompt and useful feedback on assignments, and designing sequences of assignments such that students are bound to use feedback to help them with the next thing to do;
- Increasing the ratio of formative to summative assessment, so that most assignments are for learning, not for marks; and
- Training teachers and limiting the use of part-time and inexperienced teachers without adequate quality safeguards.

REFERENCES AND FURTHER READING

Buckley, A (2013) *Engagement for Enhancement: Report of a UK Survey Pilot*. York: Higher Education Academy. Available from: http://www.heacademy.ac.uk/resources/detail/nss/engagement_for_enhancement (accessed 31 January 2014).

Chickering, AW and Gamson, ZF (1987) 'Seven principles for good practice in undergraduate education', *American Association for Health Education Bulletin*, 39(7): 3–7. [This is a succinct summary of the 'seven principles', each of which are based on extensive research evidence.]

Gibbs, G (2010) *Dimensions of Quality*. York: Higher Education Academy. Available from: http://www.heacademy.ac.uk/resources/detail/evidence_informed_practice/Dimensions_of_Quality (accessed 31 January 2014). [This is the place to start if you are interested in where all this research evidence comes from. It provides a detailed summary and references to most of the key sources.]

The following four publications are examples of the kinds of research evidence that this chapter is based on. The Hattie and Marsh article pulls together 80 studies of the vexed question as to whether there is actually any relationship between research excellence and teaching excellence. The HEPI report summarises data from one of its large-scale surveys about, among other things, students' class contact hours and independent learning hours in English universities. The Kuh and Pascarella article looks at whether prestigious universities with highly selective student entry actually provide their students with better educational provision. The Pascarella and Terenzini book has a good summary, and makes clear just how extensive and long-standing the research evidence is, but the detailed chapters are hard going.

Hattie, J and Marsh, HW (1996) 'The relationship between research and teaching: a meta-analysis', *Review of Educational Research*, 66(4): 507–542.

Higher Education Policy Institute (HEPI) (2007) *The Academic Experience of Students in English Universities (2007 Report)*. Oxford: Higher Education Policy Institute.

Kuh, GD and Pascarella, ET (2004) 'What does institutional selectivity tell us about educational quality?', *Change*, 36(5): 52–58.

Pascarella, ET and Terenzini, P (2005) *How college Affects Students: A Third Decade of Research, Volume 2*. San Francisco, CA: Jossey-Bass.

TESTA http://www.testa.ac.uk/ [This is a web site about the TESTA project, and provides the conceptual and empirical underpinnings, evaluation tools and practical advice about assessment that many institutions are now using in evidence-based attempts to improve student experience and learning.]

TESTA (2010) *Principles of Assessment*. Available from: http://www.testa.ac.uk/index.php/resources/best-practice-guides/127-principles-of-assessment (accessed 31 January 2014).

Part 3
Teaching and learning in the disciplines

Part 3
Teaching and learning
in the disciplines

15 The experimental sciences

Nathan Pike

INTRODUCTION

The experimental sciences include the diverse life sciences, which can be broadly classified within biology, as well as the physical sciences of chemistry and physics. The boundaries between these fast-moving disciplines are becoming increasingly blurred and students will often seek to undertake courses of study that provide learning in several experimental sciences. The experimental sciences also encompass fields that are burgeoning in size, such as the biomedical sciences (which provide teaching and learning in basic or applied scientific knowledge and skills that are relevant to healthcare and medical activities) and several of the systems sciences, which are themselves interdisciplinary.

Although both the diversity and number of students and practitioners in the experimental sciences are huge, the contexts of these sciences have much in common and the key issues for teaching and learning apply broadly.

This chapter sets out a number of significant prevailing contextual factors that continue to influence acquisition of learning and delivery of teaching in the experimental sciences. It discusses key learning and teaching methods within these disciplines while highlighting innovative and effective practices. Some of these issues are relatively unique to the experimental sciences whilst others also pertain to other disciplines. The aim is to at least touch on a number of the most pertinent issues facing students and practitioners working within the changing teaching and learning landscapes of the experimental sciences.

CONTEXTUAL CONSIDERATIONS

Transition into higher education and subsequent retention

The transition from secondary or further education into HE can be especially challenging for students. They often reflect that it is a time when both their social and family circumstances change drastically whilst they are also faced with the challenges of a new academic culture and a demanding and independently managed workload (Scott et al., 2012). Sensitively designed induction activities and student briefings are pivotal to supporting students through this transition.

The pursuant challenge to facilitating the transition into HE is that of supporting students to progress successfully through their courses of study. Poor preparedness in quantitative skills (including mathematics and statistics) is a strong predictor of poor retention in Science, Technology, Engineering and Mathematics (STEM) degrees (President's Council of Advisors on Science and Technology, 2012). Students routinely need special support in these subjects. Examples of such support might include bridging and remedial programmes, contextualisation of quantitative learning within appropriate discipline-specific contexts, and facilitation of team-based learning exercises. Teaching practitioners need also to ensure that they hold accurate assumptions with regard to their students' prior knowledge. The simple first steps are to familiarise oneself with the entry qualification requirements for the programmes and courses for which you teach and to be aware of differences in the academic competencies of diverse student groups.

Interrogating practice

- What proportion of your students achieved basic, moderate and advanced levels of mathematics prior to entering HE? What proportion of your students have studied biology, chemistry and/or physics prior to entering HE?
- Have you made your students explicitly aware of what they need to do to succeed in their studies? Which assessment types are new to them?
- Do you provide your students with constructive feedback on their work during the first weeks/months of their studies?

Employability

The urgent demand for increasing numbers of skilled graduates from the experimental sciences is routinely acknowledged (House of Lords Select Committee on Science and Technology, 2012; President's Council of Advisors on Science and Technology, 2012). A mismatch between employers' requirements and the graduates that Higher Education Institutions (HEIs) produce is also often lamented. There exists amongst some practitioners a view that the pure sciences need not have a vocational component and that the primary goal must always be learning of excellent quality. Of course, facilitating excellent learning and providing employability skills are not incompatible. With rising tuition fees, it is only natural that prospective students are increasingly using subsequent **employability** as the key criterion in deciding what and where to study.

Certain skills, such as familiarity with laboratory and technical equipment, or relevant field experience will be both sought after by employers and readily apparent to graduates seeking to sell their expertise in the best possible light. Other attributes such as **transferable skills** and critical thinking abilities may be less apparent to recently graduated job seekers. In an investigation conducted by seven learned societies within the biological sciences, employers' ten most sought after skills (in unranked order) were analytical and research skills; communications skills; computer and technical literacy; flexibility and ability to multitask; initiative and self-motivation; interpersonal abilities; leadership and management skills; planning and organisational skills; problem-solving and creativity; and teamwork (Biochemical Society et al., 2012). Clearly, degrees in the experimental sciences already furnish great proficiency in most if not all of these areas and, with careful consideration, can be honed to do so with even more success. A key element to this success is careful planning to embed transferable skills within curricula.

In the UK, there has in recent years been a push for the uptake by HEIs of the **Higher Education Achievement Report (HEAR)**, which is intended to assist graduates in demonstrating the range of their skills to employers. Its main purpose is to summarise and capture the totality of a student's performance whilst in HE (Burgess Implementation Steering Group, 2012). Naturally, other less-formal skills audits with students can convey similar benefits. Such audits may be managed by teaching staff but initiatives that are predominantly student-led may be equally if not more effective.

Case study 15.1: Enhancing the employability of biology graduates

BSET (Biology Student Employability Tutorials) is a novel student-designed programme aimed at improving key employability skills in Biology undergraduates while also facilitating the opportunity for students to engage in small-group learning. In developing this programme, a group of undergraduate student interns contacted a wide array of graduate employers to research the skill set that biology graduates require in order to be successful in the current market. The employers approached came from diverse sectors and were not all traditional recruiters of Biology graduates. Interviews with potential employers were conducted by telephone, Skype, email and face-to-face. Formal written responses were recorded from over 25 different employers and more informal conversations were carried out with many more.

Skills identified through this research included some expected skills, such as analytical and quantitative, teamwork, communication and leadership. Some more unexpected skills included storytelling, resilience, debating, networking and commercial awareness. One benefit of engaging students in the design process was that prospective employers were extremely willing to engage with students, more so than they might have been with academic staff, spending substantial time discussing their requirements with students.

The students incorporated the development of these core employability skills into a tutorial programme aimed at improving them. This programme now helps biology students develop a strong foundation of analytical, presentational and communication skills that will be helpful for securing employment after graduation.

The engagement of student interns to research graduate attributes from prospective employers was very well received by the employers and was highly successful. The tutorials are challenging because they use academic resources and frames of reference. The tutorials have embedded flexibility so tutors and groups can employ choice and discipline-based specificity in their use of materials. The student interns experience pronounced personal development through their experiences and all have been very successful in securing jobs themselves.

The outcome of this project was the development of a two-year tutorial programme with five tutorials in each of four semesters. In addition, there is guidance material for each tutorial, detailed staff preparation, student preparation and suggestions of how the tutorial can be structured. The programme is pitched at students in Years 2 and 3 within a four-year Scottish Higher Education Honours degree. The programme is flexible in delivery and can be tailored towards specific bioscience interests of each tutorial group. For example, tutorials regularly use primary research literature and the paper can be selected from the area of staff and/or student interest. Furthermore, because guidance materials are sufficiently detailed, the tutorials can be student-led or run by relatively inexperienced staff.

This model of engaging students in curriculum development has proven highly beneficial to our institution and to the students themselves and is one that could be easily replicated elsewhere.

(Clare Peddie and Gerald Prescott, University of St Andrews)

Interrogating practice

- List the five key employability skills that your programme engenders in your students.
- What steps could you take to highlight these skills so that they are better appreciated by your students?

Curricula: liberties and constraints

Most HEIs are autonomous institutions that, in principle, are free to determine structure and content for their courses. In practice, this freedom is often limited by both passive and active influences. Passive influences might include simple inertia whereby a curriculum changes very little mostly because the path of least resistance is to recapitulate what went before. Where a lecturer is taking on an established course or programme, or substituting for another member of staff, the scope for modifying the curriculum will again be limited. Where substantial curriculum change is possible, there is also often a lag between design and implementation because institutional validation processes and approvals from steering committees are usually required.

More active controls over the curriculum are exerted by the agencies and bodies that fund HE, by quality assurance bodies, by accrediting organisations and by employers. Funding agencies influence curricula by ring-fencing funds for direct grants to HEIs or via scholarship schemes for students to study subjects designated as being vulnerable or of strategic importance, many of which fall within the experimental sciences (Higher Education Funding Council for England, 2011). Bodies such as the UK **Quality Assurance Agency** have an integral role to play in producing **Subject Benchmark Statements** (Quality Assurance Agency for Higher Education, 2007–2008) and conducting Institutional Reviews, which evaluate institutionally set minimum thresholds for academic standards. It should be noted that an unintended side effect of ensuring quality is a tendency to encourage a homogenisation in provision and in apportionment of teaching effort across HEIs. Such agencies also routinely admit that their potential to influence the quality of provision above the pre-defined thresholds is limited.

Accreditation of degrees by external bodies is an increasing trend and, indeed, one that is often actively encouraged by governments (e.g. House of Lords Select Committee on Science and Technology, 2012). Professional organisations such as the Institute of Biomedical Science, the Institute of Physics, the Royal Society of Chemistry and the Society of Biology now routinely accredit courses within their spheres of interest and the costs of the accreditation process sometimes enjoy governmental subsidisation (e.g. Society of Biology, 2013). The influence of employers is felt through their involvement with accrediting bodies, through advice that they provide directly to HEIs and by virtue of the fact that taught programmes are increasingly being structured to facilitate **industrial placements**. Such placements can vary from relatively short extra-curricular summer internships to a dedicated and integrated year in industry, which will often result in a four-year undergraduate degree.

Internationalisation

The spirit of endeavour that characterises the experimental sciences knows no borders and cross-border collaboration is becoming increasingly common in scientific enterprises. Teaching and learning presents no exception to this trend and, particularly at postgraduate level, students seek to develop a globally informed perspective on their disciplines. **Transnational education** (in which students are based in countries other than the home country of the awarding HEI) is on the increase and many UK HEIs are opening international campuses. The countries of East Asia and the Middle East are particular hotspots for this growth. There is also a strong trend for **internationalisation** of curricula such that students can achieve a broad understanding of their field and develop inter-cultural competencies and new academic literacies that will enhance both their scientific abilities and their employment prospects.

Interrogating practice

- From an international point of view, what are the key academic and cultural differences in the teaching, learning and general conduct within your discipline?
- How could you expose your students to the experience of doing science in dissimilar international contexts?

LEARNING AND TEACHING METHODS

Large groups

The need to teach to large groups of students is common in the experimental sciences. For the most part, the size of these large groups is of the order of one to a few hundred students in a lecture theatre (or, occasionally, video-linked lecture theatres). However, the advent of the Massive Open Online Courses (**MOOCs**) has been warmly welcomed in our disciplines and it is increasingly possible to be involved in teaching student groups that are tens of thousands or even hundreds of thousands strong.

Lecturing (see Chapter 7) is perhaps the most common and well established of instructional modes. In its most rudimentary form of standing in front of a silent audience and attempting to deliver information, it is not without its problems. Indeed, it has long been said in jest (but not without some justification) that some forms of lecturing represent 'a process by which the contents of the textbook of the instructor are transferred to the notebook of the student without passing through the heads of either party' (Huff, 1954: 47). Of course, this need not be the case and the first step to a straightforward remedy is to make lectures more interactive. A broad definition of interaction should ideally be adopted such that students are free to speak both with the lecturer and, at appropriate times, amongst themselves. To encourage interaction, tell your students the rules of your lectures so that they know that it is fine to step outside of the passive behaviour to which they may be accustomed in other lectures. It is helpful to sit in on a colleague's lectures that generally receive positive feedback. (It is no coincidence that the best appreciated lectures also tend to be the most interactive!) There is huge value in obtaining constructive feedback from colleagues who agree to observe your lectures and, indeed, in developing good practice by observing the lectures of others. These practices of peer observation are becoming increasingly common and, for some practitioners such as probationary lecturers, may even be mandatory.

Remember that different students learn in different ways and, where possible, try to incorporate multiple learning aids within your lectures. In addition to text-based visual aids, the use of photographs, diagrams, graphs, short videos and physical models (e.g. molecular models to be passed around the lecture theatre) can be very effective.

Common strategies to encourage students to be active participants in lectures can be remarkably simple and include:

- Asking questions of the class and taking one or several verbal answers;
- Briefly breaking the large lecture group into smaller '**buzz groups**' to discuss an issue or problem and thereafter taking verbal opinions from a sample of these groups; and
- Surveying the whole class by asking students to raise their hands or by using flashcards.

Strategies such as these, which represent a shift towards student-centred learning in lectures, can have remarkable, positive effects on student performance (e.g. Armbruster et al., 2009). Stay flexible during your lectures and don't worry if it turns out that you have not been able to incorporate all your intended content within a given lecture. (If necessary, it is often possible to catch up in a subsequent lecture.) Facts are important within our disciplines, but concepts are even more important. Finish each of your lectures well by giving a succinct summary of the key issues so that students can start to reflect on these and incorporate them into their learning.

A strategy that uses technology to support large groups outside the lecture theatre is set out in Case study 15.2. Technological advances have driven key advances in lecturing. One such advance is 'flipping' or 'classroom inversion'. This strategy generally uses online means to provide students with the lecture content (e.g. visual presentations, videos, readings, problem sets and other activities) before the lecture. Lecture time is thus free for students to actively explore the material with lecturers and to raise queries or difficulties that can then be resolved (Mazur, 2009). **Lecture flipping** can work well for both large and small groups. An example of this approach is presented in Case study 15.3.

As already mentioned, simple real-time surveys of large classes can be conducted by asking students to raise their hands or to show flashcards. Technology can be used to arrive at similar but more nuanced results. Audience response systems or 'clickers' usually come in the form of handheld electronic devices that enable students in a class to provide multiple choice or short text answers to lecturers' pre-prepared questions. The responses can then be instantly tabulated or plotted, shown to the class and used as an indication of whether the material is being understood. The popularity of personal

Internet-enabled smartphones (which can fulfil the same function via web forms or specialised apps) means that investing in dedicated hardware is no longer essential to harness this pedagogical tool. Of course, as with all tools, it is possible to overuse clickers and cause student fatigue. They should thus be used considerately and in moderation.

Case study 15.2: Supporting a large undergraduate class using an asynchronous online forum

Large undergraduate classes can be challenging for students. Opportunities for personalised feedback are few and little adjustment can be made for students of different academic interest, academic ability or national/cultural background. How can a small number of staff provide effective feedback and support to hundreds of students?

Essential Genetics is an introductory course in Genetics at the University of Glasgow. The course is taught by only two members of staff but is taken by 300–400 students. The course is taught over 12 weeks and involves 22 lectures and two laboratory classes. The students are academically and culturally diverse and Genetics is the intended degree subject for only a small fraction.

We choose to support our students using the asynchronous online forum capability of our Moodle **virtual learning environment** (VLE). Such asynchronous forums give every student the opportunity to ask a question and involve quieter students and international students because they can take time to reflect upon and to frame their comments. Such forums can also stimulate student debate and learning and may build a sense of community.

All students can freely post questions and comments on the Essential Genetics course forum and both staff and students can respond. All authors are visible to all forum users. The students are told that any questions (scientific or course management) must be posted on the Moodle forum and that, in turn, the staff guarantee that they will check the forum frequently and regularly.

Staff activity on the forum is purely reactive: we respond to posts from students. Staff monitor the forum once a day or so and reply with short prompts or brief answers to student posts with the aim of stimulating thought and deepening understanding. As the course progresses, the students tend to post both questions and replies much more actively: by the end of the course, all students regularly monitor the forum and over a third of them have posted on it.

In formal surveys, the vast majority of students find the online forum very useful. When asked if the Facebook social networking platform would be preferable to the VLE, most students respond in the negative. They report that knowing where to go for reliable support with oversight from staff is much more important than the host environment.

Staff participation is key to catalysing student activity on the forum. Students are now requesting the deployment of equivalent forums in their other courses. We estimate that contributing to the Essential Genetics forum takes approximately 5–10 minutes of staff time per day to support over 300 students. We think that this modest commitment (which is more than offset by the release from individual course-related email messages) has a huge benefit for the student experience.

(Joseph V. Gray, University of Glasgow)

Interrogating practice

- Do your lectures employ different styles to cater to a diverse student group?
- What strategies for making lectures more interactive would work best in your context?
- If you were to use clickers, what questions could you ask of your students to establish their knowledge of the key learning outcomes?

Small groups

Teaching and learning activities that take place in **small groups** (such as tutorials, seminars and journal clubs) are very common. Done well, small-group learning can also be highly effective in increasing student learning (e.g. Wood, 2009). Particularly in situations such as tutorials that permit lecturers and tutors to work within relatively low student to staff ratios, it is essential that you have current knowledge of practical issues such as scheduling, examination formats, assignment requirements and assessment rubrics (including weightings assigned to assessable components).

Near-universal issues to discuss in tutorials include how to write a structured scientific essay; understanding plagiarism (and how to avoid committing it); searching for information (especially within academic databases); and evaluating evidence presented in the primary literature, the grey literature, the popular press and online sources.

Problem-based learning (PBL) involves the use of activities that require students to acquire new knowledge before solving a problem. These activities are now being commonly designed and utilised. PBL requires a relatively deep approach to learning and encourages students to develop the skills to acquire knowledge independently and to conduct critical analysis. Furthermore, when PBL happens in groups, collaborative learning, teamwork and additional communication skills are also developed (Allen and Tanner, 2003).

Peer-led team learning (PLTL) is a particularly powerful form of small-group learning in which more able and/or more senior students assist their fellow students by leading them through discussions, problem sets and other activities. This type of small-group learning is distinguished mainly by the fact that team leaders (who are usually trained by teaching staff in the first instance) play an instrumental role. There are tangible benefits both for the students working with the leaders (e.g. Preszler, 2009) and for the leaders themselves (e.g. Tenney and Houck, 2004).

Interrogating practice

- How would you assist small groups to work effectively without facilitation from teaching staff?
- Which group behaviours tend to enhance learning and which ones tend to detract from it?

Laboratory work

Laboratory exercises serve an integral function in bridging the gap between theoretical and practical knowledge. They should be carefully designed such that students are encouraged to do more than follow a recipe with the goal of arriving at the correct solution (or, indeed, an incorrect one). For the reasons articulated earlier in the context of PBL, simple expository laboratory activities do little to engage students. Lab exercises should ideally be driven mostly by a process of enquiry in which students have at least some opportunity (with appropriate guidance) to decide on their own experimental approaches such that positive learning outcomes are generated regardless of the overall success of the experiment. The design of such activities does require careful consideration but this effort is invariably rewarding (Adams, 2009). Non-formulaic activities also represent wonderful enhancements for the social learning opportunities that lab work provides.

Deploying simple strategies can easily lead to quick wins in teaching and learning in the lab. Postgraduate and postdoctoral assistants are often recruited to assist students as laboratory demonstrators. It is important that these demonstrators understand the key learning outcomes of the lab, of the underlying concepts, of the procedures that students will follow and of the techniques in which the students should gain experience. Best practice may often entail setting aside 30 minutes or so before the lab exercise for a discussion with demonstrators and to provide them with a brief walkthrough. Pre-lab reading materials can also be used to facilitate student engagement and students can be encouraged to do this reading by employing associated pre-lab quizzes (which can be oral, online or paper-based).

Interrogating practice

- How could you better instil in your students an appreciation of the value of enquiry-based lab work?

Fieldwork

Fieldwork presents another opportunity for enquiry-based learning and is a principal component of many of the experimental sciences. It is often less formal than other learning opportunities and, as a consequence, often results in stronger communities of learning for both students and teaching staff. It is perhaps for these reasons that fieldwork provision remains strong, even though it is often demanding in terms of financial, travel and staffing resources (Maw et al., 2011). Of course, fieldwork can be made more economical by increasing the emphasis on pre-fieldwork activities and by using mobile and online technologies such as data loggers, tablet devices, global positioning system (GPS) devices and group data sets constructed simultaneously online such that time in the field can be reduced without impacting on the quality of the experience. Fieldwork logs and reflective student diaries can also play a critical role in helping students to appreciate the transferable skills (such as communication, teamwork, experiential learning abilities, project management, risk assessment and self-discipline) which they can then highlight to prospective employers.

Interrogating practice

- What are the top three transferable skills engendered during your institution's fieldwork activities?

Technology-enhanced learning

Online resources and activities can facilitate a great deal of flexibility for students to explore materials at their own pace. Some subject matter is ideally presented online with the aid of computers and handheld devices, while other subject matter is not (e.g. that which lends itself to **kinaesthetic learning** or which would ideally coincide with the development of relevant motor skills). Well-planned **blended learning** (see also

Chapter 10) can provide a solution that represents the best of both worlds. Besides providing us with an effective means of delivering learning, online tools very often convey the benefit of allowing our students flexibility in terms of the time and place in which they learn.

Technology-enhanced learning tools can include on-demand video presentations, interactive quizzes, virtual microscopes and even virtual field trips and lab activities (Peat and Taylor, 2005). As expected, for some of the more complex activities, there are limitations to the effectiveness of online simulation (e.g. Stuckey-Mickell and Stuckey-Danner, 2007) and it is often the case that virtual labs and virtual field trips are recommended as enhancements, rather than outright replacements (Ramasundaram et al., 2005).

Case study 15.3: Classroom inversion and Just-in-Time teaching for biochemistry students

Just-in-Time Teaching (JiTT) is an example of blended learning that uses online learning to gain information to produce classroom activities tailored to students' current needs. I teach protein crystallography to second year biochemists. My overall intended learning outcome is that the students are able to read and analyse a research article describing protein crystal structures. In order to achieve this, the students need to grasp various difficult concepts linked to the technique. JiTT allowed me to move some of the practical details of the technique out of the classroom to give us more time to focus on the difficult concepts in class. Also, I hoped the pre-class work would motivate students to ask questions and discuss ideas.

The students would read through a portion of the course notes online before each lecture, complete a short reading comprehension quiz and answer a couple of open-ended questions that allowed them to comment on what they found difficult. The quizzes closed half a day before the class to allow me time to read the responses and plan the class. The class would comprise of some explanations, some clicker questions and associated peer discussion, 1-minute papers on concepts and some demonstrations with props and movies.

Feedback was collected from students in a variety of formats, including in-class quizzes and questionnaires, online questionnaires and an informal focus group. It was clear that there was a core group of the students who really liked this approach and felt it helped them learn better. In particular, they liked online course notes, the use of online and in-class quizzes to test their understanding, and the fact that the classes focused on areas of need. They also commented that spending twice as long thinking about the material (in class and out of class) increased their retention of it when they came to revise. A few students did not like the approach and preferred 'normal lectures'. Others found frustrations in the quality of the online questions (which I'm improving) and the fact that the classes didn't always address all the difficult points.

The best facet of this approach for the teacher is the increased dialogue with the students that gives you a much clearer picture of what they understand. This sometimes leaves you with some uncomfortable choices regarding content and volume, but is immensely useful. The major downside is the time taken to prepare classes and resources, although I am optimistic that this decreases over time. The major factor to be aware of is to manage student expectations as you only have time to address points that the majority need help with. Therefore, it is also important that your online learning and quizzes are clearly aligned to the key topics you would like to address in class.

(Hazel Corradi, University of Bath)

Assessment and feedback

Written examinations, essays and report-style assignments, short answer quizzes, multiple choice tests, practical and project reports, and oral and poster presentations are all common in the experimental sciences. Historically, these were often presented to students in a summative fashion (i.e. at the end of a taught programme with a view to simply obtaining a record of students' final proficiency). Happily, in recent times, there has been a decided shift towards using these assessment tools in a formative fashion (i.e. as several assessments, each of relatively modest weight and spread across a course of study such that instructors can gauge students' learning and provide timely feedback for improvement in future assessments). Of course, the ability to provide timely feedback has been improved with new technology. Online whole-class written feedback was covered in Case study 15.2. Personalised audio feedback (the subject of Case study 15.4) and video feedback (including screen-capture-based videos that contain both visual and audio annotations on students' work) can now feasibly be produced personally and with only modest effort by individual instructors (Jones et al., 2012).

Case study 15.4: Making use of audio feedback

Growing class sizes often lead to heavier academic workloads and more lag in the system between submission and return of work. Audio feedback is highly engaging for students and helps them appreciate that tutors care about their learning. Students are also much more likely to open audio files delivered online compared to collecting written feedback from a designated physical area.

Although producing audio files is relatively quick (with the rule of thumb being that 1 minute of audio is equal to 6 minutes of writing feedback), uploading them to a server and notifying students can take longer than simply annotating a written assignment. A solution to this is a simple click-record/share/listen design with no additional steps for staff or students to negotiate. A variety of technical solutions are available to provide such services, from highly expensive institution-wide commercial systems, such as Turnitin GradeMark, to low cost or free audio recording and sharing designs, such as SoundCloud (which allows direct online recording and sharing of audio files) or DropBox (which allows online sharing of audio files that need to be created on the user's local computer). Shared files can be made public or, as is more appropriate for feedback purposes, shared privately. Apart from cost, the major advantage of file sharing sites is that they can provide instructor feedback by showing when feedback files are downloaded.

Work with multiple cohorts of students on a variety of assessment types has led me to the following suggestions for best practice in the use of audio feedback:

- State the timetable for assessment and feedback explicitly and in advance so that students know submission deadlines, when to expect feedback and when to expect marks (if applicable).
- To be effective, feedback should be separated from the return of marks. If students receive their marks at the same time as or before they receive feedback, many will not look at the feedback if they are satisfied with their mark and may do so only if they want to question this mark.
- Individual audio feedback is not suitable for all types of assessed work. For example, it works better for more discursive assignments such as essays than for short exercises. Shorter exercises may be better suited to group feedback that highlights common strengths and weaknesses.
- Timing is everything: it is best to get feedback to the students quickly while their minds are still engaged with an assessment task.
- Do not send audio files directly to students: place them on a server and write a personal message in which you share a link to the file. Email is the key to sharing with large numbers of students and has been shown to be an effective channel. Finish the audio file with an open question to prompt the student to engage.

(Alan Cann, University of Leicester)

> **Interrogating practice**
>
> - How would you vary your feedback practices when dealing with large versus small student groups?

Project supervision and research training

Research projects are central to the vast majority of postgraduate degrees and, indeed, also represent the norm for a significant portion of most undergraduate degrees. Effectively helping students to develop research skills and providing students with the confidence to independently conduct novel science is a demanding undertaking that requires higher order pedagogical skills and routine reflection on the part of supervisors. Key tasks include assisting students to identify interesting research questions, guiding the design of feasible research projects, sympathetically running structured supervisory meetings, managing student expectations, providing research training, helping students to learn how to write for scientific publication, providing guidance on grant applications and lending early support in navigating the peer review system in its various contexts. It is commendable that, for the most part in our disciplines, the supervisor works alongside his or her students, helping them to learn how to learn, whilst also being a fellow inquirer seeking the mutual benefit of new knowledge.

HE practitioners working within the experimental sciences are in the fortunate position of being able to rely on extensive and context-specific pedagogical foundations in rising to the challenge of improving teaching and learning as our disciplines rapidly progress. The increasing demand for our graduates to facilitate the prosperity of our future societies means that, in achieving these ongoing improvements, we are charged with a proud task of paramount importance.

WHERE TO FIND MORE SUPPORT

Higher Education Academy (HEA). http://www.heacademy.ac.uk/resources (accessed 8 April 2014).

The BEN portal for biological sciences education from the US National Science Digital Library. http://www.biosciednet.org/portal/ (accessed 1 November 2013).

The Society of Biology. https://www.societyofbiology.org/education/teaching-resources/higher-education (accessed 1 November 2013).

The Royal Society of Chemistry. http://www.rsc.org/learn-chemistry/collections/higher-education (accessed 1 November 2013).

The Institute of Physics. http://www.iop.org/education/higher_education/stem/page_43325.html (accessed 8 April 2014).

The American Chemical Society (with particular reference to the undergraduate and graduate education links). http://www.acs.org/content/acs/en/education/resources.html (accessed 1 November 2013).

The Open Science Laboratory from the Open University. http://www.open.ac.uk/researchprojects/open-science/ (accessed 8 April 2014).

REFERENCES

Adams, D (2009) 'Current trends in laboratory class teaching in university bioscience programmes', *Bioscience Education*, 13.

Allen, D and Tanner, K (2003) 'Approaches to cell biology teaching: learning content in context – problem-based learning', *Cell Biology Education*, 2: 73–81.

Armbruster, P, Patel, M, Johnson, E and Weiss, M (2009) 'Active learning and student-centered pedagogy improve student attitudes and performance in introductory biology', *CBE-Life Sciences Education*, 8: 203–213.

Biochemical Society, British Pharmacological Society, Society of Biology, Society for Endocrinology, Society for Experimental Biology, British Ecological Society and The Physiological Society (2012) *Next Steps: Options after a Bioscience Degree*. Available from: http://www.sebiology.org/education/docs/Next_steps_web.pdf (accessed 14 August 2013).

Burgess Implementation Steering Group (2012) *Bringing it all together: introducing the HEAR*. London. Available from: http://www.hear.ac.uk/assets/documents/hear/institution-resources/HEAR-Bringing-it-all-together.pdf (accessed 14 August 2013).

Higher Education Funding Council for England (2011) *Strategically Important and Vulnerable Subjects*. Available from: https://www.hefce.ac.uk/media/hefce1/pubs/hefce/2011/1124/11_24.pdf (accessed 15 August 2013).

House of Lords Select Committee on Science and Technology (2012) *Higher Education in Science, Technology, Engineering and Mathematics (STEM) Subjects*. London: The Stationery Office.

Huff, D (1954) *How to Lie with Statistics*. New York, NY: WW Norton.

Jones, N, Georghiades, P and Gunson, J (2012) 'Student feedback via screen capture digital video: stimulating student's modified action', *Higher Education*, 64: 593–607.

Maw, S, Mauchline, A and Park, J (2011) 'Biological fieldwork provision in higher education', *Bioscience Education e-Journal*, 17.

Mazur, E (2009) 'Farewell, lecture?', *Science*, 323: 50–51.

Peat, M and Taylor, C (2005) 'Virtual biology: how well can it replace authentic activities?', *International Journal of Innovation in Science and Mathematics Education (formerly CALlaborate International)*, 13: 21–24.

President's Council of Advisors on Science and Technology (2012) Engage to Excel: Producing One Million Additional College graduates with Degrees in Science, Technology, Engineering and Mathematics. Available from: http://www.whitehouse.gov/sites/default/files/microsites/ostp/pcast-engage-to-excel-final_2-25-12.pdf (accessed 15 August 2013).

Preszler, RW (2009) 'Replacing lecture with peer-led workshops improves student learning', *CBE-Life Sciences Education*, 8: 182–192.

Quality Assurance Agency for Higher Education (2007_2008) *Subject Benchmark Statements: Biosciences; Biomedical Science; Chemistry; Physics, Astronomy and Astrophysics*. Available from:

http://www.qaa.ac.uk/assuringstandardsandquality/subject-guidance/pages/subject-benchmark-statements.aspx (accessed 8 April 2014).

Ramasundaram, V, Grunwald, S, Mangeot, A, Comerford, NB and Bliss, CM (2005) 'Development of an environmental virtual field laboratory', *Computers and Education*, 45: 21–34.

Scott, J, Green, P and Cashmore, A (2012) 'Bioscience students' first year perspectives through video diaries: home, family and student transitions', *Bioscience Education*, 20: 53–67.

Society of Biology (2013) *The Degree Accreditation Programme Handbook*. Available from: https://www.societyofbiology.org/images/Accreditation%20handbook.pdf (accessed 16 August 2013).

Stuckey-Mickell, TA and Stuckey-Danner, BD (2007) 'Virtual labs in the online biology course: student perceptions of effectiveness and usability', *MERLOT Journal of Online Learning and Teaching*, 3: 105–111.

Tenney, A and Houck, B (2004) 'Learning about leadership: team learning's effect on peer leaders', *Journal of College Science Teaching*, 33: 25–29.

Wood, WB (2009) 'Innovations in teaching undergraduate biology and why we need them', *Annual Review of Cell and Developmental Biology*, 25: 93–112.

FURTHER READING

Adams, DJ (2011) Effective Learning in the Life Sciences: How Students Can Achieve Their Full Potential. Chichester, UK; Hoboken, NJ: John Wiley & Sons.

Bryan, C and Clegg, K (2006) *Innovative Assessment in Higher Education*. Abingdon, UK: Routledge.

Handelsman, J, Miller, S and Pfund, C (2007) *Scientific Teaching*. New York, NY: Macmillan.

16 Mathematics and statistics

Paola Iannone and Adrian Simpson

INTRODUCTION

A mathematics degree aims 'to develop in students the capacity for learning and for clear logical thinking' and 'will develop [the students'] skills of abstract, logical thinking and reasoning'.

These quotations come from the publicly stated aims for mathematics degree courses from two universities which serve very different communities: the first takes students with very high qualifications and emphasises developing the next generation of researchers; the second takes students with much lower entry qualifications and has an emphasis on the development of **employability** skills. While degree programmes may have very different 'inputs' and aim for quite different 'outputs', an examination of the stated aims across the sector suggests some level of commonality: there appears to be a core of agreement that the aims of a mathematics degree involve developing certain types of analytic thinking skills.

Much of the research evidence examining teaching and learning in higher education is generic, despite concerns that many (particularly in the sciences) raise about the applicability to their own area. Joughin (2010) argues that too little account can be taken of subject context in interpreting research evidence, and mathematicians argue that the nature of knowledge in mathematics is different even from other sciences and that the teaching and assessment of mathematics may need to be considered separately (London Mathematical Society, 2010).

Clearly, there are generic issues that may apply across all (or large parts) of higher education, but these are amply dealt with in other chapters. In this chapter, we concentrate on the non-generic aspects of undergraduate mathematics emphasised again and again in different universities' aims: abstraction and analytic thinking.

Moreover, the research literature tends to have explored these more closely in pure mathematics so we will not say much that is specific about the teaching of applied mathematics or statistics. We believe the ideas of this chapter will be relevant across many sub-domains of mathematics, but note that we do not discuss mathematics taught in or for other disciplines.

This chapter is divided into three sections. First, we explore what we mean by learning to think mathematically and the research evidence for particular types of mathematical thought. Second, we examine mathematics teaching that might take account of these different ways of thinking mathematically. Finally, we look at **assessment** and the profound influence this can have on learners and teachers of mathematics.

In doing so, we recognise that teaching is a craft. There is no evidence to suggest that there is only one correct method of teaching to develop even these core analytic skills. It is more likely that the quality of teaching depends on a complex combination of teacher intention, learner preference, subject matter, institutional opportunities and constraints, assessment choices and a wide range of other, often implicit, factors.

Like others who look at education in universities, we will use the word 'innovative' occasionally – but we do so with caution. Often 'traditional' and 'innovative' are seen as code for 'bad' and 'good' by some in the education community and, occasionally, as code for 'good' and 'bad' by some in the mathematics community. Neither is right. Traditional lectures and closed book examinations are seen by many as well adapted for teaching and assessing mathematics and, to date, the evidence base for alternative forms of teaching as substantially better in achieving desired learning outcomes is lacking. Moreover, in some contexts, it is clear that both staff and students prefer traditional teaching and assessment methods.

LEARNING MATHEMATICS

There is a concern that the transition from school mathematics to a degree course in mathematics is particularly difficult. The A-level Mathematics programme has to fulfil many roles that no other A-level needs to address: in addition to acting as preparation for further study in the subject, it is also a service subject giving support for other A-level programmes (such as physics or economics) and is also often a pre-requisite for degree level study in those, and other, subjects. To balance all of these aims, among other reasons, the A-level mathematics curriculum has tended towards breadth of topic and fluency of calculation. While fluency is certainly desirable on entry to a mathematics degree, many mathematicians might prefer depth and understanding of fewer, but more targeted topics such as algebra and calculus. To some extent, the unique position of A-level Further Mathematics helps address this, but issues with the provision of this programme mean that, for many, the gap between a calculation-based mathematics preparation at school and a concept-based mathematics degree at university is too large and students struggle to develop the new ways of thinking required.

Research in student thinking tends to emphasise dichotomies: simple splits between the ways in which people think. Provided one keeps in mind that individual learners are likely to be more complicated, such dichotomies can be useful in understanding the broad issues associated with learning mathematics.

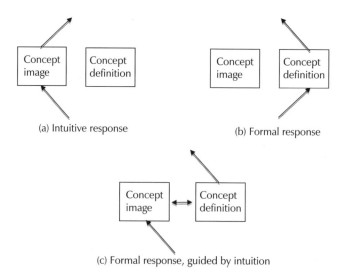

(a) Intuitive response

(b) Formal response

(c) Formal response, guided by intuition

Figure 16.1 Different forms of response using concept image and definition

One way of thinking about mathematical learning has been particularly attractive to practitioners for many years: **concept image** and **concept definition**. Tall and Vinner (1981) describe a concept image as an individual's set of mental pictures, processes and properties that they associate with a concept, and a concept definition as the form of words that specifies the concept (e.g. its formal definition).

While it is not meant to be a realistic model of cognitive functions, this idea allows us to account for some of the learning issues we see in undergraduate mathematics. Figure 16.1 suggests some crude distinctions between thinking that uses only informal intuition and imagery, thinking that uses only a definition and thinking that combines both.

In Case study 16.1 (adapted from Pinto, 1998), we see students with quite different approaches to learning real analysis. It contrasts two approaches to learning we might call 'intuitive' (using a concept image) and 'formal' (using – or trying to use – a concept definition). It indicates the need for these two approaches to be coordinated and the problems of students taking a formal approach without intuition, which might follow from a calculation-based pre-university experience. It further suggests that intuition without the ability to access the rules of 'pushing symbols' can also be restricting (albeit we might expect this to be less common amongst students).

Case study 16.1: Giving and extracting meanings in real analysis

In a traditional, lecture-based first course in real analysis, students were regularly interviewed and the researcher uncovered consistent ways in which students linked their knowledge and understanding of definitions with the construction of arguments, particularly in relation to their use of images.

The research noted two distinct strategies to developing arguments: 'giving meaning' (starting from informal ideas – concept images – and constructing arguments from that basis) and 'extracting meaning' (starting from formal theory – concept definition – and developing arguments as a form of calculation). Moreover, they found successful and unsuccessful examples of both of these strategies.

Students using a 'giving meaning' strategy who were unsuccessful tended to have some form of imagery from which they would try to reconstruct a definition, but such a reconstruction might well end up being a description of their imagery, given in some mathematical language. For example, the picture in Figure 16.2 becomes the 'definition' given as the student tries to describe it. Their imagery apparently admits only a few examples of convergent sequences – strictly decreasing ones – and their attempt to translate this into a formal definition loses the important relationship between the status of the quantifiers for ε and N.

In contrast, students 'extracting meaning' who are unsuccessful have to rely on memory and, if they forget parts or misremember them, they cannot reliably reconstruct them. For example, the student giving the definition in Figure 16.3 may seem to have a very good grasp, but further exploration seems to imply that the lack of universal quantification led the student to think that the definition refers to a particular value of epsilon.

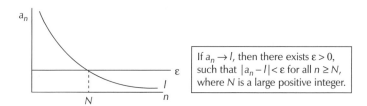

If $a_n \to l$, then there exists $\varepsilon > 0$, such that $|a_n - l| < \varepsilon$ for all $n \geq N$, where N is a large positive integer.

Figure 16.2 A less successful 'giving meaning' learner

A sequence (a_n) tends to a limit l for $\varepsilon > 0$ if there exists $N \in \mathbb{N}$ such that $|a_n - l| < \varepsilon$ provided $n \geq N$.

Figure 16.3 A less successful 'extracting meaning' learner

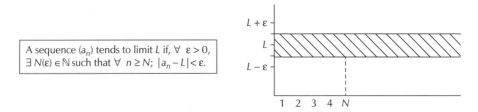

A sequence (a_n) tends to limit L if, $\forall\ \varepsilon > 0$, $\exists\ N(\varepsilon) \in \mathbb{N}$ such that $\forall\ n \geq N$; $|a_n - L| < \varepsilon$.

Figure 16.4 A more successful 'extracting meaning' learner

Successful learners in this study seemed to have some level of coordination between concept image and concept definition, the difference appearing to be only one of precedence. One student (whose definition and picture are given in Figure 16.4) talked of the need to write the definition down first 'over and over again', learning to draw the picture some time afterwards. Their emphasis was on the concept definition, but they could coordinate this with an image.

Another successful student, though, had a picture in mind and explicitly stated that he did not memorise the definition, but reconstructed it from the picture.

One can argue that the less successful learners in this case study were focused on one of the boxes in Figure 16.1, while the more successful perhaps had a balance between both (albeit still with a perceivable bias).

This study belongs to a long tradition of research into students' understanding of proving (particularly in real analysis). As other studies before, it notes the contrast between the intuitive and formal and highlights that neither, entirely on its own, is likely to be successful for many students.

Clearly expert mathematicians use both their intuition and their knowledge of results and formal rules to guide their thinking – no doubt with different mathematicians, in different subfields and at different times, using a different balance between these parts of their thinking. However, Case study 16.1 shows that not having access to the intuitions which come from a rich range of examples, counter-examples, prototypes and representations can result in students only being able to work on mathematical problems by manipulating formal language without ascribing meaning to this language (e.g. by pushing symbols). Similarly, students who are unaware of the status of the formal and reliant on pictures and metaphors will struggle with the precision required of a mathematics degree and may fall back on trying to merely mimic the formal language or, in the words of one colleague, 'write nonsense in mathematical style'.

Of course this balance between intuitive and formal extends into applied mathematics and statistics as well. Applied mathematics relies on a high degree of fluency with a wide range of calculation tools, but it also requires intuition in the form of modelling and understanding the nature and applicability of models. Again, there appears to be a large gap between school and university, with little if any emphasis on the creation or critiquing of models or understanding of the modelling process in most A-level programmes. Moreover, one can see a clear distinction in the literature between those who see modelling and applications as an area to which mathematics can be applied and those who see modelling as a way of thinking about (all) mathematics (that is, using real-world situations, in all their complexity, to allow students to encounter the need for particular types of mathematics). It is not clear that learners necessarily see this distinction.

Similarly, in statistics there is a distinction between the application of statistics to describe or draw inferences from real-world data and the development and understanding of the theoretical background of statistical techniques. The balance between these aims may well depend on the stated aims of the degree programme in which these modules sit.

So, across all domains, there is a need for students to develop particular, coordinated ways of thinking and thus, for teaching to support that development.

Interrogating practice

Can you give examples of how your intuition and formal understanding interact when you do mathematics? Look at students' written work: can you see how formal understanding and intuition interact when they do mathematics?

TEACHING MATHEMATICS

Case study 16.1 comes from research undertaken on a very traditional mathematics module: a 'definition–theorem–proof' lecture course. As mentioned earlier, we do not equate 'traditional' with 'bad': there is much to commend the lecture. Done well, it provides clear information. In mathematics, it defines the syllabus, in that a student might feel rightly aggrieved if substantial assessed material was omitted (something which may not be true in many other subjects). It can help students obtain a good set of notes. Of course, lecturers can provide notes (or gapped notes with sections to be completed in lectures) or lectures can be recorded and accessed online, but many become worried that, in doing so, important learning and teaching processes are lost.

We suggest that some of these important aspects which can be lost and may need to be emphasised in the traditional lecture, are:

- Attention;
- Modelling mathematical thinking;
- Engagement; and
- Contingency.

The often unfair stereotype of a lecture is one of very low attention, with students engaged in mindless note-taking. In fact, a good lecturer can go beyond the mere delivery of notes: they can draw attention to specific items (for example, pointing out how a part of an earlier definition appears in the middle of a later proof). The lecturer can use diagrams alongside formal derivations and point out explicitly both the links between them and the status that each holds. Some have been known to go further and develop a 'two board' system in which one board holds the formal derivations and a second board holds ideas, images, suggestions and working. This may allow the lecturer to draw explicit attention to the difference between a concept image and a concept definition and the importance of developing and integrating both.

The traditional lecture also allows an element of *modelling mathematical thinking*. Derivations are done 'live' (albeit in a time frame which, of necessity, ignores most of the deep thought processes which went into their construction). In deriving a result, a lecturer can explain how they think about the key ideas, which parts are the 'clever tricks' – unique to the situation and which simply need to be remembered – and which are applicable strategies we see in the subject again and again. For example, to show that the identity in a group is unique, one might start by imagining there are two (e and e') and using the group properties to show they are equal, then note a few minutes later that an almost identical technique appears in the proof that the inverse of a given element is unique.

Traditional lectures are also stereotyped as places of low *engagement*. There are few questions asked by the students and few questions asked to the students. The experience of many lecturers who do try to ask questions in classes is of few hands going up and those always coming from a few, generally more successful students. But this need not be the case: setting an environment in which it is not acceptable to opt out of answering can be relatively easy. In schools, mini-whiteboards are commonly used to require an answer to a question from every pupil in a class (and, if organised appropriately, allow answers to be seen by the teacher without easily being seen by other pupils). Technology is now making possible something similar in lectures with the use of 'clickers' (**personal response system**) or other form of audience response system (Rowlett, 2010). Even though these allow for only a restricted form of response, they do enhance engagement and reduce the opportunity to opt out. With the increased expectation that students come to lectures with smartphones and tablets, we may soon be in the position of having the flexibility of response of a mini-whiteboard with the ease of use of a pre-installed clicker system.

Of course, audience response leads to the need for *contingency*. The stereotype is of a lecturer following a set of notes unwaveringly. However, getting responses back from students suggesting they have significant misconceptions means that the lecturer needs to be prepared to explore an area in more depth than they allowed for, invent new counter-examples that might expose the misconception for what it is, or even unpick previous ideas to uncover the possible cause of the misconception.

To be fair, while a lecturer may be able to quickly invent a new example, a lecture is not a good place to unpick larger or deeper misconceptions, so there is a need for more opportunities for students to engage with the material and have teaching contingent on their needs. This can be achieved with **seminar** groups, which are often part of many modules in mathematics. The frequency, size and nature of those seminars vary, but it is common for seminar groups to have around 20 students who go through an exercise sheet with a seminar leader (either a lecturer or a PhD student). Such seminars can be useful to complement the lecture as they can promote group work, help students exchange ideas and allow them to get help from lecturers. However, these seminars have been criticised for the lack of structure and the variation in mode and content even across groups on the same module.

Clearly, attention, modelling mathematical practice, engagement and contingency are not exclusive to the traditional lecture/seminar model; nor is the traditional lecture or seminar always the best place to exhibit these – there are a number of innovative forms of teaching mathematics at degree level.

Case study 16.2 (Problem solving class) can appear as a good environment to develop all four of these factors in certain circumstances.

Iannone and Simpson (2012) found that 11 universities have a module with a title like 'Problem solving' on their undergraduate mathematics degree. Badger et al. (2012) provide detailed case studies of six of these, as well as an analysis of the nature of such classes and the variety of activities taking place in them. In particular, they note one issue of concern about such classes: the nature of their mathematical content. Some classes are designed to teach students to be better mathematical problem solvers (and therefore de-emphasise specific mathematical topics) while others have an explicit mathematical topic that they approach through a sequence of problems to solve. Case study 16.2 is of the former type, but there are a number of carefully developed sequences of problems of the latter type, notably for number theory (Burn, 1997) and real analysis (Burn, 2000).

Case study 16.2: Problem solving classes

The University of East Anglia introduced a problem solving module in 2012. It spans eight weeks in the first term of the first year and is compulsory for all first year mathematics students. The module is divided into two parts of four weeks each. The first is dedicated to developing problem solving techniques and the second to proof writing. Teaching is in small seminar groups (of around 20 students) where students are asked to work together on given problems coordinated by a member of faculty. There are also weekly smaller seminar sessions with 'Peer Guides' – second and third year students who have been trained to work in this environment. The problems in this module include many from Mason et al. (1982), but also some developed by the module leaders. Such problems have been grouped into different categories:

- Word problems: a problem given in narrative that needs to be translated in to mathematical language.

  - For example: what number exceeds its square by the greatest amount? What is that amount?

- Proof production: a problem for which the students need to find an appropriate statement to prove and prove it.

  - For example: a number like 12321 is called a palindrome because it reads the same backwards as forwards. A friend of mine claims that all palindromes with four digits are exactly divisible by eleven. Are they?

- Proof refinement: the statement is given and the student needs to produce a proof written in formal mathematical language.

- Open problems: a problem that does not necessarily have only one solution or could be solved at different levels.

  - For example: you are looking for a set of points in the plane satisfying the following two conditions: (1) the distance between any two points is an integer; (2) the points are not collinear.
    Can you find a set of three points satisfying these conditions? How about a set of five points? Seven points? Just how large a set can you find? Could it even be infinite?
    Extend: are points in space not all coplanar?

The module has only two lectures, one at the beginning of each section. The first lecture is an introduction to the module, its structure and assessment. The second lecture consists partly of feedback on the first coursework task and partly as an introduction to writing proofs.

Assessment is 100 per cent coursework in two parts. The first part is handed in at the end of the first section of the module and consists of a problem students have to solve. They hand in the solution to the problem and their working. The second part is a more complex problem where students are not only asked to solve the problem, but also write a proof in as polished a form and in as precise formal mathematical language as they can.

The rationale of these modules comes from the idea that the only way to learn about problem solving strategies is by 'doing' and by experiencing the strategies and proofs with the support of peers. Indeed, one factor on which the success of these modules depends is that the lecturer needs to resist the temptation to lecture! The role of the lecturer is that of a facilitator, giving minimal advice in the problem solving stage and facilitating discussion at the group discussion stage.

Students so far have had mixed reactions to this module. For some, this becomes a much appreciated opportunity to engage in depth with problems and interact with fellow students, while others are puzzled by the lack of direct instruction in a module that does not resemble the standard lecture/seminar modules they expect.

While the problem solving class tends to focus on engagement and attention, there are other teaching innovations that focus on the formal. Notably, both Houston (2009) and McConlogue et al. (2010) discuss materials designed to lead students to attend to the precision of mathematical expression. These again often emphasise the link between and status of the formal and the informal. Consider the task:

> You are given four distinct complex numbers. How do you decide whether or not these numbers lie at the vertices of a square in the complex plane? (Do not use symbols or mathematical notation in your answer.)
>
> (McConlogue et al., 2010: 13)

This requires the translation of an answer probably obtained with extensive use of mathematical symbolism into language without that symbolism (but retaining precision).

Such mathematical writing, combining rigorous symbolism with visual representations, metaphors and other forms of expression often comes to the fore in the final year project. Most universities provide some form of project module, often contributing a large portion of the final year mark and the teaching on this is different yet again. Typically a student will be provided with some one-to-one or small group supervision and be expected to study otherwise independently, write up a report on the project, perhaps present a summary verbally or as a poster and perhaps be expected to respond to questions about it.

However, we may need to be careful with introducing pockets of very different teaching. Case study 16.2 suggests that although an encounter with a very different form of teaching from that expected is relished as a challenge by some, it can be disconcerting and difficult to adapt to for others. Suddenly encountering a self-study module or project after years of lecture courses may require provision of clearer support for some students if it is not to be too great a shock.

Interrogating practice

Have you thought about what you can do in your module to help first year student to successfully move from school mathematics to university mathematics? At departmental level, can you think of strategies to help this transition in the design of your first year provision?

ASSESSMENT

Assessment is often thought of as the end of the teaching and learning process: a simple evaluation of how much of the latter took place in the context of the former. However, assessment may also be thought of as part of the process of learning and teaching. The phrase 'assessment for learning' is widely used in schools and is intended to mean the use of assessment evidence (drawn broadly) to help teachers and pupils plan forthcoming learning (Black et al., 2007).

However, one might also talk of 'assessment as learning'. In purely cognitive terms, learning involves the structuring of knowledge in memory and, as Karpicke and Blunt (2011) put it, 'a retrieval event may actually represent a more powerful learning activity than an encoding event'. That is, being assessed on something may help fix it in your mind more clearly than being taught it again. So assessment, stereotypically seen by both students and lecturers as a necessary inconvenience to tell them how much the students have or haven't learned, may actually be very valuable in strengthening learning.

A recent survey on assessment of mathematics at universities in the UK (Iannone and Simpson, 2012) suggested that by far the most common summative assessment method in mathematics was the closed book examination. Data for 43 degree courses showed that the median contribution of closed book examinations towards the final degree was 72 per cent and few departments had closed book examinations accounting for less than 50 per cent of the final degree (when averaged across all their modules). When the final year project (often representing a large portion of a final degree classification) was removed, the median contribution of closed book examinations to the final degree classification was 80 per cent.

However, there were clear variations between institutions. To some extent, this may be because, as suggested earlier, different institutions have different aims and take students with different backgrounds. But this does not account for all the variance, for example Iannone and Simpson (2012) noted that two universities, with similar entry requirements and similar views of themselves as research-intensive departments, had very different patterns of assessment. The first was disproportionately dominated by examinations – after the first year, every module delivered by the department (with the exception of the final year project) was assessed exclusively by closed book examination. The second had a disproportionately low number of closed book examinations, with at least 20 per cent of most modules across all years coming from other forms of assessment, and some modules even in the final year with no closed book examinations at all. There was no evidence of conservatism on the part of the first university; indeed, the pattern of assessment was the result of a reasoned and agreed policy in the department with the main drivers being concerns about plagiarism and the lack of validity of weekly coursework sheets. The second university had taken just as reasoned an approach to its assessment pattern, in this case wishing to emphasise the importance of developing skills of direct value to the workplace through assessment.

Of course, the second university still had a large proportion of closed book examinations in absolute terms (just under 50 per cent averaged across all modules) as did all the universities sampled. The evidence from the general assessment literature suggests that the prevalence of the closed book examination would be something that conflicts with student preference. However, it may be that this is another area where we need to take care when applying the results of the general literature to mathematics. Iannone and Simpson (2014) indicate that the sources of data in the generic research literature rarely include students on degrees in hard sciences. When mathematics students were asked – albeit in a study looking exclusively at research-intensive universities – they appeared to see the closed book examination as the 'gold standard', that is highly valued for fairness, discriminating on the grounds of ability and by far their preferred method for being assessed. This is quite at odds with the suggestions of the general literature.

That noted, the study also suggested that students would appreciate some further diversification of assessment. Despite the prevalence of closed book examinations, there are a wide range of methods in use and available. Open book examinations tend to be used in statistics and programming projects in computing courses, and most universities use some form of homework (variously called example sheets, weekly coursework, tutorial sheets etc.) that may contribute a small amount to a module mark, particularly in the early years. Marking regular coursework can be onerous and, as indicated earlier, some mathematicians express concerns over its **validity** if there is widespread collusion or copying.

However, if we take the notion of 'assessment as learning' seriously, it would suggest the need for some regular assessment like example sheets. Computer-aided assessment has been used in some areas of mathematics for many years. It has the advantages, if properly designed, of avoiding copying by providing individualised questions, improving feedback times and radically decreasing workload. The main issue is the difficulties associated with representing and evaluating answers when the intended solution is a mathematical expression. Packages like STACK (Sangwin, 2008) overcome many of these issues with the clever use of an underlying computer algebra system and a flexible question and answer design method.

Case study 16.3 shows another way in which computer-aided assessment (as well as assessment in general) can be cleverly reconceptualised. In this case, the students have to set the questions and design both the correct and distractor answers for online multiple choice tests. This fits the notion of 'assessment as learning' rather well.

Case study 16.3: The use of the platform PeerWise for assessing geometry and statistics

A team of researchers at Auckland University, New Zealand has constructed an open access platform that allows students to create and explain their understanding of course-related assessment questions, and to answer and discuss questions created by their peers (http://peerwise.cs.auckland.ac.nz). This platform is intended for use in any academic subject to implement continuous formative assessment, which is not only onerous on staff time but also allows students to assess each others' work.

In the UK, the Universities of Edinburgh and Glasgow use this platform for first year Physics modules and Liverpool University use it for a first year Chemistry module. In this case study, we describe an adaptation of this platform in first year Geometry and second year Statistics modules at Leicester University.

Both modules involve large groups of students, and opportunities for continuous assessment have in the past been restricted due to the demand they place on staff time. With the use of PeerWise, the fortnightly homework for these modules asks students to construct their own multiple choice questions to pose to their peers on selected sections of the syllabus and to critique (e.g. answer but also critically assess) their peer's questions. The lecturer of the modules acts as a moderator when the need arises and can monitor students' progress on the platform. The assessment patterns of the two modules are slightly different:

Both modules retain a large proportion of assessment by examination (in the form of a course test), but this reversed use of PeerWise includes more opportunities for continuous assessment.

The lecturer who introduced the use of this platform believes that asking the students to both provide the answers and design the questions helps them to think more deeply about the material. Part of the requirement of the fortnightly homework is that students take the questions designed by their peers to assess their own understanding and leave feedback on the questions they have answered. In this way, students also engage with peer assessment and peer learning. Moreover as the lecturer can monitor students' activity, this is also an

Table 16.1 Assessment patterns in the use of PeerWise

Geometry – Year 1	
45% course test 50% project 5% participation in PeerWise	Participation in PeerWise consists of students submitting at least two multiple choice questions every two weeks and providing feedback and comments on between six and eight questions produced by peers.
Statistics – Year 2	
20% course test 20% course test 50% open book examination 10% participation in PeerWise	Participation in PeerWise consists of students submitting at least one multiple choice question every two weeks, and commenting on four submitted by peers.

Source: Iannone and Simpson (2012)

ideal tool to quickly flag up common problems and misunderstandings, which can then be addressed in the lectures if needed.

This assessment method is relatively new, but from initial participation data it appears that general engagement with the platform is very good (though high achieving students engage with the platform more than struggling students) and the students' feedback is generally very positive.

Interrogating practice

Have you thought about the way you decided about assessment of your modules? Could you introduce, given the constraints on your module, a component of 'assessment as learning'?

CONCLUSIONS AND OVERVIEW

Our section on learning suggests that in order to achieve the aim of students with improved logical and analytical thinking, students need to develop intuitive understanding of concepts (which may involve rich sets of examples, counter-examples, representations and properties), the formal abilities to manipulate those concepts and a robust and reliable link between the intuitive and the formal. The section on teaching suggests ways in which different types of teaching might achieve this. Traditional lecturing can draw attention to both the intuitive and the formal, model how mathematicians integrate the two, and need not be as unengaging as the stereotype suggests. Other forms of teaching, such as problem solving classes, can put students in the position of modelling some aspects of creative mathematical processes in exploring problems to help develop their intuition and then, with a focus on proving and accuracy of expression, tie that intuition to the formal symbolism.

Our final section reconceives mathematics assessment as a form of learning, rather than simply an evaluation or certification process, and in doing so shows that it can help students with the process of tying the intuitive and formal together. As with teaching, the evidence suggests strong reliance on the traditional (in this case, closed book examinations) across all university mathematics departments and notes that both staff and students can see these as entirely appropriate. Even when students might value a wider range of assessment methods, the 'gold standard' remains the formal examination. But other innovative forms of assessment, such assessing knowledge through students' construction of questions, may help us address students' interest in a more varied assessment diet.

Clearly, different mathematics departments can have very different aims, but at the core they have a common interest in developing particular types of analytic thought, which constitute a mathematical habit of mind. We argue that understanding how to teach and assess mathematics comes from a careful consideration of how students learn mathematics, which may be different in many ways from how students learn in other subject areas.

REFERENCES

Badger, M, Sangwin, C and Hawkes, T (2012) *Teaching Problem Solving in Undergraduate Mathematics*. Birmingham: University of Birmingham.

Black, PPJ, Harrison, C, Lee, C, Marshall, B and Wiliam, D (2007) *Assessment for Learning*. New York, NY: Open University Press.

Burn, RP (1997) *A Pathway into Number Theory*. Cambridge: Cambridge University Press.

Burn, RP (2000) *Numbers and Functions: Steps to Analysis*. Cambridge: Cambridge University Press.

Houston, K (2009) *How to Think like a Mathematician: A Companion to Undergraduate Mathematics*. Cambridge: Cambridge University Press.

Iannone, P and Simpson, A (eds.) (2012) *Mapping University Mathematics Assessment Practices*. Norwich: University of East Anglia.

Iannone, P and Simpson, A (2014) 'Students' preferences in undergraduate mathematics assessment', *Studies in Higher Education*, DOI:10.1080/03075079.2013.858683.

Joughin, G (2010) 'The hidden curriculum revisited: a critical review of research into the influence of summative assessment on learning', *Assessment and Evaluation in Higher Education*, 35(3): 335–345.

Karpicke, JD and Blunt, JR (2011) 'Retrieval practice produces more learning than elaborative studying with concept mapping', *Science*, 331(6018): 772–775.

London Mathematical Society (LMS) (2010) *Mathematics Degrees, their Teaching and Assessment*. Available from: http://www.lms.ac.uk/sites/lms.ac.uk/files/About_Us/news/2010-04%20LMS%20Teaching%20postition%20statement%20(14%20April).pdf (accessed 11 April 2014).

Mason, J, Burton, L and Stacey, K (1982) *Thinking Mathematically*. Upper Saddle River, NJ: Pearson Education Limited.

McConlogue, T, Mitchell, S and Vivaldi, F (2010) 'Beyond templates 2: exploring students' approaches to learning on a mathematical writing course', *MSOR Connections*, 10(2): 10–13.

Pinto, M (1998) *Students' Understanding of Real Analysis*. Unpublished PhD Thesis, Warwick University. Available from: http://pqdtopen.proquest.com/#abstract?dispub=3491803 (accessed 11 April 2014).

Rowlett, P (2010) 'Ask the audience (yes, all of them)', *MSOR Connections*, 10(1): 3–5.

Sangwin, CJ (2008) 'Assessing Elementary Algebra with STACK', *International Journal of Mathematical Education in Science and Technology*, 38(8): 987–1002.

Tall, D and Vinner, S (1981) 'Concept image and concept definition in mathematics with particular reference to limits and continuity', *Educational Studies in Mathematics*, 12(2): 151–169.

17 Engineering

John Davies

INTRODUCTION: THE NATURE OF ENGINEERING AS A SUBJECT

What are some of the distinguishing characteristics of engineering as a subject in higher education?

Of course, a strong characteristic is that it is a vocational subject: a degree in engineering is a preparation for a specific career. This affects much of the thinking behind the design and delivery of engineering courses. The profession has quite a big say in content (as we shall find out in the next section), and it is common to hear academics explain, for instance, that a particular approach to running a project is designed to prepare students for the challenges they will face in industry.

Study of engineering requires a good grasp of maths and, in some areas, science. This means that universities are dependent on earlier stages of education for generating interest and ability in these subjects. But as well as these 'narrow' skills, engineers need width in their skills set: in practice they work in teams, need to communicate well, have commercial understanding, etc.

One unfortunate characteristic of engineering as a subject, especially in the UK, is that women are seriously under-represented. Women make up only about 12 per cent of those enrolling on to engineering degree courses, and many of those graduating do not go on to become professional engineers. The UK has the lowest proportion of female engineers in the EU at 9 per cent, compared with Sweden, for example, at 26 per cent (Engineering UK, 2011).

The subject of engineering is very wide-ranging in terms of scale, level of abstraction, scientific content, etc. and yet there is also a common core in terms of engineers' skills, approaches and values.

GUIDANCE ON COURSE CONTENT

UK-SPEC

Most engineering degrees are **accredited**, meaning they satisfy the requirements for the educational component in the formation of a professionally qualified engineer. The requirements are set by the relevant national bodies: the Engineering Council in the UK, Engineers Australia, Institution of Professional Engineers New Zealand, Engineering Council of South Africa, ABET (US) and many others. Internationally, there is some mutual recognition of standards. For example, the Washington Accord covers qualifications in a number of countries (including the UK, US, Canada, Australia, South Africa and Japan) at the equivalent of CEng level, and the EUR-ACE System covers European accreditation of engineering programmes.

In the UK, as an example, 'The UK Standard for Professional Engineering Competence', usually referred to as UK-SPEC (Engineering Council, 2010a), sets out the requirements. UK-SPEC defines the 'competence and commitment standard' for different levels of professional qualification and indicates the educational requirements in 'Accreditation of Higher Education Programmes' (Engineering Council, 2010b). At the heart of this are sets of 'output standards', though what are really being specified are learning outcomes rather than standards. To give an indication of standards (in the sense of level of achievement), UK-SPEC refers to the level descriptors of the **Framework for Higher Education Qualifications** (FHEQ) (Quality Assurance Agency (QAA), 2008).

In the UK, the **QAA** publishes a subject benchmark statement for all subjects in engineering (QAA, 2013), as it does for most subjects. Fortunately, for engineering the defined learning outcomes are those of UK-SPEC; therefore, the same set of generalised learning outcomes are specified by both the academic quality agency and the central accrediting body. The task of accrediting specific degree courses is licensed by the Engineering Council to professional engineering institutions (like the Institution of Mechanical Engineers) but, again, this is all based on the learning outcomes in UK-SPEC.

What industry expects

Employers vary widely in their expectations. Some employers accept completely that engineering studies provide graduates with an education, and should not be seen as vocational training. If a degree is training, it is training of the mind, not training in immediately applicable engineering skills. But others take a completely different view. I have heard employers say that after three or four years of so-called education, it is completely unacceptable that they (employers) should then have to spend money training graduates to bring them up to speed in basic engineering techniques.

The obvious point is that the answer to the question 'what does industry expect in an engineering graduate?' depends on who you are asking. That doesn't mean engineering academics should not ask the question; on the contrary it means they should ask as many people as possible. All engineering academics should make the most of their opportunities for contacts with employers in industry – it is one of the most important aspects of the job.

A number of studies have looked at how employers believe engineering degrees should be enhanced. For example, the Royal Academy of Engineering (2007) has stressed that universities and industry need to find more effective ways of ensuring that course content reflects the real requirements of industry.

> Engineering businesses now seek engineers with abilities and attributes in two broad areas – technical understanding and enabling skills. The first of these comprises: a sound knowledge of disciplinary fundamentals; a strong grasp of mathematics; creativity and innovation; together with the ability to apply theory in practice. The second is the set of abilities that enable engineers to work effectively in a business environment: communication skills; team working skills; and business awareness of the implications of engineering decisions and investments.
>
> (Royal Academy of Engineering, 2007: 4)

What students want

We've considered what the profession expects from engineering degree courses, so what about the students?

We can find out what students want, or say they appreciate, at a range of scales. At the local scale, the scale of the specific module, we can find out through the interaction in the class, and through informal and formal feedback. We return to this later, under the heading 'Evaluating practice'. At the other extreme, at a national scale, we can find out through the **National Student Survey** (NSS). This is a very influential survey that determines, among other things, league table positions. In all subjects, certainly including engineering, responses to questions like 'Staff are good at explaining things' are generally quite positive. It is questions on **assessment** and especially **feedback** on assessment that consistently throw up negative responses – even lower in engineering than the average for all subjects (Higher Education Academy, 2012).

Some other studies have involved asking students, in a more open-ended way, what they appreciate in engineering courses. Davies et al. (2006) studied submissions to a competition in which engineering students in the UK were invited to submit an essay with the title 'What makes a good engineering lecturer?'. Virtually all the shortlisted essays referred to three characteristics: that a good lecturer is enthusiastic, gives clear well-structured presentations and uses real-world engineering examples backed up by industrial experience. The same title was returned to a few years later. The top attributes this time were similar: use of real-world examples, approachability, diversity of teaching tools and enthusiasm (Collins and Davies, 2009).

IDENTITIES

An effective engineering lecturer has some combination of three identities:

- Teacher (with an active interest in student learning);
- Academic (with an active interest in research and scholarship); and
- Engineer (with an active interest in engineering practice).

The aim of this section is partly to encourage you to think about this combination in yourself and partly to discuss the situation of new staff who may be concerned about being stronger in one of these identities than the others. For example, you may have been appointed to your first lecturing job with a strong research background but little or no professional experience. Of course, your research experience has great value in itself and can benefit your students. That is partly because through your research experience you are a subject expert, and this gives your teaching credibility: you know the limits of your subject and you know how your subject is being developed. It is also because, as a researcher, you are a learner yourself, and you know what it is like to have your knowledge challenged, not in an exam (like your students) but in a discussion of your research findings, or peer review of a paper or proposal. Your research is likely to be motivated by enthusiasm and excitement for your subject and this will come across to your students. However, if you feel you are lacking practical engineering understanding you should think about strengthening it. There are various ways of doing this, from quite simple things like attending professional institution events, getting involved in contacts with employers relating to, for example, student work placements, and organising inputs to your modules from practising engineers; more significant things include consultancy, industrial secondments (which can be funded) and becoming professionally qualified (which is a realistic possibility for academics but the routes vary between professional institutions).

If you are an engineering lecturer coming straight from industry, there is of course great value in your experience of the real world. As we have discussed, students greatly value the industrial experience of those who teach them. And, for you, it is enthusiasm and excitement for real-world engineering that will come across. But remember that your industrial knowledge may become out of date after a few years unless you keep it refreshed through consultancy, etc. Then there is the academic side of things. You need to understand the importance of an academic perspective and think about how you are going to develop your own academic identity.

Either way, you are a teacher, and you need to maintain an active interest in student learning.

Interrogating practice

- How do these identities apply to you?
- If you have a need to develop in a particular area, how do you plan to go about it?

MAKING LEARNING AND TEACHING CHOICES

This section is about the choice of approaches to teaching, to creating opportunities for your students to learn.

Let's start with a 'position': a statement about how we see things. Engineering students learn in different ways, influenced by all sorts of things, including their natural learning style and what they know already. As a result of the learning opportunities and stimulation that their lecturer has provided, and through their engagement with the course material, they construct their own understanding of the subject (see also Chapter 5).

The way you make choices about your approach to teaching will be based on many things: your own learning style, the approaches that are encouraged in your school or among your immediate colleagues, your knowledge of engineering, maybe your own experiences as a student. You won't have complete freedom to teach the way you want, but you should try to be true to your personal convictions. When you take over a course from someone else, it can be nice to inherit material so it doesn't feel like you have to prepare everything from scratch, but you won't be completely comfortable about what you are doing until you have made the approach your own.

The choices that follow are presented not as rigid approaches to presenting particular parts of the curriculum, or as rival schools of thought on the best way to achieve effective learning, but as a 'palette' of options.

Lecturing

Some commentators on education like to mock the use of lectures, maybe illustrating their arguments with stories of their own terrible lecturers when they were students in the 1960s and 1970s. Certainly the idea that a lecture can somehow 'transfer' chunks of knowledge from the lecturer to the students deserves to be mocked. My view is that in the right circumstances lectures in engineering can be effective, but only as a 'starting pistol for learning'. Lectures can give the students a human face to associate with the subject. The lecturer, partly through personal enthusiasm, 'sells' the importance, relevance and essential characteristics of the subject.

Lectures (see also Chapter 7) in engineering can promote active learning, for example through interactivity, variation and effective use of technology. Of course, class size, topic and level have a massive influence.

Lectures can be interactive even with quite large groups. At the University of Strathclyde, for example, mechanical engineering students experience highly active teaching with collaborative learning while still part of a large audience group. Among the purpose-built learning spaces is a large lecture room designed for group seating so groups of students can work together as part of an interactive lecture (University of Strathclyde, 2013).

Electronic voting systems – 'clickers' – can be used very effectively to make standard lectures interactive. Russell (2008) presents some background, together with a very interesting detailed analysis of how clickers can help learning in a specific situation.

Can lectures be valuable other than in real time? Davis et al. (2009) describe a study of the effectiveness of lecture capture, including an overview of different approaches and discussion of the advantages and drawbacks. A common concern about lecture capture is that it will discourage attendance at the actual face-to-face classes themselves. But Davis et al. refer to a number of previous studies that indicate that attendance is not significantly affected, and confirm this finding themselves. They find students react positively to the availability of the resources produced.

Using a virtual learning environment

It's hard to imagine a modern engineering course without the support of a **virtual learning environment** (VLE). As in all other applications of IT, recent development has been fast. It's interesting that the spread of good practice has been instigated by innovative members of staff, and then driven by students. Feedback from students would be 'why can't everyone use the VLE like lecturer X?'. Now most universities have minimum expectations for how staff should use the VLE, including resources that should be available. This has changed things quite a lot, even on quite traditionally delivered modules. I suggested that a lecture can be seen as a 'starting pistol for learning', but many would argue that if the VLE is used properly, learning via the material made available in this way should have started well before the lecture.

Enquiry-led learning

I am using the term 'enquiry-led learning' to group together a variety of approaches with different names, all of which aim to stimulate and structure student learning in a particular way. The best known is probably **problem-based learning** (PBL). For some academics, PBL and similar approaches represent philosophical positions, strongly opposed to traditional lecture-type delivery, but the reality on most engineering courses is that both approaches exist, and can be used to complement each other.

The core characteristic is that the starting point for learning is a question, a problem, a challenge, not a set of pre-digested information imparted by the lecturer. The role of the tutor is facilitator, supporter of learning.

> PBL is characterised by an enquiry process where problems – mostly from real and complex situations – are formulated and drive the whole learning process. Learning through PBL promotes critical thinking, self-learning skills, lifelong learning, self-achievement, self-regulation, self-efficacy, communication skills and interpersonal skills for students.
>
> (Guerra and Kolmos, 2011: 4)

Most supporters of enquiry-led learning point to advantages in terms of the quality and depth of learning, but they also emphasise the development of professional skills in graduates that are ready for work. In a vocational subject like engineering, this makes enquiry-led learning very relevant.

There are some basic approaches to engineering analysis that can be explained in an engaging way with practical examples, and the direct approach may have advantages over embedding the necessary learning within a problem. However, this is not completely straightforward. There is concern among engineering employers that today's graduates are weak in their understanding of basic engineering fundamentals. 'They can't even draw a simple bending moment diagram'. But the fact is students would have learnt this in Year 1 of their course, and presumably passed assignments and probably exams that relied on this understanding. Perhaps as the course became more advanced, they lost this basic understanding, or were not capable of adapting it to a realistic problem. What's the answer? Well surely it's not to teach the same basics (even in an engaging way) again and again. I think students need to find out for themselves, in a realistic context, that this understanding is important, and to recall for themselves the basic principles and apply them, thus gaining competence and confidence with the methods. Sounds like a clear case for a problem/project/scenario!

Achieving integration and realism; developing professional skills

Projects, scenarios, investigations and other significant elements of enquiry-led learning may run through a year or semester, or be given dedicated blocks of time. Students typically work in groups. The challenge is realistic, commonly derived from industry. Across all engineering disciplines, the range of possible activities is immense: feasibility study, product or software development, design, proposal, forensic investigation, and so on.

One example of the structuring of a programme to emphasise realism and integration is the 'CDIO' approach. This is an international initiative for developing engineering education. 'The framework provides students with an education stressing engineering fundamentals set in the context of Conceiving–Designing–Implementing–Operating (CDIO) real-world systems and products.' (CDIO, 2013) The structure uses cross-cutting realistic projects to stress the context for engineering study.

A very important component of these learning experiences is the input from industry. The most realistic problem is a real one, and often the most up-to-date and context-aware guidance comes from a practising engineer. Not all engineers are good teachers, but many are excellent and love getting involved.

An area with a rich potential for project work and for broadening the curriculum and the outlook of engineering students is humanitarian engineering. Work in this area, often in conjunction with the charity Engineers without Borders, prepares students to work in a global context and highlights the role of engineers in 'providing solutions to social problems and poverty reduction, in both local and developing country contexts' (Hill and Miles, 2012).

Case study 17.1: Projects that benefit the community

In an MEng Year 4 project module in the Department of Mechanical Engineering at the University of Sheffield, students work in teams to find solutions to a real problem provided by a real customer. After using projects based on developing a product and/or a business case in a commercial context, which had varying success in engaging the students, the team moved towards projects with a greater social relevance. The project was developed to have:

- 'A strong social relevance;
- Clear interaction between students and the customer to define the need;
- Interaction with the wider community;
- Clear understanding of professional and civic responsibilities and consideration of ethical issues;
- Opportunity for social enterprise;
- Reflection on learning outcomes and social impact (both students and staff); and
- Dissemination of practice.'

(Rodriguez-Falcon and Yoxall, 2010: 63)

Examples of projects are as follows. In 'Kieron's Challenge', the brief was to make life easier for a 7-year-old boy with severe cerebral palsy, and for his family and carers. As part of this, the students met and interacted with Kieron and his family. This generated a huge emotional commitment by the students to find technical solutions to Kieron's problems and limitations. The ideas generated by the 70 students, backed up by sponsorship from local companies, led to the manufacture of several prototypes. In the following year, the project was based on supporting Sheffield Children's Hospital and its patients. After interviewing a representative of the hospital and a patient, 87 students worked on ideas aimed at solving problems within the occupational therapy and rehabilitation department. Ideas were worked up technically and prototypes manufactured. One successful example is a walking frame for children with brittle bones, which is now being used by the Sheffield Children's Hospital. In other years, challenges have been to improve the quality of life for terminally ill patients at a local hospice, and to enhance the learning experience of children with learning difficulties and disabilities at a specialist local school.

Through questionnaires used over several years, it has been possible to compare students' perceptions of the project module before and after the change to socially motivated projects. After the change, students indicated significantly higher satisfaction with the project itself, with the perceived learning achieved and with the professional outcomes. It was also seen that the nature of the project played an important role in enhancing overall student engagement. It was clear that students engaged enthusiastically with the 'customers' to determine their needs.

> 'Witnessing this type of interaction, where students use their technical skills to understand the problems, professionally and ethically approach any sensitive issues, but most of all, listen carefully to the community engaging with them, is one of the most rewarding experiences for any learning facilitator.'
>
> (Rodriguez-Falcon and Yoxall, 2010: 66)
>
> (Elena Rodriguez-Falcon, University of Sheffield)

Using laboratories and workshops

In laboratories and workshops, engineering students come into contact with the real thing: real equipment, real ways of working. The reality is not just about practice, students see engineering phenomena first-hand, and can test engineering principles and theories with real data.

Cranston and Lock (2012) describe how engineering laboratory experiments can be made more interactive using a variety of approaches, including use of large-scale wall-mounted graphs for students to plot and compare data, use of audience response systems for multiple choice questions as the experiment progresses, and follow-up materials online. Another interesting update on the traditional lab class described by Page et al. (2009) involves large-scale sharing of data. Students can upload data 'in real time, via the internet, allowing results to be available immediately for comparison with their peers', whilst still in the laboratory in front of the equipment' (2009: 37).

Virtual labs or weblabs can give remote access to real experimental equipment allowing flexible access in terms of location and time. Read et al. (2008) describe a project in which this type of access to engineering laboratories is used in supporting the learning needs of a culturally diverse student cohort as part of widening participation.

Work-based learning

With the importance of preparing for the profession, there is obvious value in engineering work experience. This is partly about being able to place engineering understanding in a practical context, but also about **employability** in its simplest form: employers tend to prefer graduates with work experience. Most guides to placements (for example, the QAA code of conduct for work-based and placement learning [QAA, 2007]) focus on the *learning* gained from a placement, but the greatest benefits may be better described as 'personal development'. Students *change* when they are on work placement.

Placements can vary in length and some are incorporated as mandatory components in courses, but the most common arrangements are summer vacation experience, or a one-year placement, taken by choice. One-year placements are usually certified as part of a sandwich degree.

Good general guidance on organising placements is provided by *Industrial Placements for Engineering Students: A Guide for Academics* (Higher Education Academy Engineering Subject Centre, 2009), especially on assessment, including examples of approaches taken by universities.

Some qualifications are entirely work-based. An example is the Engineering Gateways initiative of the Engineering Council. This is a framework for gaining the qualification that a working engineer might be lacking in order to become professionally qualified. There is guidance from the Engineering Council (Engineering Gateways, 2011) and a toolkit has been created to support universities in developing this type of provision (Engineering Council, 2012).

Interrogating practice

- What is influencing your choice of approaches?
- Do you feel your current choices are maximising the opportunities for students to learn?
- What developments do you plan to make?

ASSESSMENT AND FEEDBACK

Planning assessment

Let's start with some common problems with assessment in engineering courses. Planning and design of assessment tends to be at the level of the individual module or unit, which leads to imbalances between modules, the same learning outcomes being assessed an unnecessary number of times across a course, a lack of control of over-assessment and, at a more trivial level, bunching of assignment deadlines. Over-assessment, especially in the sense of an overload of summative (final, mark-contributing) assessment, is a problem in many engineering schools. One cause is the laudable desire to give students, especially early in the course, early feedback on their performance so they can correct misunderstandings and have a clear idea of expectations. Another cause is the commonly held belief among lecturers that 'students won't do it if they don't get a mark for it'. This means that more and more pieces of summative assessment are introduced to grab the students' attention, and students stagger from one submission deadline to the next with little time to think and sometimes no time even to attend classes.

Formative assessment simply needs to provide formative feedback. Some of the most traditional forms of engineering learning involve formative feedback like solving examples in an 'examples class' or 'tutorial', or a review of design or project work in advance of submission. Some of the more recent forms like online quizzes do the same.

Forms of assessment

University systems tend to distinguish simply between coursework and exam. Coursework in engineering can range in scale from short assignments based on lab work, to multi-discipline group designs or dissertations.

It can be argued that exams are well suited to demonstration of the mastery of basic engineering principles. There is definitely active learning as students solve problems ('study examples') with the incentive that this is the ideal way to prepare for the exam.

If you do use exams, here's a thought. The traditional exam paper offers a choice of 5 out of 8 questions, or 4 out of 6, but why? Papers where all questions are compulsory can have several advantages. Without the constraint of all questions needing to be at the same level, some questions can cover basics and some more advanced topics; and there is no need for questions to be the same length. Then a pass mark can be achieved by mastery of basic principles (rather than random and probably not fully understood bits and pieces of questions in a traditional paper), yet a mark of 80 per cent represents success in questions that require strong mastery of the material. Also, it is easier to argue that the paper demonstrates achievement of learning outcomes (though with a pass mark of 40 per cent, this is still not watertight).

Exams may be a good way of assessing understanding of more advanced analysis too, though more care is needed to ensure that the exam format does not require the problems to be over-simplified. If exams are just a test of memory – recall of facts – you should think hard about whether it is appropriate to use them.

Assessment of group work

Group work is an essential but difficult aspect of engineering courses. There are always complaints, often from good students, but usually the picture that emerges is that students understand the benefits of group work, it's group assessment that concerns them.

Many of the published examples of effective assessment of group work include some element of peer assessment. Approaches to individualising students' scores through peer assessment for work performed in teams are discussed by Russell et al. (2006) and additional benefits of peer assessment – as a learning experience for students – are identified by Davis and Austin (2012).

Feedback

Feedback and assessment are strongly linked. Engineers should understand the link well, as demonstrated in Case study 17.2. It's not just the innovative practice that interests me here, it's the thinking behind it. It is especially satisfying when we can use our understanding of engineering, not just in *what* we teach but *how* we teach it.

Case study 17.2: Feedback – an engineering concept

At Bournemouth University, the approach to feedback for students of electronic engineering is informed by consideration of feedback as an engineering concept.

In a closed-loop system (Figure 17.1), a process is controlled by the difference ('error') between the output and the target. This error is determined by feeding back the output, comparing it with the target and making any necessary adjustment to the input.

Applied to student learning and assessment, perhaps the input is student engagement, the process is the assessment task and the output is the learning. Or is it? In a control system, feedback would adjust input continuously to optimise the process, but an academic assessment task is more likely to be a discrete activity. Feedback obviously can't be used to adjust engagement with an activity

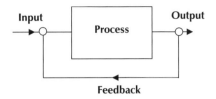

Figure 17.1 Feedback
Source: Adapted from Benjamin (2012)

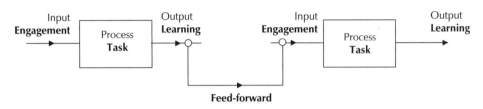

Figure 17.2 Feed-forward
Source: Adapted from Benjamin (2012)

in the past, so academic feedback must be **feedforward**, used to adjust engagement with future or ongoing tasks (Figure 17.2).

Three important and relevant qualities of engineering feedback can be identified: timeliness, appropriateness and application. How do these apply to academic feedback (or feed-forward)? Timeliness we have just dealt with. Academic feedback is most *appropriate* if it can be used by students to improve their engagement with the *next* task. *Application* is to do with whether or not students actually use the feedback they are given. Reasons for not using feedback include the delay in receiving it, not understanding it or not thinking it relevant. Timeliness and appropriateness are the responsibility of the person giving the feedback, but application rests with the student.

At Bournemouth, the result of this thinking about the fundamentals is to place emphasis on student-generated feedback. This is seen as the best way of ensuring that feedback is timely, appropriate and applied. There is support for this in the literature. Carless et al. (2010: 406) state 'in essence feedback is sustainable when it supports students in self-monitoring their own work independently of the tutor'. Gibbs (2006: 33) comments: 'Ultimately the fastest and most frequent feedback available is that provided by students to themselves from moment to moment as they study or write assignments. Investing effort in developing such self-supervision may be much the most cost-effective use of tutors' time.'

Having completed a summative assessment task, students at Bournemouth complete a self-assessment of performance questionnaire. When they submit the next assignment they provide a reflective discussion of how well the intended improvements have been achieved.

More details on the approach, and on the thinking behind it, are given by Benjamin (2012).

(Christopher Benjamin, Bournemouth University)

Feedback is obviously an important element in learning. It also attracts attention because it is one of the areas rated consistently poorly in the NSS, as we have seen. One NSS question asks whether students consider that feedback has been prompt. Mendes et al. (2011) surveyed engineering students' perceptions of feedback. Responses were that feedback should help them to identify strengths and weaknesses and provide guidance on improving performance. Students were asked 'What, in your opinion, constitutes prompt feedback?'. From the free text responses, the periods of time identified tended to range between one week (or less) and two weeks. However, over 40 per cent either did not respond to this question or gave an answer that did not relate to time at all, suggesting that not all staff and students are thinking of the same thing when they refer to 'prompt feedback'.

EVALUATING PRACTICE

Your university will almost certainly require your modules to be evaluated using a standard student feedback questionnaire. You will probably want to seek student feedback in other ways (see Chapter 9). If you are evaluating an element of innovative practice, you may want to research its effectiveness more deeply using (for example) interviews or focus groups. Then there is teaching observation. If the system you follow is based on peer observation, it may lead to useful discussions with colleagues and you may pick up a few valuable ideas when you observe others.

All this evaluation can be useful and it's obviously best to be receptive rather than defensive. Some simple pointers towards doing things in a slightly different way may be useful straightaway. But another important evaluation is self-evaluation. If you are preparing a **teaching portfolio** in your first year as a lecturer, or have already done it, you are probably sick of writing self-evaluations. There is a danger that being a reflective practitioner is seen as writing statements about yourself, but self-evaluation doesn't have to be done on a template. The most meaningful self-evaluation comes from the way you feel after a class or a meeting with students, the thoughts you have on the journey home, how you talk about your job with friends.

I was reflecting recently on a small innovation I had introduced. I found myself thinking that some aspects had gone well, some not so well, and I ended up simply saying to myself, 'well…I tried.' And it struck me that that is really the most important thing of all: that we should keep trying, trying new things even if we don't get everything right, always trying to enhance the student experience.

Interrogating practice

- How do you reflect on your own practice?
- Do you pay attention to your own feelings about how well things go?
- How do you act in response?

DEVELOPING INTERESTS IN ENGINEERING EDUCATION

There is plenty of scope to develop your interests in engineering education. This can potentially involve sharing your ideas with the engineering education community, publishing and even making engineering education your main interest ('at the expense of' technical research). However, it must be said that very few engineering academics become 'educational researchers' mainly because there is nothing in the educational background of most engineering lecturers to act as the academic basis for educational research. Also, it's a difficult area for finding funding, and engineering education research, while potentially qualifying for consideration in the **Research Excellence Framework** (REF) as 'engineering' or as 'education', actually seems to fit well with neither.

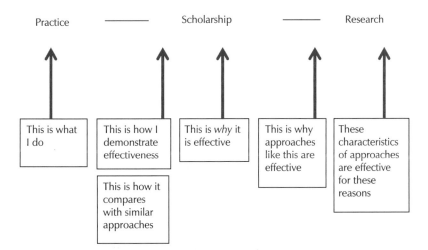

Figure 17.3 Engineering education: the practice–scholarship–research continuum

So how might you describe your interests if not as 'educational research'? I think we can define a continuum of practice–scholarship–research, and I have tried to represent the way that contributions vary across that continuum in Figure 17.3. As we move from practice to research, the outcomes become more generalisable, more of a contribution to knowledge about engineering education itself, rather than the specifics of what you do yourself.

In the UK, one contact with the engineering education community is via the Higher Education Academy. They publish a journal, *Engineering Education*, and sponsor events, including an 'EE' conference every two years. (They also have a STEM conference and a more general conference every year.)

In Europe more generally, there is the SEFI (European Society for Engineering Education, or Société Européenne pour la Formation des Ingénieurs), which publishes a journal, *European Journal of Engineering Education*, and runs a conference every year.

For serious engineering education research, the American Society of Engineering Education publishes arguably the most prestigious journal – *JEE (Journal of Engineering Education)*, and REEN (Research in Engineering Education Network) provides global connections.

REFERENCES

Benjamin, C (2012) 'Feedback for enhanced student performance: lessons from simple control theory', *Engineering Education: Journal of the Higher Education Academy*, 7(2): 16–23.

Carless, D, Salter, D, Yang, M and Lam, J (2010) 'Developing sustainable feedback practices', *Studies in Higher Education*, 36(4): 395–407.

CDIO (2013) *Worldwide CDIO initiative*. Available from: http://www.cdio.org (accessed July 2013).

Collins, K and Davies, J (2009) 'Feedback through student essay competitions: what makes a good engineering lecturer?', *Engineering Education: Journal of the Higher Education Academy Engineering Subject Centre*, 4(1): 8–15.

Cranston, G and Lock, G (2012) 'Techniques to encourage interactive student learning in a laboratory setting', *Engineering Education: Journal of the Higher Education Academy*, 7(1): 2–10.

Davis, T and Austin, S (2012) Workshop on using WebPA to assess group work. *EE2012, International Conference on Innovation, Practice and Research in Engineering Education*. Available from: http://cede.lboro.ac.uk/ee2012 (accessed July 2013).

Davis, S, Connolly, A and Linfield, E (2009) 'Lecture capture: making the most of face-to-face learning', *Engineering Education: Journal of the Higher Education Academy Engineering Subject Centre*, 4(2): 4–13.

Davies, J, Arlett, C, Carpenter, S, Lamb, F and Donaghy, L (2006) 'What makes a good engineering lecturer? Students put their thoughts in writing', *European Journal of Engineering Education*, 31(5): 543–553.

Engineering Council (2010a) *The UK Standard for Professional Engineering Competence*. London: Engineering Council.

Engineering Council (2010b) *Accreditation of Higher Education Programmes, the UK Standard for Professional Engineering Competence*. London: Engineering Council.

Engineering Council (2012) *Engineering Gateways Toolkit*. Available from: http://www.engc.org.uk (accessed July 2013).

Engineering Gateways (2011) *Engineering Gateways – Learning Whilst Earning*. Available from: http://www.engineeringgateways.co.uk (accessed March 2012).

Engineering UK (2011) *An Investigation into Why the UK Has the Lowest Proportion of Female Engineers in the EU*. EngineeringUK. Available from: http://www.engineeringuk.com/_resources/documents/Int_Gender_summary_EngineeringUK_04_11_.pdf (accessed July 2013).

Gibbs, G (2006) 'How assessment frames student learning', in C Bryan and K Clegg (eds.) *Innovative Assessment in Higher Education*. Abingdon: Routledge, 23–36.

Guerra, A and Kolmos, A (2011) 'Comparing problem based learning models: suggestions for their implementation', in JW Davies, E de Graaff and A Kolmos (eds.) *PBL Across the Disciplines: Research into Best Practice*. Aalborg: Aalborg University Press, 3–16.

Higher Education Academy (2012) *National Student Survey Discipline Report – Engineering, May 2012*. York: Higher Education Academy.

Higher Education Academy Engineering Subject Centre (2009) *Industrial Placements for Engineering Students: A Guide for Academics*. Higher Education Academy Engineering Subject Centre and engCETL, Loughborough University. Available from: http://www.heacademy.ac.uk/resources (accessed July 2013).

Hill, S and Miles, E (2012) 'What do students understand by the term "humanitarian engineering"?', EE2012, *International Conference on Innovation, Practice and Research in Engineering Education*. Available from: http://cede.lboro.ac.uk/ee2012 (accessed July 2013).

Mendes, P, Thomas, C and Cleaver, E (2011) 'The meaning of prompt feedback and other student perceptions of feedback: should National Student Survey scores be taken at face value?', *Engineering Education: Journal of the Higher Education Academy Engineering Subject Centre*, 6(1): 31–39.

Page, K, Levesley, M, Read, E, Hanson, B and Gallagher, J (2009) 'Data sharing (DaSh) for collaborative learning in laboratories', *Engineering Education: Journal of the Higher Education Academy Engineering Subject Centre*, 4(2): 37–51.

Quality Assurance Agency (QAA) (2007) *Code of Practice for the Assurance of Academic Quality and Standards in Higher Education – Section 9 Work-based and Placement Learning*. London: Quality Assurance Agency for Higher Education.

Quality Assurance Agency (QAA) (2008) *The Framework for Higher Education Qualifications in England, Wales and Northern Ireland*. London: Quality Assurance Agency for Higher Education.

Quality Assurance Agency (QAA) (2013) *Subject Benchmark Statements*. Available from: http://www.qaa.ac.uk/AssuringStandardsAndQuality/subject-guidance/Pages/Subject-benchmark-statements.aspx (accessed June 2013).

Read, E, Hanson, B and Levesley, M (2008) 'Using weblabs as a tool to support a culturally diverse student cohort', *Engineering Education – Journal of the Higher Education Academy Engineering Subject Centre*, 3(1): 52–61.

Rodriguez-Falcon, E and Yoxall, A (2010) 'Service learning experiences: a way forward in teaching engineering students?', *Engineering Education: Journal of the Higher Education Academy Engineering Subject Centre*, 5(2): 59–68.

Royal Academy of Engineering (2007) *Educating Engineers for the 21st Century.* London: Royal Academy of Engineering.

Russell, M (2008) 'Using an electronic voting system to enhance learning and teaching', *Engineering Education: Journal of the Higher Education Academy Engineering Subject Centre,* 3(2): 58–65.

Russell, M, Harotos, G and Combes, A (2006) 'Individualising students' scores using blind and holistic peer assessment', *Engineering Education: Journal of the Higher Education Academy Engineering Subject Centre,* 1(1): 50–60.

University of Strathclyde (2013) *Teaching and Learning.* http://cms.mecheng.strath.ac.uk/tandl.asp (accessed July 2013).

Dance, drama and music

Paul Kleiman

INTRODUCTION

The disciplines of dance, drama and music comprise what are normally referred to as the 'performing arts' disciplines. Each of the three disciplines, with their interlocking and interconnecting **communities of practice**, is a complex, multi-faceted, multi-layered network of identities, relationships, values, discourses and practices. The aim of this chapter is to identify some of the key aspects that are central to the effective teaching and learning of those three disciplines in UK higher education. Importantly, it does not offer 'instant answers' or 'top tips', but – especially in the 'Interrogating practice' sections – it does pose some questions. The challenge to all those engaged in teaching dance, drama and music is, importantly, to understand all these various aspects and questions as they relate to the context you are working in. The task therefore is to design, create and implement approaches to teaching and learning, and the environments in which they occur, that provide – for both students and staff – experiences and achievements of the highest quality and value.

CONTEXT

The play's the thing.

(Shakespeare)

While performance practice is an important element of all three disciplines (and the focus of this chapter), there are also significant areas of each discipline, for example theatre history, music ethnography, dance anthropology, production and technical subjects, in which the teaching, research and practice are not focused primarily on 'audience-facing' performance.

All three disciplines are taught in some very different institutions and contexts: from 'traditional' universities to small, specialist institutions, that is the dance, drama and music conservatoires. The sector now includes a growing number of private or 'alternative' providers whose courses are normally validated by an established Higher Education Institution (HEI). In the case of the universities, **learning and teaching strategies** now include a much greater focus on skills, **employability** and enterprise. In the case of the conservatoires, they have had to include a much greater focus on academic integrity and achievement alongside their historical role as providers of high quality professional/vocational training. In both cases, but particularly in some of the conservatoires, this has given rise to a number of tensions, particularly around how to combine the academic and the vocational in a way that avoids having to dilute either.

What is also clear is that each of the disciplines is in a constant state of flux and development, particularly as a result of the tectonic policy and cultural shifts within and beyond higher education. Each discipline consists of a broad and expanding spectrum of themes, subjects and methodological approaches, and each has a different profile and orientation. Nevertheless, they share some important pedagogical and methodological challenges.

In drama/theatre studies, for example, an important factor, particularly in relation to the burgeoning field of performance studies/performance research, is that not only has the discipline 'gone global' in regard to the number and location of researchers, research centres and **transnational** collaborations in and between institutions, but also there is a growing sense that a profound '**de-centering**' is transpiring (McKenzie et al., 2010: 1), with the disappearance or fracturing of a core set of discourses and practices. These shifts and changes include:

- A move away from the study of the history of drama to the theory of performance;
- Far less focus on 'the canon' of play texts, dramatists, dramatic forms and a related shift from the study and performance of plays to creating devised performance both in and, particularly, outside traditional theatre spaces;
- A move away from the study of 'plays' as artefacts of interest in themselves – or even in context – and into areas of 'performance', broadly configured;
- As a consequence, even when studying written texts, new paradigms for understanding the practices involved have been applied;
- An increased separation of research practice from professional practice;
- A far more focused set of research practices, incentives and pressures to create high-quality research outputs, including the increased acceptance and influence of discourses and practices based around 'Practice-*as*-Research';
- In response to developments in the arts world, an increasing amount of crossing of disciplinary boundaries with other creative and performing arts subjects, for example film and visual arts as well as dance and music, and away from traditional humanities subject areas; and
- The increased use and integration of information and performance technologies in and into performance.

These shifts and changes have had various and variable levels of impact across the discipline as it is taught in higher education. Similar, or parallel shifts can be observed in the disciplines of dance and music, and the 'de-centering' described by McKenzie et al. (2010) applies as much to those disciplines as it does to drama/theatre studies. That de-centering also applies to the identities of those who work as teachers, researchers and, in a significant number of cases, practitioners in those disciplines (Trowler et al., 2012).

SOME TENSIONS

In all three disciplines, there are sets of tensions in relation to learning and teaching that, even if not easily resolvable, certainly need to be acknowledged and addressed.

The temptation is to describe and perceive these tensions as either/or binary-type opposites, but in reality they usually represent the two poles of a nuanced, complex continuum. The discourses and practices of a particular teacher, course, programme or institution will be located at various and different points along a particular continuum. Some of the key tensions in dance, drama and music involve the following:

- Academic–Vocational
- Achievement–Effort
- Art–Craft
- Assessment *for* learning–Assessment *for* accountability
- **Atomistic learning–Holistic learning**
- Individual–Group
- Process–Product
- Subjectivity–Objectivity
- Teacher-led–Student-centred
- Content oriented–Learning oriented
- Theory–Practice

Some of those tensions, for example 'process–product', are part and parcel of the territory of the discipline and are normally resolved at a local level. Others, such as 'atomised learning–holistic learning' are a consequence of systemic changes, for example **modularisation**, that have had a profound impact on teaching and learning across all higher education.

In the case of modularisation, the effect has been to sort the curriculum into easily digestible, easily managed learning packages. While there are clear advantages in relation to the management of learning, a modularised (atomised) system militates against coherence and connectivity. Some argue that it is an outdated model of education that is based on a twentieth century industrial model of scientific management and focused on rationality, efficiency, standardisation, high managerial control, etc. An increasing number of programmes and institutions, in order to best meet the needs and aspirations of their students and the sort of work environments and careers they may be entering, are 'future-proofing' by moving away from a wholly modularised approach towards a more holistic, integrated one.

THE ROLE OF THE 'TEACHER'

The quotation marks around 'teacher' are quite deliberate because they signify that the roles and functions associated with that word have changed considerably and are contestable. We have moved a long way from the traditional conception of the university teacher as a singular figure of authority, possessing authoritative knowledge that s/he transmits to the student, who in turn is regarded essentially as an empty vessel to be filled with that knowledge. Those guru–disciple, master–pupil, transmitter–receiver relationships still persist, but increasingly rarely, in some areas of dance, drama and music. The general teaching and learning environment – even in the small, specialist institutions such as the music conservatoires – is characterised by a far more equal, mutually respectful relationship between the teacher and the student.

The teacher, more often than not, now acts as a **mentor**, guide and critical friend, and the student is regarded as a partner in learning. This altered relationship, while embraced by many, also challenges and indeed threatens those teachers whose academic identity is bound up with possessing authority and authoritative knowledge, and whose preferred mode of teaching is one of 'transmission'.

THE TUTOR–PRACTITIONER

A key feature of learning and teaching in dance, drama and music is the manner in which pedagogical practices and discourses intersect with professional practices and discourses. Not only do students and staff engage in performance and production projects that – to a greater or lesser extent – replicate 'real-world practices', but also a significant number of individuals combine teaching with their professional work as dancers, directors, musicians, writers, etc. This is particularly the case in relation to the relatively large numbers of part-time or hourly paid staff with active professional lives beyond education who are frequently employed in the sector. In some of the small, specialist institutions, for example the music conservatoires, the ratio of part-time teaching staff to full-time teaching staff can be as great as 20:1.

Many university teachers not only combine professional performance practice with their pedagogic practice, but they frequently use that professional practice as a focus for their research. That relationship nourishes the teaching–research nexus that plays such an important role in enhancing learning and teaching and in shaping academic identity. At the same time, it must be acknowledged that not only is there a significant amount of academic research that is not directly related to artistic/performance practice, but also a great deal of high quality artistic/performance practice that cannot be considered research (Nelson, 2013).

Part-time teachers, on the other hand, clearly bring a wealth of real-world knowledge and experience into the studio or seminar room, and students really appreciate and value the fact that they are being taught or mentored by them. However, part-time teachers, especially those with no more than a couple of hours teaching a week, can easily fall beneath the radar of institutional communication channels (they may not even have a institutional email address), and activities such as induction, assessment and programme review boards and, particularly, staff development opportunities can pass them by. Also, it is often difficult for them to be or feel part of the academic community of practice that forms around a particular course or programme, and which can play such an important role in supporting and enhancing learning and teaching. Certainly, part-time teachers need to be proactive in seeking out information, but there is also an onus on the department/faculty/institution to ensure that all staff are provided properly with the information and support they require (induction, mentors, eligibility for professional development, etc.).

The tutor–practitioner is both a higher education professional as well as an artistic professional. In regard to the former, it is essential that teachers understand the context in which they operate as teachers, and understand the roles and obligations they have in regard to their continuing professional development (CPD) and obtaining professional qualifications.

THE STUDENT AS PRACTITIONER/PRODUCER/PARTNER

One of the most significant and recent shifts in the discourses and practices of learning and teaching has been that of the role of the student. The change in the financing of higher education has fundamentally altered the relationship between the student, the teacher and the institution (Brown, 2013; McGettigan, 2013). Notwithstanding the debates about the marketisation of higher education and whether students are now 'consumers' or 'clients', that relationship has also altered as a result of genuine and valuable developments in learning and teaching and its associated discourses and practices. Those developments include student-centred learning, students as partners, assessment for learning, **immersion** learning and the focus on skills and employability.

Central to this is the notion of the student being a legitimate and active member of a community of practice (Lave and Wenger, 1991), engaging in authentic activities, discourses and practices that correspond with their chosen discipline(s), and with their needs and aspirations. Inevitably, that development has impacted on the role of the tutor who, though s/he might retain the traditional role of the 'transmitter of knowledge', becomes much more of a guide or mentor, enabling and encouraging the student to acquire not only increased knowledge, understanding and skills, but also increased authority and autonomy within that community of practice.

A recent and interesting development has been the idea of the 'student as producer' (Neary and Winn, 2009), which emphasises the role of the undergraduate student as a collaborator in the production of knowledge by working with other students and academics. In this model, students work alongside staff in the design and delivery of their teaching and learning programmes, and in the production of work of academic content and value. The aim is to enable students to take greater responsibility not only for their own teaching and learning, but also for the way in which they manage their entire experience of being a student.

MODELS OF TEACHING AND LEARNING

All education requires both the acquisition of basic knowledge and the ability to apply it in increasingly complex and sophisticated ways and contexts. The balance between acquisition and application ought to shift during the educational process from the former to the latter, although the acquisition of new knowledge and skills, through life-long learning or CPD, never ceases.

The diversity of practices and discourses within the disciplines of dance, drama and music reflects many of the tensions listed earlier and, particularly, the not uncontroversial distinction between those curricula that focus on **iterative learning** and the acquisition and application of established and recognised skillsets (e.g. the training of performers) and those that focus on and require originality and innovation (e.g. composition, choreography). Williams (2014), for example, differentiates between 'Interpretive' and 'Creative' approaches, while Towse (from the perspective of the economics of the creative industries and Intellectual Property Rights) makes a clear distinction between 'creative artists (writers, composers, choreographers and so on) and performers (actors, musicians, dancers and the rest)' (Towse, 2006).

Interrogating practice

To what extent do you:

- Develop a personalised curriculum?
- Teach small groups?
- Use the atelier (workshop) or studio principle?
- Engage in an interplay and integration of theory, practice and inquiry?
- Develop a critique of and dialogue about practice?
- Engage with e-learning and digital technologies?
- Balance skills acquisition/training with experiential/immersive learning?
- Focus on developing the autonomous learner?
- Engage in/enable/encourage reflective learning?
- Engage in research-led and professionally led teaching?
- Engage in collaborative teaching, including peer observation?
- Engage in group/collaborative/multidisciplinary/cross-level working?
- Develop/apply 'soft skills'?

The forms of practice to which these questions can be applied include the following:

- Performance/production projects: these can be internal or external and set in conjunction with industry practitioners/partners. They can be devised or directed and the role of the teacher can be that of tutor/supervisor or director.

- Studio practice/workshops: often related to practical aspects of the discipline, for example voice, movement, technique.
- Work-based learning/placement projects: learning off-site, engaging in arts/performance-based projects in the community, in and with schools, hospitals, industry, etc.
- Lectures and seminars: traditional perhaps, but they still have a role, and digital technologies enable them to be far more interactive and accessible either synchronously or asynchronously.
- Group/team-based projects: replicating or simulating real-world practice, for example allocation of specific roles.
- Master classes/practitioner talks: students clearly value the opportunity to meet, talk and work with well-established practitioners, and also recent graduates whose experiences students can relate to directly.
- Commissions/consultancy: students are commissioned by or act as consultants to industry, working collaboratively with industry partners to solve issues they identify.
- **Peer-learning**: student-to-student mentoring.

ASSESSMENT – AN ART NOT A SCIENCE

All assessment is situated in the local context, and in the particular traditions, expectations and needs of different universities, specialist institutions and academic disciplines. Theory and evidence has to be interpreted and applied within those parameters and cannot be applied simply or uniformly.

(Higher Education Academy, 2012)

Assessment and feedback in dance, drama and music appear consistently among the issues that are of most interest and concern to both students and staff, particularly in relation to the assessment of creative practice and live performance.

(PALATINE, 2008)

Case study 18.1: Feedback in musical performance

I had become increasingly aware of unresolved issues related to the feedback process that were a clear cause of dissatisfaction among students and of concern to tutors. Peer feedback is central to the undergraduate classical musical performance modules at the university: students are asked to offer informal feedback on their peers' performances in the context of group seminars and to write peer feedback as part of their performance assignments. Students, however, appeared to have a passive attitude towards the feedback process, an activity they felt tutors and examiners should be responsible for.

This attitude was most clearly illustrated by the written peer feedback assignments (concert reviews). The critical comments provided often failed to enhance the learning experience of both the students giving the feedback and those receiving it, and students received no guidance on how to change their attitude to the feedback process and improve their feedback skills. The language of assessment was also problematic, and some of the assessment categories used were either implicit or too broad and, therefore, open to misinterpretation.

Feeding the finding of my research back into teaching activities resulted in:

- Workshops that gave performance students the opportunity to reflect upon the assessment language and concepts used by tutors and examiners in musical performance;
- The structured feedback forms (SFFs) used for musical performance assessments at undergraduate levels (first and second year) were modified to be explicit and unambiguous. Three new categories were introduced to replace 'musicality' and 'performance': 'understanding of the piece as a whole', 'style' and 'approach to music';
- A new peer assessment activity was devised, which reflected the clarifications of assessment categories implemented in the SFFs;
- Using the VLE, an online Peer Feedback Database was created, which encouraged students to:
  - Engage actively with the assessment categories and language used for musical performance;
  - Gain a deeper understanding of the principles of good feedback practice and apply them in the context of peer assessment; and
  - View feedback as a mutual, dialogic process.
- Additionally, I created a structured feedback form for the peer feedback assignment designed to give students information on their use of assessment criteria, feedback principles, as well as on how to improve their feedback skills.

There was significant impact. Performance students soon reported that their engagement with the new assessment categories had enabled them to feed back to their peers in a more constructive and objective manner. The activity also demonstrated students' increased depth of participation. From a teaching perspective, it has become an invaluable tool in identifying and addressing promptly (through **formative** feedback) weaknesses in students' use or understanding of fundamental concepts related to musical performance and its evaluation. At institutional level, the impact of the work on peer feedback has been very positive. It has gained recognition (through a Teaching and Learning Award) for its ground-breaking design and innovative approach, and findings are now feeding into the development of new technology that supports instrumental learning.

The project demonstrated that peer feedback is a vital key to the development of students' independent learning. Providing guidance and structure in peer feedback activities, especially at the earlier stages of undergraduate musical performance studies, is essential to building an understanding of how to have an analytical approach to musical performance, an activity which is synthetic and creative. This understanding can give students the confidence to take charge of their own learning process and grow into imaginative and convincing performers.

(Maria Krivenski, Goldsmiths, University of London)

The increase in student numbers, staff–student ratios and group sizes, and the requirement to conform to increasingly rigid regulatory and quality assurance frameworks has been of particular significance. Assessment and feedback in higher education has been identified as a major HE policy issue, and there is considerable pressure on institutions and courses to ensure that their assessment strategies and methodologies fulfil the necessary requirements of validity, reliability and fairness. As a consequence, some of the 'traditional' approaches to assessment in the performing arts – especially learner-focused assessment and those assessment approaches whose effectiveness relies on relatively small cohorts of students – have had to be adapted or even discarded in order to meet the demands of the present conditions.

The different approaches and attitudes towards assessment within and across dance, drama and music reveal some interesting tensions and pose some intriguing challenges. It is also important to state that there are numerous examples of excellent, creative and innovative assessment practices. What is noticeable, in all three disciplines and despite or probably because of the various tensions, is both the genuine care and concern that is applied to the process of assessment, and the ongoing discussions and debates about how to enhance assessment.

Interrogating practice

To what extent do you:

- Focus your assessment processes on assessment for learning rather than assessment of learning?
- Maintain a useful and beneficial balance between formative and summative assessment?
- Ensure your assessment discourses and practices reflect the discourses and practices of the discipline?

ASSESSING PERFORMANCE

One of the defining characteristics of dance, drama and music in higher education is the engagement in the production and presentation of performance work. This can take many forms from large-scale public performances in a theatre or concert hall to intimate, site-specific performances in offbeat locations. Every performance and production is unique and the challenges of assessment are both fascinating and considerable.

The following are just some of the key challenges and questions:

- The need for assessment to engage with both process and product, acknowledging that even a performance can sometimes reveal the nature of the process;
- The need to acknowledge that 'numerous instabilities in the diversity and ephemerality of performance arts practices pose particular challenges to ideas of fixed, measurable and recordable knowledge' (Nelson, 2013);
- The need to clarify and differentiate between performance/performing (process, doing, revealing) and presentations/presenting (product, giving). Are you assessing the work or the performance of the work?
- The need to acknowledge that there are some critical and subjective aspects of performance (Does it keep us awake? Is it memorable? Is there a 'wow' factor? If you paid money to see it would it be money well spent?) that are difficult to codify in the form of clear, coherent assessment criteria (the systems of moderation and external examining act as important checks on this aspect of assessment);
- The need to resolve the contradictions between the requirement to have clear **learning outcomes** and assessment criteria, while retaining some flexibility to take account of unexpected, unintended outcomes;
- The need to recognise how our own subjective and contextualised discourses and practices impact on the way we undertake assessment;
- The need to be clear on the thorny issue of by whose or which standards is the work being assessed? Professional standards, employer standards or educational standards?
- The need to acknowledge the limitations of assessment criteria, particularly their frequent inability to encapsulate the finer points of performance work;
- The need to align learning outcomes with both curriculum content and assessment criteria (see Biggs (1999) on **constructive alignment**). But, do we start with the learning outcomes and select the most suitable piece, or do we start with the piece and hope it can meet most of the learning outcomes?
- The need to ensure that there is parity or equivalence of the amount and weight of assessment across modules and/or over time. The very nature of performance/production work is that the tasks are distributed unevenly, for example producer or technician, lead role or walk-on part. It is important that, whatever the approach to assessment, students feel a sense of fairness about assessment between and across modules and individuals.

None of these issues are easily resolvable and they undoubtedly pose a challenge, particularly in institutions such as large HEIs, in which performing arts programmes constitute only a small part of the entire programme of courses, and in which one-size-fits-all, standardised assessment frameworks apply to all degree programmes.

The challenge is perhaps encapsulated in this contribution to one of the many workshops on assessing performance organised by PALATINE, the HEA subject centre for dance, drama and music:

> The thread that runs through our task of assessing the very unscientific form we recognise as performance is one of encoding–decoding/decoding–encoding; of deconstruction and reconstruction; we pull apart so that we can understand how it was all put together, and spectating or gazing at that totality we give feedback, observation, comment and finally a grade which we think and feel is a fair and considered assessment of the work, the effort, the student at the centre of this web.
>
> (O'Keefe, 2001)

Interrogating practice

In relation to assessing performance, to what extent do you:

- Ensure there are clear, coherent assessment criteria?
- Ensure that you and the students understand the criteria?
- Ensure that the criteria are written in the discourse of the discipline?
- Clarify whether you are assessing process and/or product? Individual and/or group? Achievement and/or effort? Art and/or craft? Theory and/or practice?

ASSESSING GROUPWORK

The need for an individual to work and perform in a group context is an inescapable fact of studying and working in dance, drama and music. Yet assessment is understandably focused on an individual's achievements and efforts. It is no surprise, therefore, that there are significant tensions around the assessment of group work and, particularly, the assessment of the individual in relation to the group. One of the challenges is encapsulated in this comment by a drama lecturer in an email to the author: 'we need to encourage collaboration by finding ways of reassuring the high achievers that their results will not be dragged down by the less committed, while motivating the unwilling'.

There are no easy answers to the challenges of assessing groupwork; however, it is essential that whatever approach is utilised, it is not only made clear and understood by everyone concerned but it is applied consistently.

Case study 18.2: Engaging students in non-assessed activities

A few years ago I ran a project called 'Becoming a Music Student: Understanding and Fostering the Study Skills of First Year Undergraduates'.

The findings showed how the musical identities of students were closely connected with their experiences of assessment, evident in a mid-semester dip in confidence as students faced their first round of assessment and feedback. They illustrated too that the conventions and expectations of academic life can be mysterious to new students, fresh from the structured criteria of A-Level studies – and that bombarding them with all the information they need for university study in the first weeks of the semester may be counterproductive.

A few years later, I ran some optional lunchtime workshops on study skills, which, perhaps inevitably, reached the students who were most receptive but least in need of guidance! However, as well as learning more about the aspects of academic study that they found most bewildering (e.g. grading) these conscientious lunchtime attendees also showed me how much time and concentration the business of living independently can occupy for an 18-year-old (washing, shopping, making travel arrangements) – and for many students, having a paid job to fund those essentials – can all too easily get in the way of focusing on academic study.

In a subsequent PALATINE-funded project (the former HEA Performing Arts Learning and Teaching Innovation Network centre), completed in 2012, I picked up some of these concerns about students' engagement in departmental life, focusing on 'Engaging Music Students in Non-Assessed Activities'. The project explored the barriers and incentives to participate in departmental ensembles, attend concerts and volunteer for other activities in the department – as well as investigating students' experiences of those activities when they do engage with them.

Focus group discussions were organised with a range of students from Sheffield and two other institutions, collecting a variety of views and suggestions for developing departmental practice in this area. We also ran an online survey, inviting staff to contribute their views, so that staff and student perspectives could be compared, and differences traced over time according to length of university career.

The high level of student interest in the project was encouraging, and there was a clear sense that extra-curricular activities are an important aspect of departmental life. Students' views on levels of compulsion and credit varied: those given credit for their concert attendance or playing felt constrained by that, while those who engaged voluntarily felt that this gave the activities lower priority or status. It seems that we really can't win – but that the efforts to do so are worthwhile!

A great strength of all these projects has been in raising awareness among students and colleagues that the research tools we apply to any other intellectual problem are just as valuable in developing strategies for effective teaching and learning. Holding a Teaching Development Award brings a legitimacy to a problem because a peer-reviewed, funded project about study skills encourages all colleagues to take the findings seriously, and generates fresh data about student experience. The integration of teaching and research, and the opportunity to understand students' experiences more deeply, has been hugely valuable in my own professional development, and hopefully had at least a small impact on other people's willingness to engage with similar challenges.

(Stephanie Pitts, University of Sheffield)

THEORY AND PRACTICE

As with learning and teaching, the phrase 'theory and practice' suggests a link between two separate entities, rather than a single entity consisting of two organically inter-linked elements. The perceived separation can be particularly acute in dance, drama and music with their strong vocational and performance traditions in which skills and **critical thinking** are seen as only loosely linked, at best. However, in a higher education context, it is essential that the inter-relationship between theory and practice is acknowledged, and that students are provided with the opportunities and skills to explore, examine and experience how theoretical and practical discourses and practices intersect, inform and inspire each other (Nelson, 2013).

Interrogating practice

To what extent do you:

- Embed theory and practice, skills and criticality in your teaching?
- Articulate/demonstrate what a 'critical practice' might look like?
- Ensure practice is properly informed by critical and conceptual thinking?
- Enable students to see the value of conceptual and theoretical perspectives in enriching their own work?

THE CREATIVE CURRICULUM

Creativity has been on the agenda and in the mission statement of many institutions, and there has been a great deal of work and research around defining creativity, particularly in relation to education, and developing approaches to teaching and learning that encourage and enable students (and staff) to develop and engage in creative practices and to initiate and undertake innovative forms of teaching and learning.

The problem with creativity is that is it notoriously difficult to define; however, attempts to define it appear to coalesce around the (not unproblematic) notions of originality and novelty combined with value and utility (Mayer, 1999). The definition problem is not one that particularly concerns those who work and study in higher education. What does exercise academic minds is what place creativity has – with its associations of risk-taking, uncertainty and the ability to disturb the status quo – in the daily discourses and practices of a particular programme of study.

There is an assumption that creative arts courses must, of necessity, be creative. This is, of course, a fallacy. Replication and formulation exist alongside innovation and origination. The challenge – both for teachers and the systems in which they operate – is that, when it comes to assessment, the first two are much easier to assess than the latter two. So, in the various institutional drives for standardisation and conformity across higher education programmes, the risk is that genuine creativity, because of the complexities involved in assessing it, is driven out of the curriculum.

The learning outcomes and assessment criteria approach to teaching, learning and assessment, that is now the working language of higher education, has many positive aspects, for example clarity and transparency. But there is a natural tendency towards prescription, typically formulated as: 'on completion of this module the student *will* [author's emphasis] be able to demonstrate a, b, c, d, etc.'

That prescriptive approach to learning outcomes certainly has a place and function, particularly in relation to assessing the demonstration of competencies. However, the more that learning and teaching strategies focus on encouraging creativity and innovation (and, of course, creativity and innovation may not be the primary aim or focus), then the more learning outcomes need to evolve and become rather less prescriptive in order to allow for and map the inevitable unintended outcomes.

Interrogating practice

To what extent do you:

- Articulate a commitment to creativity/creative practice explicitly in your course documents?
- Ensure learning outcomes and assessment criteria accommodate and even encourage valuable, unexpected outcomes?
- Balance the fixed and the free through setting appropriate constraints?
- Acknowledge risk in the assessment process… and how (e.g. validating less successful, but daring/innovative work in relation to well-executed safe/formulaic work or, conversely, not validating a 'risky' but naïve rejection of artistic discourses, practices and constraints)?

THE WORLD OF WORK: EMPLOYABILITY, ENTREPRENEURSHIP AND SKILLS

The employability agenda has been an increasingly important driver of policy and practice in learning and teaching for a number of years. There is frequently an awkward fit between the performing arts disciplines and the assumptions, discourses and practices that drive that employability agenda. However, dance, drama and music graduates often do well in official surveys (e.g. the Higher Education Statistics Agency's 'Destinations' surveys, HESA 2013), due in part to the wide range of employability skills that are acquired through study and work in those disciplines.

Some of the key aspects in learning and teaching in regard to this area are:

- Enabling students to move from a focus on performance virtuosity (in any discipline) to a more complex social understanding of practice as part of a cultural/social/political/economic scene;
- Developing the conceptual shift from arts-workers to cultural entrepreneurs and social-actors;
- Emphasising and understanding the portfolio nature of employment in the arts;
- Understanding freelancing and entrepreneurialism;
- Understanding the creative industry landscape and labour market, for example supply and demand;
- Genuine engagement with the 'world of work', for example placement models, curriculum design/content;
- Developing relationships with and models of working with the arts and culture professions;
- Managing work-based learning;
- Encouraging networking with local industry contacts and attendance at professional arts events;
- Identifying, articulating and embedding the really useful key or transferable skills;
- **Internationalisation** of the student experience (this includes students studying abroad, the diversification of student cohorts and the enhancement of the curriculum).

TECHNOLOGY-ENHANCED LEARNING

Students and staff across dance, drama and music clearly utilise the standard technologies and platforms (e.g. **virtual learning environments**) associated with technology-enhanced learning (TLE). However, those disciplines are also the focus for the creative and innovative use of a wide range of digital and mobile technologies and, increasingly, social media that do not fit easily into institutional IT protocols and policies. This is particularly apparent in the extensive and varied areas of performance and production practice in all three disciplines, for example capacities for storage and retrieval of audio and/or visual files, or the use of non-standard applications and platforms.

Interrogating practice

To what extent do you:

- Integrate TEL into your own pedagogic practice?
- Keep up-to-date with recent relevant TEL developments and applications in your discipline?
- Utilise TEL in your programme/department/faculty and, if so, how?

CONCLUSIONS AND OVERVIEW

At a time when the landscape of learning and teaching in higher education is changing quite significantly, there has never been a greater focus on the act and art of learning and teaching. In this changed and still-changing landscape, the disciplines of dance, drama and music provide not only some fascinating and significant challenges but, importantly, they also provide fertile ground for important adaptations and innovations in learning and teaching.

One of the reasons for this is that, as a Dean of Studies in a music institution wrote in an email to the author: 'Students are more than ever aware of the importance of their precious 'college time'. It makes for a constructive environment and sharpens teachers and learners to think about the investment that is being made in higher education. There has always been a sense of partnership, but there seems to be a new dialogue between students and staff, and collaborative work with students seems to be at an all-time high.'

This chapter, through its identification and relatively brief exploration of the key and often complex aspects of learning and teaching in dance, drama and music, will hopefully inform future developments and assist in creating a genuine collaboration and partnership focused around learning and teaching: to the mutual benefit of all.

REFERENCES

Biggs, J (1999) *Teaching for Quality Learning at University*. Buckingham: SRHE and Open University Press.

Brown, R with Carasso, H (2013) *Everything for Sale? The Marketisation of UK Higher Education*. London: Routledge.

Higher Education Academy (HEA) (2012) *A Marked Improvement: Transforming Assessment in Higher Education*. York: Higher Education Academy.

Higher Education Statistics Agency (HESA) (2013) *Destinations of Leavers from Higher Education Survey (DLHE)*. Available from: http://www.hesa.ac.uk/index.php?option=com_content&task=view&id=1899&Itemid=239 (accessed 8 April 2014).

Lave, J and Wenger, E (1991) *Situated Learning: Legitimate Peripheral Participation*. Cambridge: Cambridge University Press.

Mayer, RE (1999) 'Fifty years of creativity research', in RJ Sternberg (ed.) *Handbook of Creativity*. Cambridge: Cambridge University Press, 449–460.

McGettigan, A (2013) *The Great University Gamble: Money, Markets and the Future of Higher Education*. London: Pluto Press.

McKenzie, J, Roms, H and Lee, CJW-L (eds.) (2010) *Contesting Performance: Global Sites of Research*. London: Palgrave Macmillan.

Neary, M and Winn, J (2009) 'The student as producer: reinventing the student experience in higher education', in L Bell, H Stevenson and M Neary (eds.) *The Future of Higher Education: Policy, Pedagogy and the Student Experience*. London: Continuum, 192–210.

Nelson, R (2013) *Practice as Research in the Arts: Principles, Protocols, Pedagogies, Resistances*. London: Palgrave Macmillan.

O'Keefe, J (2001) *Different Perspectives*. Paper and presentation notes, Assessing Live Performance Workshop, PALATINE/London Contemporary Dance School, 2 May 2001. Available from: http://78.158.56.101/archive/palatine/events/viewreport/146/index.html (accessed 9 April 2014).

PALATINE (2008) *Starting Out in Assessing Live Performance: Information Pack*. Lancaster: PALATINE.

Towse, R (2006) 'Human capital and artists' labour markets', in V Ginsburgh and D Throsby (eds.) *Handbook of the Economics of the Arts and Culture*. Amsterdam: Elsevier, 865–894.

Trowler, P, Bamber, V and Saunders, M (eds.) (2012) *Tribes and Territories in the 21st Century: Rethinking the Significance of Disciplines in Higher Education*. London: Routledge.

Williams, TH (2014) *Creator or Interpreter? Fit for Practice: an Investigation into the Employability Skills of Two Types of Performing Arts Student*. York: Higher Education Academy.

FURTHER READING

Kleiman, P (2012) 'Scene changes and key changes: disciplines and identities in HE dance, drama and music', in P Trowler, V Bamber and M Saunders (eds.) *Tribes and Territories in the 21st Century: Rethinking the Significance of Disciplines in Higher Education*. London: Routledge, 130–141.

19 | Social sciences

Fiona Stephen

Social science is, in its broadest sense, the study of society and the manner in which people behave and influence the world around us. It tells us about the world beyond our immediate experience, and can help explain how our own society works – from the causes of unemployment or what helps economic growth, to how and why people vote, or what makes people happy. It provides vital information for governments and policymakers, local authorities, non-governmental organisations and others.

(Economic and Social Science Research Council, 2013)

INTRODUCTION

Disagreement and controversy have always defined the social sciences and those whose task it is to teach in this sprawling and argumentative field have a two-fold responsibility: first to show why there can often be more than one answer to any given question; and second to ensure that students are sufficiently well informed and thus able to move beyond mere opinion, and to arrive at a considered judgement about any given problem. In this way, students should become comfortable in using analytical and critical skills and be able to identify the key questions and issues. In many subject areas, there are multiple and different narratives offering opposing interpretations. This chapter starts with the premise that teaching in the social sciences and humanities is a critical pedagogy and that the student as an **active learner** is the key focus.

THE CHANGING EDUCATIONAL ENVIRONMENT

But the study of society cannot be divorced from the demands placed upon it by society itself. Changing educational policy has placed increasing emphasis on widening participation and the need to provide graduates with the knowledge and skills to support national economic development (Dearing Report, 1997; Leitch Report, Department for Employment and Learning, 2006). The resulting increase in student numbers and diversity has brought with it a set of challenges for university lecturers. The measurement of student satisfaction with the annual **National Student Survey** (NSS) combined with various higher education league tables can be increasingly translated into financial outcomes for universities and the disciplines, particularly in the humanities and social sciences. In short, successful teaching and learning outcomes at every level are not merely intrinsically desirable but essential.

When undergraduate students arrive for their first year of undergraduate studies in the social sciences, the challenge is how to support their transition into higher education. In a period that has seen increasing student numbers and levels of indebtedness, greater attention has been paid to their material and welfare needs as they enter university. It is relatively recently that the transition into higher education and academic integration has been identified as an issue requiring attention. The need to attract students in a competitive environment, to improve student retention and achieve high levels of student achievement have all contributed to this.

Interrogating practice

- To what extent does your department's current practice take account of the needs and skills of incoming students?
- Think of three ways in which you might improve upon current practice.

In the past, there has been a tendency to attribute student difficulties with a course as problems belonging to students themselves. With the now greater emphasis on equality of opportunity, it is recognised that a long-held assumption – that all students with the required admissions grades share the same starting point – no longer applies. The challenge for lecturers is, therefore, how to engage the new diversity of undergraduate students with a series of modules that launch them successfully in the discipline they have chosen to study. In the process, there is the imperative to develop the learners' level of autonomy and critical self-confidence, aiding their transformation into active learners rather than passive recipients (a key theme of **student engagement**, as developed by Graham Gibbs in Chapter 14).

SUPPORTING LEARNING IN THE SOCIAL SCIENCES

Unlike some disciplines where there is a strictly structured knowledge basis that has to be digested and learned (for example anatomy or the case law pertaining to a particular topic), most social sciences, and increasingly the humanities, consist of a range of conceptual models and narratives that are used to inform detailed analysis and debate.

The process involved in studying these areas at higher levels, as in so many disciplines, is not about rote learning and regurgitating a set of discrete 'facts', but more about using a substantive basis for analysing, evaluating and critiquing.

In what follows, we shall be looking at four innovative ways of teaching the social sciences in a creative and student-active way: one taken from the oldest department of International Relations in the world at Aberystwyth University; another from Queen's University Belfast where the study of the Middle Eastern conflict is a conduit for examining issues relating to societal conflict nearer home; the third from the London School of Economics (LSE) where the School decided (for the first time in its history) to have a common course for all students; and the fourth even more challenging from a postgraduate programme at the University of Kent. Each in their distinctive way is dedicated to involving the student as an active and participant learner. The LSE100 is the exception in that it is cross-disciplinary within the social sciences and is designed to bring together 'hard' social scientists, such as accountants, economists and management, with the 'soft' social anthropologists, sociologists, historians and international relations scholars.

The Department of International Politics, Aberystwyth University, was an early innovator in addressing the needs of new first year students. Recognising that most, if not all, their first year intake had not had the opportunity to study international politics or international relations previously, and that they were arriving with a wide range of expectations and prior learning experiences, it was decided to introduce a core foundation module. All first year international politics students were enrolled on the module in their first semester as an introduction to the discipline and the department. The structure of the module was conceived in such a way as to challenge their expectations, avoid a didactic approach and free them from the slavish adoption of this or that textbook.

Case study 19.1: 'Behind the Headlines' in International Politics

'Behind the Headlines' (BTH) was a suitably utopian teaching project for the new millennium. It began in 2000 in the Department of International Politics at Aberystwyth University, the world's first such department and a regular source of cutting-edge innovative teaching. Today, the broad aims sound doggedly familiar: to introduce first-year students to contemporary global issues, while providing a variety of rich learning experiences. What was exceptional was the variety of ways in which relevant knowledge was delivered to students and the range of learning experiences they were offered.

BTH's other aims included the early introduction to new students of as many members of staff as possible, and the displaying of the Department's extensive research expertise. Much use was made of a notably multinational PhD community, both for their scholarly expertise and to expand the range of views with which students had to engage. Doctoral students also played a vital role as facilitators (advisers and agony-aunts) for the small, self-managed groups that were central to the learning experience.

BTH sought to sensitise students to key skills identified by the recently released Dearing Report (1997), including those related to future careers. We attempted to reach beyond the usual litany of new information sources by raising awareness about historiography, writing styles, 'reading' TV and the press, and small group dynamics.

Working in self-managed small groups was identified as a particular study skill offering useful career-related experience. 'Learning by doing' was seen as valuable in itself, while also offering excellent ('evidence based') experience to relate at career interviews. After being spoon-fed at school, however, some students resented being pushed out of their comfort zones in this way.

The empirical focus of the module changed each semester. Among the module's first headlines were: 'NATO bombs Kosovo', 'Pinochet to be extradited?' and 'Should Third World debt be cancelled?' Over time, a mix of less obvious issues was included. One 'Remembrance Day' inspired the exploration of the meaning(s) of war memorials in different countries.

Each topic (usually four sessions) was delivered through a mix of formats: traditional lectures, debates, video clips with interpretation and role playing. The final session was an interactive Forum (like the BBC's 'Question Time') but with the self-managed groups encouraged to formulate comments and questions in advance, to help group members intervene (and survive) in a large public meeting.

Assessment was in two parts. First, a reflective log written and produced by the group, analysing a self-chosen global issue (such as 'Russia after Communism'), as well as offering lessons about groupwork. Second, individuals were tested in a three-hour open book examination – the open book being their own personal compilation of material resources from the course as it progressed. Alongside traditional essay-length questions ('Is democracy a recipe for international peace?'), there were quick questions designed to test empathetic imagination as well as analytical ability ('Write a short editorial for *The Times* on the global drug trade' or 'As an adviser to the Egyptian Foreign Minister, offer five bullet points the Minister should emphasise in the next meeting with the US Ambassador').

Some students loved BTH (the variety of topics and learning experiences, and its general unpredictability). Others were troubled. The main gripes were an expressed preference for traditional modules focused on one lecturer; too much variety and innovation; and resentment at free riders in the production of the collective log. Enthusiasm also waned on the staff side. BTH was exceptionally labour intensive and it required extensive organisation both in advance and on a weekly basis.

BTH ran for six semesters between 2000 and 2003. Like other utopian projects, it was glorious in retrospect, but in the end proved too ambitious.

(Ken Booth, Aberystwyth University)

This innovative module was perhaps ahead of its time, resulting in it being removed from the curriculum at the end of only three years. There were several reasons – one being the difficulties around the issue of delivering a compulsory core module for all first year students but in a dual-language format – English and Welsh. The Welsh medium students wished to be taught on the module through the medium of Welsh in addition to delivering their assignments and writing their exams in Welsh – both these options were available to them as an integral part of the course. Apart from the cost implications of providing simultaneous dual translation for all workshop sessions, lectures and seminars, the concept of separating the students into language groups negated one of the original motivations behind the module.

With a substantial number of Welsh speaking students coming into the department alongside a wider international student mix, there was a tendency for the students to settle into two defined groups. As a department of international politics, it was felt that there was a fundamental responsibility to ensure that all the students, irrespective of language and culture, were actively encouraged to get to know each other and to benefit mutually from developing a broader cultural empathy and understanding.

Another not insignificant issue was the resulting division between members of the faculty into those who were the energetic 'champions' of the innovation versus others who were either indifferent to it or felt it was an unnecessary extra demand at the expense of their research time.

The pedagogic learning from this pilot did influence further developments in the department and was a valuable 'consciousness raising' exercise for the departmental staff about how a stimulating curriculum might be better shaped and delivered.

Role play and simulations are now common elements in many programmes of study and it is not unusual for universities to have compulsory foundation modules and programmes (see LSE100 Case study 19.3). Furthermore, in the era of student fees and the overt employability agenda, learners may be more likely to appreciate the explicit added value of such a programme. It is perhaps worth noting that a second year optional module, 'Behind the Headlines 2' had a 60 per cent take-up from the previous first year learners. This module gained excellent student evaluations and learning outcomes. However, as a case study in innovation within the curriculum, it is perhaps also a cautionary tale about how much innovation to introduce at one time.

One of the issues students complained of in the 'Behind the Headlines' case study was the lack of a unique teacher on the course and a core text book – they wanted someone who would tell them what they needed to know to be successful and to make the grade. This was despite the positive student feedback about the support they had received from the teaching assistants on the course and the ready accessibility of the academic course team. As Newman (2004) found, this is a familiar complaint. Many students are already strategic learners (taking a **strategic approach**) when they arrive at university. In many cases, their A-level programme taught them how to be strategic, tailoring their learning to meet the requirements of the assessment. The problem is that the approach has worked for them – they have been successful and arrived where they wanted to be. The initial demands of **independent** study can prove daunting.

The challenge for academics is how to encourage the students to expand their comfort zone and develop both the confidence to take risks, and a healthy scepticism towards the range of concepts and master narratives they may encounter. This is particularly relevant when teaching subjects that are controversial or politically sensitive. The whole of the learning environment is an opportunity to engage and empower students as active learners. As Giroux (1992: 141), a proponent of critical pedagogy suggests, if students are going to learn how to do all this, they need to see such behaviour demonstrated in the social practices and subject positions that teachers live out and not merely propose. The model being proposed offers a variation on the virtuous circle epitomized by Kolb's Cycle (see Chapter 5), with student **feedback** to the lecturer being the point before reflection, revision and the next orbit of the cycle. Thus assessment and feedback strategies (see Chapters 8 and 9 for a more detailed, but non-discipline specific consideration of these) can be an effective part of the process of student engagement – not simply teacher feedback on progress to the student but as part of a two-way process. This is illustrated in Case study 19.2, which focuses on the challenge of developing active learners who will engage in **deep approaches to learning**.

Case study 19.2: Teaching Middle Eastern Politics using blended learning with a web-based project

Middle Eastern Politics is an area study module with an average of 80–100 students enrolled each year. The module employs a combination of traditional and critical pedagogic approaches and is designed to encourage a spirit of critical inquiry and dialogue. New opportunities and spaces for learning are deliberately established to challenge and motivate learners. Both an explicit and implicit focus on conflict resolution through learning activities is central to the pedagogic approach on this module. The aims of the module are to provide students with an understanding of the political culture, history, institutions and current dynamics of the region; the opportunity for independent initiative through role play; computer-based learning; written presentations and conflict resolution and negotiation skills.

The students are encouraged to engage in both independent learning and group work. Active involvement with the role play combines learning with developing an understanding of the complex political dynamics within a conflict region and the demands and skills required for conflict resolution. The exercise combines face-to-face small and larger group activity with virtual online interaction (see Chapter 10) at the individual and group level. Designed to encourage small group work, writing and debating skills in a time-pressured 'real-time' context, the virtual online component keeps everyone engaged and fully participative, irrespective of whether they are on campus or not. Introducing the students to the core content of the module through the medium of 'role play' has made the range of complex material and sources more accessible and student friendly. An added advantage is that because the case study and sophisticated role-play briefs are research-led, the curriculum content is kept up-to-date in a complex subject area.

For role-play preparation, the students engage in their groups using dedicated password protected web pages for each team – planning their strategy, action planning supplemented by face-to-face group meetings and task setting among themselves. One particular advantage of the web-based element is as an ice-breaker (shyness and reluctance to speak in the classroom context is avoided), each member has a defined role and a required online part to play with contributions to make, and once the process has started, the face-to-face sessions move forward as a continuation of the virtual discussions and activities. With the course tutor as moderator, formative feedback is integral to the whole process.

In one round of the module, the Israeli team, for example, lodged over 40 communications on the message board; they approached other teams, pre-negotiated, analysed intelligence, debated infiltration, organised their portfolio and prepared press statements and position papers. On the day of the actual role play, the Israeli team successfully negotiated with the other teams; they had a clear negotiation strategy, they knew the dynamics of their own political system, as well as those of their negotiating partners, and all the rules of the game were strictly adhered to.

The mode of assessment reflects the importance attached to student input throughout the module. The **summative assessment** includes a conventional end of course written essay plus an assessed portfolio comprising three elements: a country study, a book review and the role-play analysis with supporting documentation. Although the students have worked in groups and acted in teams throughout the module, the portfolio is designed as an assessment of individual work.

The portfolio has proved extremely effective in terms of engendering different forms of writing skills, as well as incorporating student-generated resources from the role play, and an opportunity for deep learning in terms of the country study. The role-play and computer-based element of the module is perceived as a valuable and 'transforming' experience for the students – acting as a focus for a series of learning and skill-generating activities throughout the module, including the important computer-based element. There are, of course, more traditional elements in the module, such as lectures, where again the students are actively involved in the feedback cycle using Muddy Card Feedback (Mosteller, 1989) to indicate where they have least understanding.

Student evaluation has demonstrated the effectiveness of the innovation. In relation to the role-play experience, student responses have included statements such as: 'I learnt … how compromise is difficult to reach … about constraints … very helpful web-links … public speaking skills … debating skills … difficulties of real-life disputes … negotiating skills … calmness under pressure … research skills … diplomacy.'

The value of this combination of innovation in learning – the role play and computer-based learning – has been beneficial in terms of the all-round academic growth of students doing this module. They have developed new skills that have a meaningful application as much in the workplace as in a society in conflict. After each semester, students in Middle Eastern Politics have transformed *from* passive learners reluctant to participate in tutorial discussion and obsessive note-takers who over-rely on material that I distribute *to* active learners who complain there is not enough time in tutorials to debate with each other, who continue the 'dialogue' in the lecture theatre and take it into class, the common room and even down the pub.

(Beverley Milton-Edwards, School of Politics, International Studies and Philosophy, Queen's University Belfast)

Interrogating practice

Look at the assessments in a module that you are delivering. In light of Case study 19.2, what changes, if any, would you make to the assessment design or process?

The changing landscape of higher education within what is now a global market, forces the social sciences and humanities to respond to new demands and challenges, even to justify their existence. Students are less likely to contemplate substantial future indebtedness without reassurance and evidence from the relevant universities that their future prospects are encouraging and that the degree programmes they wish to pursue offer recognised value to potential employers. This does not mean the intrinsic value of study in certain disciplines is not valued, but that the curriculum designers need to be more conscious than before of the embedded skills and value contained in their programmes and in raising the students' self awareness of the attributes and skills they are developing and the transferability of these, which has been overlooked. Assessment processes in Case studies 19.2 and 19.3 highlight the value in the achieved, enhanced, outcomes for the student, as well as the added value to the actual learning process.

The increased expectations from both employers and students about future **employability** have had an impact on the entire higher education system. The reduction of government funding has created a need for institutions to plan provision in such a way as to guarantee income. This carries the danger that some disciplines may be tempted to become more strictly utilitarian in their provision and become more narrowly defined, particularly in the social sciences. The challenge of taking teaching seriously in the social sciences requires a bolder and more creative approach, one that will engender responsiveness to the outside world without becoming trapped in the latest policy priority area. It is this combination of challenges that the LSE has attempted to address with its compulsory core foundation course LSE100.

Case study 19.3: Teaching across the social sciences: LSE100 The Causes of Things

The LSE100 programme was launched formally in 2011. It is a compulsory two-part module – part one is taken in Semester 2 by all first year students and all second year students take the second LSE100 module in their first semester. It has been designed to bring real-world issues into the core undergraduate programme and to add cross-disciplinary breadth to the curriculum. Every discipline taught at the LSE brings its own perspective to bear on major public issues. Every one is continually breaking new ground and bringing forward new empirical evidence, fresh insight and new theory. Yet neither the big questions society faces, nor the methods of social sciences are neatly divided into disciplines. The challenge for students is to develop the skills and capacity to move beyond personal opinion to argument grounded in research and careful causal analysis.

The programme puts lawyers, economists, sociologists and historians in the same space and challenges them to address important questions facing society, examining different forms of evidence and assessing competing explanations presented by leading experts.

The course has been designed to build on the strengths of the LSE. The classes are interdisciplinary in the mix of students, as well as the mix of approaches, encouraging students to work and debate with fellow students from other disciplines and cultural backgrounds.

LSE100 aims, in the first instance, to give students a broader and deeper understanding of what it is to think like a social scientist. The programme presents the core elements of social-scientific reasoning and how they are applied across a broad range of social sciences. It has been designed and structured to ensure that whichever course a student is enrolled on, the programme will touch on the common themes of evidence, explanation and theory.

The LSE100 lectures explore how social scientists address important questions facing society, examining different forms of evidence, assessing competing explanations and exploring alternative ways of conceptualising problems. The lectures are followed up in small-group classes that are designed to develop an understanding of the core methodological concepts of evidence, explanation and theory, and to build and reinforce critical research and communication skills. Learning how to evaluate evidence, how to assess positions and to think critically, how to structure arguments and how to argue persuasively orally and in writing are central to the course.

LSE100 explores big questions such as 'How should we manage climate change?', 'Do nations matter in a global world?', 'Why are great events so difficult to predict?', 'What caused the financial crisis?' and 'Who should own ideas in the internet age?'

LSE100 uses learning technologies to support active learning in lectures and to provide learners with self-paced learning resources in the course **virtual learning environment (VLE)**. The course pioneered **personal response systems** (PRS or 'clickers') at the LSE with the aim of engaging students effectively in lectures while providing lecturers with real-time feedback. It also uses a texting/SMS service to elicit real-time feedback on 'muddy points' – points which students find unclear in the lecture.

The innovative approach to teaching and learning in LSE100 is also reflected in how the course is assessed. The programme uses non-numeric marks and the final mark is based on five assessments over the course. These include an essay at the end of the second semester, three in-class assessments, including a group presentation project, and a two-hour final examination. The overall mark for the LSE100 of 'Credit', 'Merit', 'Distinction' or 'Fail' is shown on the students' transcript. LSE100 has been well received by LSE graduate employers and it is felt that the interdisciplinary nature of the programme along with the new technologies and 'soft skills' development provides the participants with a distinctive edge.

(Michael Cox, LSE)

Interrogating practice

- To what extent do you understand your subject as a discipline whose borders are defined in terms of professional practices and procedures?
- How do your expectations compare with what students expect of the subject? How do you explain to them its interdisciplinary connections and coherence?

The value of **reflective practice** is widely recognised in higher education pedagogy and practice. As Cowan (1999: 18) notes reflection takes place whenever a learner analyses or evaluates one or more personal experiences and attempts to generalise from that thinking. As such, reflection or reflective practice is a fundamental critical tool. Reflective narratives provide a means for the learner to personalise learning and stimulate further development. In the social sciences, where there are usually multiple explanations for the causes of things, reflection provides the learner with a process for synthesising a personal perspective from the evidence from the multiple sources they encounter. Reflective practice is integrated into a variety of assessment processes, most often in the form of some type of portfolio or learning journal (Moon, 2000) and it is generally accepted that the activity of reflection is an essential element for successful higher level learning to take place. In the next case study, student reflection on action is integral, although the assessment process is not prescriptive. In this context, the student learners are actively listened to by the tutors who in turn reflect on the process as presented for assessment.

Case study 19.4: Political Theory and Resistance in Practice

In 'Resistance in Practice', a core module of the MA in Political Theory and Practices of Resistance in the School of Politics and International Relations at the University of Kent, students are given the option of being assessed on their understanding of current resistance movements by either writing a standard academic essay or by creating and documenting their own practice of resistance. For those that choose the latter, they are free to suggest the practices they want to develop. Students then discuss their ideas with teaching staff and, most crucially, amongst themselves, in order to refine their practices. They are presented in whatever form and available location is deemed most suitable (to date, typically on campus, although some practices have had off-campus elements). In addition, students submit documentary materials, often in the form of a reflective essay, but not always because some practices are best documented in other ways: through film; the submission of materials used in the production process; accompanying website; recordings; sketchbooks; creative writing; and so on. A successful practice of resistance is one that (a) specifies what is being resisted within the practice itself; (b) sustains the resistance with clarity and coherence; and (c) documents the practice in a manner consonant with the practice itself.

Students of politics today find themselves torn between (a) pressures deriving from a predominantly economic understanding of education ('employability') and (b) the critical and reflective perspective that the subject itself requires. In this context, it is important to ask how learners can be empowered to embrace the more active role they can play in the learning process. Given the obvious political dimension of this question, it seems essential to raise it within the learning context of politics and especially in relation to the theory and practice of resistance. Effective resistance requires those who resist to reflect on how their own position and posture is conditioned by the target of their resistance. Allowing for the possibility that our resistance is conditioned by the systems and apparatuses we wish to resist calls into question the very meaning of resistance. It is at this point where resistance assumes a very personal, 'liminal' and creative dimension, which can become the locus of **experiential learning**. Experiential learning in politics commonly takes the form of work placements or in-class **simulations**. In both cases, learners are asked to adapt to clearly defined frameworks, rules and power structures, which both enable and condition the experience that is to generate knowledge. The documented practice of resistance enables a space of experiential learning for the students, in which the influence of such frameworks and rules is temporarily suspended, thus allowing for greater creativity and reflexivity.

The maintenance of this space, however, requires challenging the traditional power dynamics between faculty and students. There are three features of the learning process that have come to be particularly important in challenging existing hierarchies. First, faculty engages with and may participate in the student practices in a variety of ways. These can range from elements of co-creation to being (relatively) passive components of a more active practice. Second, faculty present their own practice of resistance alongside student practices in order to establish solidarity with the students but also to engage actively in the learning process themselves. Third, faculty learns from student activities in many different ways; not only about the nature and scope of practices of resistance in ways that then feed into future discussions and debates but also about the best ways to facilitate the practices as a form of assessment. One group of students, for example, decided that their practices should be convened together because this in itself would mount a challenge to the individuation associated with traditional assessment techniques.

There is no doubt that enabling practices of resistance to flourish can present challenges to traditional assumptions about teaching and learning in higher education, especially those that shape views regarding assessment. However, if we want students to analyse and critically reflect on the nature and scope of resistance, as stated in the learning outcomes for this module, and we understand that experience shapes our analyses and conditions our critical responses, then it is essential to question the traditional approaches within higher education that tend to diminish the scope for student innovation and creativity in order to facilitate experiences of resistance that will engender learning.

(Stefan Rossbach and Iain MacKenzie, University of Kent at Canterbury)

These four case studies serve to illustrate some of the range of pedagogical approaches as applied in the social science context. With lecture capture and podcasts, just two examples of everyday learning technology, the challenge for academic teachers is how to maximise the value and impact of direct contact time with students, whether it is face-to-face or online. In the second section of this volume, topics such as curriculum design, assessment and approaches to e-learning are examined in more detail. The case studies offered here are designed to provide examples of pedagogy in practice with all the attendant challenges. In all four cases, the programmes of study and curriculum have been carefully designed and planned, starting with clearly defined learning outcomes for the students.

The **learning outcomes** have informed all aspects of the content, its delivery and the planned learning process. There is a clear recognition that the student engagement with the actual learning process is as integral to the success of each of the courses as the epistemology underpinning the curriculum: *how* the topics are learned about is as fundamental to the success of the learning process as the fact and detail of the formal knowledge content.

It is increasingly rare to hear students talk about 'death by Powerpoint'. The use of Powerpoint itself has become more highly developed and sophisticated. The ability to integrate film clips and other data sources has introduced the enhancement of lectures where previously there was often too much text and a tendency for some academics to simply read their slides to the students.

Along with the positive innovations made possible by the Internet and VLEs, the problems of **plagiarism** and non-authentic essays and dissertations have increased dramatically. The opportunities for such malpractice have coincided with the growing internationalisation of the student body and pressures on graduates to show an academically competitive advantage in the employment stakes. The innovations on academic courses with greater diversity of assessment techniques, if not carefully managed, can increase the opportunity for and the incidence of fraudulent work for assessment in an attempt to gain unfair advantage.

Software systems such as **Turnitin** are now essential and most institutions have clear policies and helpful guidelines for the management of assessment and processes for dealing with suspected cases of plagiarism. It is of crucial importance not only for the staff but also the students to be completely informed about these procedures and the policy of the institution governing implementation. Where graduate teaching assistants are part of the team involved in providing tutorial support for students, it is essential that they are given the necessary support and a proper induction to the course and the issues involved so that they know what is appropriate and are encouraged to refer to academic colleagues for advice and input as to how to deal with difficult issues or students.

CONCLUSION AND OVERVIEW

This chapter has focused on the diversity of intellectual activity in a small sample of the social sciences. The chosen case studies highlight innovative teaching practices within a variety of programmes and subject areas at different levels, but all share a common purpose – they are designed to create a stimulating, engaging and active learning environment in which analysis and judgement forming can flourish. The increasing presence of social media, Twitter and other newly emerging technological initiatives presents new possibilities and opportunities. The challenge for the social sciences and higher education in general is how to incorporate the best of the new, without losing sight of what is the 'essential' – which may in turn, prove to be a contested concept.

One element that is present in each of the case studies is the importance of how the assessment process is designed as an integral part of the learning experience. Assessment of student learning is a fundamental aspect of higher education and has almost immeasurable impact on student approaches to learning, university reputations and perceived academic standards. The vast resources and opportunities offered by the World Wide Web have brought with them increasing challenges, particularly plagiarism but also, in response to the threats to academic integrity and standards, more reliance on summative assessment in the form of traditional time-limited examinations. These examinations tend to focus on the ability of the learner to remember and repeat conceptual knowledge and understanding, which is at odds with the employability (and arguably also at odds with the intellectual) agenda, which would be keen to see evidence of the capability to apply the acquired knowledge in a different context and to think critically and analytically. As the **Higher Education Academy (HEA)** has identified in its report on assessment 'A Marked Improvement' (HEA, 2012: 7) and as practiced in Case study 19.4 at postgraduate level, involving the students in the assessment process is likely to help them understand the complexity of the professional judgement involved, develop a better understanding of standard setting in the discipline and enhance their self-assessment capability. In this context, the role of the academic in the development and delivery of the curriculum will be to exercise critical awareness and responsiveness while maintaining a sound disciplinary framework.

REFERENCES

Cowan, J (1999) *On becoming an Innovative University Teacher.* Buckingham: Open University Press.

Dearing, R (1997) The National Committee of Inquiry into Higher Education. Available from: https://bei.leeds.ac.uk/Partners/NCIHE/ (accessed 10 November 2013).

Department for Employment and Learning (2006) *The Leitch Review of Skills: Final Report.* Available from: http://www.delni.gov.uk/index/publications/pubs-further-education/the-leitch-review-of-skills.htm (accessed 10 November 2013).

Economic and Social Science Research Council (2013) *What is Social Science?* http://www.esrc.ac.uk/about-esrc/what-is-social-science/index.aspx (accessed 30 December 2013).

Giroux, H (1992) *Border Crossings: Cultural Workers and the Politics of Education.* New York, NY: Routledge.

Higher Education Academy (HEA) (2012) *A Marked Improvement: Transforming Assessment in Higher Education.* Available from: http://www.heacademy.ac.uk/resources/detail/assessment/a-marked-improvement (accessed 10 November 2013).

Moon, J (2000) *Reflections in Learning and Professional Development: Theory and Practice.* London: RoutledgeFalmer.

Mosteller, F (1989) 'The "Muddiest Point in the Lecture" as a Feedback Device', *On Teaching and Learning,* 3: 10–21. Available from: http://bokcenter.harvard.edu/fs/html/icb.topic771890/mosteller.html (accessed 10 November 2013).

Newman, M (2004) *Problem-Based Learning: An Exploration of the Method and Evaluation of its Effectiveness in a Continuing Nursing Education Programme.* London: Middlesex University.

FURTHER READING

Biggs, J (2001) 'The reflective institution: assuring and enhancing the quality of teaching and learning', *Higher Education,* 41(2): 221–238.

Higher Education Academy (HEA). http://www.heacademy.ac.uk/disciplines (click on the discipline title for link to subject specific resources and information).

Quality Assurance Agency for Higher Education (2007) *Subject Benchmark Statement: Politics and International Relations.* Available from: http://www.qaa.ac.uk/Publications/InformationAndGuidance/Pages/Subject-benchmark-statement-Polictics-and-international-relations.aspx (accessed 10 November 2013).

Salmon, G (2004) *E-Moderating: The Key to On-line Teaching and Learning.* London: Routledge.

20 Modern languages

Michael Kelly

INTRODUCTION

This chapter addresses issues that are central to effective learning and teaching in modern languages degrees:

- Where are students coming from?
- How are languages learned?
- What is the content of language degrees?
- What distinctive features do language degrees have?

Three case studies exemplify some effective practices in the language-learning curriculum, in content courses and in residence abroad. The discussion focuses on aspects that are particularly salient in modern languages degrees, beyond the common ground shared with other subject areas, which are dealt with in Part 2 of this Handbook. Every opportunity is taken to pose questions to the reader to prompt reflection and innovation in their own practice.

WHERE ARE STUDENTS COMING FROM? CONTEXTS FOR LANGUAGE STUDY IN HIGHER EDUCATION

Modern language degrees in the UK have traditionally been designed for British students who have spent several years learning one or more foreign languages at secondary school and perhaps even in primary school. They have accommodated students who speak a foreign language at home, as well as students wishing to learn a new language at university. In recent years, this pattern has been changing as languages have struggled to keep their place in secondary schools and applications to study language degrees have declined. As a result, teaching staff in higher education are now drawn into public debates on the need for languages in all sectors of education, and are increasingly compelled to re-examine the rationale for what they teach and how to respond to changing needs and attitudes.

Language study in British schools has been an issue in public policy for more than a decade, since an influential report from the Nuffield Foundation raised the alarm about the state of languages in the education system (Nuffield Languages Inquiry, 2000). At the same time, the government withdrew the obligation for pupils to learn languages beyond the age of 14, to the dismay of many European partners. Between 2003 and 2012, the numbers taking a GCSE language exam at 16 fell by almost a half to just over 40 per cent of pupils. This did not immediately affect A-level figures, though they dropped sharply in 2012 and again in 2013 (Tinsley and Board, 2013: 13–17). University applications have roughly followed A-level trends and have led several universities to withdraw from offering language degrees (Bawden, 2013). These developments have exacerbated the social profile of language education, which is associated with students from more privileged backgrounds studying increasingly at more prestigious universities.

The same changes are apparent in other English-speaking countries, including Ireland, Australia and the United States. A similar pattern has emerged in many other European countries, with the difference that English language studies are very buoyant while the study of other foreign languages has declined.

In response, public campaigns and government initiatives have attempted to stem the tide of retreat from languages with the involvement of numerous professional organisations. For example, the Routes into Languages programme, funded by the Higher Education Funding Council for England (HEFCE) since 2006, is designed to help increase the take-up of languages and to encourage students from a wider range of backgrounds. It now involves around 80 universities across England and Wales working with schools in their region.

The **internationalisation** of higher education is bringing new trends among staff and students. Languages departments have always had native speaker staff to teach language courses, but increasingly foreign nationals are also teaching the 'content' courses. While most languages undergraduates are British, there are growing numbers of international students studying at postgraduate level. These trends are even more noticeable in departments that include programmes in applied linguistics, interpreting and translation, and especially in English language teaching. It remains a challenge for departments to find reasons why international students might travel to Britain to study modern languages, other than English.

The English language is increasing taught as a *lingua franca* without the accompanying study of particular English-speaking cultures. Other languages may be following this path, with a sharper separation between the study of language and culture. It also corresponds to a shift in the interests of students on languages degrees. Many are showing a stronger interest in the study of language itself, including aspects of linguistics. Many wish to study three or more languages at university and some aspire to careers in the language industries, especially translation and interpreting.

Outside language degrees, students are taking opportunities to learn languages as part of their studies, as an elective module or as an extra-curricular course. Courses in university-wide language programmes and life-long learning programmes appear to be in greater demand. This is a rational choice for students who do not wish to study a full language degree, but do want to upgrade their language skills. They are able to reach GCSE-level proficiency in one year, and A-level equivalent in two years. In practice, the students who take most advantage of these language courses are international students studying in Britain and seeking to extend their portfolio of languages.

Interrogating practice

- To what extent does your department's current practice take account of the changing preferences and aspirations of incoming learners?
- Think of three ways you might improve upon your current practice to take account of learners' aspirations.

HOW ARE LANGUAGES LEARNED? THE CURRICULUM FOR LANGUAGE LEARNING

Language degrees take many different forms but all include a core element of language learning. This was the focus of the chapter on languages in the 3rd edition of this Handbook (Gray and Klapper 2009); this chapter takes a different, complementary approach. In a Single Honours degree, language learning is likely to account for around a quarter of study time, although an intensive *ab initio* course will account for more. The remainder is allocated to 'content' units and electives. In a Joint or Combined Honours degree, and in 'Minor' or 'with' degrees (e.g. Business Studies with German), the content component is proportionally smaller. Departments need to construct a curriculum that accommodates this variety.

Where all students enter the same programme, at the same level of proficiency, they can usually be taught together as a year group through their degree, and the teacher will usually know roughly what their other studies involve. But in most departments, the students are much more varied and the challenge is to design a more flexible language curriculum that meets the needs of the different types of learner (see Chapter 11). Factors to be considered are:

- What kind of contact will they have with the foreign language in the remainder of their programme?

- What kind of language study (materials, approaches, skill outcomes) will they find most relevant or attractive to their career plans or their overall interests?
- What kinds of student (year of study, level of proficiency, subject interest, rate of progression) can be grouped together in the same class?
- Practical issues such as class size, timetable constraints and availability of resources.

There are many ways of addressing these factors and Case study 20.1 outlines the solutions that have been adopted in one university.

Case study 20.1: Stages of progression in language learning

In the 1990s, Modern Languages at the University of Southampton decided that all their language teaching should be delivered by specialist language teachers. At the same time, they separated language classes from year of study, so that students would be taught with others at the same level of language proficiency, regardless of whether they were in their first, second or final year of study.

Southampton Language Stages

Students can learn a language at one of seven language stages, from absolute beginners to near-native speaker level, in a range of languages. The stages are mapped onto national qualifications as well as the Common European Framework of Reference (CEFR), which is recognised as a reference point around the world.

Students have a clear statement of what they can expect to do at the end of each stage in the main skill areas of understanding (listening and reading) and production (speaking, writing and mediation).

For example, the speaking skills achieved at each stage (**learning outcomes**) are:

1 (Good GCSE, CEFR A2) Provide and ask for simple information relating to areas of immediate concern.
2 (A-level grade C, CEFR B1) Initiate and maintain conversations and discussions relating to most everyday contexts.
3 (A-level grade A/B, CEFR B2) Engage with a degree of grammatical correctness and some spontaneity in conversations relating to most everyday topics as well as in conversations on some specialised topics.
4 (CEFR B2/C1) Engage confidently and accurately in conversations relating to everyday topics and a range of specialised ones.

5   (CEFR C1) Keep up with and participate in discussion and conversation on familiar and complex topics and present similar topics, with reasonable effectiveness and precision.

6   (CEFR C1/C2) Engage with ease in spoken interaction on complex and abstract topics, using a range of grammatical structures, vocabulary and discourse markers.

7   (CEFR C2) Converse with ease in most formal and informal situations and employ appropriate and effective strategies in managing linguistically and/or culturally complex interactions.

There are comparable descriptors for each of the other skills, which are incorporated in the course details provided to students.

In degree programmes, students must progress by at least a stage in each year of study, but may progress more quickly. In the earlier stages, students may have accelerated courses, particularly where they are already familiar with a cognate language. Students who enter university with grade A or B at A-level will begin at Stage 4 in that language.

Challenges faced

Some challenges in using the stages have been found in:

*   Mapping progression against national or European qualification levels that were designed for different purposes;
*   Applying the stages to non-European languages, especially ones that use a different writing system (e.g. Chinese, Japanese);
*   Taking account of the extensive cultural knowledge and social skills needed to achieve the higher stages;
*   Taking account of learners' different levels of proficiency in different skills (e.g. fluent speakers with little experience of writing in the language).

(Modern Languages, University of Southampton)

Interrogating practice

*   Compare the stages outlined in Case study 20.1 with your own department's learning outcomes and progression arrangements in language learning. What differences are there?
*   How does your department face the challenges identified? Is there anything in the case study that your department could learn from?

HOW ARE LANGUAGES LEARNED? THE PEDAGOGY OF LANGUAGE LEARNING

The acquisition of a second or other language has historically been the object of a great deal of research and discussion, much of which has focused on the experience of language teaching and learning (Mitchell et al., 2012). Although this is an area of considerable debate, it is generally agreed that language teachers need to be aware of key issues in language acquisition, such as:

- There are established patterns of learner progression that need to be accommodated;
- Transfers between first and second languages are inevitable and need to be managed;
- Errors and inaccuracies are a necessary part of learning and a valuable starting point for feedback;
- It is important to work with the authentic 'target' language in meaningful activities; and
- Language learning needs a combination of approaches that are cognitive (know the rules) and inductive (plenty of practice), as in learning to play the piano. At higher levels, it also needs to be reflective (language as object of study).

Many of the insights of research in second language acquisition inform the dominant communicative approach to language teaching. This has supplanted previous approaches, which progressed through a succession of grammatical forms, in order of perceived difficulty. Instead, communicative teaching seeks to equip the learner with language resources they need in order to function in the world, giving them plenty of practice in using the language meaningfully. Grammatical structures are introduced as needed, rather than as the main focus. Learners are encouraged to integrate the four language skills of listening, speaking, reading and writing, as happens in everyday life.

An important part of contemporary pedagogy is aimed at prompting learners to take responsibility for their progress so that the teacher acts increasingly as a facilitator (see Chapter 12). Students learn more effectively in this way, making better use of their time outside the classroom and developing an ability to learn that will stand them in good stead. For future language learning, in particular, students need to be encouraged to:

- Understand how languages are learnt, and develop effective strategies they can use later;
- Identify their own preferred **learning style**, and approaches that will suit them best (see Chapter 5);
- Understand the importance of affective factors, especially their relationship to the language and culture, and their motivations for learning; and
- Get involved in shaping their course, including choices about topics and materials, and personal project work.

This autonomous learning can be assisted by computer-based and online tools, previously known as ICT or C&IT, and now referred to as digital media (see Chapter 10). Computer-assisted language learning (CALL) was often the domain of enthusiasts, but has a distinguished record of innovation and is generating a great diversity of approaches (Stockwell, 2012). The digital landscape is becoming a more important focus of language learning than the classroom, and the teacher's role is to advise on the most effective ways for learners to use it. There are many digital resources that can be used in the classroom, including language learning applications and other resources that have been developed for use with portable devices, interactive whiteboards, voting systems, video links and other tools. It is a challenge for teachers to remain abreast of technological advances, which may be taken up more readily by their students.

Interrogating practice

- How does your current departmental practice take account of evidence from research into second language acquisition?
- How far do you focus on facilitating learning, as opposed to teaching?
- How could new digital tools be used in the classroom and beyond?

WHAT IS THE CONTENT? VARIETIES OF LANGUAGE DEGREES

The term 'content' is widely used by departments to distinguish between language learning and the study of linguistic, cultural and social topics. It is recognised that language learning involves content of various kinds, but generally as a means to develop language proficiency. 'Content' modules study topics in their own right using relevant conceptual approaches and methodologies.

While language degrees all have a common core in language learning, there are several different types of specialist language degree, characterised by different curriculum content. Each has a particular history and identity, and a different outcome in potential careers for students. Although they are sometimes combined in practice, the following types are generally recognised:

- Language and literature: sometimes called 'philology', especially in other European countries, established in the late nineteenth century. May involve one or two foreign languages, traditionally major Germanic and Romance languages, but other languages are growing (Slavonic, Middle Eastern and Asian languages). Canonical works now include a wider range of writers and other cultural forms, especially cinema. Linguistics also features in the content. Career outcomes: a liberal arts qualification, and entry into teaching, including English as a foreign language.

- Applied languages: language study combined with linguistics, communication studies and/or language for professional settings. Established in the 1960s, and concentrated in newer universities. May involve one or two foreign languages and study of contemporary social and political structures and the business environment. May be located in a school of business or social studies. Career outcomes: vocational emphasis, preparing for particular areas of business or the professions, also teaching (see Case study 20.2).

- Language-based area studies: established in the 1960s. Specialist study of a particular region, with social science emphasis, especially politics and economics, and including a language component. European and Latin American Studies are widely taught. Other areas include Eastern Europe, the Middle East, Africa and South Asia. Career outcomes: government agencies, non-governmental organisations and international corporate enterprises.

- Translation and interpreting: mostly established during the mid-twentieth century, though some date from the seventeenth century. Some undergraduate degrees include components of interpreting and translating, but professional degrees are postgraduate. Career outcomes: the language industries.

- Language in education: initial teacher training predominantly at postgraduate level, with a focus on pedagogy. Some Masters degrees for professional development. Career outcomes: teaching, education management.

Case study 20.2: An area studies approach to language degrees

In the 1970s, Portsmouth Polytechnic (as it was then), along with a small number of other institutions, developed a new type of language degree, distinct from the traditional model of 'language and literature'. The 'Language and Area Studies' degree programme combines language study with the study of the history, politics, economy, society and culture of the country or countries in question. The approach is multi-disciplinary and is essentially but not exclusively rooted in the social sciences. Aspects of it have since been incorporated in degrees in a wide range of universities.

Combined Modern Languages Degree

Students are invited to understand recent dramatic changes in the world while immersing themselves in other languages, societies and cultures. They study at least two languages from French, German, Italian, Japanese, Spanish, Mandarin or English as a Foreign Language. They learn to listen, read, write and speak their chosen languages accurately and fluently, and spend time abroad to experience their languages at first hand.

The first year consists mainly of core courses to ensure a firm foundation for further study. Students consolidate their knowledge of a first foreign language, and may either consolidate or undertake an intensive course in a second. They also take course units that provide an understanding of the language areas they are studying, often from a European or international perspective.

The second and final years continue the pattern of language study alongside area studies courses, which include general and comparative topics, such as:

- Business and Markets in Global Environment
- Nation, Language and Identity
- Managing Across Cultures

They also include area or country-specific courses, such as (for French):

- France's Civil Wars
- France, 1945–1995: Liberty, Equality, Fraternity?
- The French Exception: Politics and Society in Contemporary France
- Colonialism and the End of Empire in French Africa
- France in the World: Global Actor or Global Maverick?

Students spend their third year abroad.

Challenges faced

The development of these courses has been challenged by:

- Post-colonialism: why focus on European countries that built large colonial empires?
- Globalisation: why focus on particular countries, or on Europe, rather than on global patterns of political, social and economic development?
- Language focus: can a language be learned independently from the culture(s) in which they are embedded?
- Area focus: can the history, politics and economics of an area be studied without proficiency in a foreign language?
- Pressure to teach the 'content' elements of the course in English rather than French so that the unit can be made available to non-French speakers.
- Research agendas: how closely can the course reflect the research undertaken by staff teaching on it?

(School of Languages and Area Studies, University of Portsmouth)

Interrogating practice

- Compare the approaches outlined in Case study 20.2 with your own department's programme. What differences are there?
- Does your department face similar challenges?
- Is there anything in the case study which your department could learn from?

WHAT IS THE CONTENT? MULTI-DISCIPLINARITY OF LANGUAGE DEGREES

In principle, the content of a degree in languages is potentially vast, as the 2007 Benchmark Statement acknowledges (see Chapter 2 for an explanation of benchmark statements):

> The range of studies associated with languages is, likewise, extremely diverse. Study may be focused on the cultures and the literatures, both historical and contemporary, of the societies of the language concerned. It may draw upon disciplines such as linguistics in order to deepen understanding of the language. It may address aspects of history, philosophy, politics, media, geography, sociology, anthropology and economics, in order to enhance understanding of the fabric and context of societies where the language is spoken. Languages are also increasingly taught in other multi- and cross-disciplinary combinations, such as languages with business or accountancy, with law, with art and design, with computer science, with engineering, and with the natural sciences. In such combinations, the language studies undertaken are seen as adding value to the knowledge, understanding and skills acquired, and extending the range of generic skills. With such diversity and flexibility of programmes, languages are necessarily multidisciplinary and inter-disciplinary, as well as intercultural and applied in nature.
>
> (Quality Assurance Agency, 2007: 5)

Content includes the whole of the language, culture and society of the countries in which a given language is spoken. However, the rapid changes in the contemporary world, broadly summed up as 'globalisation', mean that those countries need to be understood in their interactions in a broader context, including their relations with the UK and with other countries with which students may be familiar (McBride and Seago, 2000). This is a major academic challenge.

At the simplest level, content incorporated in language learning programmes is at the level of general knowledge, including matters on which an educated person might be expected to hold an opinion. This has traditionally been reflected in language classes, where discussions are often based on analytical items in the press, and students are invited to express views on topics of current debate in written and oral work. This is relatively unproblematic for staff or students because the content does not require specialist knowledge and is not directly assessed.

At the next level, the content of language learning may be customised to match the areas of students' academic interest. In this way, students combining languages with business studies, for example, may work with business-related written and audio-visual materials that will connect with their other studies. This is the domain of 'languages for specific purposes', and teachers will be expected to develop some specialist knowledge of the subject area, to select appropriate learning resources and support learners in acquiring specialist terminology. Appropriate content of this kind is known to motivate students in their language learning.

One step further into specialisation is the approach known as Content and Language Integrated Learning (CLIL) or bilingual teaching. This involves teaching a subject through a language that is not native to the learners (Coyle et al., 2010). It takes many forms, which have different degrees of focus on learning the subject and learning the language. 'Target language teaching', often practiced in language departments, is a variety of CLIL. It entails delivering courses on the culture and society of the foreign country wholly or partly in the 'target' language. The teaching may or may not pay explicit attention to the students' language learning needs. Target language teaching of content is frequently debated in departments and different policies are adopted. The main issue is whether students are sufficiently able to understand and discuss complex content in the foreign language and whether some sacrifice of understanding is appropriate in order to develop language learning.

The next step into content specialisation is where teachers are themselves experts and perhaps researchers in the content area. Whether or not they teach in the target language, their aim is to enable students to extend their knowledge and understanding of the chosen aspects of the life of the target language countries, communities or societies. In so doing, they not only communicate expert knowledge, but also introduce approaches and methodologies from relevant disciplinary areas. For this reason, there is some debate about whether languages constitute a discipline as such, or whether this is an interdisciplinary area. In a typical department, staff are drawn from several disciplinary backgrounds. Literary specialists rub shoulders with specialists in, for example, linguistics, film, history, political science or anthropology.

This interdisciplinarity is a source of creative tension. On the one hand, it brings centrifugal pressures as staff develop stronger personal networks with teachers and researchers in cognate disciplines. They may even be drawn to move to another department in which their disciplinary emphasis (literary studies, history etc.) is the primary focus. On the other hand, the variety is a source of energy and innovation because different approaches fertilise each other and give students a portfolio of approaches to understand what makes people tick. Links with cognate disciplines can also form the basis of productive partnerships in both teaching and research.

Many examples exist of collaborative teaching and shared courses between languages and other subject areas, particularly though not only in the humanities and social sciences. Conversely, there are many examples of combined degrees with a language, where the two subjects are sharply compartmentalised and where contact between the contributing departments is purely administrative. In some subjects, it is difficult to make workable academic connections at the level of teachers (e.g. French and Mathematics). But in most cases, bridges can be built and opportunities can be taken to develop a stronger sense of integration.

DISTINCTIVE FEATURES: SUPPORTING RESIDENCE ABROAD

Language teachers have always emphasised the value of spending time in a country where the language is spoken as native. From the 1960s, language degrees routinely offered the chance for students to 'intercalate' a year abroad. From the 1970s, the year abroad became a compulsory part of most language degrees, increasingly integrated in the academic programme with dedicated pastoral support. The rationale for residence abroad is partly to enable students to improve their language skills through immersion, and partly to enable them to understand and be at ease in the culture of the country. However, the associated benefits may be even greater in fostering independence and the resourcefulness that goes with it, together with a range of **transferable skills** of communication, networking, interpersonal relations and intercultural competence (British Academy, 2012). The year also enables students to reflect on their future career options and in some cases to gain experience of a possible career path, for example in teaching or in an industrial workplace.

Since students have to bear the cost of an additional year of study, the UK government has generally provided subsidies. In practice, the majority of language students regard their year abroad as the highlight of their studies. In the small number of cases where a year abroad is not mandatory, students are required or encouraged to spend a shorter period abroad.

Universities may differ in their requirements, but there are three main routes for language students:

1   A year at an overseas university. Students study in a country where their foreign language is spoken as native, normally as part of an exchange arrangement. In Europe, the ERASMUS programme provides an administrative framework and financial support.
2   A language assistantship. The assistantship programme is led by the British Council, which sends around 2,500 English Teaching Assistants to some 14 countries in return for a similar number of foreign language assistants who come to teach in British schools.
3   A work placement. There is no national agency for finding placements and students themselves often have to take the initiative of finding placements for themselves.

These options are elaborated in Case study 20.3. Departments have to manage practical issues around matching students to suitable opportunities, meeting complex administrative requirements and assessing health and safety risks. There is a strong role for staff in advising students about the academic and personal implications of their year abroad.

Case study 20.3: The year abroad for language students

Aston University encourages and enables students on many different courses to spend a year working or studying abroad, and considers this fundamental to the University's international and **employability** strategies. A placement year or year abroad is compulsory for all students on a modern foreign language degree programme. As an integral part of the degree, students spend their third year in a French, German or Spanish speaking country, with the aim of increasing fluency and immersing themselves in a new culture and society, thus developing intercultural and employability skills.

The year abroad

Aston has a flexible approach to the year abroad, which enables students to work or study abroad, become a language teaching assistant or combine these different options. If they are studying two languages, they normally divide their time between countries where the relevant languages are spoken.

A year at an overseas university

Language students will spend a year at one or more of Aston's exchange universities in French, German or Spanish speaking countries. Current partner institutions include universities in the following locations:

- France/Belgium: Paris, Tours, Lille, Rennes, Bordeaux, Montpellier, Nouvelle-Calédonie, Brussels
- Germany/Austria: Leipzig, Frankfurt/Oder, Paderborn, Vienna
- Spain/Latin America: Santiago (Chile), Valencia, Granada, Sevilla, Barcelona

Options in further institutions and countries, for example Canada, Colombia and Argentina, are open to students of International Business and Modern Languages.

Students attend lectures and seminars at the overseas university and follow a course that complements their studies at Aston. They may also attend language programmes developed specifically for Erasmus students. They do not pay fees at these universities for their year abroad and may be eligible for funding via the European Commission's Erasmus Programme.

Work placement

A dedicated International Placement Team, based centrally in the University, runs workshops and provides advice and assistance. Students usually apply by sending a CV and cover letter to prospective employers, or they complete an online application form. If selected, they are normally interviewed, by phone or in person, by a representative from the company. The majority of work placements are paid. Most students receive additional funding support through Erasmus or the Santander programme.

English Language Teaching Assistant

The Assistantship programme is led by the British Council in the UK. The International Placement Team provides information on the range of opportunities available, running a specific session on Assistantships, and assisting with the application and interview processes. Some students also choose to take a TESOL (Teachers of English to Speakers of Other Languages) module in preparation.

Supporting the year abroad

Aston has a strong record of working with employers and universities across the world, and investing in employability. The International Placement Team provides briefings, workshops and extensive individual support, before and during students' placements. Students preparing for placement attend an International Placement Event and are put in touch with final year students who can pass on their experiences. Peer to peer interaction is further supported through blogs and student videos. In most cases, students are visited while abroad (or otherwise a Skype visit takes place), to check on progress and give help and advice.

Challenges faced

The provision of the year abroad has been challenged by:

- Time and money: can students afford to spend an additional year in their degree?
- Economics: can work placements and assistantships be obtained in times of economic difficulty?
- Health and safety: how can the department or university attenuate any risks that students may encounter?

International Placement Team, School of Languages and
Social Sciences, University of Aston

> ### Interrogating practice
>
> - Compare the opportunities outlined in Case study 20.3 with your own department's programme. What differences are there?
> - How do you support students academically while they are abroad?

Perhaps the most complex issue in the year abroad is how to incorporate the outcomes in the assessment structures leading to a degree classification. For students who have studied at a university, the issue is how to import their marks for the year. The **European Credit Transfer System** (ECTS) helps to transfer learning experiences between different institutions, but decisions on assessment are the responsibility of the university awarding degrees. The marking schemes of overseas universities are extremely diverse, and a mark of, for example, 70 per cent in the UK equates to 14 in France, 1.0 in Germany, 5 in Poland and 6 in Switzerland. Even with tables of equivalents, a particular mark is highly context-specific, depending for example on whether the course concerned was aimed at second or third year students, taught for local students or designed for foreign students. In practice, departments must decide how best to convert the mark of an overseas partner into an appropriate home equivalent.

In assessing the year spent as an assistant or on a work placement, departments have developed a range of approaches. Some simply record the successful completion of the year as a condition of graduation. Others require students to carry out academic tasks for their home institutions, such as a research project or an analytical report on their placement. Others again incorporate the outcomes of the year abroad in the assessment of final year, for example by requiring students to discuss it in assessed language assignments.

> ### Interrogating practice
>
> - How does your department address these issues about assessment?

DISTINCTIVE FEATURES: DEVELOPING INTERCULTURAL UNDERSTANDING

One of the outstanding benefits of residence abroad is to help develop intercultural awareness, understanding and competence. This is particularly promoted through direct contact with another culture, and is a distinctive aim of language degrees more broadly. The Benchmark Statement explains what this entails:

> Through their studies, their contact with the target language and associated cultures and their related studies, all students of languages will develop sensitivity to, and awareness of, the similarities and dissimilarities between other cultures and societies, and their own. In particular, their competence in the target language means that they will have an appreciation of internal diversity and transcultural connectedness, and an attitude of curiosity and openness towards other cultures. The skills and attributes they develop will include:
>
> - a critical understanding of a culture and practices other than one's own;
> - an ability to function in another culture;
> - an appreciation of the uniqueness of the other culture(s);
> - an ability to articulate to others the contribution that the culture has made at a regional and global level;
> - an ability and willingness to engage with other cultures;
> - an ability to appreciate and evaluate critically one's own culture.
>
> (Quality Assurance Agency, 2007: 8)

It is not a necessary consequence of language study that the learner becomes more interculturally adept. Some students try to bury themselves in a second culture. Some students compartmentalise their language studies. And some teachers encourage an exclusive commitment to one foreign language and culture as a means to aid learning, without contamination. Alison Phipps and Mike Gonzalez argue:

> Many of those who work in the profession today have spent their lives working with and on texts that they attempt to make fit into preconceived categories by stripping them of languages, social relations, intercultural being. There are good, pragmatic reasons for this work but what we are left with at the core of our modern language disciplines is something of a dried up husk.
>
> (Phipps and Gonzalez, 2004: 170)

My own experience has convinced me that connectedness is the default state of cultural relationships, and that efforts to 'purify' a language or culture of its foreign accretions are doomed to fail. An intercultural approach, by contrast, embraces the interrelationships between languages and cultures.

In some respects, a modern languages teaching department is a microcosm of the intercultural world, inhabited by staff and students from many different cultures. In the worst of cases, this can be a cause for resentment and suspicion, leading to hostility and infighting. In the best of cases, it can be a cause for collaboration and celebration, leading to creative development and reciprocal learning. The most powerful form of teaching is the force of example, and if academic staff in languages departments can exhibit curiosity and openness towards other cultures, they will convey this to their students.

Interrogating practice

- Does your department take an intercultural approach to teaching languages?
- How is this implemented?
- How are students supported in extending their intercultural understanding and skills?

CONCLUSION AND OVERVIEW

The discussion focuses on aspects that are particularly salient in modern languages degrees. The study of languages is deeply affected by the wider social context, particularly by the changing patterns of language study in schools and the internationalisation of higher education. Language learning remains the core component of language degrees, and research in language acquisition provides valuable insights that underpin the most effective pedagogies. On the other hand, the study of languages, cultures and societies ('content') involves a wide variety of subjects and draws on many disciplinary approaches. Spending a period studying or working abroad and developing intercultural understanding are distinctive features of modern language degrees. They both require a good deal of support in ways that extend far outside the classroom. The case studies exemplify some effective practices in the language-learning curriculum, in content courses and in residence abroad, and readers are invited to reflect on their own practice.

REFERENCES

Bawden, A (2013) 'Language degree courses in freefall', *The Guardian*, 8 October.

British Academy (2012) *Valuing the Year Abroad. A Position Statement.* London: British Academy, UCML, ThirdYearAbroad.

Coyle, D, Hood, P and Marsh D (2010) *CLIL: Content and Language Integrated Learning.* Cambridge: Cambridge University Press.

Gray, C and Klapper, J (2009) 'Key aspects of teaching and learning in languages', in H Fry, S Ketteridge and S Marshall (eds.) *A Handbook for Teaching & Learning in Higher Education: Enhancing Academic Practice.* London: Routledge, 323–244.

McBride, N and Seago, K (2000) *Target Culture – Target Languages.* London: CILT/AFLS.

Mitchell, R, Myles, F and Marsden E (2012) *Second Language Learning Theories.* 3rd edn. London: Routledge.

Nuffield Languages Inquiry (2000) *Languages: The Next Generation*. London: Nuffield Foundation.

Phipps, A and Gonzalez, M (2004) *Modern Languages. Learning and Teaching in an Intercultural Field*. London: Sage Publications.

Quality Assurance Agency (QAA) (2007) *Languages and Related Studies Benchmarking Statement*. Available from: http://www.qaa.ac.uk/Publications/InformationAndGuidance/Pages/Subject-benchmark-statement-Languages-and-related-studies.aspx (accessed 6 October 2013).

Stockwell, G (2012) *Computer-Assisted Language Learning. Diversity in Research and Practice*. Cambridge: Cambridge University Press.

Tinsley, T and Board, K (2013) *Language Learning in Primary and Secondary Schools in England. Findings from the 2012 Language Trends Survey*. London: CfBT Education Trust.

FURTHER READING

Council of Europe (2001) *Common European Framework of Reference for Languages: Learning, Teaching, Assessment*. Cambridge: Cambridge University Press.

Evans, C (1988) *Language People: The Experience of Teaching and Learning Modern Languages in British Universities*. Milton Keynes: Open University Press & Society for Research into Higher Education.

Risager, K (2006) *Language and Culture: Global Flows and Local Complexity*. Clevedon: Multilingual Matters.

Tinsley, T (2013) *Languages: The State of the Nation. Demand and Supply of Language Skills in the UK*. London: British Academy.

21 Law

Rebecca Huxley-Binns

INTRODUCTION

For most undergraduate law students, the law degree is the first step on the path to a career in the legal services sector. In England and Wales, law is studied in higher education as an undergraduate degree or by way of a Graduate Diploma in Law (GDL – also known as the Common Professional Examination or CPE) for graduates of another discipline. Legal education serves an important purpose as a prerequisite to vocational legal training and subsequent professional legal work. However, this is certainly not the only reason to study law at university. Law is interesting and intellectually stimulating. The law reaches into almost every aspect of human life: politics, business and commerce, the environment, throughout our communities, and across all ages from birth to death. Its relevance and reach are broad, and an in-depth study of law is empowering because it enables students to learn about justice, rights, obligations and freedoms, and how they co-exist and often conflict.

There is no one model of academic legal study, and some law schools offer a critical legal theory curriculum, others use **problem-based learning**, others still embed the professional qualifications, traditionally taken after the academic degree, into the undergraduate stage. With the recent emphasis on **employability** and monitoring of career destinations of graduates, many law schools have developed a more skills-orientated curriculum. In law, development of legal skills is usually achieved through a form of **experiential learning**. Given the nature of the legal advice, **simulated** rather than real-life problems are most common at the undergraduate stage.

THE ACADEMIC STAGE

Both the law degree (usually an LLB) and the GDL/CPE routes are the 'academic' stage of legal education and are regulated in terms of knowledge and skills.

All law degrees must meet the requirements of the **Quality Assurance Agency** (QAA) **Subject Benchmark** Statement for Law (2007), which provides threshold (minimum) graduate attributes of a law student. These include certain subject-specific abilities (knowledge and understanding of legal institutions, system(s), concepts, values, principles and rules), which include application and problem solving, ability to use sources and research, general transferable intellectual skills (including analysis, synthesis, critical judgement and evaluation), autonomy and ability to learn. The graduate **key skills** include communication and literacy, numeracy, information technology and teamwork.

The LLB may also be a 'qualifying law degree' (QLD) (and all GDL courses must comply with similar regulations), which allows students to progress onto the later vocational and professional training stages. QLDs are 'qualifying' for the purposes of the Legal Practice Course (LPC, for intending solicitors) and the Bar Professional Training Course (BPTC, for budding barristers) if they meet the requirements of the 'JASB' statement. JASB is the 'Joint Academic Stage Board', a joint committee of the Solicitors Regulation Authority and Bar Standards Board, the regulatory bodies for solicitors and barristers. Unfortunately for the QLD, the QAA Benchmark and the JASB requirements do not sit particularly comfortably side by side because they are not readily compatible in either content or specified outcomes. It is almost certain that either the QAA Benchmark or the JASB statement, or both, will be simplified and clarified as a result of the Legal Education and Training Review (LETR) 2013 (LETR recommendation 10, see later).

The JASB requirements for QLDs relate to the minimum credit points dedicated to a study of the foundation subjects of:

- Public Law, including Constitutional Law, Administrative Law and Human Rights;
- Law of the European Union;
- Criminal Law;
- Obligations, including Contract, Restitution and Tort;
- Property Law; and
- Equity and the Law of Trusts.

In addition, students are expected to have received training in legal research, legal principles, sources, systems and personnel, and be able to communicate, both orally and in writing, appropriately to the needs of a variety of audiences.

The law degree is a significant route into the legal services sector, particularly for those entering the solicitors' and barristers' professions. Law graduates are the largest single group of entrants to those professions (42.8 per cent of newly admitted solicitors in 2010–11 and, it is estimated, about two-thirds of those entering pupillage at the Bar. The other entrants were either cross-qualified from other professions, including other jurisdictions, or were graduates of other disciplines). Most of the other members of the legal professions (for example, Chartered Legal Executives (CILEx) lawyers, Notaries and intellectual property attorneys) are also graduates, albeit not necessarily of law.

However, by early 2013, data showed that fewer law students than in the previous four decades were directly entering the training routes to be a solicitor or barrister. This was not just because of the effect of the economic recession, but a changing legal services landscape. Although most law students embarked on their undergraduate studies intending to become a qualified lawyer – according to Hardee (2012: 11), 79.1 per cent were studying law with the intention of entering the legal profession – by the time of graduation, direct entry to the traditional professions was a minority career destination for law graduates. It may therefore be true to say that the undergraduate law degree is a servant to many masters; it serves the **QAA** in terms of **standards**; JASB for progression to certain legal careers; and the wider employment marketplace for those students entering other legal, or any of a huge range of non-legal, careers, but nonetheless bringing with them legal knowledge and skills. It is the embedding of some of those skills that is the subject of the case studies in this chapter.

REGULATION OF LEGAL SERVICES

The changing legal services landscape mentioned earlier was in part due to a new system of oversight and regulation of the provision of legal services introduced by the Legal Services Act 2007 (LSA 2007). This Act was, in part at least, designed to liberalise the regulation of legal services and encourage more competition between providers. These changes necessitated an analysis of the purpose, role and content of legal education and training. Section 1(1) of the LSA 2007 provides that the regulatory objectives of those regulating the legal services sector (in no particular order) are:

* Protecting and promoting the public interest;
* Supporting the constitutional principle of the rule of law;
* Improving access to justice;
* Protecting and promoting the interests of consumers;
* Promoting competition in the provision of services;
* Encouraging an independent, strong, diverse and effective legal profession;
* Increasing public understanding of the citizen's legal rights and duties; and
* Promoting and maintaining adherence to the professional principles.

It was section 1(1)(f) in particular that prompted David Edmonds, Chairman of the Legal Services Board, to launch the Legal Education and Training Review (LETR) in November 2010 at the Association of Law Teachers' Annual Lord Upjohn lecture. The final LETR report, *Setting Standards: The future of legal services education and training regulation in England and Wales* was published in June 2013 (LETR, 2013). Extracts from the final report and the recommendations therein will be made, as relevant, throughout this chapter. For now, within the context of the mandated knowledge and skills in the existing QLD, the report noted that the legal professions are happy with the required foundation subjects and specified skills *except* in respect of the teaching of ethics; the standards and depth of writing; and students' lack of commercial awareness. It is these recommendations that form the (very) loose basis for the following case studies. Neither the JASB, nor the QAA, nor even the LETR, mandate or propose to mandate the type of assessments on the QLD so the case studies provided here attempt to weave teaching, learning and assessment into a scheme of work for law academics and students. Regular formative assessments are the backbone to the student experience because the development of knowledge and skills is incremental towards an ultimate summative and aligned assessment.

EMBEDDING APPLIED LEGAL VALUE ETHICS IN LEGAL EDUCATION

An absolute positivist approach to learning the law simply involves focusing exclusively on the Acts and cases, which are the law. Such an approach permits little, if any, discourse into what the law ought to be: providing a limited view of the law, whence it comes and its role in society. For example, given that the media often criticise legal decisions and procedures, it is important that students of law are able to analyse those criticisms with an informed understanding of the complexities involved in answering, for example, an apparently simple question such as 'what is law?'. Providing any sort of valid answer requires the student to have enjoyed a more critical, evaluative approach to legal studies, including an analysis of the values on which the law is based and therefore, in the broadest sense, a study of values and ethics. Further, and separately from the first point, because a law degree is a prerequisite to a career in most of the legal professions, and because the regulated legal professional bodies each have a professional code of conduct, it would seem common sense that students of law grasp the intricacies of the broad ethical nature of their role as legal professionals; that said, the reasons for teaching value ethics at the undergraduate level go beyond the points made earlier. This is more fundamental than learning the compliance rules; it goes beyond offering an analysis of the positivist versus natural law distinction; and is about even more than learning to make informed ethical choices in a legal context. Because the law is normative, it is vital to embed ethics into the undergraduate curriculum because students need to be able to articulate with persuasion what ought to be done when solving legal, factual and/or ethical problems. These are some of the reasons why value ethics teaching should be explicit and pragmatic, rather than invisibly embedded in the curriculum (see Economides, 1998).

Interrogating practice

- How do you currently incorporate value ethics into your practice?
- How often do you allow time for class discussion about the fairness of the law, or the students' perceptions of justice in the topic being considered?
- What opportunities do you see for students to take an informed normative stance in relation to the law?

The QAA Benchmark (2007) already provides for knowledge of a 'substantial range of major concepts, *values*, principles and rules of that system' (emphasis added) and the JASB statement provides also for values, but not explicitly ethics: 'Knowledge and understanding of the fundamental doctrines and *principles* which underpin the law of England and

Wales…The ability to demonstrate knowledge and understanding of a wide range of legal concepts, *values*, principles and rules of English law and to explain the relationship between them in a number of particular areas.' (JASB, 2014, emphasis added).

However, it is clear that the values on which the legal system are based are not currently considered by legal education providers to be mandatory; if they were, the LETR would have had no cause to comment that: 'The centrality of … legal values…is one of the cleverest conclusions to be drawn from the LETR research data' (LETR, 2013: xiii).

Recommendation 7 of the LETR report (2013) provides that '[t]he learning outcomes at initial stages of LSET [legal services education and training] should include reference (as appropriate to the individual practitioner's role) to an understanding of the relationship between *morality and law, the values underpinning the legal system, and the role of lawyers in relation to those values'* (LETR, 2013, emphasis added).

Case study 21.1: Embedding values in the undergraduate law curriculum

Direct your students to watch and consider Harvard University's Justice with Michael Sandel, episodes 1 and 2 at http://www.justiceharvard.org

Ask them to think about how they might act in the following situation:

'Suppose you are driving through a narrow tunnel and a worker falls onto the road in front of you. There is not enough time for you to stop. If you keep straight, you will hit the worker and kill him, but if you swerve left into oncoming traffic, you will collide with a school bus and kill at least five children. What's the right thing to do? Does utilitarianism have the right answer?'

(Michael Sandel, Harvard University)

This is an important question for law students because the answer(s) necessarily involve understanding Bentham's contribution to the philosophy of law and the relationship between law, morality and society. It is likely that students will previously have encountered some notion of the 'greatest happiness for the greatest number', so this exercise builds on existing knowledge and broadens and deepens it. Episode 1, Part 2 of the Harvard Justice videos centres on the case of *R v Dudley and Stephens* (1884–85) LR 14 QBD 273, a case well known to all law students (it involved the cannibalism of a cabin boy by sailors lost at sea). Law students in England and Wales will encounter this case during their study of criminal law. Merging the criminal law on the scope of the defence of duress/necessity into a wider discussion of justice using Sandel's video is a very simple but highly effective way to broaden the main 'law' curriculum to an applied value ethics discourse. That discussion will inevitably lead students to consider the cases of *Re A (Conjoined Twins)* [2001] Fam 147 (a case involving the medical separation of conjoined twins to save the life of the stronger twin, causing the inevitable death of the weaker twin), and then to the recent decision of *Nicklinson v Ministry of Justice* [2013] EWCA Civ 961, a case which attracted media attention on the question of assisted suicide.

Interrogating practice

- What moral dilemmas do you incorporate into your teaching?
- What moral dilemmas could you incorporate into your teaching?

Whether these activities are labelled as a form of jurisprudence, value ethics or applied ethics is less important than the opportunity for students to engage in the activities themselves. It matters less whether students know that the law does not permit the defence of duress to murder, or that the defence of necessity does not extend to either murder or assisting suicide; it matters more that students are sufficiently skilled at identifying ethical conundrums, at perceiving the theories and principals which might be applied to provide a solution, and forming an opinion to which is preferable, and offering articulate justifications thereof.

By way of further example, also from criminal law, and specifically in respect of the offence of theft, tutors could introduce the concept of dishonesty in English law, and the test in *R v Ghosh* [1982] Q.B. 1053, but then embed a deeper understanding of the concept by directing students to consider the writings of, say, Nozick (episode 3 at http://www.justiceharvard.org/category/watch/) as a counterpoint to Benthamite utilitarianism. And there is even more – because Lord Lane himself raised the question in *Ghosh*, law students could first be asked to consider whether Robin Hood would be a thief in the online video, but in Sandel's words: 'Robin Hood stole from the rich to give to the poor. Is this "justice"?'. This could take students to the writings of Aristotle, and Rawls, and possibly Sen and Sandel himself. Law students might find the debate within the latter's online community interesting too (http://www.justiceharvard.org/2011/03/takeb-from-the-rich-give-to-the-poor/).

ADVANTAGES OF TEACHING VALUE ETHICS

Articulation of the justification(s) of possible solutions to a given problem develops clarity of both thought and expression that are widely regarded as the stock in trade of the lawyer. The law student might not otherwise have the opportunity to develop an open mind and tolerance that contemplating competing but equally valid values produces. Further, to learn legal rules without recourse to their history, source, gaps and omissions, without thinking critically about them, denies the reality of legal practice. Clients will have formed views about how satisfactory the law is, so law students must have the opportunity to explore and articulate their opinions about the rightness and wrongness of the law, and about their views on the difference, if any, between how the law is and how they think it ought to be.

Learning value ethics and normative approaches to the law also seems to meet students' expectations. In the experience of the author, many students have chosen to study law 'to change the world…to fight for the underdog…to challenge the way the world works…to reverse injustices…to stand up to "the man".' All of these bold intentions carry an implicit demand for a value-driven education. Students have virtuous aims for their personal and professional lives, so it behoves the legal curriculum to facilitate a study of values. It is also vital for students to learn to appreciate that 'justice' has considerable ambiguity in meaning and effect.

CHALLENGES

Some academic staff may be reluctant to lead students in discussions about what is right and what is wrong in ethical terms. They may perceive their role as to provide knowledge, and there is no ambiguity about the rightness of the content. Others may be anxious if they have not been trained in teaching ethics. Others may be nervous about the risk, actual or perceived, of indoctrinating students; or even about becoming or being perceived by the students as being a moral guide in areas necessarily sensitive and complex. These anxieties must be addressed in the curriculum formation stages. This requires agreement from the teaching team about the aims of the module (e.g. to offer an introduction to professional code compliance, or to provide a safe educational platform for students to explore value pluralism). The philosophy of the teaching team needs to be explicit and coherent. Students need to understand that the tutor is not there to provide a moral compass. There is a challenge in moving academic staff from the comfort of teaching content-heavy rules of law to facilitating very high levels of educational and affective behaviours, but the rewards are immeasurable.

Finally, a discussion of ethics is time consuming. If **modules** are over-filled with legal content, academics have a strong argument against adding value ethical debates; there simply isn't the time. The only solutions are to increase contact time or reduce the taught (and assessed) positivist curriculum. There are valid reasons for doing both – given the volume, breadth and range of law, it is not possible to teach it all over a three-year period anyway. Far more useful for students is to be confident that whatever the law is, and however it changes, they have the knowledge and skills to research, understand, analyse, apply, question and evaluate it.

ASSESSING VALUE ETHICS

The LETR recommendation 11 provides:

> There should be a distinct assessment of legal research, writing and critical thinking skills at level 5 or above in the Qualifying Law Degree and in the Graduate Diploma in Law. Educational providers should retain discretion in setting the context and

parameters of the task, provided that it is sufficiently substantial to give students a reasonable but challenging opportunity to demonstrate their competence.

(LETR, 2013)

If a value ethics approach to legal education were embedded across the foundation subjects of the degree, it could cumulate to a capstone project that involves bringing those embedded value theorists together into a single dissertation or extended essay at **levels** 5 or 6. The student could even choose the title themselves (perhaps from a list of approved topics to lift their anxiety levels, but this should not preclude a student who has an idea seeking approval to pursue it). For example, students could revisit cases such as *Miller v Jackson* [1977] Q.B. 966, *R v Brown* [1994] 1 A.C. 212 and *Williams v Roffey* [1991] 1 Q.B. 1 through the lens of Karl Llewellyn's legal realism.

EMBEDDING COMMUNICATION SKILLS INTO THE LEGAL CURRICULUM

The law exists in words. Effective communication is therefore a vital skill for a lawyer. Effective communication includes good oratory, verbal and listening skills; respect for the audience; flexibility to adapt the message to the context; and the ability to manipulate the inherent ambiguities in words.

Communication skills in a formal legal setting must be contextualised. The court system is adversarial, a term which means there are two parties (adversaries) who represent their positions by presenting evidence and calling witnesses before an independent and impartial person or group of people (usually a jury and/or judge), who decides whether the case is proven to the standard required. Articulate and persuasive presentation skills are the very least a law student needs to become an active and efficient player in the processes of law. There is congruence here too with the nature of applied ethics because it is the role of the advocate to represent his client's case within the rules of law and the rules of the court.

The LETR data revealed the most desirable skills and attributes as identified by legal services providers. Although oral advocacy was rated 15 out of 25 by the barristers and 23 out of 25 by solicitors and CILEx lawyers (LETR, 2013: 37), communication in person, attention to detail and explaining legal matters were all in the top six; in other words, well-developed communication skills. We suggest here that mooting is an excellent legal exercise that develops these desirable skills in students.

Case study 21.2: Embedding mooting skills into the legal curriculum

A 'moot' is an educational activity where students take on the role of barristers and present legal arguments on complex matters of law in an appellate (appeal) court setting. The standard format involves four students – two (one lead and one junior) presenting for the appellant and two presenting on behalf of the respondent. There are usually two grounds of appeal (legal points to be argued). The students have to spend considerable time in advance of the moot researching the law relating to their ground of appeal in order to construct and deliver a persuasive argument grounded in legal authority. The students present their submissions to the moot judge, who is often an academic from within the law school, but who will on occasion be a legal practitioner invited to appraise the students and provide a further level of reality to the proceedings.

Over the past century, mooting somewhat fell out of favour in educational circles, but it is now enjoying a resurgence as the benefits of mooting as an undergraduate learning, teaching and assessment tool are once again recognised. Nottingham Law School has embedded mooting across all three years of its undergraduate law degree and incorporated it into foundation subjects as a point of assessment to ensure all students are exposed to the benefits of mooting. In the first year, students are required to moot in the Law of Contract module, in the second year it is housed within the Criminal Law, and in the final year students are given the opportunity to select a specific Mooting module. In the first and second year modules, mooting comprises 50 per cent of the module mark (the other 50 per cent is an exam). In the final year, the assessments in the module consist of an oral moot presentation, and authorship of an original moot problem with accompanying justification.

The results achieved by the majority of students at Nottingham Law School are testament to the benefits of incorporating mooting into substantive law modules across the breadth of the degree; most students achieved higher marks in the moot than in any other assessment in the same subject, with many of these students achieving 2:1 and first-class marks in the moot. Not only does mooting provide students with skills such as the ability to research and to present, it also enhances their career prospects (and gives them something interesting to talk about at interview) and, when used as Nottingham Law School does, it allows them to excel academically in a way that is reflected in their overall degree classification.

(Jo Ann Boylan-Kemp, Principal Lecturer, Nottingham Law School)

It is incorrect to think of the moot as being only the oral presentation. Mooting has important written elements that force students to write with a different purpose than coursework or an examination, and with a different audience in mind (a judge rather than an intelligent but uninformed third party). Mooting also requires students to conduct deep research and select the strongest and most persuasive authorities in support of their submissions. Because students are limited on the number of authorities they can rely on (usually three), they have to weigh quality very carefully because quantity is proscribed. Students have to explain the law clearly and succinctly (the oral presentation is also time limited) and they have to mould a persuasive argument with a normative stance of what they suggest the law ought to be for them to succeed on the point. They have to use good reasoning skills and logic. They also have to listen. The moot is not a presentation so much as a dynamic conversation; students have to expect and should anticipate judicial interventions. They have to listen to the judge's questions and respond. It should therefore be clear that mooting provides an opportunity for deep learning.

Mooting is also an efficient tool to integrate learning, teaching and assessment. For example, the tutor can provide a short lecture on the legal content (in person, online or, say, on a podcast) in advance of the class, and then in the class, allocate students to roles as appellant or respondent to a moot question. Students would be required to make brief submissions in their groups for peers to judge and provide feedback. The whole syllabus can be learned, taught and assessed in this way, providing each student with opportunities to *practice* (**formative**) the assessments throughout the course. The benefits of this model include developing and increasing self-confidence and well-developed public speaking skills. Students can also benefit from an immediate sense of achievement and there are few teaching moments as rewarding as seeing the smile on a mooter's face for an argument well constructed. The moot requires a student to focus on a very detailed area of law and immerse themselves in it. The learning process therefore allows them to garner a sense of ownership over the problem and feel competent in their task. These are enhanced through incremental positive improvements in the formative assessments. However, it is important to meet student needs and expectations about this type of non-traditional assessment. Clear communication of the assessment criteria is vital. Mooting involves risks to student anxiety levels, which must be carefully managed. Experience also shows that mooting creates considerable student workload issues. Because of the novelty of the assessment, or perhaps because it is an individual assessment where there is no anonymity, students dedicate a disproportionate time to the preparation required. From the tutor's perspective, and in respect of the **summative** moot assessment, there are issues that need to be addressed in the moderation processes, which involve considerable allocation of resources in terms of staff time.

Interrogating practice

- How do you ensure that students can develop and practise oral presentation skills in your curriculum design?
- Do you allow time for students to offer partisan arguments about the law in a formal setting?

EMBEDDING NEGOTIATION SKILLS

Notwithstanding the adversarial nature of the court system, most legal problems never reach the court but are resolved extra-judicially (out of court) by formal or informal dispute resolution methods. These include mediation and arbitration, but often the most effective and quickest way to resolve a dispute is by negotiation. In fact, having good negotiation skills is a benefit within the law, outside the law and in one's personal life.

Negotiation is the process of achieving agreement to settle differences, usually consisting of a bargain being made or a compromise being reached, in the context that each party will seek as much of an advantage to achieve their own ends as possible. The skills needed to be an effective communicator are numerous and the tactics that can be involved are complex. For law undergraduates, however, some training on the context, behaviours, styles, processes and strategy should suffice before students are given the opportunity to enter a simulated negotiation. There is high quality and freely available information online, for example at the Harvard Negotiation programme (http://www.pon.harvard.edu/category/daily/negotiation-skills-daily/).

The following case study is another example of an approach that blends learning, teaching and assessment, this time in the context of a negotiation exercise. In advance of the activity, students should have access to two short lectures (or be asked to watch a couple of brief videos or listen to podcasts on their virtual learning environment); one dealing with the legal issues involved in the transfer of property and risk (part of contract law) and the second explaining the processes and techniques of negotiation. In the in-class exercise, students should be put into pairs/small groups and given their instructions (which would be to act for *either* Cheetham & Co *or* Bickers & Co, and it is vital students receive the correct confidential instructions, *and not both*). They would have to prepare their strategy for the negotiation and then *do* the negotiation as the tutor circulates to supervise. Follow up and feedback would be at the end of the class or during the next class, or further instructions could be given so the same case study would continue over two or more sessions to encourage deep learning. Ultimately, the students should be seeking to resolve the question of who bears the risk for the damaged goods and what remedies each party can pursue. This activity is experiential, **problem-based** and is skills-orientated learning.

Case study 21.3: Bespoke Ltd and Jeremy Clerkenwell

Common facts for both parties

Jeremy Clerkenwell, a specialist car dealer, placed an order for three brand new sports cars from Bespoke Ltd, a large car manufacturer. The contract price was £300,000 and Jeremy paid a deposit of £60,000. They agreed that Bespoke Ltd would arrange for the cars to be delivered to Jeremy's business premises.

During transportation, the vehicle carrying the sports cars travelled too fast on a newly laid road surface, causing stones to fly up and chip the windscreens and paintwork of all three of the cars.

The transporter arrived at Jeremy's business premises and Jeremy took delivery of the cars. On closer inspection, Jeremy noticed the damage to the cars and contacted Bespoke Ltd saying that he refused to pay the full outstanding balance of £240,000. Bespoke Ltd refused to accept anything less than full payment for the cars.

Bespoke Ltd instructed Cheetam & Co to negotiate a settlement with Jeremy so as to avoid going to court.

Jeremy instructed Bickers & Co to negotiate on his behalf.

Confidential instructions for Cheetam & Co

Bespoke Ltd instruct you that they are keen to receive full payment as they intend to construct a new research and development facility next to their existing factory. Full payment is required to allow construction work to start immediately.

Bespoke Ltd also instruct you that while the new facility will increase their productivity in the future, they can continue to use their existing factory for a short period to undertake similar levels of work. They could therefore delay the construction of the facility, saving them £5,000 per month. You are instructed that construction cannot be delayed for more than three months.

Confidential instructions for Bickers & Co

Jeremy instructs you that given the high specification of the cars, it will cost him £5,000 to have each car professionally repaired.

Jeremy also instructs you that, unknown to Bespoke Ltd, Jeremy has been negotiating a very lucrative agreement to ship the cars to a high-profile client in Hong Kong. The sports cars are in high demand in Hong Kong after a local movie star was filmed driving the same sports car in a new blockbuster film. Jeremy is hoping to profit from this increased demand by selling the cars for £10,000 in excess of the market price per car.

(Ryan Murray, Principal Lecturer in Law, Nottingham Law School)

COMMERCIAL AWARENESS

In the online LETR (2013) survey, 68.9 per cent of legal practitioners indicated that knowledge of the business context is important or very important to their work. 'Commercial awareness' is a term, the meaning of which is vague and the place of which in under-graduate legal education is not universally supported, however, why should students who have to learn the 'pure law' of property transfer and associated risks not also develop 'an ability to recognise clients' commercial objectives?' (LETR, 2013: para 2.75). We assert it is more reflective of any business environment to develop an understanding of the commercial realities. In a global setting, this is equally true, but cross-cultural negotiations bring their own challenges.

Case study 21.4: The University of Cumbria's use of virtual simulation

The Clinical Legal Education Association report (2007), 'Best Practices for Legal Education' identified 'sensitivity and effectiveness with diverse clients and colleagues' as a professional core deserving attention in law school. As a result, the Law department at the University of Cumbria established a virtual simulation involving a fictitious pharmaceutical company negotiating with a supplier of particular herbs for a new drug. The simulation was designed to provide students with opportunities to explore intercultural communication. The negotiation ran across two jurisdictions – the second year Law students at Cumbria represented the pharmaceutical company and a group of second year students from a German law school represented the supplier.

Prior to the simulation exercise, an introductory session on the negotiations process, techniques and the role of the lawyer in business transactions was provided. The exercise was carried out through a combination of online written and virtual live negotiations between two teams via videoconference and teleconference, all taking place within the virtual environment of SIMPLE (Simulated Professional Learning Environment). Students had to understand and interpret communications from the other team, evaluate an appropriate response, react and attempt to reach an agreement. Each week, each student was asked to reflect on the negotiation to gain an insight into their own pre-conceptions, biases and opinions; their understanding of the process itself; and their understanding of how their contribution had been perceived by others. Teams were asked to discuss their reflections if they wished and were encouraged particularly to consider and overcome any cultural differences in communication and/or strategy between the teams. Academic staff used the student experience to identify conflicts in new intercultural experiences through unobstructed observations and student interviews.

(Ann Thanaraj, School of Law, University of Cumbria)

> **Interrogating practice**
>
> - Consider a module that you teach or would like to teach where you could offer students an opportunity to communicate with students from another jurisdiction about legal matters.
> - How would you prepare students for cross-cultural communication issues? How would you encourage reflective practice from the participating students?

OVERVIEW AND CONCLUSIONS

The purpose of this chapter has been to illustrate models of legal education that embed legal knowledge and legal skills together to enhance the student's experience. We have, very briefly, reviewed some of the recommendations of the LETR and tried to show how they could be adopted into the undergraduate curriculum. We have also advocated a holistic approach to teaching, learning and assessment, going beyond aligning learning outcomes to assessment, to a method that merges the learning and the assessment into a seamless whole. We accept that the case studies featured here involve considerable challenges in implementation, not least in terms of the staff resources required to establish and operate them, however, we hope we have been able to highlight good practice, albeit only briefly, to enthuse the reader to innovate their teaching practice to benefit students learning the law.

REFERENCES AND FURTHER READING

Bone, A (2009) 'The twenty-first century law student', *The Law Teacher*, 43(3): 222–245.

Clinical Legal Education Association (2007) *Best Practices for Legal Education*. Available from: http://www.cleaweb.org/Resources/Documents/best_practices-full.pdf (accessed 14 April 2014).

Economides, K (ed.) (1998) *Ethical Challenges to Legal Education and Conduct*. Oxford: Hart Publishing.

Edmonds, D (2011) 'Training the lawyers of the future – a regulator's view', *The Law Teacher*, 45(1): 4–17.

Hardee, M (2012) *Career Expectations of Students on Qualifying Law Degrees in England and Wales*. Available from the Higher Education Academy: http://www.heacademy.ac.uk/assets/documents/disciplines/law/Hardee-Report-2012.pdf (accessed 14 April 2014).

Joint Academic Stage Board (JASB) (2014) *Academic Stage Book*. Available from http://www.sra.org.uk/documents/students/academic-stage/academic-stage-handbook.pdf (accessed 14 April 2014).

Quality Assurance Agency (QAA) (2007) *Subject Benchmark Statement: Law.* Available from: http://www.qaa.ac.uk/Publications/InformationAndGuidance/Pages/Subject-benchmark-satatement-Law-2007.aspx (accessed 14 April 2014).

Sandel, M (2011) *Take from the Rich, Give to the Poor.* Available from http://www.justiceharvard.org/2011/03/takeb-from-the-rich-give-to-the-poor/ (accessed 28 May 2014).

The Legal Education and Training Review (2013) *Setting Standards, The Future of Legal Services Education and Training Regulation in England and Wales.* Available from: http://letr.org.uk/the-report/index.html (accessed 12 April 2014).

22 | Business and management

Sarah Hamilton and Tim Stewart

INTRODUCTION

Although this chapter is titled Business and Management, it aims to be as relevant as possible to the sub-disciplines such as marketing, accounting, finance and human resources. The focus of the chapter is at undergraduate level but the content is also as relevant to postgraduate level and professional education.

Above all, this chapter aims to provide practical help to business school faculty who facilitate effective education. The main focus is on faculty new to teaching, but will, we hope, also be useful for more experienced teachers. This chapter is current at the time of writing, but a business school faculty member should expect to need to adapt and reinvent his or her educational practice and subject knowledge many times during their career.

THE NATURE OF BUSINESS AND MANAGEMENT STUDENTS

Since 2007/08, business has had the highest number of enrolments across all subject areas at both postgraduate and undergraduate levels in UK Higher Education Institutions (HEIs) (HESA, 2013). In addition, many other subject areas now offer business as a minor subject alongside another discipline like engineering, health, law or modern languages.

The majority of business students are keen to use their learning and qualifications to get a job in, or career advancement within, some sort of business (Maringe, 2006). Others will be looking for management skills or business acumen to help them prosper in another sector such as health, education, charity or public service. Increasingly, students will be planning to run their own business at some point in the future and entrepreneurship will be an important part of their studies.

One of the striking features and challenges in business education today is not only the diversity of different student backgrounds, but also the diversity of possible future opportunities they will have. One of the biggest challenges of business education is how you prepare students for jobs that do not exist yet. Many undergraduate students choose business degrees without a specific career in mind (Maringe, 2006) – it is not necessarily the case that a BSc Professional Accounting student wants to become a professional accountant. Students often choose the discipline because they recognise that the skills will be useful and transferable throughout their lives and careers. Without knowing exactly what the jobs of the future are going to be, **transferable skills** become a valuable commodity.

THE CHANGING BUSINESS ENVIRONMENT

Since the 1970s, business and management practices have continuously evolved at an accelerated pace and are likely to continue to do so (Liu, 2013). Successful business people will need to be able to adapt their knowledge and their skills to suit the continuously evolving environment. The development of **independent learning** skills and competencies, like good communication skills, are likely to be at least as important as a mastery of the discipline knowledge (see Chapter 12; Mason et al., 2009).

Traditional roles, cultures and work silos have been broken down, for example accountants are expected to understand business strategy and marketers are expected to speak in the language of finance. A particular characteristic of contemporary business education is the need to link with specialist disciplines, rather than to teach a range of sub-disciplines in a series of silos, as has traditionally been the case (Ottewill et al., 2005). It is therefore important for faculty teaching different business and management specialisms, such as HR, marketing, accounting and information management, to work together as part of an integrated team as they would do in the world of work. A fragmented business faculty that operates in silos is detrimental to the students' understanding of the integrated nature of multi-disciplinary teams in business.

THE DISTINCTIVENESS AND CHANGING NATURE OF BUSINESS AND MANAGEMENT EDUCATION

The purpose of business and management education

The debate around the purpose of business and management education is not new (Mutch, 1997; Macfarlane, 1989). Is it for the development of practitioner knowledge and skills to equip students to work effectively in a business role or does it have a higher social, moral and liberal purpose via more abstract academic study and critical evaluation of business activity?

There has been increasing emphasis on skills since the Dearing Report in 1997 (Dearing, 1997) and the Leitch report in 2006, (Leitch, 2006) to the extent that contemporary belief now takes the view that the purpose of business education is to support the acquisition of useful skills and knowledge to improve practitioner performance in the workplace (Stoner and Milner, 2008).

Business schools are responding with more applied and practitioner-relevant programmes often delivered by those with direct recent (and sometimes continued) experience of the workplace.

This has also led to many business school faculties being sourced on a part-time basis, sometimes without extensive immersion in academic communities, scholarship or **pedagogy**. Some of the challenges for these practitioner–faculties include:

- Building scholarship profiles to support their academic and teaching careers;
- Integrating into the academic community; and
- Getting the right practical support in basic classroom and assessment practices.
(Higher Education Academy, 2009a)

The practitioner–academic and traditional academic complement each other by bringing a rich variety of skills to the table that, when combined, need not be seen as a dichotomy but as an integrated and complementary approach to business education. The challenge here is for business schools to create collegiality and to reconcile the different beliefs around the purpose of business education.

Interrogating practice

- How could you work with colleagues to enhance your learning and teaching skills?
- What do you think the aims of business education should be and how does that impact on your approach to learning and teaching?

The professions

It has been common for a long time for groups of practitioners to eventually form **professional bodies** that regulate and assign vocational qualifications to specific business areas, such as human resources (Chartered Institute of Personnel and Development), marketing (Chartered Institute of Marketing) and accounting (Chartered Institute of Management Accounting). Much of the training for these professional qualifications has traditionally been done outside higher education. Increasingly, though, business schools are looking to incorporate professional body requirements into degree syllabuses. This integrated approach offers students the opportunity to gain recognition towards their membership of a professional body as well as their degree.

This can cause a tension for faculty between the requirements of the professional body and the regulatory practices of the higher education provider. There may also be tension between the professional body and the higher education provider regarding the purpose of the qualification. Professional qualifications governed by professional bodies, such as those in accountancy, are primarily knowledge and practice focused, often with an emphasis on traditional examinations. They tend to have little consideration for the requirement for critical thought and independent research as set out in the **Framework of Higher Education Qualifications** (QAA, 2008). Ultimately, balancing professional and academic standards can be challenging and it is therefore important to understand both the regulations governing the programmes and the requirements of the relevant professional body.

THE BUSINESS AND MANAGEMENT CURRICULUM

Curriculum design

The **QAA subject benchmark statements** (QAA, 2013) provide standard descriptions of what is expected to be included in particular fields of study and the outcomes in terms of abilities and skills that students should develop. They do not explicitly state the specific content of the curriculum or the methods of delivery; however, they do provide a focal point when developing learning and teaching strategies. It is likely that any **quality assurance** process for approving a new curriculum will look to see that these benchmark statements have been taken into consideration. However, there is still a significant amount of academic freedom that enables those designing the curriculum to use their academic judgement to develop the curriculum beyond the benchmark statements. This enables the curriculum to be more responsive to the changing nature of business and management education.

Business and management degrees are made up of a variety of different subject areas, which could form degrees in their own right or form topics or modules as part of a degree programme e.g. Human Resource Management, Digital Marketing. These sub-disciplines of business and management education do not have their own subject statements, but fit in with the generic business and management ones (QAA, 2007).

The freedom and flexibility this provides may also prove challenging when determining syllabus and content, with lecturers often designing content around their own research interests or areas of practical experience (Ottewill et al., 2005). The benchmark statements therefore provide only generic guidance around skills and abilities that should be developed.

Professional bodies and employers

The extent to which skills taught on business and management degrees are genuinely providing the skills that employers need has often been criticised (Leitch, 2006; Essery, 2002). The Association of Business Schools (ABS, 2013) referred to the need to design

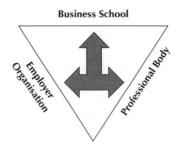

Figure 22.1 BPP University's tripartite relationship

practice into the curriculum and develop 'institutional relationships with businesses in order to deliver this aspect of their teaching' (ABS, 2013: 7).

BPP University (2013) refers to their 'tripartite relationship' with the Institute of Chartered Accountants in England and Wales (ICAEW) and an employer organisation in the construction of the learning, teaching and assessment strategy for their Graduate Diploma in Accountancy, as illustrated in Figure 22.1.

Newcastle University, Henley Business School, the University of Reading and Nottingham University Business School have partnered with PriceWaterhouseCoopers to deliver degrees that integrate professional body exams, a **work placement** with the employer and a degree qualification (ICAEW, 2013). Integration is increasing in practice and according to Lucas and Tan (2007) can lead to better academic results. Where work placements are not possible, there is a growing significance in the value of extra-curricular activities to evidence workplace skills (Higher Education Academy, 2009b).

The role of the business studies lecturer is moving beyond just teaching and now requires strong networking and interpersonal skills, working with professional bodies and employer organisations to build relationships that can enhance curriculum design, extra-curricular activities and the student learning experience.

Interrogating practice

- Have you involved relevant professional bodies and/or employer organisations in the design of your course?
- What could you do to get more involvement from the professions in curriculum design?
- Are there areas of your syllabus that would be enhanced by input from the relevant professions?

Internationalisation of the curriculum and student experience

Subjects like maths and science are broadly universal and easily cross cultural and geographical boundaries. Others, like law and health, may only be relevant to a particular jurisdiction and could be culturally specific. Business and management sit somewhere in the middle with elements of local and cultural practice but increasingly broadening out to a more global field of study (Figure 22.2). It is crucial for business education to keep up with the changing nature of business networks that cross international boundaries. Chapter 3 considers similar but broader issues around **internationalisation**.

Figure 22.2 Universal and local concepts and principles

English is the key language of business globally and many international students are keen to study business either in the UK or remotely. Business and management careers often involve a more international flavour than other subjects as organisations globalise and best practices spread around the world. Learning and teaching methods need to reflect the diversity of the cohort by adhering to inclusive teaching practices (see also Chapter 11). Curriculum content needs to ensure it covers contemporary and up-to-date tools and processes being used in global, multi-disciplinary, virtual business teams rather than UK-centric practices.

One of the key challenges for a business or management school is to create a learning experience that is inclusive in its relevance and appeal for students looking to apply the learning in different sectors, countries and disciplines.

Interrogating practice

- How do you keep up-to-date with developments in international business?
- How do you encourage your students to take an interest in business outside their own country?
- How do you ensure that students from different cultures are adjusting to education in the UK?

LEARNING, TEACHING AND ASSESSMENT STRATEGIES

Developing employability skills and reflective practice

Work-based placements

A traditional approach to developing **employability skills** (workplace competences) in the business curriculum is the use of work-based placements. These can include a whole year in practice or be a short period of time within the course of study. Work-based placements are proven to develop reflective capacity, which is an important part of professional practice (Lucas and Tan, 2007). The QAA has a **Code of Practice** around the implementation and use of work-based placements (QAA, 2012: Chapter B10). **Reflective journals** and **Personal Development Plans** and are often used in conjunction with work-based placements.

Role play

The employability agenda is driving the need for more real-world and **authentic teaching** and assessments, yet the extent to which the classroom environment can genuinely replicate the real world is questionable. We have already considered the concept of work placements, but these are not always possible or desirable. If your student is not going out into the real world how do you make the real world come to your student? One of the methods that you can try using to simulate a real-world scenario is **role play**. Role play is widely used in marketing education both in teaching and assessment (Carroll, 2006).

Some of the things you need to consider when using role play are:

- Class size – is it feasible?
- Can all students participate?
- Are you going to participate, i.e. what is your role?
- How will feedback on performance/skills be given?

It is easy to see how marketing students would benefit from role-play activities because there is a clear link to marketing specific employability skills such as negotiation, relationship building and presentation skills, but it is less obvious for other business disciplines. Haskins and Crum (1985) provide details of the role-play activity they use for cost accounting, arguing that role play is the best method for enabling the students to experience and therefore understand the complexities of human behaviour that impact on cost accounting decisions.

There is much debate over the extent to which employability skills should be extra-curricular or embedded in the programme itself. It is arguable that for business and management education, it is essential that they are embedded and that academic skills, knowledge and professional competence are also integrated (Mason et al., 2009).

Interrogating practice

- In your programme(s), are employability skills embedded or seen as an 'extra'?
- Does the extent that employability skills are embedded in the programme impact on your students' engagement with them?
- Do your learning activities enable your students to meet the employability outcomes in your teaching?

Problem solving and critical thinking

Decision making in business often requires the skills of problem solving and critical thinking.

The case method

The **case method** is designed to challenge students' thinking and give them complex situations that lend themselves to comprehensive analysis and diagnosis. The student does the analysis and diagnosis themselves rather than using a didactic approach that tells them what the correct answer should be. Cases are predominantly designed around actual business situations. Students can take on various roles in analysing the case. However, the case method is often criticised for being too rational and isolated from the conflicting demands and pressures of everyday life that managers face in contemporary and dynamically changing environments (Swiecrz and Ross, 2003).

As the lecturer, you can choose to write your own case studies and seek to get them published, alternatively you can purchase them from a variety of different companies, including directly from Harvard Business Publishing or companies like The Case Centre (formally ECCH).

Whilst the traditional case method focuses on real-life business, it is also possible to use fictional cases.

Film

The use of documentary and fiction film in the classroom has gradually been increasing. For example, Charlie and the Chocolate Factory can be used for analysing approaches to recruitment and selection (Billsberry, 2013).

The purpose of using media and video clips from films is to give students a fresh perspective and to require them to use creative thought and **critical thinking**.

Tyler et al. (2009) discuss an activity where they put students in groups and require them to source three video clips from a film or animation which they then analyse and describe to the class via a presentation explaining what each clip illustrates with relation to a specific topic in their management course.

Virtual technologies

The new generation of students is the virtual generation (Proserpio and Gioia, 2007) and they require and demand more virtual approaches to learning and teaching (see Chapter 10 for more about learning technologies).

When considering virtual learning, there are many options of which social media and blogs can be useful for engaging with the virtual generation and developing their critical thinking and decision-making skills. BPP Business School has been using Facebook and blogs in both undergraduate and postgraduate programmes. One of the key successes of the use of Facebook particularly with undergraduate students is their engagement with finding new materials and developing their own skills of research, enquiry and investigation. Communication quickly becomes two way and the students take ownership of the environment and the materials in it. Blogs have proved successful in developing the students' ability to critically reflect on their learning and their own responses and behaviours towards the discipline (Braithwaite, 2013).

Interrogating practice

- Are you making the most effective use of technology for problem solving and critical thinking?
- Review the teaching methods you currently use and consider the extent to which they engage the students in problem solving and critical thinking.

Assessment in business and management education

One of the key themes in business education is the need for 'real-world' learning experiences and employability skills. This is also true of the assessment. It is possible to plot types of real-world assessments on a continuum (Figure 22.3). Chapter 8 considers many generic aspects of assessment.

This is not intended to be a full list of assessment types but shows the varying degrees of real-world elements within different types of assessment. It also demonstrates that essays and exams are the furthest away from real world, yet often are the most commonly used. An example of a more innovative assessment that integrates employability, the real world and academic rigour is demonstrated in the London South Bank University poster in Case study 22.1.

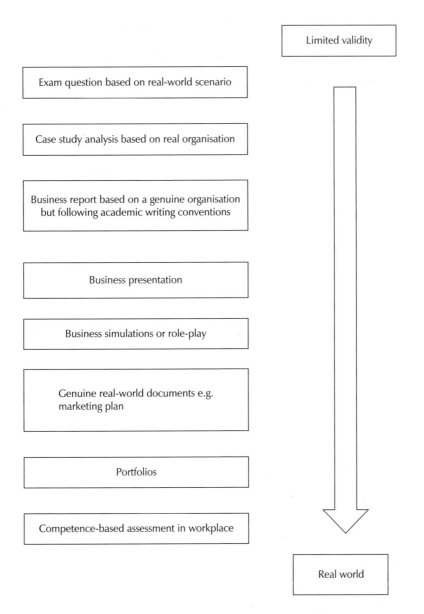

Figure 22.3 Assessment practices and their validity in the real world

STUDENT ASSESSMENT
USING DIGITAL STORY TELLING

Case study of marketing for 21st century a module focussing on contemporary issues from ethics and sustainability to post modernism

Module and Assessment Objectives:

Expose students to contemporary issues in Marketing

Facilitate research and debate on emergent controversies

Encourage the use of digital multi media presentation tools

Develop, speaking and presentation skills using digital media

Assessment Process

Answer a question linking two or three of the topics using digital software (usually PhotoStory 3).

Seminars exploring linkages between topics and debate questions

Individual consultations to refine question

Photo Story training sessions to help students produce effective audio visual presentations

Theoretical Background

"Digital Story Telling increased students" understanding of course content, willingness to explore, and ability to think critically, factors which are important in preparing students for an ever-changing 21st century" (Yang & Wu, 1012)

"The process of creating a digital story can stimulate students to carefully consider and reflect upon why they have collected selected and presented the various images or sounds this can result in deeper reflective learning" (Cox, Vasconcelos, Holdridge, 2010)

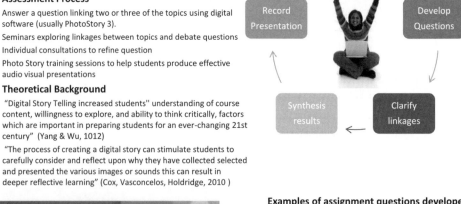

Examples of assignment questions developed successfully by students

To what extent is Corporate Social Responsibility an ethical practise?

Are traditional methods of advertising losing out to consumer centric digital media?

Post Modernism and the Future of Consumer Centric Marketing?

Student Feedback on the use of PhotoStory 3

Fun. Scary. Different. Challenging. Much harder than I thought. Creative.

Tutor Feedback on the marking of 25 minute assignments

Much more interesting than an essay, Students are engaged and engaging. They display creativity and energy.

Four years experience shows assessment is also formative as students learn to use multi media and present more effectively.

London South Bank
University

Interrogating practice

- Reflect on the real-world assessment continuum. Where do you think your assessment practices fit?
- Where do opportunities exist to make your assessments more relevant to the real world of business?

ENTREPRENEURSHIP EDUCATION

We have already seen that employability is a major theme and now we are seeing a similar focus on enterprise and entrepreneurship, which may, in part, be influenced by the growing number of small businesses in the UK and the economic downturn in 2007.

There appears to have been a natural evolution from teaching management, to leadership and now to entrepreneurship. There is a growing mindset across education and politics that entrepreneurship is not a skill that is specific to business and management education, but that all students should be taught entrepreneurship (Herrmann et al., 2008). Entrepreneurship is therefore an evolving concept, much in the same way that employability skills have been.

There are a variety of teaching methods for entrepreneurship but there is a general agreement across business educators that entrepreneurship teaching methods need to be **experiential** (Kolb, 1984) and learner centred (Gibb, 2002) and are generally more innovative and real-world orientated than found elsewhere in the business curriculum.

Learner-centred teaching methods in business and management may include:

- Projects setting up new ventures;
- Applications for new businesses;
- Presentations from existing entrepreneurs;
- Mentoring and action learning sets;
- Online virtual simulations; and
- Team-based projects.

Case study 22.2: Innovative and experiential teaching and learning

Kingston University has run an Enterprise in Action module since 2005. Delivered with the support of the national charity Young Enterprise, it has enabled some 800 students to run an enterprise during their time at Kingston.

The module is based on Young Enterprise's 'Startup Programme', through which students work in teams to establish, run and close down a micro-enterprise. This is an accelerated and intensive learning experience, telescoping the entire process into the 24 weeks between early October and late May.

The module can be studied at levels 5, 6 or 7. Learning outcomes differ in complexity and challenge by level, with different assessment tools and evaluative criteria used. Assessment methods include presentations to prospective investors, a reflective diary or blog, presentation of an annual report and accounts and reflective reports on the experience.

The variety of businesses started is wide, including both services and products: for instance authoring, e-book publishing, mending bicycles, mobile apps, news services, events organising, and self-designed and self-made goods like jewellery, desk accessories and bags for transporting cut flowers. Some students purchase and import goods, some establish shops on eBay, Etsy or other online platforms. Some focus on their personal interests or talents whilst others work more with those of their team.

Opportunities to trade are provided through trade fairs sponsored by Young Enterprise. These are showcase events in public spaces – the town's marketplace, for instance or a busy university space. The periodic fairs provide milestones through the year to help students stay on-course. Selling is frequently mentioned by students as a key learning area for them, signalling their move from consumption to active participation in creating and delivering value.

Volunteer mentors support students through the module. They are university alumni, entrepreneurs, and retired or still active business people. Many are recruited to the task by Young Enterprise, others through university placements and alumni offices. They advise and encourage students, provide feedback on pitches and sometimes find additional retail opportunities. This is most students' first experience of being mentored, and some find it difficult to use effectively.

The module begins with plenary sessions that set up the operation of the module, establish teams and start the ideation process. Regular plenaries then direct the activity and pace of the module. These are not 'chalk and talk', but project meetings when challenges are aired, milestones reviewed and feedback provided. The first trade fair is early in Semester 2, providing a strong time focus for activity.

Organising the module requires imagination and dedication. Challenges faced by staff include maintaining a diverse group of students on track with their businesses. About 120 students with varied backgrounds, experience, motivation and expectations take the module each year. A Graduate Teaching Assistant project manages, tracking the progress of teams, coordinating with the mentors and Young Enterprise, organising presentations and teams of reviewers. Teaching roles also focus on motivation as students face the realities of enterprise start-ups – including setbacks, challenges of finding funding and other

support, receiving critical feedback, learning to use mentors, delivery failures
and team bust-ups.

(Martha Mador, Kingston University)

Interrogating practice

- Reflect on this case study to identify what elements of this practice you
  might be able to use in your own teaching.
- Are there opportunities in your teaching to be more learner centred?

REAL-WORLD LEARNING AND TEACHING METHODS

It's not always possible to use such real-world experiential teaching and learning methods as evidenced in the case study, but simpler alternatives that are more feasible for
some schools and are widely used include:

- **Mentoring**
- **Action learning**
- Virtual simulations
- Extra-curricular activities

Mentoring

Mentoring is widely used in management development within business and is becoming increasingly popular in education. When designing mentoring programmes you
need to determine who will be mentors, e.g. alumni, business professionals or faculty.
Mentoring activities may include but are not limited to:

- Coaching
- Advice
- Work shadowing
- Networking
- Help with CV
- Information about the discipline

Action learning

Action learning is more of a concept than a prescribed approach to teaching, which
has been adopted by workplace trainers, professional training organisations and HEIs.

It is a technique that is valued both in practice and in education. Students work in small groups called sets to tackle real problems, take action and then to reflect back with the help of the group on what happened and what they have learnt from the experience. Action learning may be designed around group or individual projects.

Virtual simulations

Employers such as IBM use virtual worlds for their staff 'on-boarding' (induction) and the use of such technology is becoming more widely accepted in learning and training environments. **Jisc** published a useful guide for lecturers in using Second Life in teaching (Savin-Bade et al., 2009). Using virtual worlds, whilst not entirely risk free, can encourage risk taking in a safe environment. Second Life critics would argue that it does not genuinely prepare students for the real world of face-to-face human interaction. Entrepreneurship education does teach students, however, how to be more creative and innovative, how to think beyond the standard essay and exam-based assessments and how to move beyond some of the traditional classroom practices, such as two-dimensional case studies.

Extra-curricular activities

In addition to particular modules or courses, many universities offer extra curricular activities to develop entrepreneurship. These may include:

• Entrepreneur events;
• Business simulation workshops;
• Summer schools; and
• Ideas/business plan competitions.

Business schools need to develop good links with entrepreneurs if entrepreneurship education is to be grounded in the real world. If entrepreneurship education is to be embedded in the curriculum, then the development of an entrepreneurial mindset and skills in your students is something to consider when designing your learning activities.

Interrogating practice

• Is it appropriate for entrepreneurship skills to be taught to all students regardless of discipline?
• Do your teaching methods give the opportunity for experiential learning?

SPECIFIC CHALLENGES AND POTENTIAL SOLUTIONS

Challenge 1: the practitioner–academic

- Investigate the resources for Business Management educators at: http://www.heacademy.ac.uk/disciplines/business-and-management
- Attend conferences run by other university learning and teaching teams
- Look for Higher Education Authority conferences workshops and events
- Participate in peer observations as observer and observee

Challenge 2: networking and keeping up-to-date

- Write short articles for practitioner magazines such as *Marketing Week, Personnel Today* and *Management Today*
- Set up your own blog
- Work with other academics on small research projects
- Work with students as a co-author to turn assignments into articles
- Work with colleagues and share responsibility for updating each other on emerging practice
- Seek out professional conferences and seminars
- Use a professional social network tool such as LinkedIn and participate in the online discussion forums

Challenge 3: global context for curriculum and teaching

- Ensure a thorough induction/orientation for all students
- Produce a glossary of business terms
- Use diagnostic testing to help evaluate the challenges
- Allow more time for students to respond to your questions
- Put students in pairs to discuss before asking for a response
- Make more use of global companies, case studies and scenarios so they are not UK-centric

Challenge 4: employability skills and keeping it real

- Involve employers and professional bodies in curriculum design
- Conduct a review of learning outcomes related to employability skills
- Ensure employability outcomes are being assessed
- Involve the careers team in curriculum design
- Look at how work-based learning opportunities can be built into the curriculum design
- Design realistic work-based tasks into the learning activities

Challenge 5: critical thinking and problem solving

You can build opportunities into your curriculum through the following:

- Creating opportunities for basic problem solving within learning activities
- Introducing opportunities for experiential learning
- Providing critical thinking skills workshops/study skills sessions
- Modelling critical thinking skills in your own classroom and online delivery
- Ensuring critical thinking is recognised and rewarded in class feedback

CONCLUSIONS AND OVERVIEW

Business education needs to provide a balance between employability and academic skills. It needs to find a way to integrate all these components to make the student experience relevant, successful and engaging. Students are motivated by the potential job opportunities in business that their qualification might lead to. The world of business is constantly changing and, consequently, educational practice needs to keep up-to-date. The business lecturer therefore needs to engage with employers and professions to ensure business-relevant learning, teaching and assessment that develops employability and critical thinking skills.

REFERENCES

The Association of Business Schools (ABS) (2013) *The Role of UK Business Schools in Driving Innovation and Growth in the Domestic Economy.* Available from: http://www.associationof businessschools.org/sites/default/files/130516_absinnovation_web.pdf (accessed 12 July 2013).

Braithwaite, F (2013) *Leveraging Educational Value From Social Network Tools.* (unpublished).

Billsberry, J (2013) 'From persona non grata to mainstream: the use of film in management teaching as an example of how the discipline of management education is changing', *Journal of Management Education,* 37(3): 299–304.

BPP University (BPP) (2013) *Graduate Diploma in Accounting Handbook* (unpublished).

Carroll, C (2006) 'Enhancing reflective learning through role-plays: the use of an effective sales presentation evaluation form in student role-plays', *Marketing Education Review,* 16(1): 9–13.

Dearing, R (1997) *Higher Education in the Learning Society.* The Report of the National Committee of Inquiry into Higher Education (The Dearing Report). Available from: http://www.leeds.ac.uk/educol/ncihe (accessed 15 August 2013).

Essery, E (2002) 'Reflecting on leadership', *Works Management,* 7(55): 54.

Gibb, A (2002) 'In pursuit of a new enterprise and entrepreneurship paradigm for learning: creative destruction, new values, new ways of doing things and new combinations of knowledge', *International Journal of Management Reviews,* 4(3): 233–269.

Haskins, M and Crum, R (1985) 'Cost allocations: a classroom role-play in managerial behaviour and accounting choices', *Issues in Accounting Education*, 85: 109–130.

Herrmann, K, Hannon, P, Cox, J and Ternouth, P (2008) *Developing Entrepreneurial Graduates: Putting Entrepreneurship at the Centre of Education*. Available from: http://ncee.pw/wp-content/uploads/2013/12/developing_entrepreneurial_graduates.1.pdf (accessed 14 April 2014).

Higher Education Academy (HEA) (2009a) *Supporting Part-Time Teaching Staff in Higher Education: Perspectives from Business and Health. Final Report*. Available from: https://www.york.ac.uk/media/staffhome/learningandteaching/documents/postgradswhoteach/supporting_part-time_teaching_staff_in_higher_education.pdf (accessed 15 April 2014).

Higher Education Academy (HEA) (2009b) *What Can Extra-curricular Activities Do for You?* Available from: http://www.heacademy.ac.uk/assets/documents/EvidenceNet/ECAv5.pdf (accessed 20 August 2013).

Higher Education Statistics Agency (HESA) (2013) *Students and Qualifiers Data Tables*. Available from: http://www.hesa.ac.uk/content/view/1897/239/ (accessed 12 July 2013).

The Institute of Chartered Accountants in England and Wales (ICAEW) (2013) *The PwC Degree Programmes*. Available from: http://careers.icaew.com/school-students-leavers/entry-routes/university-and-higher-education/flying-start-degree (accessed 12 July 2013).

Kolb, D (1984) *Experiential Learning*. Englewood Cliffs, NJ: Prentice-Hall.

Leitch, S (2006) *Prosperity For All in the Global Economy – World Class Skills*. Available from: http://webarchive.nationalarchives.gov.uk/20130129110402/http://www.hm-treasury.gov.uk/d/leitch_finalreport051206.pdf (accessed 23 June 2013).

Liu, Y (2013) 'Sustainable competitive advantage in turbulent business environments', *International Journal of Production Research*, 51(10): 2821–2841.

Lucas, U and Tan, PL (2007) *Developing a Reflective Capacity within Undergraduate Education: The Role of Work-Based Placement Learning*. Available from: http://www.heacademy.ac.uk/assets/Documents/resources/Can't%20Tag/LucasLengTan.doc (accessed 15 April 2014).

Macfarlane, B 1989 *Business Lecturers in Higher Education: Outsider Reputations, Insider Values*. Available from: http://www.leeds.ac.uk/educol/documents/000000678.htm (accessed 10 July 2013).

Maringe, F (2006) 'University and course choice: implications for positioning, recruitment and marketing', *International Journal of Educational Management*, 20(6): 466–479.

Mason, G, Williams, G and Cranmer, S (2009) 'Employability skills initiatives in higher education: what effects do they have on graduate labour market outcomes?', *Education Economics*, 17(1): 1–30.

Mutch, A, (1997) 'Rethinking undergraduate business education: a critical perspective', *Management Learning*, 28: 301–312.

Ottewill, R, McKenzie, G and Leah, J (2005) 'Integration and the hidden curriculum in business education', *Education and Training*, 47(2): 89–97.

Proserpio, L and Gioia, D (2007) 'Teaching the virtual generation', *Academy of Management Learning and Education*, 6(1): 69–80.

Quality Assurance Agency (QAA) (2007) *Subject Benchmark Statement: General Business and Management*. Available from: http://www.qaa.ac.uk/Publications/Information AndGuidance/Pages/Subject-benchmark-statement-General-business-and-management.aspx (accessed 9 April 2014).

Quality Assurance Agency (QAA) (2008) *The Framework for Higher Education Qualification in England, Wales and Northern Ireland*. Available from: http://www.qaa.ac.uk/Publications/InformationAndGuidance/Documents/FHEQ08.pdf (accessed 23 June 2013).

Quality Assurance Agency (QAA) (2012) *UK Quality Code for Higher Education Chapter B10: Managing Higher Education Provision With Others*. Available from: http://www.qaa.ac.uk/Publications/InformationAndGuidance/Documents/Quality-Code-Chapter-B10.pdf (accessed 14 August 2013).

Quality Assurance Agency (QAA) (2013) *Honours Degree Subjects*. Available from: http://www.qaa.ac.uk/AssuringStandardsAndQuality/subject-guidance/Pages/Honours-degree-benchmark-statements.aspx (accessed 23 June 2013).

Savin-Bade, M, Tombs, C, White, D, Poulton, T, Kavia, S and Woodham, L (2009) *Getting Started with Second Life*. Available from: http://www.jisc.ac.uk/media/documents/publications/gettingstartedwithsecondlife.pdf (accessed 25 July 2013).

Stoner, G and Milner, M (2008) 'Embedding generic employability skills in an accounting degree: development and impediments', *Accounting Education an International Journal*, 19(1–2): 123–138.

Swiecrz, PM and Ross, KT (2003) 'Rational, human, political, and symbolic text in Harvard Business School cases: a study of structure and content', *Journal of Management Education*, 27: 407.

Tyler, C, Anderson, M and Tyler, M (2009) 'Giving students new eyes: the benefits of having students find media clips to illustrate management concepts', *Journal of Management Education*, 33(4): 444–461.

FURTHER READING

Hockings, C and Moore, I (eds.) (2001) *Innovations in Teaching Business and Management*. Birmingham: SEDA.

Kaye, R and Hawkridge, D (2003) *Learning and Teaching for Business: Case Studies of Successful Innovation*. London: Kogan Page.

Kotzee, B and Roger, J (2011) 'Can't string a sentence together'? UK employers' views of graduates' writing skills', *Industry and Higher Education*, 25(1): 45–52(8).

Maxwell, G, Scott, B, Macfarlane, D and Williamson, E (2009) 'Employers as stakeholders in postgraduate employability skills development', *International Journal of Management Education*, 8(2): 1–11.

McGill, I and Brockbank, A (2004) *The Action Learning Handbook*. London: RoutledgeFalmer.

Milner, MM and Hill, WY (2008) 'Examining the skills debate in Scotland', *The International Journal of Management Education*, 6(3): 13–20.

Wisker, G, Exley, K, Antoniou, M and Ridley, P (eds.) (2008) 'Mentoring, work-based and community placement support', in *Working One-to-One with Students: Supervising, Coaching, Mentoring, and Personal Tutoring*. London: Routledge, 61–74.

| 23 | # Quantitative methods in the social sciences |

Jonathan Parker

INTRODUCTION

Quantitative methods (QM) represent an oddly controversial aspect of a distinctive strength in British higher education. Undergraduate degrees in the UK emphasise preparation for and the conduct of research across most universities and subjects. This practice is particularly unique and laudable because it is expected of most students. In almost all other countries, undergraduate research is rare and restricted to a small group of elite students. This universal expectation means that research methods teaching and practice is well developed throughout the social sciences in the UK. The quality of student outcomes is consistently high across the spectrum of universities to an extent that is unknown in most countries. This high standard of undergraduate research should translate into a healthy respect for all research methods, both quantitative and qualitative. However, quantitative methods are seen to have declined into a state of crisis, with government and research councils reporting a lack of quantitative skills by university students and staff (Commission on the Social Sciences, 2003; Higher Education Funding Council for England, 2005; Lynch et al., 2007; McVie et al., 2008; Rice and Fairgrieve, 2001).

It is certainly the case that quantitative methods are not well integrated into most social science degrees. Maths anxiety makes it a daunting subject to both take and teach, and these complex skills are rarely used outside of compulsory quantitative methods modules. Consequently, quantitative data analysis is rarely practiced and seldom appears in student research. The toxic combination of a subject that is unpopular among students and staff, difficult to teach and perceived as largely irrelevant to the degree makes it particularly challenging in the social sciences. Ironically, those disadvantages mean that teachers of quantitative methods tend to work harder to keep on top of their subject, plan their classes carefully to keep students engaged, and creatively design their curricula to demonstrate the topic's relevance. Some of the most innovative practices in university teaching can be found in research methods classes because of teachers' need to cope with these difficult demands.

345

This chapter will explore the perceived crisis in quantitative methods and analyse the state of methods in the social sciences today. It will link the problems facing quantitative methods to the type of teaching that usually characterises its presence in degrees. The scholarly literature on what we know about teaching quantitative methods will be reviewed in order to find guidance on how to teach these skills in ways that may overcome the obstacles that impede it.

Case study 23.1: Every student counts: promoting numeracy and enhancing employability

This **National Teaching Fellowship Scheme** project studied factors that influence the development of undergraduate numeracy skills and their links to employability. In particular, the study examined how numeracy skills were developed across a range of academic disciplines, factors that influence that development and how the development of numeracy skills might be better supported both within and outside the undergraduate curricula. Both students and staff are generally unaware of how important numeracy skills are to employers. Factors influencing students' learning of quantitative skills include their basic conceptions of mathematics, their attitudes and approaches towards learning mathematics and levels of mathematics anxiety. Some key findings from these results include:

1   Students who view mathematics as a tool to carry out academic study, rather than just working with numbers in the abstract, are more likely to be positive about developing these skills. Showing the relevance of quantitative methods is particularly important.

   - Applying these skills through discipline-based analyses demonstrates their academic relevance.
   - Emphasising their usefulness in future employment also helps make the skills appear useful. Although some academics may see it simply as a beneficial side effect, student awareness makes them more likely to learn those skills more effectively.

2   Levels of maths anxiety are very widespread and reduce student confidence in and development of mathematical skills. Students also rate their mathematical skills much lower than their tutors do.

   - Tutors should be aware of maths anxiety, but should work to reinforce the relevance of mathematics, both to academic study and future employment, which helps students overcome this anxiety.
   - Teaching strategies should encourage deeper, rather than surface, approaches to learning by working towards applying mathematical concepts rather than rote memorisation of formula or rules.

3 Only 16 per cent of humanities and social science students in this study reported any opportunity to develop mathematical skills in their courses.

- Students must practice using these skills often and in progressively more complex ways in order to develop them, in the same way that they might continually practice and improve their writing.

Some key principles in teaching quantitative methods

- Numeracy training should occur from the start to finish in a degree.
- Numeracy should be more than a token presence and be embedded throughout the curriculum.
- Compulsory elements of quantitative training help ensure a progression of skills.
- Quantitative coursework should be **summatively assessed**.

(Nicki N. Tariq, UCLAN (lead author); Naureen Durrani, University of Sussex; Roger Lloyd-Jones, Sheffield Hallam University; David Nicholls, Manchester Metropolitan University; J. Geoffrey Timmins (emeritus), University of Central Lancashire; Claire Worthington, UCLAN)

The reluctance of both students and teachers to engage with quantitative methods means that these types of skills are not well nurtured in the social sciences. Rice and Fairgrieve (2001) found that the use of numeric data in teaching and learning in the social sciences was 'rare', and largely restricted to methods courses. They found little institutional support or recognition for the additional preparation and teaching workload that such teaching demands. Williams et al. (2004) found that quantitative methods requirements were present in Sociology degrees; however, there was little evidence of integration of a quantitative approach into substantive course teaching. In work following up these studies, Williams et al. (2008) found that for most, getting through statistics and quantitative methods was a 'necessary but unappealing' process. The range of subjects that students reported studying suggested strongly that QM teaching was focused more on knowledge of methods rather than practicing how to use them.

These problems are not limited to sociology. Adeney and Carey (2009) carried out a survey of research methods teaching in university politics departments. They found that 28 of the 53 departments responding to their survey (53 per cent) claimed to require quantitative methods. However, Parker's (2012) survey of degree requirements for all UK universities found that only 10 per cent of Politics degrees had such a requirement. Further, both studies found that there was a tendency of the research elite to avoid such requirements. If the universities with the most expertise, most resources and smallest teaching pressures choose not to require these sorts of skills, then it is hard to see why universities with fewer quantitatively trained staff and heavier teaching commitments would do so either. Responding to this deficit, the social science funding councils and the Nuffield Foundation have just begun Q-Step, a £19.5 million programme designed to promote a step-change in undergraduate quantitative social science training. The money is concentrated in **Russell Group** universities to fund new courses, work placements and pathways to postgraduate study, but it remains to be seen if this effort will spread beyond the universities receiving funding to influence the social sciences more widely.

MacInnes's (2009) report on the state of quantitative methods in the social sciences analyses the **QAA Subject Benchmarks** for each discipline, which provide a set of criteria, drawn up by the professional associations for the disciplines, for what should be included in an undergraduate degree. Only Economics and Criminology contain unequivocal requirements to teach quantitative methods as opposed to a range of methods 'appropriate' to carry out research in that discipline. MacInnes concludes that British university social science teachers do not possess the skills in quantitative methods that would allow them to teach undergraduates or read and evaluate research in their particular discipline using quantitative methods. Maths anxiety applies as much to staff as to students. When these skills are taught to undergraduates, the time devoted to teaching is not enough to give students confidence in understanding and applying these skills. Further, his review of the literature and the results of his own survey of quantitative methods teachers suggest that

> academic staff in most of the social sciences tend to draw a clear distinction between quantitative and qualitative approaches and associate this split with the epistemological division between explanation and understanding. Many view quantitative research as 'positivist' or consider it as a specialist concern of interest and relevance only to the small number of staff who use these methods.
>
> (MacInnes, 2009: 7)

These reports paint a bleak picture of quantitative methods in the social sciences, but there is much variation in their provision and status across different disciplines. Much research has occurred in disciplines such as sociology and politics, but not much systematic comparison of quantitative methods across the social sciences in the UK.

Interrogating practice

- Does your programme require quantitative methods?
- How many credits and modules do students have to take that are entirely dedicated to the topic?
- Are there other places that students are trained in or practice these skills?

CURRENT STATE OF THE DISCIPLINES IN THE UK

In order to provide a broad snapshot of methods teaching across the social sciences, a survey of degree requirements was conducted on a random sample of 40 UK universities between 2012–13. Not all universities offer the degrees surveyed, so the total number of observations varies by subject. Each university single honours degree in Business Management or Administration, Economics, Sociology, Criminology, Politics, Hospitality or Tourism was analysed. This survey analyses the **programme specifications**, handbooks, and **module** documentation in order to identify how many degrees require training of at least half a module in quantitative methods, research design or qualitative methods, and undergraduate research. The percentage of 'old' (pre-1992) universities offering the degrees was also identified because there might be differences across more traditional versus newer subjects.

The results in Table 23.1 give some indication of the variation of degree requirements across the various social science disciplines, as well as some strong areas of consensus. First, the table clearly demonstrates the nationwide commitment to research methods and undergraduate research. All disciplines except Business require methods and research in an overwhelming majority of degree programmes. While Business, a comparatively new discipline, requires methods and research in just under half of its degrees, another new discipline, Hospitality, is much stronger with requirements in a clear majority of all degrees. 'Old' and 'new' universities do not appear to differ in their provision.

The commitment to quantitative methods appears weaker than to research. Only Economics and Business require these skills in a majority of degrees. These two disciplines are also the most obvious places where quantitative methods would appear more intrinsically interwoven into the substantive teaching throughout the degree. In such cases, students would see the need for quantitative methods, practice their skills

Table 23.1 Variation of degree requirements across social science

Discipline	% Pre-1992 universities in sample	% Requiring quantitative methods	% Requiring research methods	% Requiring project or dissertation
Economics	80	100	15	75
Business	55	58	42	45
Sociology	57	40	97	90
Criminology	42	38	88	83
Politics	64	32	60	68
Hospitality	20	13	73	60

Source: author's own compilation

in subject-based work more frequently, and, therefore, more clearly appreciate the relevance of quantitative methods to their academic study and future employment. The link between other disciplines and quantitative methods is not as clear and, in many cases, is strongly contested. There is therefore less provision elsewhere in the social sciences. However, this lack of a clear link and the failure to integrate the use of numeracy throughout the degree detracts from the development of these skills, even if they are required. The need to integrate the use of number throughout the curriculum, in all years of a degree, and demonstrate its relevancy to the discipline is most clearly shown through these other disciplines. It is not enough to simply require a single module in methods to make it relevant to students.

Interrogating practice

- If you are teaching a compulsory methods module, what do the students do to develop their skills?
- Do they complete a research project later in their degree?
- Ask your colleagues what sorts of methods are used in their substantive classes. Many will be surprised at the extent to which even descriptive statistics are used in textbooks and research.

TEACHING QUANTITATIVE METHODS

Although the teaching of quantitative methods is fundamentally different from other substantive topics in that it is a skill rather than about a substantive topic, most aspects of the actual teaching do not radically differ from other subjects. The progress made in the scholarship of learning and teaching in terms of what sorts of techniques help to improve student engagement and outcomes, applies as much to quantitative research methods as to any other subject. Indeed, because of the difficulties of teaching this topic there has been more research focused specifically upon it. Many studies address specific issues, such as how much active learning to incorporate, how much online material to use, or which software is most effective. However, it is difficult to reliably determine impact that can be generalised (Garfield and Ben-Zvi, 2007). The lessons from the research, therefore, are that the basic principles of good teaching remain the same whether the subject is quantitative methods or any other substantive topic.

A set of principles for improving student outcomes in quantitative methods has been documented in the literature, although they will look familiar to most students of the scholarship of teaching and learning in higher education (Garfield, 1995; Garfield and Ben-Zvi, 2007). Most apply to higher education teaching in general:

1 **Students learn by constructing knowledge individually**. No matter how clearly a book or lesson explains or illustrates a concept, students will only understand the material after they have constructed their own meaning for what they are learning.

   Students need to clearly grasp concepts in ways that will allow them to apply them. Simply memorising formula or particular rules or axioms about probability or statistics promotes more **surface learning**, which doesn't force the students to construct a firm understanding of this knowledge. Such rote learning won't be retained much past the final exam. Getting students to explain to others the ideas being learned or show how to apply them encourages them to create a firm view of these concepts that requires deeper levels of learning. The use of group work, peer mentoring or applying concepts promotes the **deep learning** that embeds lessons more thoroughly and with better longevity.

2 **Students learn better when actively engaged**. Outcomes improve if students work collaboratively in small groups of three or four. They can solve problems, analyse data or even work on more in-depth projects, but it is critical for them to practice handling and analysing data rather than simply reading about how to do so or how to critically review other people's research. Students should learn methods in order to use them, not so that they will understand them in some future job or to just to read the literature more critically.

   This point can't be emphasised strongly enough. Students learning quantitative methods need to practice data handling. It isn't enough to teach abstract concepts. Many academics perceive quantitative methods as very relevant because you need to understand them in order to read the large amount of quantitative research in the field. Students do not see things in that way. Most of them are not going to be academics, so they don't consider reading the literature a particularly compelling reason to become more numerate, particularly because few instructors force them to analyse methods outside of methods class. Quantitative methods rarely play a fundamental role in the substantive topics in many of the social sciences, so they are not seen as a necessary skill outside of disciplines such as economics. Students need to see how they can use these concepts to handle and analyse data in order to find answers to problems that are central to their own discipline. That makes it relevant and immediate to them, which improves their motivation, promotes deeper learning and is more likely to be a skill that sticks with them past the module.

3 **Students must practice what they are learning in hands-on activities**. They need to apply ideas to new situations and use these skills over and over again. Throughout the social sciences, the art of the essay is taught and honed in almost every class that students take. The demands of learning to do high quality quantitative analysis should be treated with the same respect.

   Again, the social sciences don't treat quantitative methods as if they were nearly as difficult as writing. Students practice essays over and over again, but we expect them to master a new set of quantitative skills in just one module with one or two assessments. You have to get students to practice data handling and analysis from the beginning to the end of the degree in the same way that writing is developed if you want it done well.

Interrogating practice

- How do your students employ the methods you teach them?
- Do they conduct hands-on data analysis?
- If not, then why are they learning these methods?
- To what purpose will they use these skills?

---

4 **Students often encounter great difficulty understanding concepts of probability and statistics, and can struggle with even basic concepts.** Students often cannot quickly cover a wide amount of what seem to be, to the teachers, basic concepts of maths or probability with any assumption that they will all understand the material.

Some students will grasp the material quickly, but others will struggle with it. That is the nature of statistics, and you need to pace your lessons and curriculum appropriately. Have additional resources or guidance for students to consult if they are unsure or confused about the material. You don't have to set the pace to the slowest learner, but you do need to plan for the students to learn at different paces. There has to be space in the curriculum and help for the students who are struggling to catch up.

5 **Student learning improves if they become aware of and confront errors in reasoning.** They need time and practice to fully understand basic concepts, so classes should not be paced too rapidly. This principle is linked to the previous one, and the difficulties of learning probability and statistics are well documented.

The need for time and a curriculum presents a real challenge to teachers. There is a large amount of material and very complex skills that need to be learned and practiced. Lab and classroom time is very limited, so how can you do it all? You need to both pace the learning as well as providing substantial amounts of time for data handling, which seems an impossible task. This is one reason why it is impossible to teach quantitative methods in a single required module and why it must be a shared responsibility across a whole degree.

Some innovations in classroom practice can help address the mismatch between the amount and complexity of the material to cover and limited contact time. For example, the concept of the **flipped lecture** uses the large research consensus that lectures have limited usefulness in transmitting information efficiently. Moving this information onto a **virtual learning environment** through recorded or videoed lectures with accompanying notes can free up valuable classroom time for workshops, small group activities and more hands-on analysis of data.

> ## Case study 23.2: 'Unstuffing the curriculum': getting students actively engaged in applying methods

Dr Caroline Barnes and Dr Celia Jenkins teach sociological research methods at the University of Westminster. They have responded very innovatively to the pressures of teaching a required methods module with a limited credit allocation. They teach using the same approach as the 'flipped' lecture but apply it to the whole module in what they call 'unstuffing' the curriculum. They found that lectures were not received well by students and left little time for more interesting work, creating a deadly cycle of disengagement.

They applied the notion of the flipped lecture by removing them entirely. The class uses a workshop format in which students practice research skills as well as engaging in the broader methodological, ethical and political aspects of knowledge production. Students learn how to research by doing it and reflecting critically on this process. The heavy emphasis upon applying skills and practicing methods keeps the learning very active and relevant for the students.

The module gains more time for students to carry out their preparation and classwork by teaching over an entire year. It is assessed by: (1) 35 per cent interviews carried out by the students; (2) 35 per cent data response analysing secondary quantitative data; and (3) 30 per cent a reflective statement about the research process that compares and contrasts qualitative and quantitative methods, drawing on the wider reading around methodology and illustrating it with examples from their fieldwork. This amount of work is admirable, and

Table 23.2 Curriculum characteristics

Stuffed curriculum	Unstuffed curriculum
15 credits – 1 semester	15 credits – 1 year
Lectures and seminars	Workshops fortnightly
Lectures stultifying for both staff and students	Increased engagement by both staff and students but a lot of work
Poor attendance	Brings epistemology alive through practice of research
Students could not relate the theory of lectures to practice in seminars	'It becomes real'
Understood theory nor application well	Active learning experience but disconcerting for students regarding the uncertainty of knowledge
Passive learning experience	

could easily be accredited for double the credit allocated. The instructors are also very honest about the heavier workload it generates, but the extra work is seen as a preferable trade-off. The students are engaged and complete their assessments to a high standard, which makes up for the extra time commitment when compared to having to teach bored and uninspired students.

The schedule is as follows:

Table 23.3 Teaching schedule

Semester 1	Semester 2
Week 1: Beginning research	Week 1: Manipulating variables in quantitative research
Week 2: Making sense of research questions	Week 2: Advantages of secondary data and selecting an appropriate data set
Week 3: Generating a in-depth interview guide	Week 3: Hypothesis-testing and uni-variate analysis
Week 4: Analysing qualitative data	Week 4: Analysing quantitative data using bi-variate analysis
Week 5: Writing up research	Week 5. Preparing your report
Week 6: Reflecting on the research methodology	Week 6: Objectivity and quantitative data analysis
Week 7: Submit qualitative report	Week 7: Methodological reflections: epistemology, ontology and research

(Caroline Barnes and Celia Jenkins, Department of Social and Historical Studies, University of Westminster)

6   **Technology should be used to help students visualise and explore data**. They need to apply these tools actively in different situations rather than following rote scripts. Again, it is much better for students to manipulate, control, present and analyse their own data to promote a fuller and more lasting understanding of what they have learned.

Don't forget the importance of visual images. Students can use these in exercises and they need to learn how to effectively communicate results visually because they will have to employ these methods if they use them in assessments or their own research. It is also recognised that results can be manipulated or presented in a way to mislead the audience as to the real implications of research. Understanding good practice in visual presentation of data is a key skill in quantitative literacy.

Case study 23.3: Just plain data analysis

The political scientist Gary Klass has produced a quantitative methods text-book, along with a companion website (http://cas.illinoisstate.edu/jpda) that contains datasets from the book and other examples to use in teaching. His approach to the subject focuses on teaching statistical literacy, emphasising skills in interpreting descriptive statistics. He describes 'just plain data analysis' as 'simply, the compilation and presentation of numerical evidence to support and illustrate arguments about politics and public affairs.'

Klass argues that this approach is the most common form of quantitative social science methodology found in the research literature. He notes that it is rarely well presented in social science research methods and statistics textbooks. His book and its references pay particular attention to the presentation of descriptive data through charts and graphs, an aspect of social science research often overlooked. His numerous examples of bad practice in the media quickly capture students' attention. More importantly, he analyses why they are bad with reference to the scholarly literature on presentation, identifying statistical fallacies that can crop up when data is badly presented or misinterpreted.

The book guides students through a set of skills that appear much more practical and relevant than more advanced quantitative methods. He argues that they are much more likely to use them outside of a methods class compared to the sort of quantitative analysis that is most often taught, and this direct appeal to relevance makes this approach attractive to students.

The book provides a refreshingly clear and engaging approach to the use of numbers in public life that can engage students who are fearful of mathematics. The chapters of the book can easily be cut down or used as part of a module because he provides all the data and graphics on his website. The examples are fairly general and can be adapted across most social science disciplines for teaching.

(Gary Klass, Illinois State University)

---

7   **Students need consistent, helpful and timely feedback**. Though this advice should seem obvious, it is one of the most common student complaints and data from the **National Student Survey** confirms levels of widespread dissatisfaction with feedback. The existence of maths anxiety and general fearfulness expressed towards methods classes means that feedback is even more necessary in order to let students know how well they understand what they have learned, how they are progressing and how they might further improve. This is good practice for any teaching, but it has a particularly important role in methods teaching.

These observations from the scholarly literature on teaching quantitative methods are helpful, but similar to most general advice on teaching. The difficulty with teaching quantitative methods is that even if you follow all this advice and provide inspired and well-crafted instruction, it will not solve all the challenges facing this area. The problems faced in teaching quantitative methods are more systemic and cannot be overcome by addressing student anxiety and engaging them in the classroom. They stem from the nature of methods teaching and its relationship to the curriculum.

Case study 23.4: METAL, the Economics Network and DeSTRESS

METAL (Mathematics for Economics: enhancing Teaching and Learning) provides a selection of free learning resources designed to engage students in mathematics (http://www.metalproject.co.uk).

The project team have produced the following resources:

- Online question bank of mathematics teaching and assessment materials;
- Five interactive video units (covering ten units of study) using streaming video and animation to relate mathematical concepts to the field of economics;
- Ten teaching and learning guides that provide an extensive bank of teaching activities (for large and small groups) covering all aspects of Level 1 Mathematics for Economics;
- Economics case studies, which place mathematical problems into a real-world context; and
- An interactive website to present the teaching and learning resources, to facilitate distance learning and to foster students' autonomy and ownership of the learning process.

The Economics Network (http://economicsnetwork.ac.uk) provides an excellent gateway to a huge variety of good resources for social science teachers of any discipline. These include:

- *The Handbook for Economics Lecturers*;
- Reflections on Teaching – short case studies from economics teaching staff;
- *International Review of Economics Education* (IREE) – an international peer-reviewed journal.

The Handbook for Economics Lecturers contains a series of guides organised under the headings of:

1 Teaching
2 Assessment
3 Course design

4 Evaluation
5 Teaching assistants

This collection of guides is an excellent resource for beginning or experienced economics teachers.

DeSTRESS (Statistical resources for social sciences) is a project of The Economics Network that promotes statistical literacy across the social science disciplines by sharing, adapting and creating resources to contextualise statistics (http://economicsnetwork.ac.uk/statistics). The site includes:

- 20 professional quality short videos
- An online bank of assessment questions which you can download or customise online
- Interactive graphs
- Handouts and booklets
- Lecture slides
- External links for statistical literacy

(The Economics Network)

To undergraduates, and most postgraduates too, methods are a means to an end rather than a subject of interest in its own right. Substantive classes such as American Politics, Social Inequality, or World Development attract students because they find the topics intrinsically interesting. Research methods, however, are interesting because of what they enable you to do. They open up the dimensions of all other topics and provide a means of studying and understanding them better, as well as suggesting potential solutions to problems. That enabling role does not present too much of a problem in disciplines where these methods are core skills that students apply throughout their subsequent coursework. Economics and Psychology are not seen as having a crisis in quantitative skills because these techniques are taught and used throughout their curriculum. Students study quantitative methods because they will have to apply them in their subsequent classes. These methods are ubiquitous in these disciplines and their existence does not provoke epistemological debates. Quantitative approaches are still contested, even in these disciplines, but few academics would argue students should remain completely ignorant of them. The crucial dimension to the relationship of methods teaching to the discipline is the issue of *relevance*. The extent to which techniques learned in stand-alone methods classes are subsequently employed in further substantive courses are a clear indicator to students of how important these skills are for their discipline and their degree.

Quantitative methods should be taught by subject-specific staff so that students are given the message that it is relevant to their particular discipline. It also means that the teaching, through examples, types of application used, etc. is closely tied to its subject. Administratively, it is often difficult to offer quantitative methods taught by subject-specific staff. These classes are often taught in a service capacity by maths or statistics staff, or students across programmes are combined into one large class for efficiency. Sometimes a subject does not have quantitative specialists, though there is no reason that introductory classes cannot be taught by non-specialists (Adaney and Carey, 2009). However, these efficiencies of scale have a hidden cost through the loss of immediacy to students' home disciplines. Large, amalgamated courses reinforce the notion that quantitative methods are a stand-alone topic that has little relevance to the practice of their own discipline. The reaction of students to these courses is no different than if they were required to take a stand-alone writing course that was taught to everyone in the social sciences and taught by someone outside their particular degree.

Interrogating practice

- Are quantitative methods taught by staff from students' home disciplines?
- If not, then why not?
- If issues of resources or economies of scale require quantitative methods teaching by staff outside students' discipline, are there resources and examples in the teaching from students' home discipline?
- Are there times in the teaching when the particular interests and techniques of the students' home discipline, perhaps by staff from that discipline, can be addressed?

CONCLUSION AND OVERVIEW

Williams et al. (2004) found that the teaching of quantitative methods was widespread in sociology degrees, but there was little integration of these techniques and approaches into substantive modules. The lack of attention to or application of quantitative methods in classes throughout the degree is the most damaging aspect of teaching quantitative methods. It is this embedded culture of each discipline and how it treats quantitative methods that determines the way in which its importance and relevance is signalled to students. The complete lack of any application of quantitative methods or close analysis of them in substantive topics outside of a required methods module speaks volumes to students, regardless of any official line from their methods teachers, the department or the career officers at a university. If it isn't used outside of the single required module, then it must not be important. Its relevance and usefulness is clearly demonstrated by how often and how useful it is in analysing social science topics throughout a degree.

The importance of quantitative methods does not have to be demonstrated by incorporating highly advanced, multivariate econometric techniques across most classes, but it does require a large proportion of the teaching staff to engage with numerical data and treat research using such data as if it was a fundamental part of the discipline. Klass (2013) notes that the most widely used techniques in the social sciences are, by far, descriptive statistics. These techniques are well within the skills of higher education teachers to utilise. The use of numbers in social science is an accessible skill that is useful and important for both staff and students in order to underpin the high level of quality and commitment to research found in undergraduate education in the UK.

REFERENCES

Adeney, K and Carey, S (2009) 'Contextualising the teaching of statistics in political science', *Politics*, 29(3): 193–200.

Commission on the Social Sciences (2003) *Great Expectations: The Social Sciences in Britain*. London: Commission on the Social Sciences.

Garfield, J (1995) 'How students learn statistics', *International Statistical Review/Revue Internationale de Statistique*, 63(1): 25–34.

Garfield, J and Ben-Zvi, D (2007) 'How students learn statistics revisited: a current review of research on teaching and learning statistics', *International Statistical Review*, 75(3): 372–396.

Higher Education Funding Council for England (HEFCE) (2005) *Strategically Important and Vulnerable Subjects: Final Report of the Advisory Group*. Bristol: HEFCE.

Klass, GM (2013) *Just Plain Data Analysis: Finding, Presenting, and Interpreting Social Science Data*. Lanham, MD: Rowman & Littlefield.

Lynch, R, Maio, G, Moore, G, Moore, L, Orford, S, Robinson, A, Taylor, C and Whitfield, K (2007) *ESRC/HEFCW Scoping Study into Quantitative Methods Capacity Building in Wales: Final Report*. Swindon: ESRC.

MacInnes, J (2009) *Proposals to Support and Improve the Teaching of Quantitative Research Methods at Undergraduate Level in the UK*. Swindon: Economic and Social Research Council.

McVie, S, Coxon, AP, Hawkins, P, Palmer, J and Rice, R (2008) *ESRC/SFC Scoping Study into Quantitative Methods Capacity Building in Scotland: Final Report*. Swindon: Economic and Social Research Council.

Parker, J (2012) 'International comparisons of the integration of research into undergraduate degrees in the social sciences', *Council on Undergraduate Research Quarterly*, 32(3): 28–33.

Rice, R and Fairgrieve, J (2001) *An Enquiry Into the Use of Numeric Data in Learning and Teaching: Report and Recommendations for UK Higher Education*. Edinburgh: University of Edinburgh.

Williams, M, Collett, C and Rice, R (2004) *Baseline Study of Quantitative Methods in British Sociology*. Birmingham/Durham: C-SAP/BSA.

Williams, M, Payne, G, Hodgkinson, L and Poade, D (2008) 'Does British sociology count? Sociology students' attitudes toward quantitative methods', *Sociology*, 42(5): 1003–1021.

FURTHER READING

Rhind, D (2003) *Great Expectations: The Social Sciences in Britain*. London: Academy of Learned Societies for the Social Sciences.

Taylor, R and Scott, A (2011) 'Mathematics for economics: enhancing teaching and learning' in G Payne and M Williams (eds.), *Teaching Quantitative Methods: Getting the Basics Right*. London: Sage Publications, 140–155.

24

Art, design and media

Roni Brown

INTRODUCTION

Since the 2009 edition of this Handbook, the sector has seen significant change. Rather than rehearse these broad changes, this chapter will outline the ones that are specific to art, design and media insofar as they inform approaches to teaching and learning. This chapter endeavours to explore the challenges for art, design and media covering five thematic areas and offering potential 'solutions': (1) creativity: challenges for teaching and learning; (2) transition and the student experience in art and design; (3) space, practice and innovation; (4) assessment in art, design and media and (5) enterprise and employment.

CREATIVITY: CHALLENGES FOR TEACHING AND LEARNING

> Any act of artistic and scientific creation is an act of symbolic subversion, involving a literal or metaphorical transgression not only of the (unwritten) rules of the arts and sciences themselves but also of the inhibiting confines of culture, gender, and society. Re-thinking creativity means challenging established borderlines and conceptual categories while re-defining the spaces of artistic, scientific and political action.
>
> (Pope, 2005: 33)

Although creativity is not in any way limited to art, design and media, it is fundamental to what characterises and problematises the practice and teaching of these disciplines. Consideration of creativity as a philosophical, spiritual, material, political and economic activity is a realistic starting place for HE teachers in the development of pedagogy. Pope's (2005) comprehensive overview of creativity demonstrates the range of philosophical approaches to the topic of creativity and the divergence of views produced, for instance by the discourses of Humanism, Romanticism and Materialism.

Despite its complexity as a subject, there is some distillation of what is *at stake* in the creative process, accepting creativity as essentially dialogic – at once solved and not solved, neither divinely 'creative' nor entirely the realm of production, but something beyond (Pope, 2005: 9). Csikszentmihalyi's thesis on *flow* develops a Western conception of creativity that is based on the production of outcomes that 'have not been seen before and that make a difference in the context in which they appear' – making them significant (1996: 47). For Csikszentmihalyi, producing significant creative outcomes is underpinned by knowing the culture (internalising its values) and is reliant on the judgment of experts (for instance, teachers, curators, critics). We can therefore add to the already complex debate about creativity that it is facilitated by 'schooling' and a state of mind that is habitually disruptive (Bohm, 1998[1]). Teachers of disciplines that foster creative development will be continually gauging the maturity of the individual, the cohort and the year group in their development of complex functioning – moving between, for instance, playfulness and discipline, objectivity and subjectivity, self and other, fantasy and reality, risk and security.

The teaching and learning of creative disciplines can be characterised as contending with the following:

- Difference, plurality and independence of mind (and the uniqueness of each learning process and output) places an emphasis on teaching and learning strategies for individuals as well as groups and cohorts. Teaching and learning strategies that support **reflective practice** will be important for the transition to independent learning (for instance, see James, 2007).
- The need to build creative communities so that practice is shared, knowledge is exchanged, as are skills and resources.
- The 'vulnerability' of learners as they contend with the unknowable elements of creative practice and the idea that the self is often central to, or implicated in, the creative output. This will pose challenges to the sense of security of learners, the way they perceive the fairness of assessment and to their feelings about feedback.
- The need for creative learners to experiment across media, processes and technologies will pose challenges for teachers (in the range and currency of knowledge and skills) and organisational challenges (in terms of access to facilities that are likely to be managed by different departments).

Learning is fundamentally about discovery, making, doing and public forms of dissemination, and therefore the quality of space, technologies, materials and facilities that students have access to will be implicated in the quality of the outcomes of learning.

TRANSITION AND THE STUDENT EXPERIENCE IN ART AND DESIGN

The relationship between changes in the funding of tuition fees in 2012, and public facing information about 'student satisfaction' in the form of **Key Information Sets** (KIS;

see Chapters 2 and 3) in the same year has brought with it increasing focus on the student experience – discrete from learning outcomes and achievement. The introduction of the **National Student Survey** (NSS) in 2005 made it possible to compare the student experience between institutions and subjects, and early data showed the difference in student experience between subjects. Data for subjects within Creative Arts and Design demonstrated low scores across all areas of the survey and was especially low in the area of course organisation and management (Vaughan and Yorke, 2009: 7). Research by Vaughan and Yorke also showed considerable variation in the success of institutions in addressing student satisfaction in Creative Arts and Design, with some indication this could be related to the type, structure and scale of institution (2009: 26). Interest in 'getting under the skin' of the student experience in art, design and media has produced a range of material to support HE staff in the development of their practice. For example, see *The 3Es Project – student expectations, experiences and encounters with HE and staff perceptions* (Thomas et al., 2009); *The Student Experience in Art and Design Higher Education: Drivers for Change* (Drew, 2008); *I Can't Believe It's Not Better: the Paradox of NSS Scores for Art & Design* (Vaughan and Yorke, 2009); *Deal or No Deal: Expectations and Experience of First Year Students in Art and Design* (Vaughan and Yorke, 2012); and *How Art and Design Students Understand and Interpret the NSS* (Blair et al., 2012).

Research shows and develops the particularity of teaching and learning in art and design and supports practitioners and institutions with strategies to support creative learners. It is worth highlighting now some of the key findings of the research.

Students typically 'navigate' their learning (and the support and resources required for individualised projects) and are unlikely to be engaged in a programme of learning that is common to the group. This approach to learning will produce challenges to the way students experience the organisation and management of their studies.

> …students mentioned that they provide self-initiated projects, and are responsible for negotiating and managing their time rather than following a set timetable. This was the case for most final year students, but for fine art it was common practice throughout their whole course.
>
> (Blair et al., 2012: 4)

Students gain continuous forms of informal feedback over the length of a project often from a number of tutors. The expectation is that students will consider the advice, filter the recommendations and determine for themselves the steps they should take in the development of their work. Responses to this approach to learning (through the NSS) challenge HE practitioners to consider not necessarily a change of method, but support for students in understanding the way feedback works and the level of intellectual maturity this approach demands. From a student perspective, this approach can appear as poor communication between tutors and confusion in teaching methods. Complexity and ambiguity in the debates and concepts surrounding creative work may be comfortable territory for experienced practitioners, but for undergraduates it may turn 'the process of learning into a game that some students just don't get' (Reid, 2007).

Entry points to HE art, design and media are varied with some students having a substantial level of preparation through the Foundation Diploma in Art and Design (one-third of those surveyed), while others progress directly from A-levels or equivalent two-year qualifications. It is also important that practitioners of HE understand the learning context within schools and how this prepares students for an HE learning experience. For instance, the recent review of the National Curriculum in England (Department of Education, 2013) offers a very particular interpretation of the art curriculum that privileges the skills and media of painting, sculpture and drawing over other technologies and conceptual, thematic or multimedia approaches. It also focuses on national culture and arts heritage over internationalism and on the techniques of appreciation, fine art history and knowledge of 'great' artists over critique and analysis. Art and design are not in this sense (in this context) conceived as subjects that can transform received wisdom, understanding and culture.

The research 'Deal or No Deal' also points to the diversity of learners and their support needs. The research found that of those surveyed, just under 40 per cent believed that the availability of learning support services during their first year was relevant to them, highlighting the challenge (alongside entry profiles) to teachers to work optimally with students of such varied background (Vaughan and Yorke, 2012: 22).

The divergence between the expectation and experience of learners in their first year broadly maps onto the findings of the NSS where a significant minority of students believe that 'the deal' is not sufficiently well understood (in the areas of assessment, feedback, organisation and management in particular). Finding more consistent ways to support the transition of (different) learners into HE is a key recommendation of the research.[2] For instance, it is recommended that practitioners assess whether:

- Potential students have the opportunity to engage with the institution in various ways (e.g. through visits and portfolio interviews and, particularly for those more distant from the institution, accurate documentation regarding what is on offer).
- The institution gives students from minority groups parity of attention (the word 'minority' covers more than ethnicity – for instance, part-time and overseas students are encompassed here).
- There is good technician support in workshops.
- Students have a good understanding of what is expected of them (this applies with particular force to expectations regarding assessment).
- There is availability and engagement in tutorials and these provide formative feedback on work in progress.

There is a danger that the NSS becomes the driver for inquiries into the student experience in art and design and subsequent enhancement agendas. Students in art, design and media place a great deal of value in interdisciplinary, peer and social learning for example (Brown;[3] Vaughan and Yorke, 2012: 28). Course teams that nurture these strategies (and in doing so, develop the confidence and independence of learners) will be adopting methods that are relevant to professional practice, which compensate for the challenges posed by the pedagogy of art and design.

SPACE, PRACTICE AND INNOVATION

Discussion about teaching space within art, design and media is usually a discussion about discipline, the relationship between disciplines and changes to practice and teaching through the convergence of digital technologies. In this way, the physical environment will reflect questions of practice that creativity is essentially social, and spatial requirements whether physical or digital reflect the needs of disciplines for public forums for dissemination, debate, exchange and judgement. Little by way of innovation occurs in isolation and contemporary practice will more often than not base itself on collaborative models. An institution or department's approach to space may reflect the degree to which a curriculum is open to collaboration between groups, disciplines and types and levels of award (for a discussion about interdisciplinary models, see Blair et al., 2008). Creativity is supported by settings that are permeable, where there are internal and external flows of difference, juxtaposition, stimulus and response. Spaces for learning in art, design and media need to be adaptive (respond to how and what things are being made) and permeable (receptive to flows). These qualities are easily enough expressed; the challenges occur in the management and accountability for the use of space in fluid learning settings. Case study 24.1 on MediaCityUK illustrates the way an entirely new building confronts these challenges, creating 'low walls' between disciplines and explicit flows between higher education and industry.

Case study 24.1: MediaCityUK, University of Salford

The University of Salford opened its MediaCityUK campus in October 2011 as the new home for learning and teaching, research and innovation and enterprise across the spectrum of media and digital technologies. Occupying four floors of a building with ITV directly above, the new campus sits alongside six departments of the BBC, the largest HD studio block in Europe, a media enterprise centre, over 200 businesses from the media/digital sector and across the Manchester Ship Canal from the Lowry Theatre, the Imperial War Museum North and Coronation Street's new home.

Inside, the public ground floor gives students access to 'touch tables' and 120 micro tiles for individual broadcast or video walls, along with three TV studios, digital performance laboratory, edit suites, post-production/media technology specialist facilities and spaces configured for undergraduate and postgraduate teaching across the University's Schools and Colleges. With the open-plan academic office, emphasis on social learning and promotion of trans-disciplinary education, students learn in a dynamic and 'specialised' environment. It is a technologically advanced environment for educational partnerships, designed to draw UK and global partners from HE and industry to collaborate on research and innovation questions associated with media and digital futures.

Live briefs are key to driving an innovation eco-culture of benefit to the MediaCityUK community and to international partners such as BT, Adobe and Avid. Details of a live brief with Hewlett Packard (HP) exemplify what students are achieving through trans-disciplinary learning, which is collaborative and industry-orientated:

- Five teams of up to four students from across Media, Design, Computer Science and Business entered a competition promoting HP's Commercial Desktop PCs.
- Production of high-quality video (max 140 seconds) to engage Small/Medium Businesses (SMB) in creative, vibrant and entertaining communication of product proposition and HP strategy, using their own imagination and creative style.
- Team budget for filming with range of HP Desktops for use.
- Video placed online for HP SMB Community for a team marketing plan to promote via social media.
- Milestones: individual pitch to be selected as participant in the project; team-building; storyboarding; team pitch; filming; presentation of first edit; submission with marketing plan.
- Consistent client input and typical customer profiles from HP's SMB group.
- Judgement: how video holds attention and meets the brief; votes of HP's SMBs; quality of Marketing Plan and number of hits; delivery within budget.
- Each member of winning team awarded new Z1 workstation and £1,000 grant.
- Project supported by staff from Schools of Media, Design, Computer Science and Business and Student Life.
- Feedback from participants:

  ○ Students: 'massive boost for CV'; 'great to work with and be acknowledged by a multinational company'.
  ○ Staff: opportunity for students to pitch to industry, storyboard correctly, keep to strict industry deadlines, work in teams, demonstrate creativity/innovation to industry and for staff to work with students outside their discipline.
  ○ HP: distinctive value of five different team approaches; well-received across HP; provides a platform for further work with the University.

- Additional outputs: a student was offered an HP work placement on an animation project for future generation hardware; project videos were used in development of marketing communications and strategy for HP staff and partners.

(Andrew Cooper, Academic Director, MediaCityUK,
University of Salford)

Interrogating practice

Questions that practitioners may pose around spaces for creative disciplines include:

1   Are there spaces and/or informal learning activities that provide opportunities for year groups to exchange skills and knowledge?
2   How are the opportunities for curatorial space exploited to disseminate the work of art, design and media students?
3   How are technical resources managed in ways that exploit (within means) access to the widest range of creative processes and media?
4   How does the learning environment, curriculum and management structure promote opportunities for collaboration between disciplines?

ASSESSMENT IN ART, DESIGN AND MEDIA

In higher education, the likelihood of feedback providing unambiguous, categorical feedback to the student about the exact standard of all aspects of their work or how to improve it is very low indeed with almost all feedback requiring interpretation.

(Price et al., 2010: 279)

This statement offers a concise appraisal of the complexity of feedback (and assessment), pointing to the highly nuanced nature of language when it comes to the judgment, appraisal and onward development of learning. The authors are not referring to a particular subject, yet practitioners of art, design and media will readily identify with the idea that assessment is highly problematic.

The challenge for practitioners exists in the nature of creativity and its relationship to learning (and assessment). Elliot Eisner's work (2009) analyses the cognitive processes of creating work (concept formation, imagination, realisation) and the necessary role of dialogue and the judgment of experts to ascertain the relative importance of the work as art. Eisner also reminds us of the limitations of language to express what we know and more so when knowing is sensory or tacit. Research conducted by Shreeve (2009), Blair (2007) and Orr (2010) demonstrates that while it is commonly accepted that student work is assessed by the shared language and tacit knowledge of practitioners (in ways that occur in professional practice), to students this can appear obscure and confusing – or worse – a question of what teachers like and dislike.

Practitioners of HE art, design and media will find research about assessment of design by Cowdroy and Williams (2006) and assessment of fine art by Orr revealing (2010). Both create **pedagogy** around assessment that acknowledges what is authentic to creative practice/practitioners and at the same time formulate ways to make assessment accessible and meaningful to students in the development of their practice.

Despite the alignment of curriculum, learning outcomes and what was required for assessment we had to acknowledge our reliance on our own intuitive understanding of what creative ability is, our assumption that our students understood what we understood by creative ability and our tendency to assess students' creative ability on the basis of what teachers like.

(Cowdroy and Williams, 2006: 98)

A respondent in Orr's research comments on being utterly and profoundly moved by a piece of student work and comments:

…how do you measure that kind of intellectual[ism]? You have to make part of that judgment with your heart if you like, which is what art and stuff is about so there clearly is a role for that and maybe you can't write criteria.

(Orr, 2010: 12)

In this research, as well as that by Blair on the 'crit' (2007), practitioners are encouraged to draw on the forms of dialogue relevant to professional practice, but reconstruct them as explicit learning processes. Practitioners are encouraged to use methods of assessment and feedback as ways to develop the pedagogic literacy of students – to share and develop the language and criteria by which judgment is made and dwell on the difficulties of language in assessing sensory, experiential phenomena. Drew and Shreeve (2005) refer to this as 'assessment as participation in practice' – creating a community of practice where informal, continuous and divergent forms of assessment are conceptualised and decoded in ways that support learning and professional development.

Interrogating practice

1 Does assessment language (for instance, learning outcomes) help students to understand expectation? (This is complex and varies according to creative discipline but would, for instance, unpick conceptualisation and the intellectual work of creativity; schematisation and idea development; and realisation through making skills, editing, giving point to, etc.)
2 Have assessment teams discussed and unpicked the language of assessment and do they share a common interpretation of it and agree how it is applied to level and phase of learning?
3 Is the language and practice of assessment discussed with students as part of their understanding of pedagogy and particular form of professional practice?

(Continued)

4 Do feedback mechanisms (formal and informal) consistently reinforce and embed the language of assessment?

5 The basics: does feedback support development as well as offer judgment? Is it timely? Are there opportunities for students to discuss the feedback (and unpick the language)? Are assessment and feedback building confidence and supporting a growing sense of learner independence? Are students adopting the language of assessment in their critiques of their own and others' work?

Case study 24.2: Research on the group crit: how do you make a firing squad less scary?

Why research the crit?

The relationship between achievement and feedback, and the fact that effective feedback improves achievement, is well documented (Taylor and McCormack, 2004; Hattie and Timperley, 2007). This is especially true of written feedback. However, in art and design education, feedback will take place in an often emotionally charged face-to-face meeting where verbal criticism, both negative and positive, takes place in front of an audience. The forum for this feedback in art education is the Group Crit (**Crit**, Art Crit or Group Critique) in which students are expected to present and perform. It is the students' reception and perception of this oral feedback in today's quality-focused context, which is at the heart of this research.

How was the research conducted?

The research explores the impact of verbal feedback on achievement in art and design education via a survey taken amongst 60 undergraduate art and design students at the University of Wolverhampton in 2009/10. The survey collected both quantitative and qualitative responses and identified a fundamentally emotional and fear-focused perception of the Group Crit, one that was opposed to its supportive and bespoke dynamic intentions. Material was gathered from the survey, emails exchanged with colleagues and Q&A discussions following presentations of this survey at conferences (Higher Education Academy Teaching and Learning Conferences at the University of Sunderland in 2010, and Ravensbourne in 2011). The majority of students had little experience of the Group Crit model prior to higher education and the research shows that students are often 'intimidated, scared and frightened' by the type of feedback they gain in the Crit and of being 'made' to contribute vocally to group sessions. These same students, unfamiliar with the Crit method, define themselves as separate; often alienated and differentiated from others and their peers as a consequence of the Crit.

What did the research find?

1   Deep concerns amongst students towards being criticised; they expressed emotional and fear-focused responses towards feedback, amplified by the public nature of the Crit. Indeed, one respondent wrote in response to a question on how to improve the Crit – 'how do you make a firing squad less scary?'

2   The Crit model is the opposite of the prescriptive teaching style students have previously encountered and whilst, on the whole, students value the Crit and (verbal) feedback, it appears to be the least successful model for those who are struggling the most. These students have nothing or little to present and feel ignored. For some students, the process is divisive, the effect is to split those students for whom the process works and those for whom it does not.

What can practitioners do to create a positive Crit experience?

It is important to guide participants in highlighting the 'more positive' elements of their work produced and in being constructive with feedback that shares best practice and listens to students. There is also a need for transitional skills into higher education and an exposition of the teaching and learning styles, not prescriptive education but self-efficacy, independent and innovative learning.

Provisional conclusions regarding the improvement of feedback for the students are:

• Greater contact and individualised support
• Smaller groups (seminar model)
• More peer-to-peer feedback opportunities
• More one-to-one tutorials

Feedback can be improved by:

• Explaining the Crit
• Timing the Crit
• Exploring the student role and voice
• Providing clear guidelines relating to the role of feedback in the environment of the Crit
• Transparency – how all feedback relates to the grade awarded and to improving achievement

The full article can be found in *Networks*, http://arts.brighton.ac.uk/projects/ networks/issue-18-july-2012/the-art-group-crit.-how-do-you-make-a-firing- squad-less-scary

(Peter Day, University of Wolverhampton)

ENTERPRISE AND EMPLOYMENT

At the time of preparing the 2009 Handbook, the outcomes of *Creative Britain: New Talents for the New Economy* (Department for Culture, Media and Sport, 2008) were in the course of being implemented. Among the many recommendations were those aiming to develop awareness of creative careers among young people (the Arts Council England Bridge Organisations began in 2012); proposals to create new kinds of training environments targeted at where there are skills gaps (the National Skills Academy for Creative and Cultural Skills opened in Purfleet in March 2013); the need to promote diversity among creative industry employers (for instance, through vocational training and apprenticeships); ways to encourage closer links and knowledge exchange between higher education and the creative industries; and measures to support innovation and the digital economy (through Knowledge Exchange Hubs, such as 'The Creative Exchange'). These initiatives provide resources and partnership opportunities for HE creative innovation, enterprise and employment.

In addition to the findings on employment and skills were those concerning the support needs of new and small creative businesses. For instance, it found:

> ...that the proportion of creative small firms using formal business planning techniques is just 35 per cent, fewer than one in five business managers in the music industry have any professional mentoring in business techniques, and a third of creative businesses with an annual turnover of more than £1 million have no explicit financial goals... this absence of business planning and training has been raised consistently throughout the industry consultation of the Creative Economy Programme.
> (Department for Culture, Media and Sport, 2008: 24)

The range and quality of case study material, for example *Looking-Out Case Studies: Effective Engagements with Creative and Cultural Enterprise* (Higher Education Academy Art Design Media Subject Centre, 2009) suggests that art, design and media courses regard relationships with employers as fundamental to the pedagogy of creative disciplines. The use of 'live' projects; the practice of full-time, visiting and associate lecturers being themselves drawn from industry; and the integration of placement opportunities and units that specifically address professional practice point to a curriculum that values the way it prepares students for employment.

Research conducted by Ball et al. (2010) provides the most recent and comprehensive analysis of creative careers, analysing the destinations of 3,500 art, design and media graduates qualifying between 2002 and 2004. The research found that although graduates valued their creative education (and perceived their creative ability to be most valuable to employment), there were notable gaps. 'Just over half the graduates (52 per cent) felt their course had prepared them very or fairly well for the world of work' (Ball et al., 2010: 9) and specific gaps were noted in IT and business skills, networking and client-facing skills. Despite the scale of micro- and small businesses within the creative sector, the research found that entrepreneurship skills were the least well developed and 'also perceived to be the least important for career development' (Ball et al., 2010: 9).

Practitioners will find *Creating Entrepreneurship: Entrepreneurship Education for the Creative Industries* (Higher Education Academy Art Design Media Subject Centre, 2007) a valuable resource identifying the barriers and inhibitors to entrepreneurship education; the range, type and distribution of curriculum models; and the areas that require advocacy and debate, framework and policy. Case study 24.2 provides an example of entrepreneurship education at the University for the Creative Arts that is available to students in addition to their accredited learning. Creative Challenge provides a specialist focus on social enterprise and sustainability.

Case study 24.3: Creative Challenge – a social and environmental entrepreneurship programme at the University for the Creative Arts

The Creative Challenge (http://www.creativechallenge.info) is a trademarked and unique social and environmental entrepreneurship programme that empowers students to develop their creative, entrepreneurial and employability skills, and at the same time helps them consider how they can use these skills to address the increasing number of global challenges. The programme has developed over a number of years with the active support of various University for the Creative Arts (UCA) academics and industry stakeholders. It is managed by the university's Research and Enterprise Department as an extra-curricular opportunity for UCA students from all disciplines and years of study.

Through workshops, written work, presentations, lectures and tutorials, students are taken through a programme of personal and professional support to develop their skills and ideas, resulting in a competitive pitch to a panel of senior academics and industry professionals, and an industry work placement. It thus supports creative arts students interested in environmental and social entrepreneurship in making a positive difference – that is to effect social change while sensitive to, or directly working with the environment. Impact can be achieved through non-profits, private companies and government. Students are introduced to the concept of the triple-bottom line (people, planet, prosperity) and are helped to broaden their understanding from value chains to value circles.

The programme has three elements:

1 Personal development workshops that help students to focus and critically reflect on their studies, their ambitions and making a positive contribution;

2 Practical workshops exploring employability, entrepreneurial skills and understanding commerce and exchange, including Intellectual Property Rights; and

3 Master classes and workshops that prepare students to utilise elements 1 and 2 to develop innovative ideas to effect positive change that is recognised and valued by others and has the potential for realisation.

A key part of Creative Challenge is the contribution of inspirational guest speakers, business skills experts and personal development facilitators.

Key points

- Pedagogy: constructivist, activist, critical, humanist, creative, problem and project learning, placement
- Values: sustainability, socially aware, entrepreneurial, holistic, empowerment, democratic, challenging, integrity and authenticity
- Brand: engaging, aligned and sensitive to the subject matter, industry standard and professional
- Engagement: strong tripartite communication between students, academics and industry, long-term vision and relationship building, adaptation, learning communities
- Skills development: entrepreneurial, business, art and design application, critical and holistic thinking, listen, presentation, sustainability and Intellectual Property.

Student feedback:

- Kane O'Flaherty, Graphic Communication, 2010/11: 'The Creative Challenge pushed my creative flair, enhanced my technical skills, and increased my self-confidence. It changed my way of thinking and guided me to apply things to reality in a functional manner. Thanks to the Creative Challenge I feel that I found myself as a designer.'
- Alexandra McEwan, MA Book Arts, 2012/13: '...the experience of presenting was invaluable. You are put under pressure, with real people asking you unscripted questions and this is what it is like in the real workplace. Presenting to a panel was the most valuable part of the process.'
- Susan Toft, BA Fine Art, 2012/13: '...I learnt so much from it in all sorts of areas, from implementing ideas to how I can become entrepreneurial myself.'

(Uwe Derksen, University for the Creative Arts)

CONCLUSION AND OVERVIEW

Restrictions on space and time necessarily place limitations on the range of material that can be covered in this chapter. There are significant omissions worth mentioning here owing to their centrality to teaching and learning in art, design and media. The diversity of the student and staff community provides the points of difference and connection in which creative practice thrives. In this sense, diversity is pursued for social, cultural and creative reasons. Practitioners will find a range of materials that explore progression and widening participation at UK Art and Design Institutions Network (UKADIA) and an exploration of internationalisation in art and design can be found in Harley et al. (2008). The designation of the chapter (adopting art, design and media over other options) may imply a conventional or rigid grouping of disciplines. It is therefore worth stating the extent to which the boundaries of these disciplines are overlapping with others (business, marketing, technology) or combine with others (ecology, social science, engineering) to create highly specialised fields, new services and experiences (information can be found in Universities UK (2010)).

Despite the omissions, the chapter attempts to create a sense of the underpinning nature (and particularities) of teaching and learning in art, design and media in a changing disciplinary and higher education context. It will at least provide a sense of the scale and complexity of the challenge for practitioners – and a discursive setting for organisational and professional development of the disciplines.

NOTES

1   Bohm in *On Creativity* (1998) discusses the idea of intelligence as being when the perceptual field is free of conditioning by any established patterns of reactive and reflective thought so as to process new 'ratios' – 'fitting'.
2   See the 'Template for assessing the quality of the student experience' in Vaughan and Yorke (2012: 57).
3   Brown's unpublished 2011 research into the student experience at the London College of Communication found that opportunities to learn with peers, across courses, was the most frequently cited enhancement theme expressed by students.

REFERENCES

Ball, L, Pollard, E and Stanley, N (2010) *Creative Graduates Creative Futures*. London: Council for Higher Education in Art and Design, and University of the Arts London.

Blair, B (2007) 'At the end of a huge crit in the summer, it was "crap" – I'd worked really hard but all she said was "fine" and I was gutted', *Art, Design and Communication in Higher Education*, 5(2): 83–95.

Blair, B, Cummings, A, Dunbar, T, Hayward, D and Woodman, J (2008) 'Bau-wow! A model for creative practice, thinking, research and innovation in the 21st century', in L Drew (ed.) *The Student Experience in Art and Design: Drivers for Change*. Cambridge: Jill Rogers Associates and the Group for Learning in Art and Design (GLAD), 65–98.

Blair, B, Orr, S and Yorke, M (2012) *How Art and Design Students Understand and Interpret the NSS*. Group for Learning in Art and Design (GLAD) and Higher Education Academy. Available from: http://www.heacademy.ac.uk/resources/detail/disciplines/Art%20 and%20design/GLAD_report_April2012 (accessed 9 April 2014).

Bohm, D (1998) *On Creativity*. London, Routledge.

Cowdroy, R and Williams, A (2006) 'Assessing creativity in the creative arts', *Art, Design and Communication in Higher Education*, 5(2): 97–117.

Csikszentmihalyi, M (1996) *Creativity: Flow and the Psychology of Discovery and Invention*. New York, NY: Harper Collins, 47.

Department for Culture, Media and Sport (DCMS) (2008) *Creative Britain: New Talents for the New Economy*. Available from: http://webarchive.nationalarchives.gov.uk/+/http:// www.culture.gov.uk/images/publications/CEPFeb2008.pdf (accessed 9 April 2014), 24.

Department of Education (DoE) (2013) *The National Curriculum in England Framework Document*. Available from: https://www.gov.uk/government/uploads/system/uploads/ attachment_data/file/210969/NC_framework_document_-_FINAL.pdf (accessed 15 April 2014).

Drew, L (ed.) (2008) *The Student Experience in Art and Design: Drivers for Change*. Cambridge: Jill Rogers Associates and the Group for Learning in Art and Design (GLAD).

Drew, L and Shreeve, A (2005) 'Assessment as Participation in Practice', in C Rust (ed.), 12th ISL *Symposium Improving Student Learning through Assessment*, Oxford: Oxford Centre for Staff and Learning Development, 635–654.

Eisner, EW (2009) *What Do the Arts Teach?* Lecture at Vanderbilt University, November. Available from: https://www.youtube.com/watch?v=h12MGuhQH9E&noredirect=1 (accessed 13 May 2014).

Hattie, J and Timperley, H (2007) 'The power of feedback', *Review of Educational Research*, 77: 1.

Harley, A, James, S, Reid, E, Reid, S, Robinson, H and Watson, Y (2008) 'The third space: a paradigm for internationalisation' in L Drew (ed.), *The Student Experience in Art and Design: Drivers for Change*. Cambridge: Jill Rogers Associates and the Group for Learning in Art and Design (GLAD), 167–188.

Higher Education Academy Art Design Media Subject Centre (2007) *Creating Entrepreneurship: Entrepreneurship Education for the Creative Industries*, The Higher Education Academy Art Design Media Subject Centre and the National Endowment for Science, Technology and the Arts.

Higher Education Academy Art Design Media Subject Centre (2009) *Looking-Out Case Studies: Effective Engagements with Creative and Cultural Enterprise*. Available from: http:// www.heacademy.ac.uk/assets/documents/subjects/adm/looking-out-case-studies- effective-engagements-with-creative-and-cultural-enterprise.htm (accessed 15 April 2014).

James, A (2007) 'Reflection revisited: perceptions of reflective practice in fashion learning and teaching', *Art, Design and Communication in Higher Education*, 5(3): 179–196.

Orr, S (2010) 'We kind of try to merge our own experience with the objectivity of the criteria: the role of connoisseurship and tacit practice in undergraduate fine art assessment', *Art, Design and Communication in Higher Education*, 9(1): 5–19.

Pope, R (2005) *Creativity: Theory, History, Practice*. London: Routledge.

Price, M, Handley, K, Millar, J and O'Donovan, B (2010) 'Feedback: all that effort, but what is the effect?', *Assessment in Higher Education*, 35(3): 277–289.

Reid, E (2007) 'The problem with cultural capital in art and design higher education', in L Drew (ed.), *The Student Experience in Art and Design: Drivers for Change*. Cambridge: Jill Rogers Associates and the Group for Learning in Art and Design (GLAD), 141.

Shreeve, A (2009) *Assessment in Art and Design*. CLIP CETL, University of the Arts London.

Taylor, MJ and McCormack, C (2004) *Juggling Cats: Investigating Effective Verbal Feedback in Graphic Design Critiques*. Australian Council of University Art and Design Schools New Policies – New Opportunities.

Thomas, B et al. (2009) *The 3Es Project – Student Expectations, Experiences and Encounters with HE and Staff Perceptions*. Available from: http://www.adm.heacademy.ac.uk/projects/adm-hea-projects/the-3Es-project-student-expectations-experiences-and-encounters-with-he/ (accessed 15 April 2014).

Universities UK (2010) *Creative Prosperity: The Role of Higher Education in Driving the UK's Creative Economy*. London: Universities UK.

Vaughan, D and Yorke, M (2009) *I Can't Believe It's Not Better: the Paradox of NSS Scores for Art & Design*. Group for Learning in Art and Design (GLAD) and the Higher Education Academy. Available from: http://www.adm.heacademy.ac.uk/library/files/adm-hea-projects/glad-nss-project/nss-report170310.pdf (accessed 15 April 2014).

Vaughan, D and Yorke, M (2012) *Deal or No Deal: Expectations and Experience of First Year Students in Art and Design*. Higher Education Academy and HEAD Trust. Available from: http://www.heacademy.ac.uk/resources/detail/disciplines/art-and-design/deal_or_no_deal_report (accessed 13 May 2014).

FURTHER READING

Eagleton, T (2008) *Literary Theory: An Introduction*. 3rd edn. London: Blackwell.

Steiner, G (2010) *Grammars of Creation* (e-book edition). London: Faber and Faber.

Sternberg, RJ (1999) *Handbook of Creativity*. Cambridge: Cambridge University Press.

Winnicott, DW (1982) *Playing and Reality*. London: Routledge.

25

Sport-related subjects

Richard Winsley and Richard Tong

INTRODUCTION

Sport-related subjects are one of the top ten most popular subjects studied at university. Since the first edition of this Handbook in 1999, the numbers of students graduating annually with sport degrees has doubled, now exceeding 10,000. This chapter will review the context in which sport is studied, types of provision, types of students studying on the degree programmes, how the subject is taught and assessed, and **employability** opportunities for graduates. It will also consider future challenges and opportunities.

CONTEXT

In the early 1980s, there were only a few institutions offering degrees in sport-related subjects, however universities soon saw the potential to increase student numbers in this area. The original degrees were traditionally based in Physical Education (PE) Colleges with the curriculum being dominated by the practical aspects of sport science. Other programmes subsequently developed in science faculties to offset the decrease in the number of applicants for science-based degrees. These programmes were dominated by laboratory-based work focusing on biology, biochemistry and nutrition of sport and exercise. The third phase in the evolution of sport-related programmes was in Leisure and Recreation Departments. These degrees tended to have a curriculum based on leisure management and recreation studies, in contrast to sport science. In 2000, the first Benchmark Statements in Hospitality, Leisure, Sport and Tourism (HLST) were produced and these were later refined in 2008 (Quality Assurance Agency for Higher Education, 2008).

As there are a wide range of sport-related programmes nationally, the Benchmark Statements use the Council of Europe definition where sport means 'all forms of physical activity which, through casual or organised participation, aim at expressing or improving physical fitness and mental wellbeing, forming social relationships or obtaining results in competition at all levels' (Council of Europe, 2001, Article 2, European Sports Charter).

The initial titles used for sport-related degrees were normally Sports Science, Sport Studies, Human Movement Studies or Leisure Management. This trend continued until the turn of the century when more specific titles evolved, which reflected more closely the content of the degrees. Most recently, sport degrees have evolved in more specialised areas, such as sport nutrition, sport biomedicine, sport psychology, sport and exercise medicine, sport coaching, sport development, sport conditioning, etc.

In 2005, the British Association of Sport and Exercise Science (BASES) began to endorse undergraduate sport and exercise science degrees to ensure that the content reflected the title of the award. The key endorsement criteria that a programme must meet are:

- Programmes should engage students for a minimum of 10 per cent of student effort time in each of the three disciplinary areas of Biomechanics, Physiology and Psychology;
- A minimum of 5 per cent of student effort time should be dedicated to providing students with exposure to the inter-disciplinary study of sport and exercise science;
- A minimum of 150 hours (total) of practical field-based/laboratory experience, across the three discipline areas, should be included in the programme;
- Programmes must include at least 5 per cent of student effort time in 'research methods';
- Students must complete an independent study; and
- The programme team must comprise at least two BASES Accredited Sport and Exercise Scientists (British Association of Sport and Exercise Science, 2005)

Currently there are 35 BASES-endorsed programmes in the UK, but other organisations, such as the UK Strength and Conditioning Association, the British Association of Sport Rehabilitators and Trainers, the British Psychological Society and UK Sport, also endorse or accredit programmes.

Interrogating practice

- Reflect on your programme design and consider if it is possible or appropriate to gain endorsement or accreditation from an external organisation, if not already recognised?

As the subject has matured to become an established part of the degree programme portfolio of many institutions, so competition for undergraduate students has now reached saturation point, and hence in recent years there has been a significant increase in the number of Masters programmes offered. Initially generic sport and exercise science Masters degrees were developed, but students now have the opportunity to study more specialist Masters programmes, such as Sport Psychology, Sport Physiology, Sport Biomechanics, Sport Nutrition, Sport Culture, Sport Management, Sport Coaching, Sport and Exercise Medicine, etc. Although graduates from undergraduate degree programmes in sport science possess excellent transferable and analytical skills, graduates often need to undertake a specialist postgraduate programme to gain employment in their preferred area.

Following the rapid growth of the discipline, a plateau in applications to study sport in the UK has now been reached. Competition rates for gaining a place on sport-related degrees has fallen from the heady heights of over 1:30 in the early 1990s to a more realistic 1:5 to 1:10. In the remainder of this chapter, we will focus on Sport and Exercise Science degree programmes because this is the predominant title used for studying sport-related subjects in the UK.

What is sport and exercise science?

Sport and exercise science (SES) is the application of scientific principles to the promotion and enhancement of sport and exercise-related behaviours. SES comprises of three parent disciplines: biomechanics, physiology and psychology. Other aspects of sport science are often included, such as performance analysis, nutrition, motor control, sport sociology, sport management, health, etc., thus it is clear that the discipline covers a diversity of content.

Curriculum design

SES is a relatively new subject in higher education institutions and there is no set curriculum. BASES-endorsed programmes comprise of at least 30 per cent of physiology/biomechanics/psychology combined with elements of laboratory work and an independent research project. Hence, all programmes have slightly different curricula reflecting the chosen emphasis of the degree and staff expertise. Some programmes place greater emphasis on health and exercise, coaching, performance, nutrition or physical education, whilst others are more focused on research or the application of sport science to elite performers or exercise participants.

Sport and exercise science students

The demographic profile of students enrolling onto SES programmes appears to have its own unique character. Data available from an HEA commissioned report into the HLST sector within the UK (Walmsley, 2011) illustrates these key attributes. The number of students wishing to study this subject area remains relatively buoyant, coming on the back of strong growth during 2007–2010, which saw a 17 per cent increase in enrolments on to SES degree courses. The majority of students enrol on undergraduate programmes, with postgraduates accounting for just over 4 per cent of the market share. Typically, the students enrol full time (92 per cent), but this hides a marked divide between the undergraduate and postgraduate populations, where the latter has nearly 50 per cent part-time students compared to just 4 per cent for the undergraduate programmes. Arguably this echoes the simple financial reality facing many students as they try to afford to complete postgraduate study by combining this with paid employment.

Although there will inevitably be variation between institutions, the data reveals that sport science degree programmes in the UK are generally studied by young men. Student gender balance data indicates that males outnumber females by nearly 2:1 (64 per cent male versus 36 per cent female; Walmsley, 2011). These data are unsurprising when interpreted in the context of sport being perceived as male dominated with regards to participation, cultural status and as a career destination (Hargreaves, 2003). Whether males are being actively or implicitly encouraged to study sport science and conversely if females are being overtly or covertly discouraged from studying the subject is unknown. With judicious use of female role models in university marketing materials and school outreach work, this gender imbalance can start to be addressed, but the prevailing societal attitudes cannot be avoided. On a positive note, akin to what is seen at school, female students' academic performance on SES degrees is generally stronger than that of males (Howatson and Dancy, 2009).

The typical age of a SES student is between 18 and 24 years old, with only 5 per cent of students aged over 30 years old (Walmsley, 2011). It is understood that sport, as a specific subset of physical activity, is seen as the preserve of the young in light of its portrayal in the media and wider society (Phoenix and Sparkes, 2006), but whether this dissuades older adults from studying on these types of programmes is unclear. Anecdotally, mature students enrolling on SES undergraduate programmes are often either ex-armed forces returning to study, those seeing the degree as a stepping stone to becoming a teacher or coach, or retired professional athletes. Although numbers are small, having mature students on a programme is welcomed because they bring a diversity of experience, offer considered opinions, demonstrate good self-discipline and have a professional attitude to their studies, which can be shared with their younger peers. Offering part-time, distance learning or work placement opportunities are all features that make courses more attractive to mature entrants and these permutations should be considered.

Interrogating practice

- How does your department deal with the diversity of experience of incoming students?
- How can you challenge students coming from different backgrounds?

Historically, international students are not drawn to studying sport science at under-graduate level in the UK, with them accounting for less than 3 per cent of the undergraduate population (Walmsley, 2011). With many universities' international recruitment drives focusing on China and Asia, these are ironically barren areas for recruitment to sport science due to the low status of the subject in these countries. However, recruitment from countries such as Australia, New Zealand, North and South America, South Africa and Russia, where the cultural kudos of sport science is viewed differently, has started to prove more fruitful. The place of HLST subjects to develop the multi-cultural intelligence and awareness in their students has been well argued (Caruana and Ploner, 2011) and in a future market place with increasing cross-border career opportunities, students are only going to be disadvantaged if universities do not help nurture this global view.

LEARNING STYLES IN SPORT AND EXERCISE SCIENCE

The debate about learning styles – what they are, how they might be asessed, how they're adjusted – is on-going and has been eloquently and critically explored by Coffield et al. (2004).

Research into the predominant learning style in SES students has received limited attention, but some data are available from the work of Peters et al. (2007), which indicated that students demonstrated a preference for **auditory**, **kinaesthetic** and group learning styles. Data from associated sources, revealed that when classifying learning preference according to the VARK (Visual, Auditory, Reading/Writing and Kinaesthetic; Dunn and Dunn, 1992) classification system, in human physiology students there was a clear predominance of **visual** learners (approximately 50 per cent), an equal mixture of auditory and **reading/writing** preference learners (approximately 20–30 per cent each), with the minority of students (approximately 5 per cent) preferring the kinaesthetic learning style (Dobson, 2009). Other data, also from human physiology students, reported that a significant proportion of students use a multimodal sensory learning style (Breckler et al., 2009), underlining the importance of providing learning opportunities in a variety of formats. As has been described earlier, the variety in content within SES degrees – ranging from pure cellular physiology, to applied mathematics within biomechanics, to the epidemiology of obesity, to racism within sport or the global politics of world sporting organisations – does support the idea that a multimodal learning approach may be the most appropriate. Using the learning styles approach described by Kolb (1984) to categorise academic disciplines, (see Table 25.1) indicates that the diversity of content in a well-rounded sport and exercise science degree is likely to appeal to all types of learner. What is also apparent is how the generic SES academic disciplines span both the pure and the applied domains. For example within an exercise physiology module, students will be taught about the processes of cellular biochemistry along with the application of these processes in fuelling exercise.

Table 25.1 Classification of sport and exercise science academic disciplines within the Kolbian schema of learning styles

Learning styles	Abstract	Concrete
	Hard pure sciences	*Soft pure sciences*
Reflective	Biomechanics	Sport and exercise psychology
	Exercise physiology	Sport sociology
	Hard applied sciences	*Soft applied sciences*
Active	Biomechanics	Sport and exercise psychology
	Exercise physiology	Coaching/teaching
	Sport and exercise psychology	Sport rehabilitation/therapy
	Sport rehabilitation/therapy	

Source: Adapted from Fry et al. (2003)

LEARNING DELIVERY FORMATS

A variety of delivery formats are used within SES degree programmes, each appealing to a preferred student learning style and allowing for the expansion in subject-specific knowledge alongside the development of independent learning. Rather than describe all the excellent practice that is being employed, a brief discussion of those formats that predominate in SES programmes seems appropriate.

Lectures

Whole group lectures are commonly used within most SES programmes (see Chapter 7). Group size may vary from 20 to over 250 in any class, typically with a PowerPoint presentation being used, supported with external video and audio content to illustrate key points. The duration of any one lecture varies between one to three hours, thus the ability to keep the students engaged and actively learning throughout demands that the lecture be divided into manageable chunks, have a clear focus and use a variety of media. Although this style of teaching is arguably best suited to the auditory and reading/writing learners, the media used will allow the visual learner to be well accommodated. The use of in-class tests, worksheets or short rest breaks allow the learning to be broken into segments, which has been shown to help maintain attention by the learners (Gibbs and Habeshaw, 1998). Modern technology, such as text messaging or personal response systems in lectures now allows opportunities to assess students understanding or to allow them to request points to be clarified anonymously. Post-lecture guided reading, review quizzes and Internet links all serve to underline the responsibility of the student towards their own independent learning.

Case study 25.1: Using learning technology in exercise and sport

A letter from the US

In the US, the use of computers starts in kindergarten. Thus, from the age of five, students expect technology to be an integral part of both their learning and social environments. How does one compete for their attention against the ever present temptation to check email, Facebook, texts or any of the numerous social networking outlets while we are educating them? We use as much technology and interactive pedagogy as we can.

A common thread for teaching exercise science needs to be its application, but in order to provide an application an understanding of the basics of biological sciences is needed. Herein lies the challenge: how do we keep the attention of the student who is eager to learn application, but does not yet understand the basics? We combine basic science with application for each lesson and we use technology as a tool to do so. During my exercise physiology class, we have a theme of the day. I might use the example of American football, with the class topic being anaerobic energy production. I start the class with a You-Tube video of a football match and we watch the play for about five minutes. I then introduce the science of anaerobic energy production. I do not use Power-Point presentation to do this, instead I write a word document that is projected on to the screen at the front of the classroom. I direct students to their textbooks for visual diagrams of the topic and ask them to produce their own word documents on the topic, thus requiring the students to actively write in their notebooks. This exercise may take about 10 minutes, but no more as I find students start to lose focus. Next, I put students into groups of four and ask them to discuss how what they learned about the anaerobic energy system relates to American football players. Finally, and they know in advance that this will happen, one of the groups will come to the front of the classroom and, using the YouTube video, apply the anaerobic energy system to a football match.

Another approach is the use of online discussion boards. I post a question on our virtual classroom platform – at Colby-Sawyer it is Moodle. The students are given strict guidelines on how they are to post on the forum – the post needs to be between 200–250 words, be grammatically correct and contain at least one reference from a peer reviewed journal. The deadline is typically at midnight, the night before class. The following class is then structured around the forum discussion. Throughout the class, I pull up numerous student posts, which results in a whole class centred on student responses obtained through using learning technology.

No longer are university students willing to sit passively in the classroom. They want interaction, they want connection and they want to know how it relates to the real world.

(Kerstin Stoedefalke, Colby-Sawyer College, NH, US)

Interrogating practice

- Reflect on the quality of the student engagement in your last lecture or seminar. How can you enhance the student engagement before, during and after your next session?

Laboratory practicals

One of the unique aspects of sport science is that the student is able to translate the theoretical learning received in the lectures with hands-on data collection in a laboratory session. The student acts as their own subject, collecting data about themselves, which brings a personal involvement in the learning process as they observe that they have responded to the exercise, just like the textbook or lecturer described. A recent census on the use of laboratory practicals as a teaching tool across 64 UK-based HE institutions showed that these were most favoured in physiology-related modules, but were heavily used by both biomechanics and psychology teaching (Smith, 2011). This active applied learning makes the students the centre of the learning experience (Michael, 2006) and allows the kinaesthetic and the visual learners to concrete their understanding, but frequently because the data collected is subjected to further mathematical analysis, this allows all of the learning styles represented in Table 25.1 to be served. Examples of laboratory sessions with preparatory and reflective follow-up tasks can be found in Eston and Reilly (2008). This applied learning through laboratory practical work is duplicated across exercise physiology, biomechanics and sport and exercise psychology and it is well received by the students.

Another commonly used strategy is the pooling of student data collected within laboratory sessions, both within a module cohort but also across the years, so that a descriptive database of normative data accumulates. This gives greater statistical power to any subsequent data analysis, provides more scope for cross-group comparisons, but allows the student to see how they have done against others on the same degree programme – which for some students is surprisingly motivational.

Interrogating practice

- Since students are often assessment driven, how do you encourage students to complete formative or non-assessed tasks that will benefit their learning?

Problem-based learning

Problem-based learning (PBL) is regularly used within sport science degrees. At its very narrowest, it may centre on just using a single discipline's knowledge to address the question, for example, 'A coach is concerned that her players seem to "choke" when faced with a high-pressure competition. What psychological tools can the sport psychologist use to address this issue?' Better still, but logistically difficult to arrange, is when the PBL is multidisciplinary. For example, a group of students might be set the challenge of providing a multidisciplinary approach to help an athlete prepare for running the Marathon des Sables in which they would have to address:

- Exercise physiology – physiological demands of the race, assessment of current fitness profile, running efficiency, thermoregulation, acclimatisation procedures, etc.;
- Training science – devising a suitable training programme for the athlete;
- Sport psychology – ensuring optimal motivation, coping strategies and social support;
- Sport nutrition – ensuring that an optimal nutrition and hydration strategy was followed before, during and after training or the race;
- Biomechanics – analysis of running gait, shoe cushioning dynamics;
- Sport therapy – injury prevention and rehabilitation strategies;
- Sport history/socio-cultural – historical background to the race and its place as a positive or negative influence for Morocco; and
- Sport organisation – the infrastructural, logistical and developmental challenges and solutions to resolve in hosting the race.

As with all PBL, this helps the students understand the interconnectedness of the knowledge sets so as not to silo knowledge into convenient, but arguably restrictive, compartments. It also encourages them not just to learn facts for facts sake, but to understand the applied use of this knowledge so that the 'how to' – the procedural knowledge – is also developed (Michael, 2006). Finally, this inquiry-based and active learning approach allows them to reflect on their own learning strategies, thus developing their understanding that content and process are inseparable components of learning (Massialis, 1985).

Experiential learning

Exposing students to the challenge of working with individual athletes, teams, or different populations in order to develop their applied skills is an effectively used strategy seen in many programmes. This real-life situational learning develops the 'art' of being a practitioner to complement their theoretical understanding. It is not just restricted to the sporting setting, but is also used in modules with a clinical/health focus, providing experiential learning with patient groups or sedentary adults for example.

Examples of experiential learning include placements with:

- Sport psychologists for an elite soccer team
- Clinical exercise physiologists in a cardiac rehabilitation department
- Research scientists within sport science academia
- Strength and conditioning coaches in a professional rugby club
- Sport nutritionists for a rowing development squad
- Biomechanists within the armed forces

Although there is unarguably a logistical burden with arranging placements in external organisations or bringing athletes or patients to the university, when managed successfully both parties benefit. The students not only recognise the importance of these placements in developing their professional skills and understanding, but also for their employability prospects.

Case study 25.2: Reflections of my placement year as a student intern

The industrial placement programme has proven to be an invaluable experience and integral part of my career development within sport and exercise sciences.

My placement was undertaken at the Children's Health and Exercise Research Centre (CHERC) at the University of Exeter, where I worked as a Research Associate, being involved in a wide range of projects. This took place after undertaking my first two years of undergraduate study at the University of Bath. During these first two years at Bath, I was introduced to many new concepts in sport science but the placement year allowed me to consolidate my understanding of the information I had learnt, most importantly how to apply this to real-life situations.

I was assigned a variety of tasks such as assisting the research projects being undertaken, preparing laboratory space and the necessary equipment and materials, participant recruitment and care, performing experimental procedures, running protocols and reviewing of the data. It was a hugely rewarding experience because I was treated and utilised as a full and trusted member of the research team, performing tasks that actively contributed to the centre and its research output. This opportunity gave me a true insight into the world of research, and has motivated me to pursue this as a career in the future.

(Owen Tomlinson BSc, MSc, University of Exeter)

Resourcing and costs of delivery

Sport and exercise science degrees are not cheap to deliver. They require a variety of different types of learning space – gymnasiums, swimming pools, resistance training facilities, laboratories, interview rooms, outdoor sports fields/tracks, lecture theatres and treatment rooms to name but a few. In addition, the equipment purchase costs, technical support and annual maintenance costs are considerable.

However, the diversity of learning environments that the sport science degree student is exposed to gives variety to their course, exposes them to learning in new situations – often cited as an intended learning outcome – and allows them to develop a breadth of generic and subject-specific skills, many of which help them in their future careers.

Employability

What do SES students go on to do when they graduate? One of the advantages of the discipline is that it does have a vocational slant and career paths are available in both the sport and the health sectors. Indeed, approximately 20 per cent of 2011 UK SES graduates found initial employment in sport-related industries (Higher Education Careers Services Unit (HECSU), 2012). For students wishing to stay in the sporting world for their careers, the following are common job destinations:

- Sport nutritionist
- Sport psychologist
- Sport administration (national governing bodies)
- Sport performance analysis
- Sport equipment development
- Sport physiologist
- Strength and conditioning coach
- Personal trainer, health and fitness trainer
- Sport coaching
- Sport marketing and brand management

In addition, a number of students move from SES degrees into teaching and physiotherapy career paths. The route into teaching requires successful completion of an additional year on a PGCE course, and by-and-large leads to physical education teaching, but becoming a science, maths and primary teacher are also seen. The path to becoming a physiotherapist is also well trodden, especially with the introduction of the MSc accreditation pathway into physiotherapy, which is increasingly available in many physiotherapy schools. Similar opportunities are available in sport therapy. Encouragingly, a number of students move into medicine after finishing their SES degrees. Once again the graduate entry scheme into medical school has facilitated this, but the open mindedness of these schools to take students from SES backgrounds is to be welcomed, and arguably reflects the acceptance of sport medicine as a discipline within the medical hierarchy. Initiatives such as 'Exercise is Medicine' by the American College of Sports Medicine and the British Association of Sport and Exercise Medicine serve to underline this fact. Reciprocally, SES degree programmes now see medical students intercalating to the degree after completion of their intermediate medical studies.

Careers relating to health include clinical exercise physiologist, cardiac physiologist, health trainer, exercise and health psychologist, general practitioner exercise referral scheme coordinator, health advisor, etc. The fact that SES degrees equip students with knowledge about exercise science as much as sport science means that the graduating student is well placed to secure employment in these types of careers. With many governments trying to get their populations more physically active, there should be an increasing demand for graduates with this knowledge and skill set.

However, there is a disproportionate mismatch between the number of career opportunities within the sector and the number of SES graduates each year. For example, there were over 8,500 SES graduates in 2011 in the UK (HECSU, 2012) and the majority of these graduates ended up in careers unrelated to sport and exercise science. After accounting for those staying in sport, education and health careers, 70 per cent of SES undergraduates went into careers outside the sector (HECSU, 2012). Rather than see this as a failing, it should be seen as a positive aspect of the degree – graduates who wish to stay in the sector are very well placed, conversely those who wish to follow a different career path are also highly employable. Consequently, SES graduates become accountants, journalists, advertising executives, civil servants, architects, blue chip company managers, bankers, charity workers, pharmaceutical company representatives, lawyers, etc. The growth in sport law is an interesting development, being a diverse field covering employment, media, injury and construction law sectors; it thus provides a wide variety of choice to budding lawyers and consequently explains its attraction as a career.

So why are SES students so employable? A recent joint Confederation of British Industry (CBI) and Universities UK commissioned report (2009) reaffirmed the responsibility that universities have to equip their students with the necessary skills to make them attractive to potential employers. Namely, the following skills were highlighted as being vital:

- Positive attitude
- Self-management

- Teamworking
- Business and customer awareness
- Problem solving
- Communication and literacy
- Application of numeracy
- Application of information technology

In 2013, the *Daily Telegraph* listed sport science as one of the top ten recession-proof degrees (*The Telegraph*, 2013), which is unsurprising when considering the generic and employability skills that are developed by the students during their SES degree programmes. Referring back to the earlier section on learning delivery formats, it is clear to see how the variety of learning challenges used in SES degrees help to develop the attributes listed. In addition, it is also suggested that these employment skills are developed through students' participation in sport *per se* during training and competition, thus the SES graduate represents a highly employable asset to prospective employers.

CONCLUSIONS AND OVERVIEW

The challenges facing sport and exercise science are no different to those facing other subject areas in higher education, namely, economic pressures, national and international competition for high quality students, governmental policy, student and parent expectations, current and future demographic trends, the expansion of learning technology, graduate employability, accessibility, etc. However, as the subject has grown exponentially since its conception in the early 1980s, these pressures are now more than ever relevant to SES degrees because many institutions have the subject as a cornerstone of their business planning models and need them to succeed.

We are now seeing a plateau in the number of applicants against an expansion in the number of programmes and this is causing recruitment issues at several universities. In parallel, recent UK government policy that has allowed universities to recruit more than their student allocation, if applicants achieve specific high grades, further affects those universities with a lower intake profile. As other subject areas are having difficulty with recruitment, some SES departments are being required to recruit more students to ensure the university reaches its target. Finally, as for all subjects studied in higher education, the change in future demographics will affect universities – the anticipated decrease by 10 per cent in the number of 18-year-olds by 2020 will challenge SES departments to meet recruitment targets. Whether this perfect storm of recruitment pressures will force some SES departments to retract or at worst close is still to be played out, but inevitably the landscape of choice will look different in the coming years.

Linked with the widening access agenda and student expectation, sport science providers are being required to offer a more flexible and accessible curriculum – this manifesting itself in the expansion of foundation degree programmes, distance learning and block delivery formats that are becoming increasingly available. Alongside these expectations are the increased technological and resource demands that virtual learning environments and digital technology place on universities. However, SES lends itself as an attractive subject for online and virtual delivery and the subject must harness the opportunity that developments, such as **MOOCs**, and **iTunes** University, present as a shop window to attract new students.

The worldwide popularity of sport as evidenced by participation levels, television coverage, newspaper column inches, spectator numbers and sport clothing sales demonstrates that the entity has both interest and meaning for people. The resultant career opportunities coming from the industry will need informed and employable graduates and those from SES programmes are natural entrants into these careers. In addition, the importance of being physically active throughout life is now recognised by governments and the medical world alike. Once again, SES provides the perfect arena to develop the evidence base underpinning this and to educate about why and how this can be achieved. In her 2012 Christmas speech to the nation, Her Majesty the Queen highlighted the importance of sport and health in maintaining the country's well-being. Hopefully, the legacy from the 2012 Olympics will ensure that sport and exercise science still has the potential to maintain its position in the top ten most popular subjects studied at university.

REFERENCES

Breckler, J, Joun, D and Ngo, H (2009) 'Learning styles of physiology students interested in the health professions', *Advances in Physiological Education*, 33(1): 30–36.

British Association of Sports and Exercise Science (2005) *BASES Undergraduate Endorsement Scheme*. Available from: http://www.bases.org.uk/Undergraduate-Endorsement-Scheme-BUES (accessed 5 November 2013).

Caruana, V and Ploner, J (2011) *Critical Review of Contemporary Practice in Internationalisation within the HLST Subject Communities*. Available from: http://www.heacademy.ac.uk/resources/detail/disciplines/business/critical-review-caruana-dec2011 (accessed 3 July 2013).

Coffield, F, Moseley, D, Hall, E and Ecclestone, K (2004) *Learning Styles and Pedagogy in Post-16 Learning: A Systematic and Critical Review*. Learning and Skills Research Centre: London.

Confederation of British Industry (CBI) and Universities UK (2009) *Future Fit: Preparing Graduates for the World of Work*. London: CBI.

Council of Europe (2001) *Recommendation No. R (92) 13 Rev of the Committee of Ministers to Member States on the Revised European Sports Charter*. Available from: https://wcd.coe.int/ViewDoc.jsp?Ref=Rec%2892%2913 (accessed 23 July 2013).

Dobson, JL (2009) 'Learning style preferences and course performance in an undergraduate physiology class', *Advances in Physiological Education*, 33(4): 308–314.

Dunn, R and Dunn, K (1992) *Teaching Secondary Students Through their Individual Learning Styles*. Needham Heights, MA: Allyn and Bacon.

Eston, R and Reilly, T (2008) *Kinanthropometry and Exercise Physiology Laboratory Manual*. London: Routledge.

Fry, H, Ketteridge, S and Marshall, S (2003) 'Understanding student learning', in H Fry, S Ketteridge and S Marshsall (eds.) *A Handbook for Teaching and Learning Higher Education*. London: Kogan Page, 9–25.

Gibbs, G and Habeshaw, T (1998) *Preparing to Teach* (4th edn.). Trowbridge, UK: Cromwell Press.

Hargreaves, J (2003) *Sporting Females: Critical Issues in the History and Sociology of Women's Sport*. London: Routledge.

Higher Education Careers Service Unit (HECSU) (2012) *What Do Graduates Do?* Available from: http://www.hecsu.ac.uk/assets/assets/documents/WDGD_Oct_2012.pdf (accessed 31 July 2013).

Howatson, G and Dancy, P (2009) 'An examination of the changing profile of sport science students and the impact on degree outcome', *Journal of Hospitality, Leisure, Sport and Tourism Education*, 8(2): 143–147.

Kolb, DA (1984) *Experiential Learning Experience as a Source of Learning and Development*. Upper Saddle River, NJ: Prentice Hall.

Massialis, BG (1985) 'Discovery- and inquiry-based programs', in TN Postlethwaite and T Husen (eds.) *The International Encyclopedia of Education*. Oxford: Pergamon Press, 1415–1418.

Michael, J (2006) 'Where's the evidence that active learning works', *Advances in Physiological Education*, 30(4): 159–167.

Peters, D, Jones, G and Peters, J (2007) 'Sports students' approaches to studying and their learning styles', *HLST Special Edition Newsletter*.

Phoenix, C and Sparkes, AC (2006) 'Young athletic bodies and narrative maps of aging', *Journal of Aging Studies*, 20: 107–112.

Quality Assurance Agency for Higher Education (2008) *Subject Benchmark Hospitality, Leisure, Sport and Tourism*. Available from: http://www.qaa.ac.uk/Publications/InformationAnd Guidance/Pages/Subject-benchmark-statement-Hospitality-leisure-sport-tourism-2008. aspx (accessed 29 July 2013).

Smith, M (2011) 'Exploring laboratory and field-based practical provision within sport science-related undergraduate programmes', *Link 28*. Hospitality, Leisure, Sport and Tourism.

The Telegraph (2013) *Ten Recession Proof Degrees*. Available from: http://www.telegraph. co.uk/education/educationpicturegalleries/9852535/Ten-recession-proof-degree-subjects.html?frame=2472756 (accessed 29 July 2013).

Walmsley, A (2011) *Report on Hospitality, Leisure, Sport and Tourism Higher Education in the UK*. Oxford: Higher Education Academy's Hospitality, Leisure, Sport and Tourism Network.

26

Nursing, health and social care

Julie Williams and Maria Joyce

INTRODUCTION

This chapter introduces the key aspects of learning and teaching relevant to educators in nursing and professions allied to health and social care. In response to changes in policy, demography and health and social care delivery, the context is continuously dynamic and one that can bring challenges to the education of the future workforce. This necessitates developing curricula that both acknowledge and reflect these changes whilst maintaining academic rigour. This chapter therefore looks at the implications for healthcare professional education in response to policy agendas. Health and social care provision is a closely governed industry and these regulatory processes are discussed both in their capacity to impact on service delivery and the education of the professional workforce.

The authors work in a city university within the large rural county of Lincolnshire. This geographical location brings its own challenges with a countywide catchment area for nursing, health and social care practice experiences, within community locations and several acute hospitals. The socially and culturally diverse population has impacted upon the local economy with both the rapid influx of populations from the European Union and UK migrants moving from poorer industrialised areas to rural and coastal neighbourhoods. This has brought different challenges to the provision of health and social care with the changing expectations of the public and the services commissioned on their behalf.

POLICY AND PRACTICE CONTEXT

Recent changes to health and social care commissioning have resulted in new models of service provision. These changes influence and ultimately transform educational curricula, thus developing and advancing practitioners in response to the social and political environment. The key drivers for change include political factors, economic influences, socio-cultural changes, social trends, environmental changes, technological developments and changes in health and social care policy, regulation and legislation. These require newly qualified practitioners to have sufficient transferable skills and competencies to enable them to work in any environment, including increasingly complex settings.

Health and social care services are subjected to a number of quality assurance measures and include external scrutiny by agencies such as the Care Quality Commission (CQC), Trust Development Agency (TDA) and Monitor (the sector regulator for health services in England). Educational establishments are likewise subjected to regular monitoring from statutory and regulatory bodies, such as the Health and Care Professionals Council (HCPC) and the Nursing and Midwifery Council (NMC) to ensure educational standards and compliance with performance expectations. Individual practitioners are also subject to regulation to ensure public safety and that continuous learning can be evidenced. Additionally, there is a requirement to evidence and demonstrate currency of individual practitioner competence and, where this falls short, investigatory procedures are evoked to address deficits.

The professional regulatory body for nurses, the NMC, and for allied health practitioners and social workers in the UK, the HCPC, set the direction for the standards of degree level education and thus the context and content of educational programmes (Health and Care Professionals Council, 2012; Nursing and Midwifery Council, 2010). Similar regulatory frameworks exist in Europe and Australia, such as the Nursing and Midwifery Board of Australia. Government, Department of Health (DH) and statutory directives highlight the need to enhance the quality of learning experience in nurse education and mandates an equitable balance between theoretical and practice learning (Department of Health, 2012a; Nursing and Midwifery Council, 2010). The HCPC also maintains standards for proficiency and conduct, both in practice and education. The Approved Education Institutions (AEIs) are accountable for both aspects of this educational provision. These agencies hold and maintain the professional register and approve education and training programmes, including regular monitoring of educational standards. Therefore, educational institutions, such as universities, are a vital interface between academic staff, health and social care practitioners and the future workforce, i.e. students.

The involvement of service providers in designing and delivering the curriculum is beneficial to enhancing the integration of theory and practice and facilitating multi-professional, multi-agency working. This impacts on education programme design, focusing the curriculum so that all qualifying health and social care practitioners are deemed fit for both practice and purpose, with competencies that align across the whole healthcare system. The practitioner should also be fit for award and this element is managed and upheld in the AEIs by their internal quality assurance mechanisms and through joint external scrutiny with partner organisations and regulatory agencies.

Recent policy directives concentrate on patient safety as the underpinning philosophy for all health and social care service provision, including integrated individually tailored care packages. In the UK, the driving force for nursing has seen the publication of a national strategy that emphasises leadership as a focus for enhancing a culture of compassion throughout the workforce. This agenda has permeated across all health and social care professions and has become a benchmark for high quality care (Department of Health, 2012a).

The drive for improved patient care has been led by government policy calling for stronger public participation across the health and social care sector and within programmes of education leading to professional registration and beyond. Guidelines of good practice standards set out the service user experience in terms of what the public can expect (Department of Health, 2010, 2012b; Goodrich and Cornwell, 2008; National Institute for Health and Care Excellence, 2011). The term 'service user' is generally seen to include people using health and social care services as clients, patients, parents, guardians and/or carers and can be represented by members of the public individually or as groups or communities. In response, the National Health Service (NHS) has been listening to the voice of the service user in order to improve services, promote choice and assure access to services. Thus the differing experiences and opinions held by service users inform and assist future decision-making, service provision and educational strategies. Service users are also involved in education of students, including participating in the experiences of candidate recruitment through to teaching and assessing students, both on a formal and informal basis. They are seen as key to bridging the gap between theory and practice, thus enabling students to better understand the experiences of service users.

KNOWLEDGE, SKILLS AND ATTITUDES

The everyday practices, roles and attributes of professionals working in the health and social care arena are complex in nature, diverse by speciality and often unconscious to the person experiencing them. This acknowledges that there are significant social, cognitive and behavioural aspects encapsulated in all professional practices. In particular, nurse education has an eclectic theoretical knowledge base and draws from learning experiences in practice with and from other professions, such as medicine, thus rendering it a complex educational endeavour (Williams, 2010). Evidence-based educational and professional practice (EBP) continues to evolve as research becomes increasingly accessible through new mediums and technological advances. EBP practice advances knowledge and supports reasoning, which ultimately influences the standard of care that students of health and social care educational programmes subsequently deliver.

Educational strategies such as 'learning to learn' (Wingate, 2007), 'academic literacy' (Lea and Street, 2006) and the focus on communities of practice in the Australian context (Hirst et al., 2004) facilitate the acquisition of appropriate and relevant knowledge and skills throughout the international academic community. For nursing specifically, nurse lecturers and clinical mentors are engaged in two fundamentally different knowledge-based activities giving rise to divergent orientations, priorities and dispositions (Williams, 2010). In this way, vocationally orientated professional education involves more than the benevolent transfer of knowledge and the passive recipient of information. The challenge for educators is to ensure the task of *transforming* (Brookfield, 2000; Mezirow, 2000), not merely *transferring*, subject knowledge into discipline-specific performance is tangible, transparent and achievable.

Case study 26.1: Adding an international context to learning in the development of social work

The Erasmus Mundus programme – MA Advanced Development in Social Work (ADVANCES) – is designed to promote outstanding levels of practice skills so practitioners can confidently respond to the challenges facing societies across the world. It is delivered by a consortium of five Universities – from Denmark (Aalborg), France (Paris), Poland (Warsaw), Portugal (Lisbon) and the UK (Lincoln). The programme offers scholarships to applicants from within, and external to, the EU with students originating from countries such as Germany, Poland, Palestine, Malawi, Thailand, Australia, Jamaica, Pakistan, Zimbabwe and Ukraine.

Such a rich and diverse group brings its own educational and pedagogical challenges. One solution has been to draw upon and explore the notion of Threshold Concepts; what are the areas of knowledge that enable the individual to move from 'studying social work' to be 'being a social worker'? We have therefore focused upon the search for these transformational constructs, identifying differences and commonalities, and promoted a learning environment in which each participant is actively educating the other members of the group. This complex task is being done in a language other than their own, using the common medium of English. Their ability to embrace the complexity of linguistic nuances and to explain ideas to each other is a wonder to behold and a testimony to the power of international education.

(Nigel Horner, Head of School – Health and Social Care,
University of Lincoln)

The university plays a significant role in enriching health and social care services by educating the future workforce and through being a springboard for innovation and enterprise. Professional education beyond initial registration, clinical practice and the research endeavour all share common priorities in order to ensure the required knowledge maintains its relevance and currency in a rapidly changing and challenging environment. To meet these challenges, academics need to guide and nurture their students' endeavours to achieve mastery of a flexible approach to knowledge acquisition throughout their careers. By paying attention to detail when considering the requisite knowledge, skills, motivations, context and learning styles that underpin curriculum development, educators will build educationally valuable relationships.

Considered in light of the changing employability status of new graduates, nurse educators have potentially very broad spheres of influence, therefore being empowered to act within the boundaries they set is crucial. Nurses are traditionalists *par excellence* and research suggests that the urge for cultural and professional perpetuity is so strong that they place significant emphasis on the importance of historical anecdotes of practice-based nursing experiences. Through the medium of personal storytelling, the ability to relate theory to practice is enhanced and goes some way to inducting students into the world of nursing. In this way, the use of tales depicting personal practice experiences are highly valued by nurse educators as a means of promoting and endorsing reconciliation between theoretical propositional and practice-based knowledge, thus attempting to mediate between the two very different worlds they occupy. Such 'tales from the sluice' are perceived as ways in which disciplinary knowledge can be acquired, transmitted or formed (Williams, 2010) and have utility in the education of nurses.

Learning to become a health or social care professional requires individuals to demonstrate self-motivation and maturity. Being able to articulate a deep understanding of all experiences of learning enables practitioners and students to develop ideas in order to build knowledge. Such elements of self-awareness include the ability to reflect and educators should guide learners in these endeavours. Any time 'built-in' to an educational programme for reflection may also be used for deconstruction after stressful experiences and the use of a **reflective journal** can be an important tool for learning and enable the student to see their own self-development and recognise that learning has taken place.

There are two basic forms of reflection: 'reflection-on-action' and 'reflection-in-action' (Schön, 1987). The word 'action' is vital. Commonly, reflection-on-action involves mentally revisiting past events to gain insight and understanding of personal behaviours in order to improve professional competence. Reflection-in-action enables practitioners to demonstrate the skills of self-examination of personal behaviours as well as the behaviours of others during an event or interaction (Schön, 1995). An active process, reflection is structured through the use of a model or framework, of which there are many (Gibbs, 1988; Johns, 2000; Kolb, 1984). As a basis for learning, it links together new and old experiences, as well as providing insights and opportunities to challenge accepted values and behaviours. The reflective process enables individuals to question their actions, make sense of them and use what is learnt to challenge and develop existing professional practices. In this way, students use reflection to increase awareness of their practices and increase personal confidence in their professional roles.

Health and social care educators need to regularly review the reflective sources available to them in order to enhance their academic achievements and professional practices because reflection can inspire creativity and differential modes of thinking. Self-efficacy is an important part of the way you see yourself and how you manage your academic practices and is thus crucial to your success, both academically and professionally.

Health and social care professionals will often be required to extend their learning beyond their initial registration, therefore continuous learning is commonplace and needs to be facilitated around their working life. Continuing professional development (CPD) encompasses a combination of approaches health and social care professionals undertake to learn, keep up-to-date and practice safely. It is managed in a variety of ways and professional regulators set out how the practitioner can achieve these mandated requirements in order to maintain their professional registration. Such learning experiences expose students to styles of teaching and learning that may not be familiar to them, such as guided-learning, self-directed learning or **problem-based learning**. Strategies to support students following these **flexible learning** approaches will need careful consideration and often will require non-traditional mechanisms for formative and summative feedback. This can be achieved by the practitioner keeping and sharing a learning log of their CPD activities and using a variety of learning experiences, such as personal tutor conferences, discussion groups and other forms of social media which enhance communication. The NMC states that all those completing a notification to practice form must comply with the 'Post registration and education practice (PREP) standards' (Nursing and Midwifery Council, 2011).

Recent UK strategies and directives such the Chief Nursing Officer's vision for nursing (Department of Health, 2012a), known colloquially as the '6 Cs of Nursing', has set an agenda that encompasses and embraces values-based teaching and learning. Curriculum development, approaches to teaching, and learning outcomes must demonstrate how these 6 Cs are evidenced. Care, Compassion, Competence, Communication, Courage and Commitment form the bedrock for measuring quality in healthcare services and students of these professions are tasked with making every contact count and providing evidence of learning that validates the acquisition of these values.

LEARNING, TEACHING AND ASSESSMENT

Learning has been transformed from traditional methods of face-to-face teaching through to multi-digital use of a range of technological advances, with national policy strategies providing guidance on using technology in both adult and children's learning settings (Department for Education and Skills, 2005; Higher Education Funding Council for England, 2009). Existing technology is continuously improving with the use of the **virtual learning environment** (VLE) and new emerging technologies such as cloud computing, digital storage, mobile learning (see also Chapter 27) with smart phones and tablets, use of apps, learning analytics, open content and research repositories. It is now commonplace in higher education institutions to use virtual and remote laboratories and wearable technology that can send messages and communicate with other staff and students to enhance their learning. Traditional face-to-face teaching methods can be routed through online and distance modes, and delivered either independently or in a blended forum. **Blended learning** merges virtual and physical learning through formats ranging from supplementing classroom learning to delivering teaching through learning management systems, as seen in distance learning formats. Success depends on the presentation and standardisation of materials, equitable access to the learning opportunity and presenting a range of online learning tools to meet varying learning styles.

Interrogating practice

- What teaching methods do you use for your module?
- Do these methods align with the assessment?

The academic landscape is changing with increased use of social media and mobile learning alongside the use of advanced learning technologies. The speed of change means it can be hard to keep up-to-date with how to use these to best effect whilst understanding the extent to which they can enhance student learning. New and creative approaches to using this technology are constantly being explored in both advancing teaching and enhancing learning. Learning Landscapes (Learning Landscapes in Higher Education, 2010) are those where university and academic staff engage with students on all issues relating to the teaching, learning, research and administrative environment and are gaining momentum nationally and internationally. These promote discussion and timely responses, and therefore more effective management of expectations. Initiatives such as Student as Producer at the University of Lincoln (http://studentasproducer.lincoln.ac.uk) emphasise the role of the students as collaborators in the production of knowledge.

Case study 26.2: Engaging experienced learners

Joanne joined the nursing programme after twenty years as a support worker working with older people. Struggling to come to terms with the academic elements of her nursing programme, she excelled at achieving her clinical competencies. Passionate about caring, she approached her tutors pleading for help to 'become the best nurse she could be'.

The ethos of the university and the nursing programme was to work in partnership with students to enhance their learning and to engage participation in their education, at every level. Joanne was advised to seek out campaigns that she could join as well as canvassing local health care providers for involvement, including applying to become a 'Care Maker' (http://www.nhsemployers.org/campaigns/care-makers-hub/what-are-care-makers). Joanne was nominated to work with the local acute NHS provider services on their strategic plan to integrate older people's care services across the county. Joanne's enthusiasm and passion was rewarded when her nomination was successful and she became a member of the Joint Services Older People's Strategic Board. Such engagement in both theory and practice elements of her studies will enhance Joanne's chances of building a very successful career.

(Chris Craggs, Senior Lecturer, University of Lincoln)

The **National Student Survey** (NSS) in the UK enables final year students to comment on their experiences at university. The data arising from the NSS is used as an indicator of quality, performance and overall satisfaction with programmes of education. Results are published annually, enabling year-on-year and university-by-university comparisons to be made, assisting future applicants in making informed choices when selecting their place of study.

The introduction of simulated learning and skills suites has significantly increased opportunities to develop and practice competence in skills relevant to health and social care education in a controlled environment. Learners are able to demonstrate these skills at levels ranging from basic to advanced, across many disciplines, prior to starting a placement. Simulation can be used for teaching and assessing skill acquisition using modes of low fidelity, such as wound sites, through to online interaction with high fidelity 'manikins' enabled for surgical procedures (Moule et al., 2008). It is recognised as enabling students to gain confidence and competence through unlimited practice and feedback without patient involvement and before being placed in a real-life setting. The intention is to reduce errors and improve patient safety (Donaldson, 2009). Early recognition of students' learning needs and potential deficits enables individual action plans to be developed, with a focus on the requisite minimum standards to be achieved in relation to knowledge, skills and attitudes. Mentors and students can then work together in the completion and achievement of these individualised learning plans, with a clear focus on the required outcomes, the processes and the time scales necessary for success (Williams, 2010).

Interrogating practice

- To what extent do you operate a shared curriculum with mentors in practice?

Policy has embedded simulation within the nursing curriculum with a prescribed number of practice hours available for use in simulated learning (Nursing and

Midwifery Council, 2010). The technological advances have increased exponentially and have resulted in this format of teaching, learning and assessment gaining popularity. Whilst these points bring many positive aspects to the use of simulated learning, there are several challenges. The rising level of technological advancement incurs increasing costs related to extending bespoke facilities, upgrading and replacement of equipment requiring on-going maintenance. The scope of the high fidelity manikin must be matched by a similar level of skill in the educator using the equipment. Simulation cannot replace real-life learning with real patients, but can enable the practitioner to develop a competent technique that can then be enhanced by practical learning.

Assessment has a role in ensuring quality and safeguarding academic standards, both within the organisation from where the assessment originates but also as a national comparison against other similar organisations. This national standard is upheld by the **Quality Assurance Agency for Higher Education** (QAA). The QAA regularly reviews all UK higher education providers using a quality code as a framework for standards, which are publicly available. For the European dimension, the Bologna Agreement Declaration (1999) provides an international framework through which academic degrees can be easily recognised and compared. This model promotes the mobility of students, academic staff and researchers throughout Europe and ultimately contributes to high quality teaching with a European dimension.

Assessment may be **formative** or **summative**, with formative intended to aid the learning process and summative designed to measure how much learning has taken place. Formative assessment works best when used periodically with feedback given to the student on their progress, including the identification of any additional learning needs and the steps needed to address them. Summative assessment is essential in ascertaining that all required levels of knowledge have been achieved and requisite standards met. The method of assessment used must be relevant to the expected learning outcomes. The different assessment formats employed must lend themselves to determining the level of achievement across different outcomes and learning for different purposes.

Interrogating practice

- Thinking about the assessment you give, does it provide added value to the practice setting or enhance skills development?

Assessment can take place through online submission of assignments, online tests, online journals, discussion summaries and peer reviews, with benefits including 24-hour access to learning content and equitable provision of learning materials. Assessment in practice is used to test competencies that cannot be readily tested or examined via conventional methods, such as written assessments or examinations. Professional skills and attributes can be assessed in real-life situations using a framework of work-based competencies relevant to the health professional being assessed. The recording of these learning experiences is often performed through direct observation and assessor judgement and/or the compilation of a portfolio of evidence that can be used to illustrate that learning has taken place.

Assessment is an essential part of the teaching and learning process and is used to support motivation of students, create learning opportunities and provide learning feedback to students and the teacher, as well as maintenance of standards and quality, both internal to the course and external in relation to the organisation. While all these mechanisms are an essential part of the assessment process, their functions can be achieved within different timescales.

Inter-professional education (IPE) is distinguishable by its focus upon the different professional groups learning about and from each other to improve practice and health care (Royal College of Nursing, 2007), whereas multi-professional education (MPE) focuses on the common content of learning. IPE has been advocated by the World Health Organisation (WHO) since 1988, supporting the principle that the earlier health and social care professionals worked together the sooner they would collaborate effectively in teams (World Health Organisation, 1988). IPE is effective in both clinical teaching and theoretical lectures and should be embedded within the curriculum.

For some educational programmes, cohort group sizes are getting bigger. For commissioned and vocationally orientated programmes, such as nursing, this has resulted in less time spent on small group teaching and more lectures delivered to large groups. The impact of economic and financial constraint has meant lower staff–student ratios and evoked criticism in terms of having the potential for disadvantaging some students by having a detrimental effect on educational attainment. Approaches to learning and teaching must be reviewed as a direct response to the growth in class size, with approaches to small group teaching not readily transferring to large group lecture settings. Curricula will consequently need to reflect the prevailing social, political, educational and professional doctrine of the times (Williams, 2010).

ROLES SUPPORTING LEARNING

Personal academic tutors

University teachers of health and social care educational programmes generally come with a wide range of interests and experiences grounded in their professional practice and experiences. However, the more generic skills of providing pastoral support constitute a significant element of student learning in higher education. This pastoral support is normally provided through a system of assigned personal academic tutor roles. Undertaking the personal academic tutor role provides educators with enhanced understanding of how they can have a personal impact on improving the learning situation and experience for students (Booth and Anderberg, 2005), as well as being a mechanism for improving their personal confidence in developing their own teaching performance.

Lecturer practitioners

Health and social care curricula and programmes of education require balance between theoretical and practice-based learning. Curricula based on empirically generated knowledge combined with **practice-based** skills and know-how will generate graduates who are fit for purpose and practice. Educator roles that traverse theory and practice can be challenging and complex, as in the case of preparing practice educators to embrace additional roles that directly affect the initial registration of students (Nursing and Midwifery Council, 2008), known as the 'sign-off mentor'. The requirement to achieve significant levels of competence in both the field of higher education as well as maintaining expertise in the practice field has enabled the growth of lecturer practitioner role in the education of health and social care students. The introduction of the lecturer practitioner has contributed to the success of the level of attention given to skills acquisition in educational programmes leading to registration in the health and social care fields.

Clinical support roles

Mentors/Practice assessors

The Nursing and Midwifery Council (NMC) standards for supporting learning and assessment in practice (Nursing and Midwifery Council, 2008) outline a framework that identifies key competencies for those in key roles in the education and training of healthcare professionals. This developmental framework identifies the knowledge and skills that nurses and midwives will need in order to support students undertaking NMC-approved recordable qualifications. The required knowledge and skills competencies are based on four stages of knowledge acquisition ranging from stage 1 to stage 4, as shown in Table 26.1. As clinical practitioner roles change, so do the requirements to support learners in diverse and challenging professionally qualified roles.

The word 'mentor' can be traced as far back as when Odysseus, in his absence, assigned responsibility for taking care of his son to a man named 'Mentor'. The name 'mentor' subsequently became synonymous with an individual who acts as a teacher, guardian, advisor and 'critical friend'.

The NMC, as the regulatory body for all qualified nurses in the UK, outlines the key role responsibilities of mentors in the nursing professional (Nursing and Midwifery Council, 2008), which include:

- Supervision of learners in learning situations;
- Organising and coordination of learning activities in practice;

Table 26.1 NMC standards for supporting learning and teaching in practice

NMC stage of mentorship	Required knowledge	Recorded on a register
Stage 1	All nurses and midwives must meet the defined requirements of the Code: standards of conduct, performance and ethics for nurses and midwives.	No
Stage 2	The standard for mentors. Must have successfully achieved all of the outcomes of this formal qualification.	Yes: local mentor register
Stage 3	The standard for a practice teacher for nursing or specialist community public health nursing. Must have successfully achieved all of the outcomes of this formal qualification.	Yes: local mentor register
Stage 4	The standard for a teacher of nurses, midwives or specialist community public health nurses. Must have successfully achieved all of the outcomes of this formal qualification.	Recorded on the NMC register on application and payment of the relevant fee.

Source: Nursing and Midwifery Council (2008: 20)

- Setting and monitoring learning objectives;
- Assessing skills, attitudes and behaviours of learners;
- Evidencing learners' achievements;
- Providing constructive feedback;
- Liaising with others about learner-specific performance;
- Identifying concerns; and
- Agreeing actions about concerns.

In addition, a number of authors have identified characteristics and role-specific responsibilities of mentors in healthcare learning environments. The following provides an insight to the multifaceted nature of the mentoring role, as Walsh (2010) provides from a synthesis of authors' views:

- Role model
- Energiser
- Envisioner
- Investor
- Supporter
- Standard prodder
- Teacher–Coach
- Feedback giver
- Eye opener

- Door opener
- Ideas bouncer
- Problem solver
- Career counsellor
- Challenger

This list is not exhaustive and clearly distinguishes a mentor as a knowledgeable professional practitioner who spends considerable time and effort to advance the profession to which they belong by sharing their knowledge, skills and expertise with learners, no matter what the educational circumstances.

Interrogating practice

- Who else supports learning in practice and how is assessment managed?

LEARNING SUPPORT

University education requires learners to demonstrate a set of skills that may have been difficult to achieve throughout their pre-university experiences. This has the potential to disadvantage some students. Acquiring the skills of academic writing, referencing, time management and accessing and sourcing literature should be strongly advocated by academic staff and can often be seen as elements of core learning support provided by universities.

Where students have an educational psychologist's diagnosis of a specific learning need, such as **dyslexia** or dyspraxia, or because English is their second language, their needs will need to be met by a number of supportive strategies, such as recording lectures (be mindful that lectures are intellectual property), additional time in summative assessments (such as examinations), advance publication of lecture notes, to name just a few. Those with dyspraxia may have difficulty with typing, writing and practical skills and may require the assistance of an amanuensis, commonly known as a scribe. Identifying learning difficulties early in the student's educational experience will significantly enhance their ability to succeed with their academic studies and achievements.

ACHIEVEMENT AND PROGRESSION

Much attention has been paid to the retention, progression and attrition rates of students studying health and social care, especially in relation to undergraduate pre-registration programmes of study. Reasons for failure to complete are various, often interlinked and usually down to more than one factor. Glogowska et al. (2007) noted that failing to achieve success and make suitable progress amongst health and social care students can be as a result of failing to reach the required minimum standard in either, or both, academic and practice competencies, thus contributing to high levels of attrition and spoiled career ambitions.

To better the chances of cohort success in educational programmes, universities need to pay attention to their recruitment and admission policies and procedures. Such strategies must sufficiently take account of how best to communicate and support applicants, and equally important is how to manage student expectations of their chosen educational programme, especially in relation to the required commitment for attendance and conformity to mandated regulated standards. Pre-programme criminal record checks, subsequent annual declarations and occupational health assessments can help determine individual suitability and fitness to practice as a healthcare student. Strategies such as pre-admission literacy and numeracy assessments and the facilitation of diagnostic assessment can help in the early detection and recognition of the need for increased support for some students (Williams, 2011).

Interrogating practice

- What recruitment methods are used for your programme?
- How do the recruitment and selection processes test for evidence of the skills and attitudes expected of those graduating within the profession?

Some students may hide their vulnerabilities and anxieties by assuming a deliberate and calculated approach to their studies. Such **surface approaches** to learning can have a negative effect and students may disengage from their learning and be more unlikely to seek the help they need. These barriers to achievement and progression can manifest in, for example, numerous applications for deferral of assessment submission dates or in some cases non-submissions. Debriefing and regular constructive feedback on progress plays an important role for everyone involved with an underachieving student (Robshaw and Smith, 2003).

Within both practice and educational settings, mentors and teachers need to be aware of the significant commitment required by all participants when contributing to student learning, achievement and progression. What is reflected in everyday nursing practice, in contrast to classroom learning, often reveals a very different experience for the student (Duffy, 2003). Thus, failing to progress in either theoretical or clinical endeavours may be as a result of students' preconceived and unmatched expectations. Regular reviews of progress with personal academic tutors can help counter any potential problems and provide opportunities for additional pastoral support. Learning and teaching relationships therefore need to acknowledge the students' perspective and provide encouragement and positive reinforcement on a holistic level, fostering motivation and progression where possible (Williams, 2011).

Students with disruptive behaviour, who display negative attitudes towards staff and service users and who, despite advice and support, continue to fail in their understanding or performance of the professional requirements of healthcare practitioners, may find themselves subject to the judgement of a professional suitability panel. The outcome of such may invoke a termination of studies for the student concerned. Unresolved conflict can negatively influence the student's learning experience and that of others, and should not be ignored. Determining the ways in which any negative situations can be rectified, finding compromise and most importantly, helping students learn from the experiences are core role responsibilities for educators. This includes empowering students to take responsibility for their actions and concluding with positive observations, examples or praise. Students who fail to make the requisite progress, for whatever reason, should be helped to find an alternative pathway for their future studies and/or career choices.

QUALITY OF EDUCATIONAL OUTCOMES

Paying attention to all aspects of the educational experience, including the learning environment helps to create a strong sense of shared purpose. Implementing robust support mechanisms, setting policies that are consistent with good practice and having realistic expectations for individual performance will enhance the student experience. Ultimately, while some students will inevitably fail, or be discontinued due to professional unsuitability or misconduct, providing a holistic approach to students and their educational experience can facilitate success (Williams, 2011).

Despite this, there can be incidences of academic malpractice to be dealt with – one of the most common offences being plagiarism. Whilst research in this area in health and social care education is sparse, Harper (2006) noted that the evidence does suggest that dishonesty in academic settings can translate to dishonest and unethical behaviour in professional health and social care practice settings. Educational programme teams should aim to develop strong relationships with placement partners in order to protect the public by supporting link lecturers, mentors and students in their respective roles in potentially delicate circumstances such as these. The inference here is that addressing malpractice issues in a fair and consistent manner may help prevent misconduct in the healthcare professions. Institutional policies and procedures must therefore be clearly laid down and accessible to all students at the beginning of their studies (Williams, 2011).

OVERVIEW

This chapter has discussed key aspects of nursing, health and social care education in higher education settings. It has considered the policy and practice context within which the competent practitioner demonstrates the required knowledge, skills and attitudes in all environments. The chapter provides an insight into the many different approaches that may be utilised in teaching and assessing students across health and social care educational programmes. Crucially, we have included details of the roles that support learning in both classroom and practice settings and how to manage the achievement and progression of students with competing demands in complex learning environments.

REFERENCES

Booth, S and Anderberg, E (2005) 'Academic development for knowledge capabilities: learning, reflecting and developing', *Higher Education Research & Development*, 24(4): 373–386.

Brookfield, SD (2000) 'Transformative learning as ideology critique', in J Mezirow and Associates (eds.) *Learning as Transformation: Critical Perspectives on a Theory in Progress*. San Francisco, CA: Jossey-Bass, 125–147.

Department for Educaton and Skills (DfES) (2005) *Harnessing Technology: Transforming Learning and Children's Services*. London: The Stationery Office.

Department of Health (2010) *Equity and Excellence: Liberating the NHS*. London: The Stationery Office.

Department of Health (2012a) *Compassion for Practice. The Vision and Strategy for Nurses Midwives and Health Care Staff*. London: The Stationery Office.

Department of Health (2012b) *The NHS Constitution*. London: The Stationery Office.

Donaldson, L (2009) *The 2008 Annual Report of the Chief Medical Officer: Safer Medical Practice*. London: The Stationery Office.

Duffy, K (2003) *Failing Students: a Qualitative Study of Factors that Influence the Decisions Regarding Assessment of Students' Competence in Practice*. London: National Medical Council.

Gibbs, G (1988) *Learning by Doing: A Guide to Teaching and Learning Methods*. Oxford: Further Education Unit Oxford Brookes University.

Glogowska, M, Young, P and Lockyer, L (2007) 'Should I go or should I stay?,' *Active Learning in Higher Education*, 8(1): 63–77.

Goodrich, J and Cornwell, J (2008) *Seeing the Person in the Patient*. London: Kings Fund.

Harper, M (2006) 'High tech cheating', *Nurse Education Today*, 26(8): 672–679.

Health and Care Professionals Council (HCPC) (2012) *Standards of Education and Training*. London: HCPC.

Higher Education Funding Council for England (HEFCE) (2009) *Enhancing Learning and Teaching Through the Use of Technology: A Revised Approach to HEFCE's Strategy for e-Learning*. London: HEFCE.

Hirst, E, Henderson, R, Allan, M, Bode, J and Kocatepe, M (2004) 'Repositioning academic literacy: charting the emergence of a community of practice', *Australian Journal of Language and Literacy*, 27(1): 66–80.

Johns, C (2000) *Becoming a Reflective Practitioner: A Reflective and Holistic Approach to Clinical Nursing, Practice Development and Clinical Supervision*. Oxford: Blackwell.

Kolb, D (1984) *Experiential Learning: Experience as the Source of Learning and Development*. Englewood Cliffs, NJ: Prentice Hall.

Lea, MR and Street, BV (2006) 'The "Academic Literacies" model: theory and applications', *Theory into Practice*, 45(4): 368–377.

Learning Landscapes in Higher Education (2010). Available from: http://learningland-scapes.blogs.lincoln.ac.uk/files/2010/04/FinalReport.pdf (accessed 9 November 2013).

Mezirow, J (2000) 'Learning to think like an adult: core concepts of transformation theory', in J Mezirow and associates (eds.) *Learning as Transformation: Critical Perspectives on a Theory in Progress*. San Francisco, CA: Jossey-Bass, 3–32.

Moule, P, Wilford, A, Sales, R and Lockyer, L (2008) 'Nursing students learning through simulation: a randomised study of non-eqivalent groups', *Nurse Education Today*, 28: 790–797.

National Institute for Health and Care Excellence (NICE) (2011) *Quality Standards for Service User Experience in Adult Mental Health*. London: NICE.

Nursing and Midwifery Council (NMC) (2008) *Standards to Support Learning and Assessment in Practice: NMC Standards for Mentors, Practice Teachers and Teachers*. London: NMC.

Nursing and Midwifery Council (NMC) (2010) *Standards for Pre-Registration Nursing Education*. London: NMC.

Nursing and Midwifery Council (NMC) (2011) *The PREP Handbook*. London: NMC.

Royal College of Nursing (RCN) (2007) *The Impact and Effectiveness of Interprofessional Education in Primary Care*. London: RCN.

Robshaw, M and Smith, J (2003) 'Keeping afloat: student nurses' experiences following assignment referral', *Nurse Education Today*, 24(7): 511–520.

Schön, DA (1987) *Educating the Reflective Practitioner: Toward a New Design for Teaching and Learning in the Professions*. San Francisco, CA: Jossey-Bass.

Schön, DA (1995) *The Reflective Practitioner: How Professionals Think In Action*. San Francisco, CA: Basic Books.

Walsh, D (2010) *The Nurse Mentor's Handbook: Supporting Students in Clinical Practice*. Maidenhead: Open University Press.

Williams, J (2010) *Pride and Prejudice: the Socialisation of Nurse Educators*. PhD thesis, University of Lancaster.

Williams, J (2011) 'Dealing with failing and problem students', in: A McIntosh, J Gidman and E Mason-Whitehead (eds.) *Key Concepts in Healthcare Education*. London: Sage Publications, Chapter 9.

Wingate, U (2007) 'A framework for transition: supporting 'Learning to Learn' in higher education', *Higher Education Quarterly*, 61(3): 391–405.

World Health Organisation (WHO) (1988) *Learning Together to Work Together for Health. Report of a WHO Study Group on Multiprofessional Education of Health Personnel and the Team Approach*. Geneva 796: WHO.

Medicine and dentistry

Colin Lumsden and Lucie Byrne-Davis

INTRODUCTION

This chapter is an overview of some important issues that are specific, but not exclusive, to medical and dental undergraduate and, to a lesser extent, postgraduate medical education. The chapter introduces important concepts that must be considered when educating the doctors and dentists of tomorrow and builds upon ideas introduced elsewhere in the text. Reading of several of the chapters in Part 2 is highly recommended, as is reading of the chapter equivalent to this in the third edition (Feather and Fry, 2009), especially in relation to assessment and problem-based learning. Using case studies in medical and dental training, we show how technology can be used to address a range of current concerns.

BREADTH, DEPTH AND OUTCOME

Medicine and dentistry have recently seen a much greater level of scrutiny by the **General Medical Council** (GMC) and **General Dental Council** (GDC) and a shift to outcome-based curricula. The de facto outcomes for medicine can now be found in the *Tomorrow's Doctors* (GMC, 2009) document, which sets out the minimum competencies of newly qualified doctors. The GDC published their *'Preparing for Practice'* and *'Standards for Education'* documents in 2011 and 2012, respectively, outlining the outcomes to be achieved and stipulating the educational rigour required for first registration. Every UK medical and dental school must demonstrate how these outcomes are to be achieved and assessed. Regulatory professional bodies have increasingly taken on a role in quality and their requirements highlight many current issues in health professional undergraduate education. Medical and dental schools must not only ensure the maintenance and assessment of academic standards, but they are also held accountable by these regulatory bodies, which are in turn accountable to the Department of Health and ultimately the general public. Overall, HE quality assurance practices also pertain, including those run by the **Quality Assurance Agency** (QAA).

Both specialities – medicine and dentistry – must ensure that students and trainees not only understand relevant factual knowledge but are able to put this knowledge into practice with patients. Universities are therefore required to satisfy themselves and prove to external bodies that those graduating are of a sufficient standard to begin practice. Medical trainees currently undergo a further period of close supervision (Foundation Year 1) before they are able to gain full registration to the medical register. This is then followed by a period of supervised training dependent upon their speciality; however, dental students must be ready to practice safely and competently on graduation from university, although the vast majority undertake a Foundation Training Year to work in the NHS. Undergraduates from both professions are therefore expected to be proficient in a plethora of skills that are necessary to practice safely and engender trust in the public. The GMC (2009) aimed to define this range by pointing to vertical themes within curricula in its publication *Tomorrow's Doctors: Outcomes and Standards for Undergraduate Medical Education*. The themes are 'the doctor as scholar and a scientist', 'the doctor as a practitioner' and 'the doctor as a professional'. These include, but are not restricted to, the attainment of:

- Knowledge in the key areas of physiology, anatomy, pathology, pharmacology, psychology, etc.
- Diagnostic skills to be able to recognise patterns of disease, illness and abnormality;
- Evaluative skills to be able to find and analyse scientific data on best practice, innovations and research;
- Practical skills in order to examine, investigate and treat pathological conditions in patients (including prescribing skills);
- Communication skills to ensure the development of good patient rapport during consultations;
- Professional behaviours expected within the specialities; and
- Life-long learning skills and the ability to demonstrate competence through reflective practice and self-evaluation.

The GDC has similar expectations but also specifies management and leadership outcomes with respect to the dental team and the requisite surgical skills. It can therefore be seen that education in medicine and dentistry covers the full gamut of skills, from the attainment of basic scientific knowledge through to the modelling of professional behaviours expected of those entering the professions. These extremely complex requirements necessitate specific methods to ensure the trust of the public and the safety of patients. Healthcare professions are at a pivotal point in time in view of the very real concerns expressed in the final Francis Report, published in February 2013. The report identified serious failings at the Mid-Staffordshire NHS Trust and considered why the problems at the Trust were not identified and acted on sooner, with 290 recommendations designed to change a culture where cost control came ahead of patient safety, and to make sure patients come first by creating a common patient-centred culture across the NHS (Francis Report, 2013).

Arguably, trust in the healthcare professions is at an all-time low and it is incumbent upon HE institutions to ensure graduates are able to practice holistically, with the best interests of the patient at heart, rather than cede to the pressure to achieve and maintain targets that may not best benefit the patient.

These challenges are set against a backdrop of the most accelerated development of technology in history. This affects both professions and training for them. This chapter focuses on three technological solutions that address many of these concerns in different ways. They offer solutions to safe clinical practice for students; collating and accessing multiple assessment outcomes and mapping these to curriculum outcomes; and ensuring more uniform learning opportunities for geographically dispersed students.

THE USE OF SIMULATION IN MEDICAL EDUCATION

This section aims to offer the inexperienced medical educator something of a practical model and guide for undergraduate medical **simulation**, as well as raising issues associated with its use. Readers may also find it helpful to look at Chapter 26 in relation to simulation.

Simulation can be defined as the technique of imitating (recreating in a safe environment) a situation or process through a suitably analogous situation or apparatus, in order to gain skills, whether technical, clinical or non-technical. Medical simulation encompasses a variety of modalities from role play (with or without **simulated patients**), and part task trainers (i.e. lifelike models of body parts, such as an IV cannula insertion arm, airway head, etc.), through to whole body simulators and virtual patients. The increase of simulation in undergraduate and postgraduate medical education is driven by a variety of factors. Reasons include concern about the ethics regarding practicing on patients, the reduction in training hours and traditional resources (e.g. certain patient groups) and the availability of increasingly authentic simulators. Simulation is also favoured in assessment because it allows the training and assessment of greater numbers of trainees and increases the standardisation and quality assurance of assessments. Simulation also allows for training with greater safety for both patient and trainee.

Case study 27.1: The spectrum of simulation for medical students

The Royal Preston Hospital uses its purpose-built skills laboratory high-fidelity simulation suite with medical students during three years of their training. Within these sessions, students are challenged with a variety of clinical presentations that vary in complexity and in the focus of the subsequent debriefing (Issenberg et al., 2005). As students progress through the years, the focus of the encounters moves from clinical management to their non-technical skills (human factors).

This case study describes the critical steps and considerations of a typical fifth year session, with a discussion about human factors, along with the concepts and pedagogical processes underlying simulation.

Why simulation?

A Best Evidence Medical Education (BEME) systemic review (Issenberg et al., 2005) examined evidence that suggested simulation-based medical education complements, but does not duplicate, the education occurring on clinical placement. It is a form of **experiential learning**, which prepares the students for genuine encounters, with the learner being an active participant within a controlled safe environment. The opportunity for repetitive performance and practice reduces time to pass through various stages of competence for technical skills (conscious to the more 'automatic' unconscious competence). This occurs alongside raising participants' awareness of error, underpinned by feedback about personal cognitive performance under stress.

Simulation is a safe environment in which high risk/low occurrence situations can be encountered (such as resuscitation), or low risk/high occurrence encounters (such as the patient with asthma). It is a safe environment where mistakes can be made and learnt from without consequences for patient safety. As simulation is dynamic, with expert facilitators and technicians, encounters can be varied to reflect either student expertise or a specific targeted training encounter. It can bridge the gap between theory and **problem-based learning** and the real clinical environment, with the debrief being a key element in the experiential process. Through performance coding (i.e. rating) and video debriefing, students can begin to understand their approach to a patient and their team within potentially stressful situations. This highlights processes within the learner's control, such as perception, meaning and insight (Kneebone, 2003) – key concepts linked closely with human factors. Students are encouraged via experiential learning, through Kolb's learning cycle (see Chapter 5) with multiple visits to the simulation centre. This enables them to move through the cycle and facilitate active experimentation in a safe controlled learning environment.

Why teach students human factors?

Human factors are a crucial aspect of patient safety education, authoritatively defined as:

> Human factors refer to environmental, organisational and job factors, and human and individual characteristics which influence behaviour at work in a way which can affect health and safety.
>
> (Health and Safety Executive, 1999: 2)

With adverse events occurring in the NHS in more than 10 per cent of hospital admissions in 2003; 6,800 negligence claims in 2008–2009 (Association of Surgeons of Great Britain and Ireland, 2010); and between 60–70 per cent of these errors being non-technical (DeAnda and Gaba, 1990, 1991), an early understanding and teaching of these clinical knowledge and non-technical factors in parallel is crucial to them having a lasting impact on patient safety. The 2009 World Health Organisation (WHO) document emphasised the importance of patient safety training for medical students. Within this guide, simulation was identified as a learning tool that should be embedded within medical school curricula. By Year 5, the emphasis is primarily on human factors, unless technical or knowledge elements are a cause for concern.

Preparation

Authenticity of simulation is very important. This covers both physical authenticity, which is the degree to which the simulator looks and feels like the real thing, and functional authenticity being how real the actions and competencies feel compared to those in real life. Frequently part task trainers and 'Resusci Annie' full-bodied simulators are regarded as low fidelity when used by themselves. Hybrid simulators, such as those in Preston, enable the use of a mannequin with human-like physiology and signs, with the integration of computer technology to mimic true physiological responses. Despite this, fidelity will rarely be complete because simulators are never totally isomorphic with the real thing. Consideration of the following factors can enhance authenticity and thus increase fidelity. Fidelity can be increased with consideration of the following:

1 *Scenario design*: clinical validity is of key importance. Design needs to reflect reality, with consideration given to the history and supporting materials such as GP letters or admission notes, drug charts or IV charts. Fifth year sessions encompass presentations from acute severe asthma to shock as a result of anaphylaxis and sepsis.
2 *Physiological parameters*: starting parameters and their progression, along with mapping of the patient's condition and the response to treatment.
3 *Role play*: what role plays will be provided by both the facilitator in the room (nurse/another doctor/family member), and the patient (second facilitator as voice of the mannequin or even more realistically 'wearing' a part task trainer or even simpler simulation device)?
4 *Supporting staff*: what support will be offered when requested and how rapidly that assistance will appear. Will this vary depending upon student competence?
5 *Simulation environment*: where is the simulation going to be set? The fifth year sessions are set in the Medical Admissions Unit, wards or emergency department. The set therefore has to be manipulated to be as close to this

as possible. Equipment available should match that in reality as closely as possible. It is also possible in some circumstances to use a specially adapted part of the real setting. Many of Roger Kneebone's publications about simulation consider ways of increasing authenticity.

6   *Style of debrief*: in the fifth year sessions we code performance based upon both clinical and human factors elements. This allows for a targeted video debrief which facilitates **reflective practice**.

All of these considerations must be scripted and discussed by facilitators prior to the student arriving. This requires training, provided on site by permanent clinical simulation technicians and through faculty development courses.

Practice

Fifth year students attend three sessions within the Oncology, Skills and Simulation block. They are provided with the required knowledge prior to the session either via a lecture or through an interactive mobile learning package delivered through their tablet device. The session is run with six to eight students attending at a time, allowing practice in groups of three or four. The design of the simulation centre facilitates observation through one-way glass with audio feed, in a separate debriefing room. This enables students to observe and assist with debriefing their colleagues. Students are pre-briefed as to what to expect and are given an orientation to the mannequin and simulator.

During the simulation, authenticity and thus immersion is increased through the use of smell ('fart' spray/stink bombs), sight (fake vomit/blood/make-up) and audio (patient microphone and telephone connected to the control room). This is important to enable learning about human factors. The authenticity should be as high as possible to create the greatest opportunity for immersion in the simulation, thereby increasing **validity** and **reliability**. Students gain feedback 'in' action on their management through the alteration of the mannequin and its physiology.

Debrief

Feedback 'on' action is the single most important feature of simulation-based practice. Feedback also appears to slow the decay of acquired skills and allows learners to self-assess and thus monitor their own progress toward the acquisition of skills and behaviours. Feedback encourages looking at 'how' the student behaved/managed the patient. It is equally important to look at the 'why', which is better uncovered through the style of debrief (Fanning, 2007). In the student sessions, all feedback/debrief is **formative**. Several behavioural marking scores such as the surgical NOTSS (Non-Technical Skills for Surgeons) have been developed (http://www.abdn.ac.uk/iprc/notss), although some question their predictive validity, reliability and feasibility (Sharma et al., 2011).

Conclusion

Laurillard comments that learning is not only the responsibility of the teacher to create the conditions in which understanding is possible, but it is also the students' responsibility to take advantage of the opportunity (Laurillard, 1993). Student feedback from sessions is incredibly positive. Not only do they gain simulated experience in dealing with acutely ill patients, but they also start to develop an understanding of teams, the principles of leadership and follow-ership, along with the importance of situational awareness and the traps of task focus. With such importance attached to patient safety, the introduction of 'human factors' to students should heighten their awareness within the clinical situation. Simulation that strengthens cognitive awareness of personal behaviour is key to increasing reflective practice, which is the cornerstone of good medical practice. As such, simulation is a core part of a curriculum that teaches ethics and law, communication skills, safe prescribing, patient-centred practice and clinical knowledge.

(Sarah Wood, Jacky Hanson, Mike Dickinson and Mark Pimblett,
Lancashire Teaching Hospitals NHS Foundation Trust)

Interrogating practice

- What are the costs and benefits of high fidelity simulation?
- Where could you increase the use of simulation in your practice and what resources would be required?
- What experience(s) have you had delivering or receiving feedback on directly observed practice? Were there benefits to you as learner or tutor?
- Think of experiences you have had when human factors contributed to a poor or a good outcome. Might prior simulated practice and its emphasis on reflection and debriefing have helped mitigate poor or support good outcomes?

CONTINUOUS ASSESSMENT AND THE DEVELOPMENT OF PROFESSIONAL COMPETENCE

Case study 27.2 illustrates how technology-supported approaches can be blended into a fully integrated 'assessment for learning strategy' (see Chapter 8), and used to develop professional competence in dental undergraduates. Such approaches can provide a personalised, valid, full transferable portfolio able to inform postgraduate development. They also capture the assessment of both technical and human factors skills. The case study therefore has applicability across the two specialities and in other health-related professions.

Case study 27.2: Developing professional competence using integrated technology-supported approaches in dentistry – LIFTUPP

Context

Dental education represents a perfect case study to develop professional competence because upon graduation dentists are required to be able to undertake independent practice. Until recently, dentistry embraced the traditional model of clinical education, which establishes the development of professional competence through appropriate attainment in only two domains, namely clinical skills and knowledge. Furthermore, these domains have been traditionally assessed in isolation leading to a student graduating 'knowing a lot', and 'being able to do a lot', but not necessarily knowing 'why they do it'.

Modern concepts define professional competence as 'the habitual and judicious use of communication, knowledge, technical skills, clinical reasoning, emotions, values, and reflection in daily practice for the benefit of the individual and community being served' (Epstein and Hundert, 2002).

This definition highlights the need for assessment across multiple domains and is one that has been embraced by the General Dental Council (GDC, 2011, 2012). 'Standards for Education' (GDC, 2012) states the educational requirements a provider must demonstrate in order to make their programme 'sufficient'. Standard 3, Requirement 16 states:

> To award the qualification, providers must be assured that students have demonstrated attainment across the full range of learning outcomes, at a level sufficient to indicate they are safe to begin practice. This assurance should be underpinned by a coherent approach to aggregation and triangulation…
>
> (GDC, 2012)

Overall, addressing these stakeholder requirements presents multifaceted challenges in curricula and assessment, which by implication brings the need for reform and innovation in educational philosophy, educational approaches and curriculum management.

Objectives

To address these challenges, our objective was to create a learning design that could:

1   Demonstrate student attainment and understanding in all of the outcomes required (including professionalism) in a way that was objective, defensible, reliable and acceptable to all stakeholders;
2   Provide a system for holistic skills development and progression by altering learner self-regulation through appropriate feedback and real-time access to personal developmental data;
3   Allow for reliable gathering of student clinical data in extended clinical environments;
4   Facilitate programme development, staff development and external inspection;
5   Provide a dedicated portfolio that highlighted the continuing training needs of the new graduate, as well as producing a new graduate who is aware of their own training needs;
6   Allow for rapid integration and triangulation of existing Bachelor of Dental Surgery (BDS) curricula, including systems of assessment; and
7   Be grounded in current best pedagogical practices.

It became clear that the only solution was to use technology-supported learning.

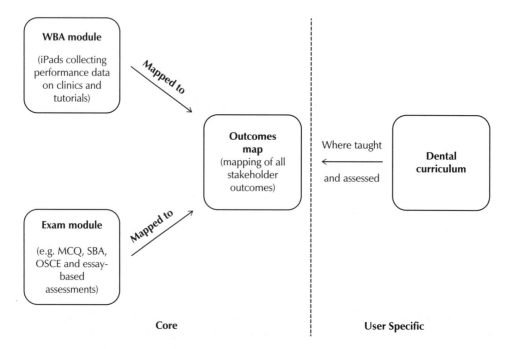

Figure 27.1 Simple representation of the Learning Design and how it relates to the core and individual curriculum

The Learning Design

The design comprised the Core and the User-Specific curriculum (Figure 27.1). The Core began with an Outcomes Map, containing a relational database of the requirements of all the stakeholders in dentistry, including the GDC and the QAA. Two bespoke modules were then aligned to this map: a web-based Exam Module to run paper-based examinations, comprising an examination database and a sophisticated quality assurance cycle; and a Work-Based Assessment (WBA) Module designed to capture the best practice in clinical assessments, based on iPads. Crucially, all the questions in both modules are aligned in a relational database to the Outcomes Map. Sitting off the Core is the User-Specific Curriculum, which is 'plugged in' to the Outcomes Map by identifying where any required stakeholder outcomes (including postgraduate) are taught and assessed.

The fundamental aspect of this learning design is full integration, which could only be realistically achieved through the use of technology. All clinical assessment, knowledge-based assessment, stakeholder outcomes and curricula are mapped together in a relational database. In this way, a detailed curriculum map can be automatically generated showing where any stakeholder outcomes are delivered, even down to individual exam questions and specific parts of WBAs. Full portfolios can be created based on triangulated holistic performance against key outcomes, rather than independent print outs of exam results and number of treatments carried out. A web-based interface was created to allow students and staff instant access to timetables, longitudinal performance activity, portfolios, detailed feedback and comparator data all in one integrated place.

iPads and assessing professional competence

Prior to this project, student clinical data were collected as paper records and were considered in isolation from other domains. Often these data represented single spot assessments and it was impossible to deduce continuous longitudinal performance. In order to design a solution, we did not wish to simply translate existing paper WBA forms onto tablet devices (iPads); we wanted to be innovative using technology. Using mobile technologies and a database, WBA could be continuous and triangulated on all clinics, and so we no longer needed to complete the whole WBA, for example we could just continuously and longitudinally record some of the stages of the Direct Observed Procedure (DOPs) seen on that occasion because, with time, the database structure would assemble the full picture. Furthermore, all the traditional WBA formats could be desegregated from their pure forms and split into individual observations to test understanding, for example one aspect of the Case Based Discussion that we handled in isolation is 'justification for, and knowledge of appropriate Special investigations'. This change in format meant that multiple students could be assessed simultaneously with a single iPad. Moreover, we also developed a six-point scoring system based on developing learner independence (Crossley et al., 2011), referred to as 'developmental need indicators'. When combined with the desegregated WBA approach, and the ability for each student to see their personalised longitudinal data, the developmental need indicators acted to give the learners high levels of specific **feedback** that enabled them to address required changes to their self-regulation (Butler and Winne, 1995) and develop in the areas needed through deliberate practice (Ericsson, 2004). A further advantage of this approach is that because we were now collecting upwards of 3,000 data points per student from multiple staff, over multiple clinics, we were able to make highly defensible decisions over progression, as well as monitor how individual members of staff were assessing students. This later feature enabled us to undertake targeted training for staff to reduce the effects of marking bias that have frequently plagued WBA approaches.

One of the most important features of the system is collecting continuous multi-assessor data through the iPads. To illustrate, consider the assessment of professionalism. This is an area where there is not even an agreed definition, a situation that makes the assessment of professionalism difficult. However, if there are data from a number of individuals, who have adjudged the student to be professional on multiple occasions in different settings, then the accumulation and use of expert opinion is a process that is defensible in law under the doctrine of *Stare Decisis* (Shapiro et al., 2002). Further, data collected are pushed from the iPads to the server over Wi-Fi after each and every clinic, regardless of location. The data from this and the Exam Module are automatically collated to produce a valid and transferable skills portfolio against the required stakeholder outcomes.

Choice of platform

The web was chosen to run the Exam Module and the interface to allow maximum user access. The WBA Module required a portable, Wi-Fi-enabled electronic device to allow staff to assess clinical ability across multiple centres and encourage staff to assess multiple students concurrently as they moved about the clinic. The iPad was chosen in 2010, primarily because it was the only tablet available of a sensible size. However, the iPad brought with it a number of useful security features, such as encryption and remote wiping.

Evaluation and impact

Enhancing teaching and learning

The enhancement of teaching and learning has been evidenced for both students and staff. From the student perspective, we have moved from a system where clinical competence was frequently measured on the basis of a prescriptive number of tasks to be completed, for example you must undertake

50 fillings, to one that is based on personal quality, consistency, range of experience and demonstrable evidence of student reflection following feedback. Moreover, there has been a positive change in student independence and evidence of their striving to attain it, as witnessed through an improvement in personal action plans and student performance in assessments. From the staff perspective, there has been a noticeable change in attitude to the value of feedback and its format of delivery, as well as the importance of giving students accurate feedback, rather than avoiding it through not wanting to 'upset' or 'demotivate'. This change has been reflected in simple analyses of staff calibration data and written feedback comments given to students, but a number of surveys will be conducted to more fully understand the magnitude of these changes.

A further area of educational impact has resulted from access to large quantities of data. Whereas before there were a number of end of year assessments and some 'spot clinical tests', there are now thousands of data points per student. This is an active area of research and we are developing algorithms to look at the developing patterns of performance and give students early interceptive feedback of their need to make changes. Furthermore, early data suggest that it may be possible to predict the number of sessions needed for the learner to achieve the required standard, opening the possibilities for reactive timetabling. One demonstrable outcome, thus far, has been our ability to defend progress decisions at all levels. The triangulated longitudinal data was so robust that the university was able to support the decisions, even in areas of professionalism.

Advantages and challenges

The advantages have been manifold, and are further reaching than simply fulfilling the stakeholder requirements. Students now leave the University of Liverpool Dental School with a valid, fully transferable **portfolio**. This highlights quality and consistency across all domains and outlines areas where students may need further experience. One of the most beneficial advantages has been in curriculum management. Programme leads can now triangulate exam and clinical performance together in an unprecedented way to recognise which outcomes are not being met, and hence which parts of the curriculum have potential weakness. Clinical data collection is now instantaneous and hence analyses can be carried out at any time. This enables staff to analyse performance, highlight weakness and provide targeted training at multiple points through the year. Assessment setting with integrated **blueprinting** has become simple, as all questions are aligned to outcomes. A bespoke quality assurance cycle and exam setting system have also ensured a question bank of a high quality. Financially, we estimate that the approach has saved the work of one administrator and two clinical teachers, amounting to a saving of approximately £120k per annum in the school alone. Further savings are made across the university due to the simplicity in gaining evidence for Progress and Fitness to Practice decisions, and of course paper saving.

The main challenge has been encouraging clinical staff to change their teaching practice. The iPad application itself required very little training, but ensuring staff used a consistent marking system and gave appropriate feedback proved to be an ongoing issue. The data provided by the project certainly helps to identify outliers and hence improve the quality assurance of the system. One of the unexpected challenges has been the difficulty of having so much data and how to present it in a simple and meaningful way. There has been no roadmap for how to interpret complex patterns of data and so we are currently devising methods of analysing student performance across multiple areas.

There were inevitable security challenges as the iPad app had been designed to collect patient hospital number, date of birth, gender and ethnicity. These data points were felt to be important because they would not only allow demonstration of the student experience over patient mix, but also enable longitudinal research over changing patient flows and disease change. In order to adhere to NHS concerns over Clinical Governance, iPads were set up to be encrypted and remotely wiped. Further, the clinics 'own' the iPads, rather than the staff or the students, and therefore no iPads (and hence data) ever leave our control.

Measuring impact

The most dramatic effect has been in the **National Student Survey (NSS)**. This independent survey is completed by final year graduates, and in the section of 'Assessment and Feedback', student satisfaction has improved by almost 30 per cent over the last five years. There are a number of focus group studies being undertaken to understand the teaching and learning impact on staff and students, along with a number of quantitative data analysis studies to develop better algorithms for progression analysis. There is also an intention to liaise with the postgraduate sector to further refine the transferable skills portfolio.

Future developments

The learning design has become known as the Longitudinal Integrative Fully Transferable Undergraduate to Postgraduate Portfolio (LIFTUPP). Eight out of 16 UK dental schools will shortly be using LIFTUPP, opening the possibility for national standards in assessment and massive exam question and data sharing to enable better training of dentists in the future. In theory, the LIFTUPP learning design is appropriate to any situation where it is necessary to demonstrate that individual learning outcomes have been met, and a transferable portfolio is needed.

(Luke Dawson, Ben Mason, Colette Balmer,
Liverpool Dental Hospital, Liverpool; Phil Jimmieson,
Computer Science Dept., University of Liverpool)

Interrogating practice

- Have you considered what 'professionalism' means in medicine, dentistry or other healthcare professional education?
- What are the costs and benefits of continuous assessment in higher education?
- How could mobile technology allow better assessment of professionalism in your higher education context?
- Is the triangulation and aggregation of all assessment data against outcomes a more reliable measure of readiness for practice than finals examinations?

ADDRESSING VARIATION IN LEARNING OPPORTUNITIES

In this final section, we explore in Case study 27.3 how issues such as geographically dispersed students and equitable treatment of students can be addressed through the introduction of a large-scale mobile learning (m-learning) technological solution to facilitate the more uniform delivery of the medical curriculum.

Case study 27.3: The use of m-learning at Manchester Medical School

Manchester Medical School (MMS) has the largest student population in the UK. From the third to the fifth years of the medical degree programme, students are based at one of four 'Health Education Zones' (HEZ). Each HEZ comprises a Teaching Hospital, the surrounding District General Hospitals and General Practices where students gain experience of clinical practice. This geographical distribution of the student community, in addition to unreliable access to learning materials at different locations, resulted in students being unable to optimise their learning opportunities within these clinical settings. We sought to both improve the student experience and make it more uniform. In doing this, there were a number of important implementation considerations:

Technological

- Devices: which to select and how to address security in the clinical workplace?
- Wi-Fi: how to address the reliable provision of Wi-Fi at multiple National Health Service (NHS) institutions?

Educational

- What learning materials are required and how should they be produced?
- How can the implementation be evaluated?

Solving the technological challenges

Due to the lack of availability of dependable mobile devices in 2011, each third year student was loaned an Apple iPad2 tablet for the duration of their degree, which was then gifted to them on their graduation. The devices were configured by the Faculty of Medical and Human Sciences IT Services with security features that included an obligatory passcode and the deletion of all information from the tablet following ten incorrect attempts. Code of conduct agreements were signed by students upon receipt of the tablets and information governance was additionally addressed through agreements with each participating NHS institution.

A dramatic improvement in Wi-Fi connectivity across the participating NHS institutions was seen following the introduction of the iPads to the student community. The number of hospitals with full Wi-Fi coverage improved from four in December 2011 to 18 out of 19 hospitals by July 2013.

Enhancing the educational benefit

Our students needed to be able to reliably access standardised resources and learning materials to complement the curricular content as required. They – and we – were concerned with parity of experience and equitable access. This was a major issue in such a distributed learning environment. The use of mobile technology facilitated the provision of:

- Bespoke, interactive m-learning packages created by MMS learning technologists working with clinical staff – these can be viewed from any operating system and not exclusively on an iPad;
- A video library of lectures, which can be downloaded for offline viewing when Internet access is unavailable;
- Access to downloadable applications (Apps), such as BMJ Best Practice and the British National Formulary (BNF);
- A wide range of electronic downloadable texts covering most of the required reading for the programme;
- Electronically distributed forms replacing the need for paper-based forms, for example evaluation, feedback, assessment, etc.;
- Centrally managed timetabling pushed directly to users' devices; and
- An electronic portfolio, skills and patient case logging.

These actions have opened up a huge array of resources that students can access to complement their studies according to their own needs and learning styles. These include:

- Access to the Apple App store containing a vast collection of medical resources from reference resources, medical calculators, 3D anatomy applications, etc.;
- Access to productivity Apps, such as note-taking, mind mapping, spreadsheets, presentation applications, as well as reference management tools available at all times;
- Video resources from the wider Internet but also instructional videos provided by the institution;
- Access to eBook publications with the ability to annotate and create learning aids, such as Flash cards for revision; and
- Access to new Apps designed to push content to users, such as abstracts and indeed downloadable journal papers;

In addition, benefits to teaching and learning resources include:

- The use of emerging and increasingly sophisticated student response systems to improve student interaction in previously didactic sessions;
- The production of multimedia texts and resources by teachers, for example Prescribing skills handbooks, Assessment handbooks, Clinical Neurology and Anatomy to date. (These texts have been made available free of charge to a worldwide audience. The books themselves contain interactive elements, as well as video, audio and formative assessment elements);
- The increasing use of video conferencing for institutional meetings and student support when face-to-face meetings are not possible at short notice; and
- The use of inbuilt video cameras for use in recording, for example in communication sessions and simulation in order to provide accurate and meaningful feedback on student performance.

This plethora of resources and innovations has created almost infinite possibilities for students and tutors. The flexible learning pedagogy allows students to access resources whenever and wherever they wish, and in addition they are able to select resources that best suit their needs and learning preferences.

As with any new intervention, a thorough evaluation is essential to ensure a continuous cycle of improvement. The MMS m-technology multidisciplinary research group has been established for this purpose. To date, three surveys, due for publication in 2014, have been completed exploring the impact of this iPad introduction on student learning and further research is ongoing.

The benefits of this approach

Students now have the opportunity, afforded through mobile devices, to take advantage of learning materials as required, permitting them to optimise how they spend their working time and access 'just-in-time' learning experiences. The rapid and almost ubiquitous access to mobile devices means that students who are not part of an institutional provision such as this can still have access to this myriad of resources. Institutions should recognise this and ensure their students are accessing the best possible peer reviewed resources rather than accept the existence of an informal 'hidden' mobile curriculum (Ellaway, 2014).

The success of this implementation is due in no small part to its scale. A pilot trial could not have achieved the same results, for example neither the significantly improved Wi-Fi at NHS institutions distributed across North West England, nor the integration of the tablet devices into the students' daily lives through instilling their sense of ownership, could have been achieved.

In conclusion, this large-scale m-technology implementation has facilitated and standardised the provision of bespoke, required learning resources to enhance curricular delivery for a geographically distributed population of students.

(Jane Mooney and Tim Cappelli, Manchester Medical School)

For further information, see UCISA Best Practice Guide, *Mobile learning: How mobile technologies can enhance the learning experience* (http://www.ucisa.ac.uk/publications/effective_use.aspx)

Interrogating practice

- Could the implementation of a similar approach by your institution help to enhance the student experience?
- What technological and educational considerations do you consider would be key in successful implementation in your context?
- Can you think of other ways to make the most of these technologies in an educational or healthcare setting?
- What challenges are posed by this shift in the way educational resources are accessed?
- Why do you think such technological advances are described as 'disruptive technologies'?

CONCLUSIONS AND OVERVIEW

Medicine and dentistry provide unique challenges to the newly qualified educator. Changing public attitudes to these professions, regulation by professional bodies and a recent history of high profile malpractice have only served to heighten challenges. The practice of these professions is therefore changing, and education for that practice must change too. This chapter does not attempt to cover the full gamut of applicable educational approaches and issues, rather it references other chapters and focuses on how technology is helping to address these challenges. It does this by presenting three case studies that discuss relevant educational and professional issues, as well as being brief 'how to' guides. The case studies highlight how simulation can aid students to be better equipped for practice on graduation (including both technical and 'human factor' elements); how required learning outcomes can be better mapped and assessed across the curriculum and in a variety of settings; and how student learning in situations of diverse opportunity can be enhanced as well as made more uniform. Thus the case studies address key issues to enhance student learning and outcomes and show how higher education can better demonstrate that required outcomes have been achieved. While these issues and solutions to them are of particular interest to medicine and dentistry, many of them have applicability elsewhere in higher education.

REFERENCES

Association of Surgeons of Great Britain and Ireland (ASGBI) (2010) *Patient Safety: A Consensus Statement, Friday 23rd October 2009 at the Royal Institute of Architects, London.* Available from: http://www.asgbi.org.uk/en/publications/consensus_statements.cfm (accessed 9 April 2014).

Butler, DL and Winne, PH (1995) 'Feedback and self-regulated learning: a theoretical synthesis', *Review of Educational Research*, 65(3): 245–281.

Crossley, J, Johnson, G, Booth, J and Wade, W (2011) 'Good questions, good answers: construct alignment improves the performance of workplace-based assessment scales,' *Medical Education*, 45(6): 560–569.

DeAnda, A and Gaba, DM (1990) 'Unplanned incidents during comprehensive anaesthetisa simulation', *Anesthesia & Analgesia*, 71(1): 77–82.

DeAnda, A and Gaba, DM (1991) 'Role of experience in the response to simulated critical incidents', *Anesthesia & Analgesia*, 72(3): 308–315.

Ellaway, R (2014) 'The informal and hidden curricula of mobile device use in medical education', *Medical Teacher*, 36(1): 89–91.

Epstein, RM and Hundert, EM (2002) 'Defining and assessing professional competence', *Journal of the American Medical Association*, 287(2): 226–235.

Ericsson, KA (2004) 'Deliberate practice and the acquisition and maintenance of expert performance in medicine and related domains', *Academic Medicine*, 79(10): S70–S81.

Francis Report (2013) Available from: http://www.nhsemployers.org/The-Francis-Inquiry/Pages/Francis.aspx (accessed 23 January 2014).

Feather, A and Fry, H (2009) 'Key aspects of teaching and learning in medicine and dentistry', in H Fry, S Ketteridge and S Marshall (eds.) *A Handbook for Teaching and Learning in Higher Education* (3rd edn.). London: Routledge, 424–448.

General Dental Council (GDC) (2011) *Preparing for Practice.* London: GDC.

General Dental Council (GDC) (2012) *Standards for Education.* London: GDC.

General Medical Council (GMC) (2009) *Tomorrow's Doctors.* Available from: http://www.gmc-uk.org/education/undergraduate/tomorrows_doctors_2009.asp (accessed 19 June 2014).

Health and Safety Executive (HSE) (1999) *Reducing Error and Influencing Behaviour.* HSG48, London: HSE Books.

Issenberg, SB, McGaghie, WC, Petrusa, ER, Gordon, DL and Scalese, RJ (2005) 'Features and uses of high fidelity medical simulations that lead to effective learning: a BEME systematic review', *Medical Teacher,* 27(1): 10–28. http://www.bemecollaboration.org/Published+Reviews/BEME+Guide+No+4/ (accessed 27 January 2014).

Kneebone, R (2003) 'Simulation in surgical training: educational issues and practical implications', *Medical Education,* 37(3): 267–277.

Laurillard, D (1993) *Rethinking University Teaching. A Framework for the Effective Use of Educational Technology.* London and New York: Routledge.

Shapiro, M and Sweet, AS (2002) *On Law, Politics, and Judicialization.* New York, NY: Oxford University Press.

Sharma, B, Mishra, A, Aggarwal, R and Grantcharov, TP (2011) 'Non-technical skills assessment in surgery', *Surgical Oncology,* 20(3): 169–177.

World Health Organization (WHO) (2009) *Patient Safety Curriculum Guide for Medical Schools.* Available from: http://www.who.int/patientsafety/education/curriculum/EN_PSP_Education_Medical_Curriculum/en/ (accessed 23 January 2014).

Glossary

This glossary provides two types of information. First, it provides the reader with simple explanations and definitions of technical and educational terms used in the disciplines covered in this book. Second, it provides a dictionary of many commonly used abbreviations and acronyms. The glossary has been carefully assembled by the editors. In the text, the first mention in each chapter of a glossary item appears in **bold**. The entries reflect current usage in higher education in the UK.

academic practice Term used to describe the collective responsibilities of academic staff in higher education, namely those for teaching, learning and communicating the subject, discipline-specific research/scholarship, enterprise, academic management activities and for some service requirements.

access course A qualification (Diploma) for non-traditional, usually mature, students as a route into higher education and recognised by the QAA.

accreditation Certified as meeting required standards (e.g. an accredited programme is one that has been approved by an external body as meeting certain standards or criteria).

achievement motivation A desire to succeed at a task (e.g. obtaining high grades, even when the task does not inspire interest (*see also* extrinsic motivation, intrinsic motivation).

achieving approach to learning *See* strategic approach.

action learning An approach to learning involving individuals working on real projects with the support of a group (set) which meets regularly to help members reflect on their experience and to plan next actions.

active learning Process of engaging with the learning task at both the cognitive and affective level.

activity theory Analysing activity (especially in the workplace) as a complex phenomenon that is socially situated. May be used in relation to learning and teaching (*see also* situated learning).

adult learning theory   A range of theories and constructs claimed to relate specifically to how adults learn. Includes self-directed learning. Much of the work on reflection and experiential learning is also part of this area. Concerns over validity of some of the theories and that some aspects are not distinctly applicable to adults.

affective domain   One of the major areas of learning, the learning of values.

aims (learning aims)   At the top of the hierarchy of descriptions commonly used to define a learning experience. They are intended to provide the student, teacher and other interested parties with an understanding of the most overarching general statements regarding the intended consequences of a learning experience (*see also* objectives, learning outcomes).

amotivation   Absence of tangible motivation.

andragogy   The theory of adult learning, associated with the work of Malcolm Knowles.

AP(E)L   Accreditation of prior learning. Taking into account previous 'certificated' learning gained either as a whole or part of a programme, towards all or part of a new qualification. Also the counting of experience (experiential) towards obtaining a qualification.

appraisal (as used in higher education) also **performance appraisal**   A formal, regular, developmental process in which the one being appraised is encouraged to review and reflect upon performance in the workplace. Usually based on a focused interview with a peer, head of department or line manager. At the interview, objectives (linked to strategic aims of the department) are set and development needs identified. Performance against these objectives is reviewed at the next appraisal interview.

approaches to learning   *See* deep, surface and strategic approaches to learning.

approaches to studying inventory   A device used to identify student approach to study.

Asperger's Syndrome   Severe and sustained impairment in social interaction, and the development of restrictive, repetitive patterns of behaviour.

assessment   Measurement of the achievement and progress of the learner (NB wider definition in North America).

asynchronous learning   A student-centred teaching method that uses online learning resources to facilitate information sharing outside the constraints of time and place among a network of people

atomistic learners   An approach to learning building up from fine-grained factual information and detail, sometimes these learners may lose sight of the 'big picture' and implications for understanding concepts and theory (*see also* holistic learners).

auditory learning   Learning by using auditory materials and hearing (*see also* kinaesthetic learning, visual learning).

authentic teaching/assessment   Situating teaching and assessment in real world issues, problems and applications.

autonomy (of student learning)   Commonly refers to students taking more responsibility for and control of themselves and their learning, including being less spoon-fed. May also include elements of students taking more responsibility for determining and directing the content of their learning (*see* engagement).

blended learning   A mix of face-to-face and online learning.

blueprinting (of assessment)   Ensures that assessment tasks adequately sample what the student is expected to have learned.

Bologna Magna Charta Universitatum   Dating back to 1988, a document signed by 430 European universities, pledging to reform structures of their institutions in a convergent manner, towards a common framework of comparable degrees to include 'diploma supplement' (HEAR in the UK), quality assurance and elimination of obstacles to mobility of students and staff. More countries have since become signatories.

buddying scheme   A peer support scheme in which support for new students is provided by existing (more senior) students.

buzz group   A small group activity, typically within a large group, in which students work together on a short problem, task or discussion. So called because of the noise the activity generates.

case method   A group learning activity in which students are presented with a case study depicting a genuine business scenario. They identify the business problems and ways they might be addressed through enquiry and analysis. Primarily facilitated rather than directly taught.

code of practice   A series of system-wide expectations covering an area, usually based on accepted best practice, often set by regulatory bodies.

cognitive domain   The major area of learning in most disciplines, to do with knowledge, understanding and thinking.

communities of practice   The community is made up of those who share common understandings and practices (e.g. in a discipline) and who may extend or create knowledge by virtue of shared practices and discussion (e.g. in the case of those working in the profession).

competence   Most contemporary use in education relates to performing a task or series of tasks, with debate over how far such activities also require underpinning knowledge and understanding. (1) May be used generically to mean demonstrated achievement with respect to any clearly defined set of outcomes. (2) Is used to indicate both a high level of achievement and just acceptable level of activity. (3) Something that a person in a given occupational area should be able to do.

concept definition   The form of words that specifies the concept (e.g. its formal definition).

concept image   An individual's set of mental pictures, processes and properties that they associate with a concept.

constructive alignment   Ensuring, at least, learning outcomes, teaching methods, learning activities and assessment are compatible with each other.

constructivist   A number of theories attempting to explain how human beings learn. Characterised by the idea of addition to, and amendment of, previous understanding or knowledge. Without such change, learning is not thought to occur. Theories of reflection and experiential learning belong to this school.

core skills   *See* transferable skills.

course This term is used to refer to both smaller sized units of study (modules) and, confusingly, to larger units encompassing a set of modules which comprise a programme of study (*see also* module, programme).

credit accumulation and transfer (CATS) Assigning a numerical value to a portion of learning, based on a number of notional learning hours earning one credit point. Thus modules can be said to be worth 30 credits and rated at say level 7 (Masters). Used as a currency for purposes of transfer and equivalence (*see also* ECTS).

crit (critique) A form of formative and/or summative assessment widely used in art and design. Usually conducted orally and led by the learner's input.

criterion-referenced assessment Judges how well a learner has performed by comparison with predetermined criteria.

critical incident (analysis) An event that, when reflected on, yields information resulting in learning from experience.

critical thinking (thinker) Critical thinking is the attempt to ask and answer questions systematically using words like what, who, where, when, how and why and phrases such as what if, what next, taking the process through description, analysis and evaluation.

de-centering Delegating responsibility for the approaches to the locality where the expertise is situated.

deductive teaching/learning Working from general premises. (In language teaching, presenting grammar rules in isolation and encouraging learners to generate specific examples based on the rules.)

deep approach to learning Learning that attempts to relate ideas together to understand underpinning theory and concepts, and to make meaning out of material under consideration (*see also* surface approach, strategic approach).

degree-awarding powers (DAP) Powers awarded to higher education providers to allow them legally to award UK degrees (and hold university title) and recognised by UK authorities (UK and Scottish Parliaments, Welsh and Northern Ireland Assemblies). Such providers hold overall responsibility for academic standards and quality of the qualification. QAA advises government on DAP and university title.

DELNI Department for Employment and Learning in Northern Ireland (http://www.delni.gov.uk).

diagnostic test A test used (possibly at the start of an undergraduate module) to identify weaknesses (e.g. in grammatical knowledge or numeracy), with a view to addressing these in a more focused manner.

didactic teaching A style that is teacher-centred – often prescriptive, formulaic and based on transmission.

disciplinary specificity Characteristics of a discipline that affect what one can do when teaching it; comprising socio-cultural and epistemological characteristics of the discipline.

distance learning Learning away from the institution, as exemplified by the Open University. Most often, students work with learning resource materials that can be paper-based, on videotape, available on broadcast TV or accessed online. Nowadays, all the opportunities afforded by technology (e.g. interaction) are used.

domain   A particular area (type) of learning. Much associated with categorising learning outcomes and the use of hierarchical taxonomies within each domain. Considerable dispute on the number and range of domains and the hierarchies of learning within them. The original three domains identified are cognitive, affective and psychomotor.

dyslexia   A specific learning disability that manifests primarily as a difficulty with written language, particularly reading and spelling. The most common disability in higher education.

EMI/Q (extended matching item/question)   A written assessment (e.g. testing diagnostic investigation and reasoning). Each question has a theme from which lists of possible answers are placed in alphabetical order. The candidate is instructed to choose the best matching answer(s) to each of a series of scenarios, results, etc.

employability   A set of achievements, skills, understandings and personal attributes that make graduates more likely to gain employment and be successful in their chosen occupations.

engagement   *See* student engagement.

European Credit Transfer System (ECTS)   A standard system for describing student attainment in HE across the European Union based on 60 ECTS credits for one year full-time study. In England, Wales and Northern Ireland, 2 credits = 1ECTS (*see also* credit accumulation, transfer).

evaluation   Quantitative and qualitative judgement of the curriculum, and its delivery, to include teaching (NB different usage in North America).

experiential learning   Learning from doing. Often represented by the Kolb Learning Cycle.

external examiner/examining   External examiners are part of UK universities' self-regulatory procedures and play a key role in maintaining standards between institutions in a particular discipline. Usually distinguished members of the profession who have the respect of colleagues and students alike. For taught courses, they typically act for a fixed term. They play a similar role in examination of postgraduate dissertations and theses, leading discussion in viva voce examinations. Forms a key part of quality assurance processes.

extrinsic motivation   Typifies students who are concerned with the grades they achieve, external rewards, and whether they will gain approval from others (*see also* Achievement motivation, Intrinsic motivation).

facilitator   As opposed to teacher, tutor or mentor, a role to encourage individuals to take responsibility for their own learning through the facilitation of this process.

fair (of assessment)   Fair with respect to (1) consistency between different markers; (2) transparency and openness of criteria and procedures; and (3) procedures that do not disadvantage any group of learners in the cohort.

FAQ   Frequently asked question.

feedback   Oral or written developmental advice on 'performance' so that the recipient has a better understanding of expected values, standards or criteria and can improve their performance (*see also* formative assessment, feedforward).

feedforward   Refers to information about student work and progress that focuses on future actions rather than past mistakes. The purpose of feedforward is to ensure that feedback clearly informs students' future learning.

fieldtrip/fieldwork   Practical or experimental work away from the university designed to develop practical skills (e.g. observation of natural environments), which may be for a single session or coherent period of study lasting several days. Most common in life and environmental sciences, geography, civil engineering and construction.

flexible learning   Often used interchangeably with the term 'open learning', but may be distinguished from it by the inclusion of more traditional modes of delivery (such as the lecture). Designed to ease student access and choice.

flipped lecture   Lectures that are premised on the understanding that students will have done all the preparation (e.g. reading, group work, question formulation, watched screencast lecture) beforehand, so that they come to the timetabled (lecture) session prepared to enter into interactive work around the preparatory work. The lecturer then focuses on the learning process and the areas where students need more help or testing understanding.

focus group   A technique for pooling thoughts, ideas and perceptions to ensure equal participation by all members of a group. Requires a facilitator. Some versions of the method aim to obtain a consensus view, others the weight and thrust of opinion. More accurately called nominal group technique.

formative assessment   Assessment that is used to help teachers and learners gauge the strengths and weaknesses of the learners' performance while there is still time to take action for improvement. Typically, it is expressed in words rather than marks or grades. Information about learners may be used diagnostically (*see* summative assessment).

foundation degree   Two-year vocational degree to level 5. May be topped up for the award of Bachelor's degree (level 6).

Framework of Higher Education Qualifications   *See* level and QAA.

franchising arrangements   Where an institution outsources authority and responsibility, through a legally binding agreement, for aspects of university provision, for example accreditation or responsibility for recruiting teaching staff.

G20 countries   A forum set up in 1999 to bring about cooperation and consultation across the 20 major economies of the world.

General Dental Council (GDC)   The UK professional body that regulates (and registers) all dental professionals in the country. Protects the public from unqualified dental professionals (http://www.gdc-uk.org) (*see also* professional bodies).

General Medical Council (GMC)   The UK professional body that regulates (and registers) doctors and ensures good medical practice. Promotes and maintains the health and safety of the public by ensuring proper standards in medical practice (http://www.gmc-uk.org) (*see also* professional bodies).

global learners   Learners who situate their problem solving within the wider context of the world at large, thus developing higher level knowledge, understanding and critical thinking skills.

graduate attributes   The distinctive qualities, skills and understandings that each university considers its students will have on successful completion of their studies.

graduate demonstrators/teaching assistants (GTAs)   Typically doctoral students who assist with teaching (e.g. facilitating seminars or demonstrating in laboratories/ workshops).

grounded theory   A term used originally by B. Glaser and A. Straus (*The Discovery of Grounded Theory: Strategies for Quantitative Research*, Chicago, IL: Aldine, 1967) to describe a research method in which theory or models are developed systematically from data rather than the opposite way around.

HE   Higher education

HEA   Higher Education Academy (http://www.heacademy.ac.uk).

HEAR   Higher Education Achievement Report (http://www.hear.ac.uk).

HEFCE   Higher Education Funding Council for England (http://www.hefce.ac.uk).

HEFW   Higher Education Funding Council for Wales. (Gyngor Cyllido Addysg Uwch Cymru) (http://www.hefcw.ac.uk).

HESA   Higher Education Statistical Agency (http://www.hesa.ac.uk).

Higher Education Review   A periodic process managed by the QAA to inform students and the public whether a provider meets the expectations of the higher education sector for (1) setting and/or maintenance of academic standards; (2) the provision of learning opportunities and (3) information; and (4) the enhancement of the quality of students' learning opportunities (*see also* UK Quality Code).

holistic learners   An approach to learning in which learners start from the 'big picture' and may not always realise that some processing of finer-grained information and detail is necessary to understand and apply concepts and theory (*see also* atomistic learning).

immersion learning   Student interaction with authentic language through long periods of exposure to the second language.

independent learning (study)   Often used interchangeably with the terms 'open learning', 'self-directed learning' and 'autonomous learning'. Has a flavour of all these terms. Often associated with programmes of study created individually for each learner.

induction   Initial period of work or study during which basic information is provided through short courses, small group activities or one-to-one meetings. The purpose is to equip the students or staff members with background information so that they may become effective in their study or in their role as soon as possible.

inductive teaching/learning   Working from particular cases to general conclusions. (In languages, learners identify recurrent use and pattern in context and work towards the formulation of rules).

industrial placements   A learning experience offered to students to assist them to gain applied knowledge, understanding and skills through an extended period of time based in industry.

institutional review   *See* Higher Education Review.

instructor presence   A term popular in the US where it denotes the active and visible presence and participation of the instructor as a guiding hand in an online course.

International Student Barometer (ISB)   Student survey (questionnaire) that tracks students' expectations, perceptions and intentions across three areas – academic structure, student services, and infrastructure – to enable individual institutions to ascertain what is working well and not so well. Primarily aimed at international students. Commercial survey run by iGrad and customised to the needs of different institutions.

international students   Students who travel to a country different from their own for tertiary study. In the UK, international students are those other than 'home' students (who study in the UK and will be UK and EEC nationals).

internationalisation   Curriculum materials/design that include content and approaches to promote student awareness of working/living in different countries and aid employability in a global job market. Also used to refer to the diversity of staff and students.

interpersonal domain   One of the major areas of learning, the learning of behaviour involved in interacting with others.

intrinsic motivation   Typifies students who enjoy a challenge, want to master a subject, are curious and want to learn (*see also* achievement motivation, extrinsic motivation).

iterative learning   Learning to acquire high-level skills by practicing particular tasks over and over again.

iTunes   Popular music and video playback software by Apple. Also allows users to subscribe to podcasts.

IWB   Interactive whiteboard.

JAMES (Joint Audio Media Education Support)   A joint audio, media and educational support body, which provides links between the media industry and education, accreditation, and careers support and advice.

Jisc   Organisation which supports digital technologies for education and research at national level (http://www.jisc.ac.uk).

Jorum   A free online repository service for open educational resources produced by the UK further and higher education community (http://www.jorum.ac.uk).

key information set (KIS)   The KIS provides comparable sets of information (on the Unistats website) about full or part-time undergraduate courses. They contain the items of information that prospective students have identified as most important to inform their decisions (*see also* Unistats).

key/core/transferable/common skills   *See* transferable skills.

kinaesthetic learning or tactile learning   A learning style in which an individual's knowledge acquisition is enhanced by touching, manipulating or doing as distinct from listening, watching, reading or writing (*see also* visual learning, auditory learning, read/write learning).

laboratory/practical class   A type of teaching session, usually included in curricula in experimental sciences, biomedical sciences and engineering disciplines, which is broadly intended to offer training in techniques and learning how to carry out experimental investigations.

learning agreement/contract   A contract drawn up between teacher and learner, whereby each agrees to take on certain roles and responsibilities (e.g. the learner to hand in work on time and the teacher to return corrected work within a specified period of time). May specifically concern setting out the learning outcomes the learner undertakes to achieve.

learning and teaching strategy   What an institution, or parts of it, wishes to achieve with regard to learning and teaching, how it will achieve it and how it will know when it has succeeded.

learning centre   A centre to which students may go to gain support for their learning, for example using online resources.

learning community   *See* communities of practice.

learning cycle   Theory describing the stages of learning from concrete experience through reflection and generalisation to experiment towards new experience, often attributed to David Kolb.

learning log(book)   A journal in which learners record their reflections on learning activities.

learning objectives   *See* objectives.

learning outcomes (intended learning outcomes [ILO])   Specific statements that define the learning students are expected to have acquired on completion of a session, course, programme, module, or unit of study.

learning style   Used to describe how learners differ in their tendencies or preferences to learn. Recognises learning differences, a mix of personality and cognitive processes.

legitimate peripheral participation   Describes newcomers who later become experienced members and eventually old timers of a community of practice or collaborative project.

level (of award)/level descriptor   Used to describe a hierarchy of learning outcomes across all domains, usually in HE levels 4, 5 and 6 in undergraduate programmes and 7 (Masters) and 8 (doctoral). Most commonly follows classification from QAA (the Framework of Higher Education Qualifications).

licensing   A term often used synonymously with accreditation, especially in Europe. May also relate to 'license to practice' associated with some professions.

life skills   Psychosocial abilities that enable individuals to deal with challenges of everyday life, notably cognitive, personal and interpersonal skills.

lifelong learning   Learning from 'cradle to grave'. The modern world requires continuing professional development, constant updating and so on, irrespective of age.

MCQ   Multiple choice question.

mentor   A peer who supports and advises a new student or member of staff by helping him/her to adapt to institutional culture, acting as a sounding-board for ideas and encouraging reflection on practice.

meta-cognition   Refers to the processes that allow people to reflect on their own cognitive abilities, i.e. know what they know or to think about their thinking. It includes knowledge about when and how to use particular strategies for learning.

mixed skills teaching/testing   The integration of the four language skills (listening, speaking, reading and writing) in tasks that replicate real-life language use (e.g. relaying written stimuli orally, making a written note of a spoken message).

moderation   The process for assuring that grades awarded are fair and reliable and that marking criteria have been applied appropriately and consistently.

module   A discrete unit of study, credit-rated, assessed and part of a larger award-bearing programme of study. (The term 'course' is sometimes used interchangeably.)

MOOC   Massive Open Online Course

multimodal learning   A multimodal learning preference is a preferred way of learning new information or material that incorporates several different styles of learning. Different modes of learning are combined, such as visual and auditory.

National Committee of Inquiry into Higher Education (NCIHE)   The Dearing Committee, set up under Sir Ron (later Lord) Dearing by the Conservative Government in 1996 to make recommendations for the next twenty years about the purposes, shape, structure, size and funding of higher education. Reported in July 1997. The report commented on aspects such as organisation of programmes, quality matters, staff development and funding. Still influential.

National Science Foundation   A US independent agency of the federal government responsible for promotion of progress in science and engineering by supporting programmes of research and teaching.

National Student Survey (NSS)   An exit survey in the UK of final year undergraduate student satisfaction on their total student experience, widely translated into university league tables.

National Survey of Student Engagement (NSSE)   A student survey used in the US and Canada, but finding application in the UK now. Focuses on critical thinking, course challenge, collaborative learning and integration.

National Teaching Fellow (NTF) and **National Teaching Fellowship Scheme (NTFS)** A national award under the NTFS to an individual staff member (usually academic but also others in supporting roles) in an HEI in England, Wales or Northern Ireland to recognise excellence in teaching and facilitating student learning (*see also* HEA).

norm-referenced assessment   Judges how well the learner has done in comparison with the norm established by their peers.

NUS   National Union of Students (http://www.nus.org.uk).

objectives   Originally developed by educational psychologists and known as behavioural objectives. Definition and use have become less and less precise in recent years. Their meaning has ranged from exact, measurable outcomes of specific learning experiences to more generalised statements of learning outcomes. The term may be distinguished from or used interchangeably (but loosely) with the term 'learning outcomes'.

Offa   Office for Fair Access (http://www.offa.org.uk).

OIA   Office of the Independent Adjudicator (http://www.oihe.org.uk).

OMR (optical mark reader)   Special scanning device that can read carefully placed pencil marks on specially designed documents. OMRs have in the past been frequently used to score forms, questionnaires and answer-sheets.

open learning   Learning flexibly with regard to pace and location. Usually associated with delivery without a tutor being present. Will often allow learning in order of own choice, in a variety of media and may also imply no entry barriers (e.g. no prior qualifications).

open source   Describes software available for free distribution and whose source code is available for free modification by users.

oral examination   *See* viva voce examination.

OSCE (objective structured clinical examination)   Clinical assessment made up of a circuit of short tasks known as stations. Several variations on the basic theme exist. Typically, candidates pass through a station where an examiner grades them according to an itemised checklist or global rating scale.

OSLER (objective structured longer examination record)   Clinical assessment with some similarity to an OSCE, but involving one or more long case.

passive learning/approach   As opposed to active. Learning or an approach to learning that is superficial and does not involve full engagement with the material.

pedagogy   The practice and method of teaching and study, and the research of it.

peer assessment   Assessment by fellow (peer) students, as in peer assessment of team activities.

peer support   A system whereby students support one another in the learning process. Students may be in informal groups or more formal, designated groups (as in SI groups).

peer tutor/tutorial   Tutorial facilitated by fellow students (peer tutors).

peer-led team learning (PLTL)   *See* peer support.

performance indicator (PI)   Measure of achievement of individuals or organisations, often expressed in terms of quantitative outputs.

personal development plan (PDP)   A range of formal and/or informal mechanisms that promote reflection by an individual of their learning, performance and/or achievement and that can encourage planned personal educational and career development (*see also* progress file).

personal response system   Individualised electronic means of 'voting' (e.g. indicating a preferred answer), often used in large classes ('clickers').

placement   Placing students outside their home institution for part of their period of study, often work placement in which the student 'learns on the job'.

plagiarism   Presenting others' work as one's own.

portfolio (teaching portfolio)   A personal collection of material representing an individual's work (e.g. to demonstrate achievement and professional development as a university teacher).

Postgraduate Research Experience Survey (PRES)   A survey of postgraduate researchers. In the UK used to inform institutions about perceptions of learning opportunities and supervision with the aim informing improvements (http://www.heacademy.ac.uk/pres).

Postgraduate Taught Experience Survey (PTES)   A survey of postgraduate taught students in the UK to collect feedback on the student experience and enable institutions to identify areas of teaching strength and those for improvement (http://www.heacademy.ac.uk/ptes).

practice-based skills   Skills learned in practice rather than in the classroom.

probation   The initial phase in employment with a new organisation in which a member of staff 'learns the job'. In higher education, this usually involves periods of formal training and development; often the probationer is supported by a mentor. Many institutions set formal requirements that staff are expected to meet for satisfactory completion of probation.

problem class   Typically a session in the teaching of mathematics, engineering and physical science in which students work through problems and derive solutions with the support of a teacher and/or tutor/demonstrator. Not to be confused with PBL sessions.

problem-based learning (PBL)   A pedagogical method introduced in the 1960s, much used in medicine. Curriculum design involves a large amount of small-group teaching and claims greater alignment with sound educational principles. Learning and teaching come after learners identify their learning needs from a 'trigger' in the form of a scenario ('the problem').

professional bodies, associations or societies   Organisations created by a Royal Charter to support a specific profession. Support their members and can also ensure that professional standards are upheld. Many professional bodies offer accreditation via membership that can be a requirement of being allowed to practice certain professions in the UK, for example doctors.

professional doctorates   A field of studies that is a professional discipline. It is a research degree with a significant taught element, plus a research project published as the thesis.

programme of study   An award-bearing collection of modules or other teaching and learning, typically running over a defined period of time (e.g. BA, MEng).

programme specification   A succinct way of describing the attributes and outcomes for a named programme of study, written to follow QAA guidelines.

progress file   A term given prominence by the NCIHE. Comprises a transcript, or formal record of academic achievement, and a developmental aspect enabling students to monitor, plan and reflect on their personal development (*see also* personal development plan).

project-based learning   This is a teaching method in which students gain knowledge and skills by working for an extended period of time to investigate and respond to a complex question, problem or challenge.

psychomotor domain   One of the major areas of learning, the learning of certain types of skill.

QAA (Quality Assurance Agency for Higher Education)   The UK body that safeguards academic standards to ensure students have the best possible learning experiences (http://www.qaa.ac.uk).

QAA subject benchmark statements   *See* subject benchmarking.

quality assurance   An ongoing process by which an institution (programme, department, school or faculty) monitors and confirms policies, processes and activities, and by which quality is maintained (and enhanced).

Quality Code   *See* UK Quality Code for Higher Education, QAA.

quality enhancement   Refers to all the activities and processes adopted to improve and develop the quality of higher education and the dissemination of good practice.

rationalist   The belief that reason is the basis of knowledge.

read/write learning   Preference for learning based on words and text-based input and outputs (*see also* kinaesthetic learning, auditory learning).

Research Excellence Framework (REF)   The system for assessing the quality of research in UK HEIs. It replaced the Research Assessment Exercise (RAE) and was completed for the first time in 2014. Amongst other things, the funding bodies intend to use the assessment outcomes to inform the selective allocation of their research funding to HEIs, with effect from 2015–16 (http://www.ref.ac.uk).

reflection   Consideration from description to analysis of an experience or of learning to enhance and improve understanding and practice.

reflective journal   A journal or log book often required as part of a work placement in which a student will regularly describe and reflect upon their learning and how they have been putting into practice in the workplace the generic and discipline-specific skills that may have been taught at university. Aims to encourage thinking about what has been learnt and how.

reflective practitioner   Someone who is continually involved in the process of reflecting on experience and is capable of reflecting in action, continually learning from experience to the benefit of future actions.

reliable/reliability (of assessment)   A test that is consistent and precise in terms of factors, such as marking, quality of test and test items. The assessment process would generate the same result if repeated on another occasion with the same group, or with another group of similar students, or if repeated with other markers.

research-led teaching   One style of incorporating research into teaching where students learn about research findings, the curriculum content is dominated by staff research interests and information transmission is the main teaching mode.

reusable learning objects   A new conceptualisation of the learning process: rather than the traditional 'several hour chunk', they provide smaller, self-contained, reusable units of learning.

role play   A planned learning activity where participants take on the role of individuals representing different perspectives (e.g. a mock interview) to meet learning outcomes, related to empathy or to expose participants to a scenario in which they will have to take part 'for real' in the near future.

Russell Group   A member organisation of 24 leading UK universities committed to maintaining the very best research, an outstanding teaching and learning experience for students and strong links with business and the public sector, almost all of which have medical schools (http://www.russellgroup.ac.uk).

SAQ (structured/short answer question)   Also known as modified essay questions or short answers. SAQs test knowledge recall in a directed, but non-cueing manner.

scaffolding   Help and support of various types provided for students when they learn new things or are struggling.

SEDA   Staff and Educational Development Association (http://www.seda.ac.uk).

self-directed learning (SDL)   The learner has control over educational decisions, including goals, resources, methods and criteria for judging success. Often used just to mean any learning situation in which the learner has some influence on some of these aspects.

semester   A period of study in a modular programme of study, over which a set of modules are taught. Typically the academic year is divided into two semesters of equal length. Semester length varies across the sector.

seminar   Used with different meanings according to discipline and type of institution. May be used to describe many forms of small group teaching. Traditionally one or more students present formal academic work (a paper) to peers and a tutor, followed by discussion.

SFC   Scottish Funding Council (http://www.sfc.ac.uk).

SI (supplemental instruction)   Originates in the US. A means of supporting learners through the use of trained SI instructors who are also students. SI instructors take the role of facilitator and operate within a framework determined initially by the course leader. Usually SI instructors are more senior students selected for the role.

signpost   Statements in teaching sessions that help students to see the structure and direction of the teaching, and the links. Typically in a lecture, signposts will be used to give the big picture and then to signal the end of one section, the start of the next and where it is going.

simulated patient (SP)   An actor or other third party who role-plays the part of the patient in a clinical encounter with dental, medical or similar students.

simulation   Often associated with role play, but increasingly used in the context of ICT. A learning activity that simulates a real-life scenario requiring participants to make choices that demonstrate cause and effect.

situated cognition/situated learning   Learning and understanding often relates to and arises from (social) contexts. Those working in similar contexts (e.g. a discipline or profession) develop understanding about that context (*see also* Community of practice). In the case of language learning, assistance with vocabulary would be offered in the context of the environment rather than the other way around (*see also* activity theory).

small group teaching   A term used to encompass all the various forms of teaching involving 'small' groups of students, ranging from one-to-one sessions to groups of up to 25 (or even more) students. Includes tutorials, seminars, problem classes.

social presence   In online learning, where the online learning space features and encourages authentic human interactions between students and between students and teaching staff. In contrast to a resource-led approach, a course with a high degree of social presence would see students learning through group participation and open exchange between course members.

socio-cultural   Approaches to learning that emphasise the interdependence of social and individual processes in the construction of knowledge – associated with the ideas of Vygotsky.

soft skills   A broad range of generic skills required for learning and employment, for example managing one's workload, communicating well, learning independently, problem solving, working effectively with others.

Spellings Commission 2005   A US government commission set to investigate outcomes of college and university education, focusing on four areas: access, affordability, standards and accountability.

standards   The term used to refer to levels of student attainment compared to criteria (or comparators).

strategic approach to study (strategic learning)   Typifies students who adapt their approach to learning to meet the needs of the set task. Intention is external to the real purpose of the task because it focuses on achieving high marks for their own sake, not because they indicate high levels of learning. Also known as the achieving approach.

student engagement   Has various meanings. In learning, the active interaction between the time, effort and other resources invested by both students, their teachers and institutions so as to optimise the student experience, enhance learning outcomes and the development of students. Can encompass students as partners (*see also* students as partners).

student response system   This is a type of interaction using a wireless device 'clicker', to create interactivity between a presenter and his/her audience.

students as partners   Students, institutions (and policymakers at national level) working together for the benefit of the student experience. Implies students should be involved and consulted about virtually all aspects of their institution and their courses, implying two-way operation of responsibilities.

subject benchmarking   A collection of discipline-specific statements relating to undergraduate programmes, as published by the QAA. Covers all the main disciplines.

summative assessment   The type of assessment that typically comes at the end of a module or section of learning and awards the learner with a final mark or grade for that section. The information about the learner is often used by third parties to inform decisions about the learner's abilities.

supervision   The relationship between a student and supervisor (member of staff) to facilitate learning and discovery, and to model professional behaviour.

supervisor   Person (often disciplinary expert) responsible for facilitating the work of students, usually project work and research.

surface approach to study   Learning by students that focuses on the details of the learning experience and is based on memorising the details without any attempt to give them meaning beyond the factual level of understanding (*see also* deep approach, strategic approach).

synchronous learning   Refers to a learning environment in which everyone takes part at the same time. Lecture is an example of synchronous learning in a face-to-face environment, where learners and teachers are all in the same place at the same time.

teaching portfolio   A personal document containing information about one's teaching activities, commentary and supporting evidence. Will include detailed personal reflection on practice and identify areas for enhancement. May also include student feedback and evaluative input from mentors and colleagues.

team teaching   A system whereby learning is designed, delivered and supported by two or more teachers who may share the same session.

threshold concepts   Critical concepts in each discipline, the misunderstanding of which may impede student learning. Developed by Erik Meyer and Ray Land.

transferable skills   A collection of skills associated with employability. Variously includes communication, numeracy, learning to learn, values and integrity, use of technology, interpersonal skills, problem-solving, positive attitudes to change and teamworking.

transnational education (TNE)   All types of HE study programmes, courses or educational services (including distance learning) in which the learners are located in a country different from that of the awarding institution.

Turnitin   Plagiarism software commonly used in HE.

tutorial   Used with different meanings according to discipline, type of institution, level and teaching and learning method. Involves a tutor with one or more students. May focus on academic and/or pastoral matters.

UCAS   Universities and Colleges Admissions Service (http://www.ucas.ac.uk).

UK Professional Standards Framework (UKPSF)   UK descriptors that set out four levels of expertise in relation to teaching and supporting student learning. HEA accredited programmes and professional development routes align to the descriptors (*see also* HEA).

UK Quality Code for Higher Education (The Quality Code)   Sets out the expectations that all providers of UK higher education are required to meet. The Quality Code has three elements covering academic standards, academic quality and information about higher education provision. Published by the QAA (*see also* Higher Education Review, subject benchmarking, levels).

Unistats   An independent website for comparing sets of information about undergraduate courses in the UK and designed to meet the information needs of prospective students (http://unistats.direct.gov.uk) (*see also* key information set).

UUK   Universities UK (http://www.universitiesuk.ac.uk).

valid/validity (of assessment)   Adequacy and appropriateness of the task/test in relation to the outcomes/objectives of the teaching being assessed (i.e. it measures what it is supposed to measure).

VARK   Acronym that stands for four modalities used for learning information: visual (V), aural/auditory (A), read-write (R) and kinaesthetic (K) (*see also* the four separate entries).

video-conference   A synchronous discussion between two individuals or groups of people who are in different places but can see and hear each other using electronic communications.

virtual learning environment (VLE)   An online education system that models conventional in-person education by providing equivalent virtual access to classes, class content, tests, homework, grades, assessments and other external resources. It is also a social space where students and teacher can interact through threaded discussions or chat.

visual learning   Visual learners learn best by seeing things in a pictorial format (*see also* kinaesthetic learning, read/write learning).

Vitae   A UK network-based organisation that works in partnership with HEIs, research organisations, funders and national organisations to meet society's need for high-level skills and innovation and produce world-class researchers (http://www. vitae.ac.uk).

viva voce examination ('viva')   An oral examination, typically at the end of a programme of study. One part of assessment strategy if used in undergraduate programmes. Significant part of assessment of postgraduate research degrees in the UK. May be used to test communication, understanding, capacity to think quickly under pressure, reasoning and knowledge of procedures.

work-based learning   A type of curriculum design allowing content and learning to arise from within real working contexts. Students, usually employees, studying part-time and using their workplace to generate a project. Unlike PBL, work-based learners are working on real problems in real time.

work placement   *See* placement.

Index

Diagrams and tables are given in *italics*.

LIBRARY, UNIVERSITY OF CHESTER